Teaching Representations of the French Revolution

Teaching Representations of the French Revolution

Edited by

Julia Douthwaite Viglione, Antoinette Sol, and Catriona Seth

Modern Language Association of America
New York 2019

Library of Congress Cataloging-in-Publication Data are available from the Library of Congress.

ISBN (cloth) 978-1-60329-465-2
ISBN (paper) 978-1-60329-400-3
ISBN (EPUB) 978-1-60329-401-0
ISBN (Kindle) 978-1-60329-402-7

Options for Teaching 47
ISSN 1079-2562

Cover illustration of the paperback and electronic editions: *La Liberté armée du Sceptre de la Raison foudroye l'Ignorance et le Fanatisme*, drawn by Simon-Louis Boizot and engraved by Jean-Baptiste Chapuy. Source: Bibliothèque Nationale de France.

Published by The Modern Language Association of America
85 Broad Street, suite 500, New York, New York 10004-2434
www.mla.org

Contents

Part III: Writing the Revolution

Part IV: The Revolution in Art and Mass Media

Acknowledgments

We have enjoyed discussing the French Revolution and its heritage with students and colleagues. Our teaching and research informed our vision. During the preparation of the book, we were greatly helped by the suggestions and enthusiasm of all the authors. We would like to thank the readers whose supportive preliminary reports and pertinent comments encouraged us to go through with the project. Our gratitude also goes to Sister Mary Helen Kashuba for her graciousness as well as to James C. Hatch, senior acquisitions editor at the MLA, who answered our queries with efficiency and thoroughness and was an invaluable link with the Publications Committee. We hope that the volume will give inspiration to current and future generations, whatever their background, age, or area of study.

Julia Douthwaite Viglione, Antoinette Sol, and Catriona Seth

Introduction

The Revolution for Today's Readers

That "the French Revolution" is in the singular could be considered misleading, because the Revolution was not one event but a complicated web of often brutal actions, interactions, and reactions. Although rooted in local causes in metropolitan France, it ended up affecting peoples and governments worldwide. Allies became enemies and vice versa. France moved from an absolute monarchy to a constitutional monarchy to a republic. The Revolution put an end to a seemingly immutable order and gave birth to a new one in blood and pain. To say it was a confusing, turbulent, and violent time is an understatement.

One reason for the confusion around *revolution* is semantic. Given its origins in the astronomical realm, as referring to celestial bodies that revolve in space before returning to their original positions, the word used to describe the revolt ignited in 1789 has confounded expectations since 1791 at least. In September 1791, many observers celebrated the revolt's successful end: since the new constitution had been written and approved by the king, the centuries-old divine monarchy had effectively come to an end; the regime of absolute kings was now officially *ancien*: former, redundant, passé. What more could anyone want? Why did a movement that began with demands for fiscal responsibility and judicial reform snowball into an increasingly radical attack on wealth, inherited privilege, and the Catholic Church? Is such restless (some might say reckless) disregard for authority a feature of all modern revolutions, or was it particular to the uprising that exploded one summer in Paris? The jury is still out.

The events of 1789–99 in France were momentous not only because they put an end to a monarchy by beheading a king—the English Civil War had achieved that a century earlier—but also because they had profound implications for the whole of Europe and the world. The Revolution inspired efforts from the redrawing of borders to the creation of the Rights of Man, which remain a template for humanity in the twenty-first century. It was contagious, quickly spreading to neighboring lands and inspiring the Latin-American demands for independence and the Italian drive toward unification (*Risorgimento*) that rocked established orders in the decades that followed. It also led to mass emigration of certain social classes—namely, the nobility and the clergy—who sought refuge by traveling across the Alps or the Ural Mountains, traversing the Channel, or embarking on the long ocean passage to America.

Our goal in this volume is to foreground the French Revolution as both a body of materials and a repertoire of ideas to spark the teaching of humanities in the twenty-first century. The volume considers as self-evident the primacy of a cultural studies approach to teaching. This means that, instead of focusing on intellectual history (the great thoughts of great men), as some scholars are wont to do, our contributors marry a healthy respect for philosophical idealism with a pragmatic eye for urgent social issues. Readers will learn about the influence of political theories penned by famous writers such as Jean-Jacques Rousseau and Edmund Burke, and they will also discover how the period was lived and remembered by lesser-known members of society. Although most of us work in the United States, one might consider us as descendants of the United Kingdom–based Birmingham school of cultural theory and inspired by its leader, the Jamaican-born scholar Stuart Hall, who demanded that culture be taught not simply as something to appreciate or study but also as a "critical site of social action and intervention" (qtd. in Procter 2). We position the volume this way in order to bridge past and present: to show how revolutionary debates generated the controversies over free speech and access to work and fair wages that remain unresolved today, not to mention the nexus of concerns surrounding religious worship and freedom of dress in the increasingly global public sphere. The desire to strengthen bonds of fraternity among citizens takes on unexpected complications when our neighbors are just as likely to be Muslim, Buddhist, or atheist as they were once likely to be either Catholic or Protestant.

The French Revolution is an essential part of many courses: it is obviously a keystone in European history, but it is also relevant to the study of other, non-European movements, including the American Revolution of 1776–80, the Arab spring of 2011, and recent upheavals in Ukraine, Tunisia, and Syria. In literature, the study of classic texts by writers active in Europe during or after the tumult, such as William Blake (1757–1827) or Victor Hugo (1802–85)—both of whom are discussed in this volume—could be completed by the study of authors who were born afterward or in faraway places: people such as Giuseppe Parini (1729–99), an Italian; Harriet Beecher Stowe (1811–96), an American; or Alejo Carpentier (1904–80), a Cuban. Scholar-teachers from diverse backgrounds suggest how to teach the French Revolution to audiences ranging from young children to community college juniors, from advanced students in military history to aficionados of Haitian, Spanish, or German literature. They use eclectic sources, from material written or published at the time (archives, books, but also prints and all kind of ephemera) to objects (painted plates, flags), music, celebrations, and games. Their topics cover the map, but all are animated by a similar optimism about human potential.

The Revolution in Politics, Religion, and the Arts, from 1789 to Today

If only for a moment, the French Revolution offered an opportunity for the previously voiceless to be heard. Women, working men, and some people of color dared to speak up or write down their views, and sometimes those views influenced legislation. In the Revolution's early days, there was hope of equal participation of the sexes in the political and public realm. This brief taste of agency nevertheless led to a conservative backlash that hindered women's participation in civic affairs and professional life until the third quarter of the twentieth century; the French were among the last of the Western powers to give women the vote, in 1944.

Along with understanding how divorce law and abolitionism made their way into the French legal system, readers should grapple with the conflicts inherent in the First Republic's rigorous secularism. Just as the Napoleonic code (*Le code civil*, 1804) put women firmly under men's legal coverage, the empire reinstated slavery in the colonies. Yet just as the empire lost power over the colonies, neither Napoleon's will nor the example of the duchesse d'Angoulême (sole survivor of Louis XVI and Marie-Antoinette's children) ever really succeeded in raising church attendance to Old Regime levels. Once the men had lost their habit of going to mass, no manner of female or priestly encouragement, so the story goes, could get them to return (Hufton). Catholicism would never again reign supreme as it did under the absolute monarchy. It is not surprising that the resentments left by the split of church and state continue today, as the recent acrimony over *laïcité* in the Fifth Republic shows.

French *laïcité*, born of the Revolution, is a militant secularism quite unlike the "live and let live" attitude of the Anglo-American tradition, which means your Manchester or New York neighbors might be Sikhs sporting a turban, Hassidic Jews, or niqab-wearing Muslims. In France, the all-in-one women's swimsuit nicknamed the burkini has been banned from the beaches at Cannes, and simply by wearing a niqab or a burka outside your home, you are in breach of the law and liable for a hefty fine.

The January 2015 terrorist attacks in Paris—against the satirical magazine *Charlie Hebdo*, on-duty police officers, and clients of a kosher supermarket—have become subsumed, in popular memory, into a single attack against the periodical that famously published caricatures of Muhammad. This is because beyond the killing of individuals, French men and women felt that their values were being attacked—and not just any values: those the Revolution fought to impose, in particular freedom of expression and thought. One of the primary outcomes of the terrorist attacks in Paris in January and November 2015, and in Nice on the highly symbolic date of 14 July 2016 (the French national holiday and the anniversary of the storming of the Bastille), has been to force the French government to grapple with religious belief as a value concomitant with equality before the law. This grappling has raised tensions on both the left and the right and is pushing events toward outcomes that remain unknown. Staff members of the Hôpital Bichat-Claude Bernard in Paris, to give one example, are now required to sign a *charte de la laïcité* ("a charter of secularism")—which means that a doctor, once employed, cannot demand to be allowed to wear a kippah or hijab or to engage in religious propaganda of any kind.

This reaction can be seen as part and parcel of France's revolutionary heritage. Political satire reached its apogee during the Revolution, although it was already a traditional way of exposing weaknesses of the state by revealing the debauched and corrupted private lives of powerful men. Satirical pamphlets, libels, and anecdotes superimposed political relationships onto sexual ones. Deregulation of the press during the Revolution led to a profusion of often short-lived periodicals. Until then, there had been few venues for counterdiscourse beyond satirical images and pamphlets, which aimed to discredit official versions of events and also to undermine religious and monarchical authority. Robert Darnton, in his comprehensive study of the genre, *Devil in the Holy Water*, points out that satire was a way for the French to make sense of the "larger sphere of famous people and great events" (5). He adds that the making of meaning is "conveyed primarily by myths and symbols" (6). Those meanings may be hard to decipher for readers in the twenty-first century, because of their dependence on current events. But even if a specific referent is obscured by time, the accumulation of stereotypes and clichés—used and recirculated—are easily understood by the target readership, as we see in the study of *Charlie Hebdo* (Conroy's essay in this volume).

Power, dogmatism, privilege, entitlement, and hypocrisy were—and are still—the bread and butter of the satirical press. Lynn Hunt points out that political pornography accounted for half the obscene literature produced after 1789 ("Pornography" 307). Homosexuality, denoting nature in disorder, was a common charge against the nobility as well as against the clergy. During the French Revolution, political and pornographic satire were often combined; hyperbolic and excessive by nature, they made respected authorities into fair game for criticism and thereby "de-sacralized" both throne and church (Baecque 165).

The famous or infamous French political newspaper *Charlie Hebdo,* like its fellow publication *Le canard enchaîné* ("The Angry Rag"), can trace its genealogy to this tradition, as Melanie Conroy's essay in this volume shows. *Le canard*, as it is affectionately known, offers topical political commentary and often reveals scandals through probing journalism couched in deliberately provocative terms. It seeks to reveal the dark underbelly of power: clandestine commissions, insider dealing, and nepotism. It has a faithful band of readers who rejoice in its punning headlines and running attacks on whoever stands out as needing to be taken down a peg. *Charlie Hebdo* made its mark by being offensive to anyone who wields any form of power and to all the religions of the Book—not just to Islam. It thrives on poor taste and disregard for what most people consider to be the common bounds of decency, not only knocking down political figures and making jibes at religious authority but also making ageist, sexist, or racist jokes:

it is an equal-opportunity offender of sensibilities. It can also espouse the true French tradition of *gauloiserie* ("bawdiness")—the sort of nudge-nudge-wink-wink humor of farce—and *esprit* ("wit"). The tradition shares some characteristics of the revolutionary pamphlets and cartoons. The satirical weekly, targeting political figures as well as religious ones, is difficult to understand without context. After the tragic events of January 2015, when the offices of *Charlie Hebdo* were subjected to a terrorist attack and journalists were murdered during an editorial meeting, about half a million articles (the count from an Internet search) attempted to explain not only the how and why of the event but also the cartoons themselves.

For the French, understanding the satire was beside the point. They took to the streets in hundreds of thousands all over the country to protest the murder of Charb (Stéphane Charbonnier), Bernard Maris, Honoré (Philippe Honoré), Cabu (Jean Cabut), Tignous (Bernard Verlhac), Georges Wolinski, and others as well as what those murders represented: an attack on free speech. The French shared and celebrated their outrage at the attack on the institution of free speech and freedom of the press. Voltaire's *Traité sur la tolérance* (1763), thanks to its very title ("A Treatise on Tolerance"), became a best seller two hundred and fifty years after its initial publication and was accompanied by affirmations of "Je suis Charlie" 'I am Charlie' from around the world, a slogan shared on social media, beamed on buildings across the world, and worn on badges by Hollywood actors and statesmen after the killings in an illustration of how much Enlightenment ideals remain alive. Freedom of the press, closely allied to the republican ethos, is the sine qua non of French democratic public life. As the French scholar and philosopher Jean-Jacques Delfour writes, "Each drawing is a provocation, that is to say, a call to question a prejudice, a presumption, a tacit compromise." The image as signifier is transgressive in order to get at an unconscious or hidden truth. Political satire, as practiced by *Charlie Hebdo* and its predecessors, rages against inequality, dogmatism in all its forms but especially religious dogmatism, and hypocrisy in the anticlerical revolutionary tradition: strategies whose roots lie in the late eighteenth century. An attack against secularism, *laïcité,* is an attack against the French Republic and all it stands for. Students need to see these connections in order to make sense of France's tolerance of truly offensive images and the fact that the fierce protection by the French of the right to transgress sensibilities—be they religious, societal, or political—reaches back to the foundational myths of the Republic itself.

Identity politics, or what is called, with a shudder of distaste, *communautarisme*, appears to be creeping back onto French soil and threatening the solidarity of the people. Seen in the long-term view from the original conception of a *république*, this complaint, with its manifest object of villainy—observant Muslims—makes more sense. Just as the First Republic deputies removed all signs of religious power from the French countryside in 1794, the Fifth Republic still wants to be first in her people's hearts. The thinking goes like this: The state offers such a generous range of social support, and people used to be grateful; but now these newcomers are dividing against one another in the name of religion and ambition (Alderman). The nerve! *Quel culot!* The hostility toward visibly religious Muslims wearing burkas—or Jews with twisted sidelocks, or Catholics with cassocks—is simply a condition of being *républicain*. It grows out of the ingrown peasant *méfiance* ("distrust") of outsiders; the republican scorn for organized religion, a scorn traditionally promoted by the state schooling system; and an Enlightenment belief in universalism, all of which are inherited from the past. Divisive accoutrements and belief systems, it is claimed, menace the cherished ideal of the *res publica* and dreams of civic harmony. Some observers throw up their hands over the present stalemate, lamenting the seemingly inexorable rise of xenophobic sentiment in a "morose" society (Mathy 3). Others express cautious optimism over the "pluralist belonging" or "alternative visions of republicanism" that are emerging in some immigrant neighborhoods (Newman xxxii, 91).

When we turn our sights to aesthetics, the Revolution holds value as an event that influenced styles of dress, from the ephemeral—a haircut à la Titus or a Phrygian cap (*un bonnet rouge*)—to the enduring vogue for jeans and trousers, which has made us all sansculottes. It coined turns of phrase, such as *Ça ira* and the slogan *liberté, égalité, fraternité*, which is still the motto of the French state. It has inspired and continues to inspire literary and artistic works, oil paintings, mangas, and hip-hop music, as the essays in this volume illustrate. All sides in the original conflict used mass media—caricatures and periodicals but also ceramics, coins, and other ephemera. The entrepreneur Pierre-François Palloy, for example, lined his pockets by selling souvenirs of the Bastille cut from the prison's stones. Richard Taws describes the business: "Operating in the dynamic tension with the empty Bastille site but distinct from it, Palloy's work did not demand that travelers make a pilgrimage to the Bastille but promised instead to multiply the absent Bastille and bring it directly to the people"

(98). These values of openness and transparency, the acts of sharing and worshiping state-oriented ceremonies, were new to everyone and bewildering to many.

Theater featured large in the revolutionary environment, and the connection between politics and art was never more evident than on the stage. Revolutionary theater combined different modes—the sentimental, neoclassical, utopian, and fantastic genres—to political ends, and famous plays from the past were adapted and reinterpreted accordingly. It was a medium that seemed capable of reaching all, in the new, classless society where a good number of the citizenry nevertheless remained illiterate (Kennedy 35–39). Melodrama's popularity may have derived from its power to reflect the turbulence that was playing out in the streets of Paris, where a rich, newly inclusive cultural environment existed. It may have only existed for a while, partly as a consequence of the 1791 deregulation of theaters and the more oppressive legislation that followed, but as Logan Connors remarks in his essay, it was "a powerful collective experience," in which some women playwrights, provincials, and radicals attained success beyond their wildest dreams.

Virulent after the early, sterile years of Louis XVI's marriage to Marie-Antoinette, when their union produced no children, scandal sheets (*libelles*) and cartoons played a role in driving a wedge between the French people and their once-beloved royal family. One of the recurring themes was to denounce the queen's involvement in public affairs, as Melissa Deininger's essay in this volume shows. Political caricature was potent, brutal, and sharp. It belonged to a combative tradition of satire, such as the mazarinades, which criticized the actions and attitude of Regent Anne of Austria and her right-hand man, Cardinal Mazarin, during the 1650s. Like the mazarinades, revolutionary caricature and theater were heavily context-dependent for interpretation: they drew their power from audiences' sense of indignation over lived experience rather than from classical learning. Their visual character appealed to all segments of the population, including those who could not read, who were on the receiving end of political messages they could not have deciphered in the papers. This immediacy helped build a wider base for public debate, which, once confined to Versailles, now commonly took place on Parisian streets. Some ephemera attained hitherto unknown levels of sophistication: witness the royalist newspaper *Les actes des apôtres* ("The Acts of the Apostles"), launched in 1789, whose elaborate caricatures were accompanied by detailed explanations that savaged left-wing policies through allusion to sources such as Rabelais, Homer, and the Scriptures, before it went out of print in 1792.

The consequences and trauma of the violent political upheaval can be seen in genres such as emigration literature, sentimental novels, and memoirs, all of which enjoyed success in the first half of the nineteenth century; their popularity emerges clearly in the essays by Pratima Prasad and by Ourida Mostefai. Every family had its story of suffering and grief to be shared, and each chose its own way to mourn. While aristocrats and intellectuals had access to a broader variety of reading material, the memoirs of common folk must be understood as growing out of their oral legends and limited sources—that is, almanacs, breviaries, and saints' lives (Steinberg 430–36). Along with women, people of color participated in the political process more than they ever had before, both in France and colonial Saint-Domingue. Once they came face to face with angry rivals, these newly enfranchised political actors had to deal with the backlash that followed. An abrupt wave of conservativism reversed the liberal legislation passed during the 1790s, on subjects such as marriage, divorce, and slavery.

The revolt in Saint-Domingue, the first successful overthrowing by slaves of a colonial government, left inspiring and painful traces in the visual arts, as anyone who has seen images of the Bois-Caïman ceremony or Anne-Louis Girodet's striking 1798 portrait of Deputy Jean-Baptiste Belley will attest. But the violence of what would come to be known as the Haitian Revolution delayed the abolitionist movement in France for two decades. Of course the Haitians had been dealt a hand much worse than that of the French people. The financial yoke put on the fledgling nation in 1804 was sufficient to grind down the Haitian economy for more than twenty years, and the French government refused to recognize the Haitian state until reparations were made. It may seem strange to us, but for many years historians regarded the slave uprising as a typical massacre, a deplorable skirmish between blacks and whites, or an otherwise "invisible event," as Ronan Chalmin notes in his essay in this volume. Scholars today consider the Haitian Revolution a hugely important turning point in history. Still, debates prevail about the timing and origins of its inspiration, as Marlene Daut explains in this volume. Haitian events manifested hopes set alight by revolutionary legislation passed in Paris, but they also derived from reports on Louis XVI and his actions (Ogle 89–91). Mixed-race inhabitants of Saint-Domingue (*les gens de couleur*) were initially pleased with the king, speculating—erroneously, as it turns out—that his feeble support for the white landowners was part and parcel of his distaste for slavery. Scholars are now examining the nuances of historical meaning as expressed by Haitian writers themselves. New editions of once forgotten texts are helping readers understand how 1 January 1804, a momentous date, was experienced on local ground.

The Revolution in the Academy Today

Over the past thirty years or so, historians, by studying the use of imagery, songs, costume, theater, and symbolism, have produced exciting insights into the revolutionaries' efforts to invent a new national identity. This academic trend, which has become prominent since the 1970s, supports models of historical interpretation that explain political change in terms of language, rhetoric, and symbols as well as biography, economics, and class consciousness. Such work has breathed fresh life into revolutionary studies by liberating historiography from narratives about great men and great deeds, from arguments about the existence or nonexistence of the bourgeoisie, and from the dry socioeconomic detail that had so long characterized the field. Yet some critics remain unconvinced.

Perhaps the most outspoken criticisms have been voiced by Rebecca Spang in the United States and by David Andress and Colin Jones in Britain. In essays written years apart and from very different angles, they contend that the new, cultural history has neglected the question of human agency—whether of individual or group—and overestimated the extent of societal transformation wrought by the Revolution. By focusing on discourse, imagery, symbols, and metaphors, cultural history has tended to interpret the Revolution as a vast and somewhat disembodied network of collective thought or images without explaining how these linguistic and visual systems became meaningful to particular people. This approach skirts the traditional search for causes by presuming that there are connections in the air, but those connections may or may not be supported by factual evidence. Moreover, if cultural historians' approaches have supplanted earlier methods such as biography and economic analysis, they nevertheless left intact the stark demarcation between the Old Regime and modernity familiar to us since Marx.

Spang, Andress, and Jones call for ways of writing history that will complement the excellent corpus to date by casting light on the people who drove the action. Some written traces of popular sentiment exist and remain unexplored, Jones reminds us, and he provides an eye-opening study of attitudes toward Robespierre in July 1794 to prove it. Working with documents from the Archives Nationales, the Archives de la Police, and elsewhere in French libraries, scholars in literature and history can sometimes provide a corrective to the unexamined assumptions people make. Although historians associated with the new cultural history embrace this demand for studies of reception or consumption, the call for a renewed emphasis on so-called real people and real things must be considered carefully. Ideally, one should not only be attentive to discourse as an agent of social change but also seek answers about how particular individuals, groups, and institutions shaped their culture.

Contrary to the utopian claims of the patriots, the Old Regime did not end in 1792. Darrin McMahon, Gérard Gengembre, and Dale Van Kley have all illustrated how tensions between revolutionaries and royalists drew on differences of opinion that had long coexisted under the Old Regime and flared into ferocious polemics only with the 1790 attacks on the Church. It is important, alongside the writings of republican sympathizers, to recuperate the little-known texts of émigrés and Catholic loyalists. Their education enabled them to pen articulate reflections on revolutionary events, but their politics made them anathema to the Marxist approach that long dominated history departments in France.

Contemporary thought on the Revolution seeks to resist the long-held notion that the Old Regime simply collapsed (and moreover that this collapse was somehow inevitable) under the weight of its legendary decadence. Instead, through an exploration of the so-called losers of history—people such as émigrés, noblemen, the clergy, and practicing Catholics, as well as women and people of color—today's scholars seek to restore greater texture to history writing and thus heighten the sense of contestation and contingency that surely typified this epoch in France, the rest of Western Europe, and beyond.

Despite these somewhat populist assumptions, the essays in this volume wisely refuse to hold up any one historical agent as the victim. They strive to capture the evolution of political feelings as a tug-of-war between forces that all have some claim on the truth. A ruthless desire for results not only motivated the mobs of July 1789 and September 1792, it also drove routine judicial practices of the Old Regime. If complainants were sufficiently wealthy and well-connected, they could rapidly dispatch wayward children, adulterous wives, or upstart rivals to convents, prison, or—worse yet—to *le Mississippi* or French Guyana. Students should know that New Orleans was originally colonized by people who went there against their will, sent abroad by lettres de cachet or deportation following arrest or phony recruitment scams (Canetti; Heinrich 5–13). If the revolutionary state proved somewhat incompetent to manage the nation's finances through the printing of paper assignats, it arguably performed better than the bank set up during the Regency by John Law with the duc d'Orléans's backing (Harris 14). Similarly, if the work of the radical journalists Jean-Paul Marat and Jacques Hébert can be faulted for stirring up the masses to commit horrific acts of brutality in September 1792, so too the oppressive arm of royal censorship and government-approved persecution of non-Catholics must be held accountable for some shocking mistakes (Linton).

Equally important to revolutionary historiography is an understanding of the period's literary production. Nineteenth-century scholars such as Eugène Maron (*Histoire littéraire de la Révolution* [1856]) and Georges Duval (*Histoire de la littérature révolutionnaire* [1879]) laid the groundwork with their research on revolutionary oratory and journalism. Maron, however, dismissed fiction published during the Revolution as unworthy of serious study, and Duval claimed that none of the novels contemporaneous with events bore any traces of the tumult (147). A disparaging attitude toward revolutionary literature ran through the influential works of nineteenth-century critics and kept this corpus fairly untouched by readers until the mid-twentieth century. Inspired by the linguistic turn in historiography and supported by new reference tools and databases, a first wave of scholars began scrutinizing this material. Malcolm Cook's 1982 book-length study launched this development by analyzing revolutionary fiction organized by genres such as pastoral and allegory. Henri Coulet, Béatrice Didier, Lynn Hunt (*Family Romance*), and Allan Pasco contributed to a rediscovery with their studies of fiction writers previously considered to be second-rate, and their evidence demonstrates literature's importance to the rapid cultural changes that marked the 1790s.

Some of this work reveals ties to the culture wars of the 1980s–1990s and the dominance of literary theory, French or otherwise, in the American university. Hunt's *Family Romance of the French Revolution* caused a stir by appropriating Freudian theory to understand dysfunctional families in life and literature. Borrowing from speech act theories and performance studies as articulated by J. L. Austin, Judith Butler, and others, the theoretically rich discussions of Marie-Hélène Huet and of Cecilia Feilla have illuminated revolutionary theater. However, other critics may have been led astray by French theory, because, as Ieme van der Poel has remarked, it was not originally written for an academic audience. Authors such as Hélène Cixous and Jacques Lacan saw themselves as primarily a literary avant-garde and used a very French fondness for punning and wordplay in their writing. To foreign readers, that style "made their thought seem more profound than it probably was" (van der Poel 14).

For the moment, a reliance on clever theories is the exception, not the norm, in revolutionary studies. Most scholarship we have surveyed aims to produce finely hewn historical contextualization about the vast network of readers and writers who bought, consumed, and shared writings of the period. Putting fiction into dialogue with period newspapers, political writing, and oratory can sometimes reveal epiphenomena of importance. Studying literature alongside life writing and court documents can add new dimensions to the Terror by showing how the victims and their families used the printed word to fight back against unfair sentencing and imprisonment (Fairfax-Cholmeley). These examples and the essays in this volume show how today's researchers and teachers are trying to create precise and historically accurate interpretations for relatively unknown works of literature, as well as émigré writings, published from 1789 to 1794. Such historical methods may well provide the most useful approach, at least until the contours of this massive field come fully into sight.

All this scholarly activity is good news for the humanities classroom. Yet so far no one book synthesizes the many new stories, sources, theories, and methods that have been created. It seemed to us that a volume was needed to offer both specialists and nonspecialists a panel of ideas on how to teach this vital field. As a glance at any newspaper will reveal, we live in a world of propaganda, advertisement, and political extremism, in which acts of terrorism and revolt seem to take place on a daily basis. Such acts can today inflame emotion worldwide almost instantaneously, thanks to minute-by-minute video footage spread on social media. This volume suggests ways to help students understand how those phenomena developed, as well as topics such as universal human rights, slavery, and privilege. It provides precise examples and broad ideas to assist the teacher in leading students to analyze the coded language in period texts and to see the hidden messages in paintings. It incites readers to consider the particularly ruthless nature of the many revolutions that have rocked France, the perennial problems of mob violence, and the wider question, Do the ends ever justify such means?

How to Read This Volume

This volume is organized in six parts. Part 1 explores historical contexts through a narrative chronology as well as essays on perspective and memory. It encompasses materials as diverse as battle plans, sites of memory (*lieux de mémoire*), banlieue culture, and rap music. Part 2 examines problems of human rights and the role played by classical rhetoric in revolutionary ideology. Essays discuss what liberty, slavery, and freedom might have meant to inhabitants of French colonies overseas. New ideas emerge about teaching colonialism, gender, and *le patrimoine* ("heritage"). Part 3 looks at how the Revolution was interpreted in diverse literary genres in France, Germany, the United States, and other countries. Essays focus on useful, if unfamiliar, texts that teachers should know, including short stories, novels, poetry, plays, and letters. Part 4 explores the seismic shifts that the Revolution set off in the arts; it studies traditional artworks such as paintings and drawings and, less commonly studied, celebrations and porcelains. Revolutionary images came in all media, from educational playing cards to propaganda prints, coins, and cartoons. The materials gathered here indicate that the Revolution was one of the most mediated events in occidental history. The essays in part 5 consider the global reach of the Revolution in time and space. It includes studies on the Haitian Revolution and thoughts on how to understand Spanish, Greek, and German reactions to events from the 1790s to the 1820s. Echoes between the French Revolution and subsequent ones around the world can be discerned in voluntary or forced emigrations, religious strife, and anxiety over the mob.

Edited by professors from a variety of backgrounds and intellectual traditions, and with wide experience in researching and teaching the revolutionary period, the essays form a truly interdisciplinary volume. Though it proposes only a selection of sources and approaches, it will be useful to readers in fields such as French language, colonial and postcolonial studies, theater, art history, cultural and military history, media studies, digital humanities, political science, and literature. All its sections bring a personal touch to the issues by presenting real-life experiences with students who hail from different nations and walks of life. Whether they are in a French-language class, a summer school, a theater workshop, or a history seminar, we can learn from our students.

The essays in this volume are all a bit traditional in that they insist on the importance of close reading and linguistic analysis of individual texts.

They give evidence of impeccable historical background research. But in spirit they are creative and brave and aim to inspire and instruct through a personal, energetic connection with other people. They invite teachers to relive the excitement of the Revolution with objects, music, art, and celebrations, as well as accurate maps of French military actions across the Continent. Observing how events can reverberate through time and space beyond their origins, to ends that change radically over time, is both heartening and alarming. It reveals the unpredictable nature of human affairs. Revolution is a shape-shifter, meaning many things, peaceful and violent, to many people.

Our own experience confirms that one can mobilize students with a subject like this. Although it is impossible to trace a student's vocation to one particular class the student took in college, classroom observations and correspondence with former students, sometimes years after their graduation, have proved that they sometimes do become more public-spirited from exposure to materials like these. Once people learn about rights, they usually become keen to keep theirs. And once their rights are secure, they may ponder the rights afforded to other people, whether close to home or far afield, in Africa, North and South America, or Europe, where illegal aliens, homeless refugees, indigenous peoples, and the urban poor are all existing in conditions one would not wish on a dog.[1] One could pair up testimonials of real-life experiences with the theoretical language of revolution, as Jeffrey Champlin, Habiba Boumlik, and Robin Kietlinski have all done in their classes, whether they were teaching in Palestine, Vermont, or New York City. With more civic-minded citizens in the world, we will all be better off.

The volume takes a deliberately synthetic approach: we consider the period 1789–99 as an opportunity to highlight the many networks, narratives, causes, effects, and codes traded among friends and foes during those years. It is crucial to remember that these things arose from a world that no one ever thought could change. There is no single critical orthodoxy that dominates our efforts, although a certain historicism is present, as the different critical references show.

Translation Issues

In teaching the French Revolution, one cannot ignore issues of language and translation. Although translations open up the area for nonnative speakers, they are once removed from the source. There are at least four types of translation—linguistic, cultural, temporal, and aesthetic—and all four are relevant here. Translation and commensurability are major concerns for teachers using German sources, some of which can be read only in the original. In his essay in this volume, John Pizer undertakes a study of Goethe, Hölderlin, and the Brothers Grimm and shows, among other delightful surprises, how the French fairy tale "Little Red Riding Hood" evolved into a Jacobin-inspired tale called "Little Red Cap." In the Grimm Brothers' "Little Red Cap," the wolf doubles as a revolutionary agent who battles for survival with a hunter who represents German royal authority. Amir Minsky discusses a text that is itself a multilayered translation, both literally and metaphorically: he examines the intersection among travelogue, propaganda, and eyewitness accounting in Joachim Heinrich Campe's "Letter from Paris" (1790) and argues that Campe, a Prussian, translates for a German readership not only the events of the early Revolution but, more important, the emotional energy that made it so infectious.

Jennifer Gipson illuminates the changing meanings a text can acquire over time for different audiences; she studies "La Marseillaise noire" (1867; "The Black Marseillaise"), written by a free man of color, the French-speaking Creole Camille Naudin. To follow the poem's reception from its native New Orleans to other locales in later years, she writes, students must learn to look closely at what was recorded, how it was recorded, who did the recounting, and why. Matthew Lau's essay highlights how lives are constructed in print and on the stage, by studying two orators famous for their crowd followings, Georges Jacques Danton (1759–94) and François-Dominique Toussaint Louverture (1743–1803), as they are brought to life in the plays *Danton's Death* (1835), by Georg Büchner, and *Monsieur Toussaint* (1981), by Édouard Glissant.

Conceptual translation is an idea that cuts through both print and visual media. Consider the essay in this volume by Ourida Mostefai, who studies émigrés of the 1780s and 1790s alongside immigrants of the early-twenty-first century. Illuminating the tortuous ways they express identity and belonging, she unearths the painful realities of what it means to be French even today. Or look at the essay by Beth Wright, an art historian who analyzes the multisensory effects of material designed to teach the Revolution during the tumult, including masterpieces by the painter Jacques-Louis David and the pallid corpse of his most famous subject, Jean-Paul Marat (1743–93). Katherine Astbury and Giulia Pacini both take on the issue of translating concepts for unexpected audiences, in their essays on the radical prints collected by Baron Ferdinand de Rothschild and on the talking plates of common faience, which are now considered priceless collectors' items. Links between political ephemera of yesterday and today are explored by both Séverine Rebourcet and Melissa Deininger. An intriguing example of how concepts fail to translate can be seen in the essay by Yvonne Fuentes: when France's great hero Napoleon arrived in Spain, he was hated, and satirists had a heyday pointing out his many flaws. These are a few ways students can be invited to think about revolution indirectly, through its artifacts.

Interpretive Relations among the Essays

The division of the volume into five parts is arbitrary, of course, and the ways to combine the essays are endless, but a certain logic runs through our organization. Astbury's essay on strip-cartoon technology clearly belongs alongside Amaya Martin and José Martin-Pereda's essay on the optical telegraph: both involve ways of seeing. But first readers should learn from Beth Wright how to open themselves, as contemporaries theorized that one should, to enable art to speak to "all the senses at once."

The nexus of work on black liberation struggles in our book is strong: Gipson's exploration of black New Orleans speaks directly to the essays on Haiti by Daut and by Chalmin. Chalmin's essay, by approaching the French and Haitian Revolutions through their legendary figures and the writing of great philosophers, makes an intriguing sparring partner for Daut's. Chalmin's story has a beginning (Paris) and a consequence (Saint-Domingue): it is linear, leading from the *métropole* to the colony. Daut, on the other hand, contends that the slave revolt on Saint-Domingue exploded in a separate world, that it was motivated primarily by local resentments, and that it must be understood as part of the dynamic and unpredictable tug-of-war among France, her colonies, and other foreign powers that culminated in the creation of the new state called Haiti in 1804.

For those interested in knowing how ordinary people weathered the wars of revolutionary France, we recommend reading Christopher Tozzi's "new military history" alongside Erin Myers's essay on Hugo's *Quatrevingt-treize* and its famous battle scenes. A real-life example of such tensions comes to light in Prasad's memories of teaching veterans from American wars in Iraq and Afghanistan as they showed up in her Boston classrooms. Also timely is Conroy's comparison of the biting political satire of the 1790s and the recent past, using the case of *Charlie Hebdo* to show how some French artists try to live up to what are currently known as republican commitments.

Rights are a concern for essays in part 2 but in other parts as well. Take the eye-opening work of Rosa Mucignat and Sanja Perovic, who trace little-known connections among the highly secretive radical networks located in Italy, Greece, and Germany. The people of these networks, like the sansculottes of 1789, tried to fashion a new world out of rights that they considered revolutionary. The circle of Joseph Johnson, studied by J. B. Mertz, contributes to our appreciation of radicalism and makes a British philosophical connection to Champlin's essay. Champlin's approach to teaching Burke and Rousseau is noteworthy for its political acumen but especially remarkable in that Champlin teaches in Palestine. One has to believe that the Palestinian students, with the very land under their feet subject to change ownership, given the demanding expansion of aggressive Israeli settlers, have a take on property rights that is very different from—and much more visceral than—that of American students (Kershner).

The texts and approaches brought together in the list of must-reads by the volume editors span the Atlantic and the Alps. Julia Douthwaite Viglione suggests ways to teach a provocative fable of 1789 about a hungry wolf and a complacent stag, and she seeks to prod students to make connections across the centuries and oceans, with La Fontaine's wolf fables from the court of Louis XIV as well as with American concepts of social or Internet predators. Antoinette Sol opts for the quieter genre of domestic fiction, as penned by Marie Françoise de Kéralio (née Abeille). Yet she shows how seemingly innocuous letters exchanged among lady friends yielded very useful information for readers trying to make sense of the political events going on in 1790–92. Catriona Seth reminds us of the importance of Germaine de Staël's works as a means of making sense of life during the Revolution but also of reflecting on the use of fiction to write history.

Diversity—political, socioeconomic, and ethnic—can be found at home as well as abroad, as we are reminded by Boumlik and Kietlinski, eighty percent of whose students at LaGuardia Community College are people of color, many of them recent arrivals to the United States. Such students bring firsthand knowledge and valuable testimony to the study of the Déclaration des droits de l'homme ("Declaration of the Rights of Man"). Gender also casts a different light on things; it would be interesting, for example, to juxtapose Tozzi's advice on teaching military history with Dominica Chang's views on women's service in revolutions past.

Amy E. Wright's suggestions for teaching the cult of *liberté* as it migrated across Latin America may become a classic, in that they show how to survey the changing spirit over vast spaces of time and space. In their synchronic study of ideas moving through western and southern Europe, Mucingnat and Perovic's essay on the "French Revolution effect" could be juxtaposed with Mostefai's study, which zeros in on the movement of ideas among two antagonistic places, former colonies and France, over time. Where Mostefai traces arcs leading from other countries in and out of France, as people are forced to flee or return home, Mucignat and Perovic focus on the activities of radicals who aspired to attain revolution on their own soil. Whether it is in Italy, Germany, the Netherlands of the 1790s, or Mexico in the 1810s, thousands of people aspired to the egalitarian goals of 1789. Luckily for us, they wrote as well as organized movements.

Yet cynics may still ask, Is it possible to inspire students to become more engaged with their communities through historical artifacts? Is it prudent? Will social media make democratic aspirations flower in exciting new ways in the future or create a population obsessed with consumer goods and narcissism? In answer, we invite you to read these essays out of sequence in the days and years ahead and to follow your own curiosity. After all, this volume is meant as a revolutionary gesture: an act of solidarity with you, the reader.

Notes

Translations from the French are ours, unless otherwise indicated.

1. Describing his son's torture by the Macedonian police for being without the proper papers, Bajlam Nazirov states, "Even dogs are treated better than that. Here we are nothing" (Douthwaite, *Rousseau* 216).

Works Cited and Recommended

Alderman, Liz. "Au Revoir, Entrepreneurs." *New York Times*, 22 Mar. 2014, p. BU1.

Andress, David. "Can Culture Really Explain Politics? 'Interdisciplinary' Historiography, Enlightenment, and Revolution." *The Interdisciplinary Century: Tensions and Convergences in Eighteenth-Century Art, History, and Literature*, edited by Julia V. Douthwaite and Mary Vidal, Voltaire Foundation, 2005, pp. 260–69. SVEC 4.

Baecque, Antoine de. "Pamphlets: Libel and Political Mythology." *Revolution in Print: The Press in France, 1775–1800*, edited by Robert Darnton and Daniel Roche, U of California P, 1989, pp. 165–76.

Baker, Keith Michael, editor. *The French Revolution and the Creation of Modern Political Culture*. Vol.1, Pergamon Press, 1987.

———. *Inventing the French Revolution.* Cambridge UP, 1990.

Bourdin, Philippe, and Cyril Triolaire. *Comprendre et enseigner la Révolution française: Actualité et héritages.* Belin, 2015.

Canetti, Elias. *Crowds and Power.* Translated by Carol Stewart, Penguin Books, 1962.

Cook, Malcolm C. "Politics in the Fiction of the French Revolution, 1789–1794." *Studies on Voltaire and the Eighteenth Century*, vol. 201, 1982, pp. 233–340.

Coulet, Henri. "Existe-t-il un roman révolutionnaire?" *La légende de la Révolution*, edited by Christian Croisille and Jean Ehrard, Éditions ADOSA, 1988, pp. 173–83.

Darnton, Robert. *The Devil in the Holy Water; or, The Art of Slander from Louis XIV to Napoleon.* U of Pennsylvania P, 2009.

Delfour, Jean-Jacques. "*Charlie Hebdo* et le mythe révolutionnaire de la République." *Club de Mediapart*, 14 Jan. 2015, blogs.mediapart.fr/jean-jacques-delfour/blog/140115/charlie-hebdo-et-le-mythe-revolutionnaire-de-la-republique.

Didier, Béatrice. *Écrire la Révolution, 1789–1799.* PUF, 1989.

Douthwaite, Julia Viglione. *The Frankenstein of 1790 and Other Lost Chapters from Revolutionary France.* U of Chicago P, 2012.

———, editor. *Rousseau and Dignity: Art Serving Humanity.* U of Notre Dame P, 2017.

Duval, Georges. *Histoire de la littérature révolutionnaire.* E. Dentu, 1879.

Fairfax-Cholmeley, Ian. "Defense, Collaboration, Counter-Attack: The Role and Exploitation of the Printed Word by Victims of the Terror, 1793–1794." *Experiencing the French Revolution*, edited by David Andress, Voltaire Foundation, 2013, pp. 137–54. SVEC 5.

Feilla, Cecilia. *The Sentimental Theater of the French Revolution.* Ashgate Publishing, 2013.

Furet, François. *Interpreting the French Revolution.* Translated by Elborg Forster, Cambridge UP, 1981.

Furet, François, and Mona Ozouf, editors. *A Critical Dictionary of the French Revolution.* Translated by Arthur Goldhammer, Harvard UP, 1989.

Gengembre, Gérard. *La contre-révolution ou l'histoire désespérante.* Imago, 1989.

Harris, Seymour Edwin. *The Assignats.* Harvard UP, 1930.

Heinrich, Pierre. *La Louisiane sous la Compagnie des Indes, 1717–1731.* Librairie Orientale et Américaine E. Guilmoto, 1908.

Huet, Marie-Hélène. *Rehearsing the Revolution: The Staging of Marat's Death, 1793–1797.* U of California P, 1982.

Hufton, Olwen. "The Reconstruction of a Church, 1796–1801." *Beyond the Terror*, edited by Gwynne Lewis and Colin Lucas, Cambridge UP, 1983, pp. 21–52.

Hunt, Lynn. *The Family Romance of the French Revolution.* U of California P, 1992.

———. "Pornography and the French Revolution." *The Invention of Pornography*, edited by Hunt, Zone Books, 1993, pp. 301–39.

Jones, Colin. "The Overthrow of Maximilien Robespierre and the 'Indifference' of the People." *American Historical Review*, June 2014, pp. 688–713.

Kennedy, Emmet. *A Cultural History of the French Revolution*. Yale UP, 1989.
Kershner, Isabel. "A Bolder Israel Plans to Expand Its Settlements." *New York Times*, 25 Jan. 2017, p. A1.
Linton, Marisa. "Citizenship and Religious Toleration in France." *Toleration in Enlightenment Europe*, edited by Ole Peter Grell and Roy Porter, Cambridge UP, 2000, pp. 157–74.
Manjoo, Farhad. "How Social Networks Stole Trump's Limelight." *New York Times*, 2 Feb. 2017, pp. B1+.
Maron, Eugène. *Histoire littéraire de la Révolution*. 1856. *Internet Archive*, 7 Feb. 2016, archive.org/details/bub_gb_bidSePyo51AC.
Mathy, Jean-Philippe. *Melancholy Politics: Loss, Mourning, and Memory in Late Modern France*. Pennsylvania State UP, 2011.
McMahon, Darrin. *Enemies of the Enlightenment*. Oxford UP, 2001.
Newman, Andrew. *Landscape of Discontent: Urban Sustainability in Immigrant Paris*. U of Minnesota P, 2015.
Ogle, Gene E. "The Trans-atlantic King and Imperial Public Spheres: Everyday Politics in Pre-revolutionary Saint-Domingue." *The World of the Haitian Revolution*, edited by David P. Geggus and Norman Fiering, Indiana UP, 2009, pp. 79–96.
Ozouf, Mona. *L'homme régénéré: Essais sur la Révolution française*. Gallimard, 1989.
Pasco, Allan H. "Literature as Historical Archive: Reading Divorce in Mme de Staël's *Delphine* and Other Revolutionary Literature." *EMF: Studies in Early Modern France*, vol. 7, 2001, pp. 163–200.
Procter, James. *Stuart Hall*. Routledge, 2004.
Spang, Rebecca. "Paradigms and Paranoia: How Modern Is the French Revolution?" *American Historical Review*, vol. 108, no. 1, February 2003, www.fd.unl.pt/docentes_docs/ma/amh_ma_2130.pdf.
Steinberg, Ronen. "Terror on Trial: Accountability, Transitional Justice, and the *Affaire Le Bon* in Thermidorian France." *French Historical Studies*, vol. 39, no. 3, August 2016, pp. 419–44.
Taws, Richard. *The Politics of the Provisional*. Pennsylvania State UP, 2013.
Van der Poel, Ieme. "France and the United States in Contemporary Intellectual History: An Introduction." *Traveling Theory: France and the United States*, edited by Van der Poel et al., Associated University Presses, 1999, pp. 11–28.
Van Kley, Dale. *The Religious Origins of the French Revolution*. Yale UP, 1996.

Part I

Historical Contexts

Julia Douthwaite Viglione, Antoinette Sol, and Catriona Seth

A Narrative Chronology of Events in Revolutionary France

The date most often used for the beginning of the Revolution is the storming of the Bastille prison on 14 July 1789. But significant events prepared that day. First and foremost, the French state faced an economic crisis that the finance ministers Charles-Alexandre de Calonne and Jacques Necker tried in vain to solve. Second, unrest in the legal profession had led to the dismissal, exile, and reinstatement of the Paris and Bordeaux parliaments by King Louis XVI. Third, poor harvests and fear of famine had spread through the country and caused peasant and urban riots. Last but not least, thanks to the loosening of censorship laws, publishers began mass-producing political journalism and pamphlets in ways that had rarely if ever been seen in France before, and readers quickly became enthralled by tracts such as Abbé Emmanuel-Joseph Sieyès's *What Is the Third Estate?* (*Qu'est-ce que le tiers état?*), a demand for improved representation of commoners in the upcoming convocation of the Estates General, an advisory body to the king that had last been summoned in 1614. These and more are all paving stones on the road to the Fourteenth of July.

There are several ways of teaching the events of the French Revolution, the most common being to explain its various movements by the governing bodies in power. On 17 June 1789, the Estates General declared itself the National Assembly. That designation lasted only three weeks, until the deputies, who had come from all over the kingdom, refocused their energies on creating a new constitution for France and thus adopted the name Constituent Assembly. In rural areas from 17 July through early August, a general panic broke out, leading to an agrarian insurrection known as the Great Fear (*La Grande Peur*). During its tenure from July 1789 to October 1791, the Constituent Assembly voted an end to all privileges, composed the Declaration of the Rights of Man (Aug. 1789), nationalized church property, imposed an oath to uphold the civil constitution for the clergy, and issued assignats, a new paper currency. In May 1790, the Paris municipal government was reorganized into forty-eight local sections, and the traditional guilds were abolished, as were internal trade barriers. During this time, political clubs such as the radical Jacobins and the Cordeliers were formed, and the assembly abolished nobility and titles. In the summer of 1791, an upsurge of anti-Bourbon sentiment suddenly came to a head. The king and queen, who had been living under virtual house arrest in the Tuileries Palace, tried to flee to the east but were arrested at Varennes on 21 June 1791. They were escorted by armed guard back to Paris and returned to the Tuileries, where surveillance of them was increased. News of the royal family's failed escape attempt launched a further exodus of the wealthy, which further weakened their ranks, which had already been depleted in 1789–91. These emigrations robbed the nation of much of its financial and military might. Later that fall, slavery was abolished in continental France, and the Constituent Assembly, after finishing the constitution, dissolved itself to become the Legislative Assembly.

Under the Legislative Assembly from October 1791 through September 1792, those who had fled France were declared traitors and forfeited their holdings if they did not return. The Girondins, a party that counted among its members former ministers of the court of Louis XVI, military officers, and lawyers, made up the political majority of the Legislative Assembly and formed a ministry. Food shortages continued, as did riots. In the colonies, equal rights for free blacks and mulattoes were decreed in April 1792. War was declared against Austria. The Legislative Assembly, faced with the growing threat of the Prussian army, which was deploying significant troops on the eastern border, declared a national emergency and granted itself special powers. There was a division of power and struggle among the assembly, Paris's municipal government, and the Provisional Executive Committee, which was led by the flamboyant orator Georges Danton. Although the royal family was isolated in the Temple after the bloody attack on the Tuileries on 10 August, fears of conspiracy and foreign invasion inflamed the situation and brought about the September Massacres in Paris (2–7 Sept.), where over a thousand prisoners—mainly petty criminals but also Catholic nuns and priests—were killed by rioters. Unexpectedly, the French troops defeated the Prussians at Valmy.

The Legislative Assembly became the National Convention, which promptly declared a republic on 22 September, symbolically giving birth to a new era: it is the starting date for the new republican calendar, which was used in France until the early years of the nineteenth century. The convention began to debate the fate of Louis XVI, who was put on trial. On 21 January 1793, the new republic beheaded the monarch, who had been found guilty of treason. War was declared against a lengthening list of enemies without: England and Holland (Feb. 1793) and Spain (Mar.).

Meanwhile civil conflict was disrupting life in the republic and hindering military recruitment efforts. Eventually the government suppressed uprisings in Lyon, Marseilles, and the Vendée region in western France, but bitter memories of the mass drownings, infernal columns, and other repressive tactics used to stamp out dissent would haunt this time. In the spring of 1793, the convention formed the Committee of Public Safety, whose members came from the three opposing factions, the Montagnards, the Girondins, and the moderate Marais. This committee formed the de facto executive government and, at the start of summer, published a new constitution. In response to foreign threats, the convention issued an order for a general mobilization (*levée en masse*). In September 1793 the Revolution hit its most radical point in the political continuum with the decree of the Law of Suspects, which endowed the Committee of Public Safety with powers to arrest and punish. Over the ten months that followed, summary trials were followed by mass executions of people accused of a wide variety of crimes, mainly of betraying the Republic.

During this period, called the Terror, Marie-Antoinette was tried and beheaded in October 1793, and the sister of Louis XVI followed in May 1794. (The heir apparent to the Bourbon throne, the nine-year-old dauphin, Louis-Charles, would die in prison under mysterious circumstances. Only his sister, Marie-Thérèse-Charlotte, then fifteen, would survive.) In October 1793, women's political societies were banned. After a purge that had put the leading Girondins to death in the autumn of 1793, in February and March 1794 an internal power struggle occurred. More arrests and executions followed in quick succession, including former members of the convention, popular Montagnard orators, and journalists, among them Jacques-René Hébert, Camille Desmoulins, and Danton himself. On 4 February 1793, the abolition of slavery was extended to the colonies. In the summer of 1794 during the republican month of Thermidor (from late July to mid-August), infighting resulted in the arrest and execution of Maximilien Robespierre, Louis-Antoine de Saint-Just, and Georges Couthon. Many scholars consider the execution of Robespierre and his cohort on 27 July (9 Thermidor) as signaling the Revolution's end.

The convention tried to deal with the aftermath of the Terror by releasing prisoners from the crowded jails, purging militants from its ranks, punishing the most notorious leaders of repressions in the Vendée and Lyons, and closing the Jacobin clubs. A year and a half after Jean-Paul Marat, the Revolution's most famous martyr, was conferred a hero's honors, including internment in the stately Pantheon, his body was disinterred and publicly dishonored. The economic situation was dire, and there were more food riots. On 23 September 1795, the convention ratified the Constitution of Year III, which founded a new governing body called the Directory (*le Directoire*).

A group of five men made up the Directory from October 1795 through 9 November 1799. Along with a bicameral legislature, these five tried to lead the nation during what is considered one of the most unstable and volatile moments in French history. The insurrection in the Vendée was finally extinguished, and Napoleon Bonaparte, named head of the French army, won a series of spectacular victories (at Lodi, Arcole, and Rivoli). Internal discord plagued the Directory until Napoleon seized power in the coup d'etat of 18 Brumaire and established a three-man executive committee, the Consulate, with him as first consul. This is another date that some historians mark as the end of the Revolution.

On the whole, historiography has had a fairly favorable view of the Revolution, seeing it as a milestone in the birth of modern democracy, acknowledging the posterity of the Declaration of the Rights of Man, and underscoring important developments like the partial abolition of slavery. Contemporaries of the Revolution felt that they were undergoing a sea change. Although the memories of the massacres (some claim they were acts of genocide) in Lyons, the Vendée, and other regions left long-burning resentments and many crimes unpunished, since the Third Republic the Revolution has enjoyed a rather positive image in French history books. Its bicentennial in 1989 saw a terrific flourishing of scholarly and popular writing, films, and art inspired by the spirit of 1789, but it also saw the rise of efforts to capture the lesser-known stories of the royalist, Catholic, and peasant citizens who disagreed with reforms and fought to keep their traditional ways intact. Subsequent generations, from those born in the aftermath of the troubled times of the Revolution, to current freedom fighters in repressive regimes the world over, have treated it as a benchmark of often violent struggle in the name of democratic ideals.

It is beyond the scope of this book to provide an exhaustive account of how the Revolution inspired or forced change in countries around the world, and such a narrative would prove inadequate in any case, given the rapid pace with which new knowledge is emerging—about Haiti especially. The direction of political currents—from center to periphery, for example, or from metropolis to colony—is also a topic fraught with controversy and one that is inspiring exciting research today, as is clear in the essay in this volume by Rosa Mucignat and Sanja Perovic and in the illustrated atlas by Pierre-Yves Beaurepaire and Silvia Marzagalli. The essays gathered in the part titled "Global Reverberations" will doubtless pique many a reader's curiosity about the connections between people in countries as far-flung as Holland, Italy, the United States, Mexico, Greece, and Haiti, and a history of all that movement has yet to be written (if such a feat is even possible). We certainly hope, as editors, that readers will find the diversity of approaches and examples thought-provoking and that the authors' reflections will lead to further research.

Works Cited

Beaurepaire, Pierre-Yves, and Silvia Marzagalli, editors. *Atlas de la Révolution française: Circulation des hommes et des idées, 1770–1804.* Cartography by Guillaume Balavoine. Éditions Autrement, 2010.

Sieyès, Emmanuel-Joseph. *What Is the Third Estate? Pages*, U of Oregon, pages.uoregon.edu/dluebke/301ModernEurope/Sieyes3dEstate.pdf. Posted for the course Modern Europe, taught by David M. Luebke.

Lauren Pinzka

Teaching the French Revolution as Myth and Memory

For students who have come of age during an era replete with terrorist killings, never-ending war, and near financial collapse, it is timely to remember another volatile period: the violent political and cultural upheaval that was the French Revolution, during which France's relation to its past was profoundly and forever altered. My cultural studies course Myth and Memory in Modern France embraces Pierre Nora's theory of cultural memory and aims to sensitize students to the way that revolutionary memory has reverberated around the globe. This topic is explored in greater depth in part 5 of this volume. My course, through its focus on how materials are recycled and repurposed over time, makes students into partners in learning and reveals the relevance of 1789 for our time. I normally go beyond the limits of the French Revolution to the historical memory and mythmaking of war, colonialism, and nationalism, but in this essay I limit my discussion to works specifically recalling France's revolutionary past.

My gateway course is geared for students who have achieved high proficiency in French, but it could also be taught in a variety of humanities programs entirely in English, as all the works taught can be found in translation. The reading list could easily be reduced to lighten what is an ambitious syllabus. For example, limiting the course to the French Revolution and its sequels in the nineteenth century could easily constitute a satisfying version of the course.

I begin my course with a discussion of historical myth and memory in a universal context, drawing on the students' own experiences, then applying the ideas of Roland Barthes and Pierre Nora. I devote two weeks to a study of the French Revolution itself, then move to the revolutions of 1830, 1832, 1848 and 1870–71 to see how the revolutionary past was reappropriated at each of these turning points. After pursuing the Vichy government's national revolution, I conclude with the upheaval of May 1968, whose symbols and discourse are some of the most compelling evidence of the enduring influence of 1789. In examining these crucial events through literature, film, art, song, and pamphlets, the students assess the influence of the French Revolution on the media and explore how the bloody upheaval of the period was continually distorted and reified as each new era reached into its past for justifications, inspiration, and models. These documents compel us to ask whether the inscription of the past into history somehow repeats its components, filters the past anachronistically, or adds important psychological, heroic, and ideological dimensions. We consider whether the response to historical events differs with gender and experience and attempt to answer how a culture memorializes its violent past. In this essay I provide an overview of my course and devote special attention to two fleshed-out examples: Andrzej Wajda's film *Danton* and excerpts from Gustave Flaubert's *L'éducation sentimentale (Sentimental Education)*. By considering these two cases in depth, I demonstrate the value of my approach and show how it can successfully work with a literary work as well as with a film.

Throughout the course, I assign background reading on key historical events. A thorough but concise introductory text is Peter McPhee's *The French Revolution, 1789–99*. Avoiding an overly dogmatic point of view on the Revolution, McPhee presents competing theories without insisting on a definitive answer to its causes and aftereffects. Later in the course, I assign Alice Conklin, Sarah Fishman, and Robert Zaretsky's *France and Its Empire since 1870*, an equally readable and balanced account.

I begin the semester with an introduction to the process of and function of mythmaking during the French Revolution, addressing how the French view the 1789 Revolution and which myths have inscribed it into their national memory. In *Mythologies*, Barthes elucidates the process by deploying the Saussurian notion of the relation between a signifier, which is in itself empty of meaning, and the signified, which is the concept or material object it connotes. The signifier and signified together become a sign carrying the weight of all its signifieds. Myths are created in a two-part process: first a signifier is emptied of its content, then it is given a new meaning, as a sort of shorthand that consciously or unconsciously serves the political purposes of its user. The sign is now impoverished, losing its rich panoply of meanings, and becomes cemented to one concept. In the case of a myth, the meaning of a word is already constructed and imposed, its rich past amputated (189–90). A concept can be attached to many signs or what Barthes calls forms. For example, liberty can be attached to the flag, to the French Revolution, to the Statue of Liberty, to the Constitution of the United States, but the many forms become reduced to a limited number of concepts. The repetition of a concept is an indication of its mythic character (193). Through mythification, the concept is simplified and made to appear natural and innocent, whereas in fact it carries a political bias, usually that of the dominant ideology (217). I give as early examples of Barthes's mythologies the chapters titled "La croisière du sang bleu" 'The "Blue Blood" Cruise' and "Le pauvre et le prolétaire 'The Poor and the Proletariat.'

We also read Nora's chapter "La fin de l'histoire-mémoire" 'Between Memory and History,' to understand the term *lieux de mémoire* ("realms of memory") sites around which national memory has solidified (xvii), of which we study many associated with the revolutions of France. Nora's explanation of the terms *memory* and *history* complement and enrich Barthes's semiotic explanation. Just as the signifier attaches itself to multiple signifieds, the memory appropriates details in a blurry, evolving manner, locating them in space, in gestures, in images, and in objects (xviii). For Nora and his *nouvelle histoire* ("new history") colleagues, on the other hand, history is an intellectual process of analysis, reconstruction, and representation of the past that seeks to transmit values and create an awareness of a nation as a collective project and whose true purpose is to transform, petrify, even destroy and suppress memory (xix, xxiii, xx). Barthes might have spoken of the dominant ideology of the bourgeoisie seeking to obscure other voices so as to create a national mythology. In Nora's *Les lieux de mémoire*, material, symbolic, and functional memory sites are recuperated as the process of reification is carefully unraveled ("Fin" xxxiv). The selections from Nora's monumental work, which I intersperse throughout the term, demonstrate his contention that a maximum of meaning is captured in the minimum of signs (xxxv), as we can see in any topic from "La Marseillaise" to the Communards' Wall.

We are now ready to delve into myth and memory sites associated with the first French Revolution. After discussing McPhee's book, we read Jacques Julliard's analysis "Le peuple" 'The People.' The French journalist brilliantly elucidates the use of *peuple*, one of the terms key to revolutionary mythology, ambiguously describing the *populus* (meaning the nation), *plebs* (the notion of class distinctions), and *vulgus* (the bottom rungs of society) (186). The word gains much of its strength from designating the whole (an entire population) and a part of that whole (the poor) (188). Jean-Jacques Rousseau's use of the term as the origin of political sovereignty is one of the many connotations of the word (Julliard 195). In another chapter from Nora, we analyze the revolutionary calendar as a failed project to create a new collective memory in a radical rupture with France's Catholic and royalist past. We also consider the revolutionary mythology of songs such as "La Carmagnole" and "Ça ira" 'It Will Be Fine' and read Michel Vovelle's analysis of the political twists and turns of "La Marseillaise" as patriotic anthem since the French Revolution. The "Déclaration des droits de l'homme et du citoyen" 'The Declaration of the Rights of Man and of the Citizen,' Maximilien Robespierre's "Discours sur le jugement de Louis XVI" 'Speech on the Judgment of Louis XVI,' and Andrzej Wajda's film *Danton* complete my unit on 1789. Key to my discussion is the role of language, a subject explored by Jeffrey Champlin in this volume. Since the 1983 Polish film is a particularly strong illustration of the appropriation of myth and historical memory, I elaborate on some potential topics of discussion about it.

Not only did the polemic that arose after *Danton*'s release illuminate the mythic status of the French Revolution and the hold that the historical events in question still have on France today (McAllister 64)[1] but also its obvious allusions to Wajda's native Poland or perhaps to the Stalinist show trials (69) point to Barthes's emphasis on the political goals behind mythmaking. In a critique of the film, Regina Janes states that to control the present, one must control the representation of the past, since innocent viewers take art for history (306). Although the first scene of the film depicting a young boy reciting the Déclaration des droits de l'homme is fictitious, we are treated to the usual signs associated with the French Revolution, integral to the mythology surrounding that event: bread lines, revolutionary police, the threat of arrest, packed prisons, and guillotines

(McAllister 65). Most important, the film begins and ends with Georges Danton's first riding in a carriage, observing a guillotine, one of the most famous symbols of the Revolution, then dying underneath the blade of the guillotine. Other visual images dominate: "body parts, feet, broken heads of statues, broken heads of men, naked bodies of a boy and man," all meant to evoke horror and a decidedly negative view of the Terror (Janes 296), reinforcing Barthes's point about myth in the service of political ideology. Appearing in the film is Jacques-Louis David's painting *Le serment du jeu de paume* (*The Tennis Court Oath*), providing another visual representation of the Revolution that can be discussed further in the context of artistic representations of historical events. (Beth Wright's essay in this volume specifically addresses the visual arts.)

Wajda, who adapted his movie from *The Danton Case* (*Sprawa Dantona*), by Stanisława Przybyszewska, discards the traditional emphasis on the people as chief political actors. Instead, he reduces his story to one of the other great myths of the Revolution, that of the *frères ennemis* ("enemy brothers") Robespierre and Danton (McAllister 66). Most striking is the treatment of the "people who form a smiling or oppressed or cheering mass, an undifferentiated backdrop to the important activities of people whose names we know. They huddle pathetically over fires; they line up stoically and silently for bread; they cheer wildly when Danton returns to the city." The people appear to be innocuous, except in an early scene where sansculottes ominously search carriages entering Paris (Janes 296). Paul Coates notes that the power of the crowd is undercut by Wajda's choice to interweave images of the people with that of Danton (295).

True to Barthes's analysis of myth, the signs are stripped of most of their rich past. The causes of the Revolution, the deletion of Danton's role in the September Massacres, a misrepresentation of Robespierre's position on freedom of the press (McAllister 65), and the failure to cite the foreign wars responsible for the existing famine are just some of the historical elements missing from the film. In their place, Danton and Robespierre seem to stand in for the conflict between the rights of the individual and the state.

It was commonly believed, given the timing and distortions of the film, that the mythical French Revolution served to criticize General Wojciech Jaruzelski's imposition of martial law to crush Solidarity's push for political freedom in Poland. The character of Danton reminded contemporary viewers of Lech Wałęsa, a resemblance that Wajda denied. But Janina Falkowska insists that the scenes that include peasants in line for bread, with spies listening in on them, are clear references to Poland from the 1960s and 1970s (103–04). Coates concludes that Wajda's overriding desire is to portray revolution as nightmare, complete with menacing soundtrack (338), to condemn the Soviet abuses in the Poland of his childhood (300): "a typology of revolution whose master-narrative is less the French prototype than the later Bolshevik version" (294).

The subsequent French revolutions of 1830 and 1832 can be successfully examined in the context of the mythology of 1789. A particularly rich subject of study is Eugène Delacroix's *La Liberté guidant le peuple* (*Liberty Leading the People*), painted in 1830 and depicting the goddess of liberty leading the people over a barricade and fallen footsoldiers. She famously brandishes the tricolor flag and a bayoneted musket. Alain Jaubert's short documentary named for the painting provides a valuable companion teaching tool. The students enthusiastically read passages from Victor Hugo's *Les misérables*, volumes 4 and 5, which recount the failure of the June 1832 rebellion while referencing the victories of 1830 and 1848. Although the barricade symbolizes heroism and hope in the Delacroix painting, it is a scene of defeat and even treachery in Hugo's work, as in *L'éducation sentimentale*. Unlike in Flaubert's novel, misery and idealism are displayed in equal parts in *Les misérables*. Hugo's remarks on the 1848 debacle as well as his belief in the barricades as a symbol of France's future serve as an excellent segue to a discussion of Flaubert's novel.

Published in 1869, *L'éducation sentimentale* dramatically departs from both Wajda's reverential approach to the French Revolution and from Hugo and Delacroix's idealized views of the barricades.[2] Whereas Wajda wielded myths and inaccurately portrayed events perhaps to attack Stalinism and to extol the Solidarity movement, Flaubert used the same tools of mythmaking but with the opposite intention: to demythify the 1848 revolution, which had reappropriated many of the great myths of 1789. True to Barthes's theory of mythology, the nineteenth-century author's antimythification can be seen as a creation of a new revolutionary myth to undermine revolutionary activism in the service of bourgeois values. Flaubert "could not resist the temptation to let his accumulated bile overflow in what amounts to an almost militant debunking of all the nonsense and turpitude he associated with politics," writes Victor Brombert (157).

Chief among Flaubert's techniques are the deployment of formidable symbols of revolution, an attention to historical accuracy, a creation of a typology of revolutionary participants, and most of all an emphasis on the people as political actors. Throughout the description of the uprising, memories of 1789 are reactivated for the reader as they undoubtedly were for the participants of the time. Red-capped men sing "La Marseillaise" or "Les Girondins" (314), Paris is suddenly replete with barricades, an armed man in a Phrygian cap proclaims to a citizen that he must once again do his revolutionary duty (317), and on nearly every page are repeated references to the people as an indistinct entity. Flaubert then goes further, creating his own symbol of the revolution with his magnificent *fille publique* ("wench") who, after the sacking of the Tuileries, takes on the pose of the Statue of Liberty, an image that Brombert deems a comment on politics as a form of prostitution (134–35). In Vaheed Ramazani's analysis of the image of the prostitute, "she is a figure for revolution, but a figure degraded by repetition, circulation, over-use: a cliché" (124).

The novelist is, moreover, incomplete in his description of the events that he himself witnessed: "[T]he novel . . . offers, uncharacteristically, the standard material for official accounts and folk memory of the 1848 Revolution" (Wetherill 25).[3] Like Wajda, who provides no background information to the viewer, Flaubert portrays events that have no context, again divesting symbols of their rich history, in the words of Barthes. Julia Douthwaite explains that Flaubert reproduces "caricatural images of the dominant social types of the late 1840s. Three distinct social circles emerge: . . . discontented youth chez Deslaurier, the shifting allegiances of ambitious bourgeois chez Arnoux, and the smug complacency of powerful industrialists and politicians chez Dambreuse" (41). Individual language and descriptions of décor mark their social class and reveal class pretentions (41–42). Like Wajda, Flaubert appeared interested in creating a typology of revolution, a reductionist tack at the core of mythmaking.

On the other hand, Flaubert's portrayal of *le peuple* is very different from that of Wajda's. Stefan Jonsson notes, "Flaubert effectively liquidates 'the people' as a credible political ideal; it only exists as "a cover-up for the pursuit of private ambitions and collective delusions" (68). The author strips all nobility from the revolution as people laugh at the sight of death, making a mockery of political ideals. His protagonist, Frédéric, watches the crushing of the rebellion, fascinated, extremely amused, as if at a night at the theater. The people, "deux masses profondes" 'two dense masses' (Flaubert 318), are deprived of political agency, rational interests, and, of course, individuality (Jonsson 70).

The sacking of the Tuileries provides the most dramatic take on revolutionary action. Flaubert offers a cruel parody of revolutionary solidarity with characteristic bestialization of human comportment: "C'était le peuple . . . des gens disparaissaient dans cette masse *grouillante* qui montait toujours, comme un fleuve refoulé par une mare d'équinoxe, avec un long *mugissement*. . . . On n'entendait que les *piétinements* de tous les souliers" 'It was the people . . . some disappeared into a *swarming* mass that kept rising, like a river forced back by an equinox tide, with a long roar [*mooing sound*]. . . . One could only hear the *stamping* of all the shoes' (319–20; emphasis mine). After a terrifying description of excess, destruction, and mayhem, the antiproletarian character Hussonet exclaims that he finds the common people revolting, to which Frédéric replies that he finds them sublime (322). All individuality lost, the participants are available for disparagement or idealization by the bourgeois protagonists, whose parallel reactions negate each other. Flaubert makes repeated use of *on* ("one") for *le peuple*: "one" was beating up a few bourgeois (315); "one" was tearing off gates, casting iron, rolling cartridges (316).

Jonathan Culler insightfully explains Flaubert's innovative narrative technique to debunk revolutionary mythology: "rapid shifts of perspective which prevent one from determining who speaks or from where" (118). This strategy allies with mythmaking, because the source of the image is unclear, as if events are spontaneous and unmediated. For example, Frédéric steps on the hand of a fallen sergeant and then observes the scene of revolutionary pillage, drinking, and fighting. The impersonal "Cela faisait rire" 'It provoked laughter' (Flaubert 318) that follows makes the inappropriate reaction as impersonal and detached as possible, denying an attribution to his character that would help the reader identify with him or would illuminate his motives. "Flaubert's characters are poor reflectors in that they do not compose the world for us, do not organize it in ways that reveal new possibilities of feeling and perception" (Culler 129). They are not the expected "repositories of meaning" of more conventional fiction (134). In reading *L'éducation sentimentale*, we are witnessing a unique form of narrative mythmaking and memorializing that undercuts itself on every page.

I next spend several classes on the Commune, whose symbols again recall 1789. As with Wajda and Flaubert, Hugo's "L'année terrible" and Arthur Rimbaud's "L'orgie parisienne ou Paris se repeuple" ("The Orgy") provide contrasting views on the events of 1871. Hugo's poem is a classic work of 1870s mythmaking: the author celebrates the Frankish roots of French culture and poeticizes the construction of a French identity.[4] He both traces France back to its origins and creates a vision of Paris under siege during a war against its historical brothers. Rimbaud provides an ironic, degraded vision of Paris as a prostitute in the throes of revolution, the antimyth par excellence. We also listen to "Le temps des cerises" 'The Time of the Cherries,' one of France's most famed revolutionary songs. The cherries of the title are believed to be a metaphor for the good times that lie ahead if the 1870 revolution succeeds. The song has lived on in the French memory as a symbol of revolution akin to that of the tricolor flag or "La Marseillaise," the national anthem.[5]

The Vichy period, one of the most compelling sequels of the nineteenth-century revolutions, is brilliantly discussed by Philippe Burin. I also study the famous song of the French resistance, "Le chant des partisans"; the fascist journal *Je suis partout*; *Le Pierrot Noir* , a langorous take on French collaboration; and finally, Christian-Jaque's wartime version of it, *Boule de suif* (1945). Christian-Jaque's film is an especially effective demonstration of the appropriation of national revolutionary myths. Boule de suif, the heroine of Maupassant's short story situated during the Franco-Prussian war, becomes a symbol of French resistance to the Nazified Prussians.

I conclude the course with *Mai 68 dans le texte,* compiled by Emmanuelle Loyer, and *Nés en 68* ("Born in '68"), a film directed by Olivier Ducastel and Jacques Martineau in 2008.[6] The film re-creates for the modern viewer the revolutionary discourse of May 1968, which overtly references previous revolutions. We see how the events of that spring are remembered today in France as well as how they preserved France's revolutionary past. Providing a historical counterpoint to the film, Loyer assembled primary documents from the period in the form of pamphlets, declarations, petitions, slogans, police reports, press releases, and so forth. The juxtaposition of the film memorializing the event and our analysis of the language and mythmaking of the time provides an excellent conclusion to the course. We see the hold that the French Revolution has continued to exert centuries later. The use of historical memory and myth to political ends can be no clearer than in the 1968 uprising, which had as its goal the radical transformation of French society. The revolutionary spirit of 1789, still a driving force in the early twenty-first century, retains its significance as a subject of inquiry.

Notes

Translations from the French are mine, unless otherwise indicated.

1. French leftists have generally preferred Robespierre as the revolutionary hero, while the *annalistes* have rehabilitated Danton. The uproar over Wajda's

film (so upsetting to President Mitterrand that he left the auditorium) reignited debate over competing mythical versions of the Revolution (McAllister 66). Wajda answered his critics by saying that facts are for the historians, positing that the truth is unknowable (McAllister 70; Martin 65).

2. In an advanced course, it would be possible to read the entire novel, but in an introductory level literature course I often assign the last two pages of part 2, chapter 6, and the first thirty pages of part 3, chapter 1. I then skip to the last three pages of part 3, chapter 5.

3. See Doyle 39 for a discussion of some of Flaubert's more interesting omissions.

4. After the humiliation of the French defeat at the hands of the Prussians, the 1870s became a rich period of patriotic mythmaking, during which many simplified versions of French history became anchored in the national consciousness.

5. To complete my study of the Commune, we read Rebérioux. The history of the Communards' Wall in the Père-Lachaise Cemetery exemplifies the relation among public sentiment, historical memory, and the exigencies of a political moment. I add to this work Barthes's "Un ouvrier sympathique," from *Mythologies* (63–64), to complement the varying takes on the proletariat explored in the course of the semester.

6. For nonreaders of French, mai68inenglish.com/ is an excellent resource, providing English translations for the 1968 posters.

Works Cited

Barthes, Roland. *Mythologies.* Éditions du Seuil, 1957.

Brombert, Victor. *The Novels of Flaubert.* Princeton UP, 1966.

Burin, Philippe. "Vichy." Nora, *Lieux*, vol. 2, pp. 2469–87.

Christian-Jaque, director. *Boule de suif.* Artès Films, 1945.

Coates, Paul. "'Where Id Was . . .': *Danton* according to Georg Büchner, Stanislawa Przybyszewska, and Andrzej Wajda." *Commitment and Compassion: Essays on Georg Büchner*, edited by Patrick Fortmann and Martha B. Helfer, Rodopi, 2012, pp. 283–302.

Conklin, Alice L., et al. *France and Its Empire since 1870.* 2nd ed., Oxford UP, 2014.

Culler, Jonathan. *Flaubert: The Uses of Uncertainty.* Elek Books, 1974.

Danton. Directed by Andrzej Wajda. Gaumont, 1983.

Douthwaite, Julia. "The Uses of History in Tocqueville's *Souvenirs* and Flaubert's *L'éducation sentimentale.*" *Romance Languages Annual*, vol. 4, 1992, pp. 40–46.

Doyle, Natalie: "Flaubert's *L'éducation sentimentale*: 1848 as Parody." *Australian Journal of French Studies*, vol. 28, no. 1, 1991, pp. 39–49.

Falkowska, Janina. "The Historical Discourse in *Danton.*" *The Political Films of Andrzej Wajda: Dialogism in* Man of Marble, Man of Iron, *and* Danton. Berghahn Books, 1996, pp. 102–10.

Flaubert, Gustave. *L'éducation sentimentale.* Gallimard, 1952. Vol. 2 of *Œuvres.*

Janes, Regina. "Danton Does Not Sing *La Marseillaise*: Andrzej Wajda, Jean

Renoir, and Their French Revolutions." *Studies in Eighteenth-Century Culture*, vol. 25, 1996, pp. 293–307.

Jaubert, Alain, dir. *Liberty Leading the People*. Encyclopaedia Britannica Educational Corporation, 1991. DVD-ROM.

Jonsson, Stefan. "The Invention of the Masses: The Crowd in French Culture from the Revolution to the Commune." *Crowds*, edited by Jeffrey T. Schnapp and Matthew Tiews, Stanford UP, 2006, pp. 47–75.

Julliard, Jacques. "Le peuple." Nora, *Lieux*, vol. 1, pp. 185–229.

Loyer, Emmanuelle. *Mai 68 dans le texte*. Broché, 2008.

Martin, Marcel. "La nouvelle 'affaire Danton.'" Review of *Danton*, directed by Andrzej Wajda, *La revue du cinéma*, Apr. 1983, pp. 63–66.

McAllister, Elaine. "Film as Historical Text: *Danton*." *Literature and Film in the Historical Dimension*, edited by John Simons, UP of Florida, 1994, pp. 63–73.

McPhee, Peter. *The French Revolution, 1789–99*. Oxford UP, 2002.

Nés en 68. Directed by Olivier Ducastel and Jacques Martineau, Pyramide Distribution, 2008.

Nora, Pierre. "La fin de l'histoire-mémoire." Nora, *Lieux*, vol. 1, pp. xvii–xlii.

———, editor. *Les lieux de mémoire*. Gallimard Quarto, 1997. 2 vols.

Ramazani, Vaheed K. "Historical Cliché: Irony and the Sublime in *L'éducation sentimentale*. *PMLA*, vol. 108, no. 1, 1993, pp. 121–35.

Rebérioux, Madeleine. "Le Mur des Fédérés: Rouge 'sang craché.'" Nora, *Lieux*, vol. 1, pp. 619–49.

Vovelle, Michel. "*La Marseillaise*: La guerre ou la paix." Nora, *Lieux*, vol. 1, pp. 85–135.

Wetherill, P. M. "Flaubert and Revolution." *Literature and Revolution*, edited by David Bevan, Rodopi, 1989, pp. 19–33.

Christopher Tozzi

Teaching the Revolution through a Military Lens

How many students in a course on the French Revolution can identify the major military events and figures of the period? That question may seem irrelevant in the wake of the rich scholarship that has appeared during the last several decades on other key dimensions of the Revolution, such as mass media, human rights, and religious freedom, which the essays in this volume deal with. Teaching military history might appear to be at odds with helping students understand topics now deemed more intellectually significant than they used to be.

Yet military history need not detract from other aspects of the French Revolution. On the contrary, the French revolutionary army and wars can serve in the classroom as a fruitful entry point for studying other topics and for engaging students who might otherwise not be inclined to take a course on the Revolution in the first place. Used properly, military history can leave students with a richer, fuller grasp of the revolutionary era.

Why Military History?

Many academic disciplines trace their intellectual roots to a liberal Enlightenment tradition that is dismissive of war. As Hans Joas (29–42) has shown, the overarching trend on college campuses in recent decades has been to place military history low on the list of teaching priorities. Yet in this respect universities are not responding to the wishes of many of their students, who express consistent interest in courses on military history (Ewers).

That interest is likely due in part to the presence of veterans on campuses. The federal government reported in 2013 that over one million veterans were pursuing higher education, a figure it expected to grow by twenty percent in succeeding years ("Who?"). For men and women who have pursued military careers, military history is the basis for a personal connection to subjects such as the French Revolution (Lynn, "Embattled Future").

The popularity of military history among the public at large also contributes to students' demand for military history in their courses. Wars, armies, and military technology fuel a huge publishing industry, to say nothing of television shows, films, and cable news. One might argue that these media narrow students' viewpoints by inclining them to believe that war is necessarily a significant component of the study of the past. That argument may be valid, but it is not a reason to view the teaching of military history negatively. Teachers have much to gain by showing students that military events are deeply intertwined with social, cultural, economic, and political affairs, even if popular representations of military history do not always make this relation clear.

Military History as the Key to Continuity

Given the scholarship of the last several decades, the French revolutionary wars and the revolutionary army may seem to have little importance in the history of the Revolution as a whole. Yet that military events and institutions are among the most continuous features of revolutionary history makes them valuable in the classroom.

The revolutionary war, which the National Assembly initiated in April 1792 by declaring war on the king of Hungary and Bohemia—by which the deputies meant the Holy Roman emperor, Leopold II—continued in one form or another virtually uninterrupted until Napoleon's defeat at Waterloo in June 1815. The war therefore "ended up as the common denominator of the Revolution," as François Furet observed (72); therefore the otherwise discontinuous phases of the Revolution were connected by war. The French revolutionary army was one of the few things that the revolutionaries never disbanded or radically reformed. Political regimes, religious accords, administrative organizations, and laws on institutions such as slavery varied widely over the course of the revolutionary period, but the army remained fundamentally stable, despite a series of incremental reforms pursued by succeeding administrations.

The details of the war and the French revolutionary army (to say nothing of the armies of competing states or of antirepublican French factions) are beyond the scope of this essay, but teachers seeking an overview may take advantage of a rich set of works on this topic. Frederick Schneid's introduction to *European Armies of the French Revolution* offers a concise yet thorough summary of the revolutionary wars. The first chapter of the same book, also authored by Schneid, summarizes the institutional history of the French revolutionary army to great effect ("French Army"). For a more detailed narrative of the war, T. C. W. Blanning's *The French Revolutionary Wars, 1787–1802* remains a touchstone, and John Lynn's *Bayonets of the Republic* surveys the makeup of the French army in impressive detail. Samuel Scott's *Response of the Royal Army to the French Revolution* offers perhaps the most complete and original analysis of the institutional history of the army during the Revolution.

French Revolutionary Military History in the Classroom: Some Examples

There are also works of scholarship that combine military history with other dimensions of the Revolution. None of them focus on the war or the army for the sake of military history but instead use the military context as a research tool for uncovering broader themes.

For example, the military history of the Revolution offers an excellent foundation for exploring social change in the classroom. A teacher might begin by discussing the relation between the army and society during the Enlightenment. As Michael Roberts argues in introducing the military revolution thesis, the emergence in the seventeenth century of more sophisticated military technology fueled demand for new classes of people to enlist in the army, which had traditionally been the province of the military nobility (23–24), because the new weapons and strategies required expertise that was not a part of a typical aristocratic education. The extent to which changes in military technology opened up new career opportunities for nonelites was limited under the Old Regime, but the changes help explain why the Ségur Ordinance of 1781, which restricted most officers' commissions in the army to nobles, exempted the artillery and engineering corps, where nonaristocratic men trained in mathematics were crucial (Lucas 101).

Once the Revolution began, the army's role in driving social change increased dramatically. The emigration of thousands of noble officers created new opportunities for men of humble origins to pursue wealth and political status by enlisting as officers. As Rafe Blaufarb shows, it also transformed the army into a cauldron for experimenting with revolutionary notions of merit, since the regiments and volunteer battalions became one of the first institutions in France where talent took precedence over lineage as the basis for promotion.

In addition, as both Jean-Paul Bertaud and Lynn (*Bayonets*) demonstrate, the army became a proving ground for new ideas about democracy and political expression (see Champlin's essay in this volume). The revolutionaries extended universal voting rights to soldiers well before they granted them to all men in France, yet they also sought to soften political debate among the troops by banning political clubs. Changes such as these make the revolutionary army a fruitful point of entry for discussing the key social and political changes effected by the Revolution.

Even troop movements and tactics on the battlefield, topics not usually considered to be of much value outside military academies, exemplified revolutionary social reform. A close look at some of the major battles of the Revolution, for example, such as Valmy in 1792 and Fleurus in 1794, reveals how unimportant cavalry proved for French forces on revolutionary battlefields. That trend, which constituted a sharp departure from the Old Regime, can be explained partly in terms of the revolutionaries' wish to make men more equal by reducing reliance on socially prestigious cavalry squadrons, partly because of the short supply of nobles trained as cavalrymen. The revolutionary generals adopted tactics focused on unsparing frontal assault, to demonstrate the devotion and self-sacrifice that French leaders expected of soldiers as well as of republican citizens in general.

The cultural history of the revolutionary era is likewise inseparable from the military context. A lesson on Norbert Elias's famous "civilizing process" thesis about prerevolutionary Europe might include discussion of the ways in which this process affected the army under the Old Regime. Noble officers, like their civilian counterparts, were keen to prove that they were civilized; they adopted effeminate dress and conveyed their servants to battlefields (Bell 30). Old Regime military history offers opportunities for studying the complex theme of pacificism during the eighteenth century, which in turn shows the intellectual diversity of the Enlightenment. Philosophes such as Voltaire wrote frequently about warfare but not always to denounce it, as the traditional understanding of the Enlightenment would expect. Enlightenment thinkers sometimes approved of war, a reality illuminated perhaps most clearly by the declaration in the *Encyclopédie* that the "art of war is . . . the greatest of all" (7: 985).

The revolutionaries' rejection of the Old Regime culture of war, and of aggressive war in general following the National Assembly's "declaration of peace" of May 1790, exemplified their dismissal of aristocratic culture (Bell 108). In its place they instated a new military culture that entailed strict separation between the military and civilian spheres. Martial glory assumed less importance when the French reconceptualized war as a necessary evil that someday would be ended instead of an ordinary feature of international politics. The Napoleonic regime moderated the existential theory of warfare but left intact the notion that a universal and lasting peace was possible. Napoleon also advanced the program of using the army as a model for civilian society and culture by, for example, requiring many civilian officials to dress in military garb (Bell 191, 230, 244). These changes exerted a lasting influence not only on France but also on the many regions across the globe affected by the Revolution.

Revolutionary military history can also help students understand and interpret the political history of the Revolution. The debates between the spring of 1790 and April 1792 regarding whether France should go to war against its enemies, and what type of war it should wage if it did, offer an excellent starting point for studying the political radicalization of the Revolution as well as nuancing the thought of some of its political leaders. For example, depictions of Maximilien Robespierre as a bloodthirsty dictator, the image students are likely to have from popular representations of the man, are at odds with his famous observation that France should avoid foreign war because "no one likes armed missionaries" (Bell 208). The declining popularity of the king, the rise and fall of the Girondins, and the Montagnard consolidation of power can also be explained, in part, by the debate over the war and France's poor military fortunes at its outset (Guiomar 16).

Teachers seeking to explain the Reign of Terror may also find the revolutionary war to be a good point of departure. As Mona Ozouf shows, the argument that the Terror came in response to military crisis overlooks the chronology of the relation between the war and the Terror. It was not until the summer of 1794, when French armies finally triumphed on the battlefield, that the revolutionaries began intermixing the rhetoric of the war and the Terror to suggest that the second was caused by the first. For students, Ozouf's essay is an excellent exercise in interpreting historical evidence. It is also an opportunity to expose more advanced students to historiographic debate, since Ozouf responds to a range of other historians since the nineteenth century who have written about the Terror.

Lessons for the Present

The themes of the French Revolution continue to influence present-day societies. The military dimension of the Revolution has been influential as well. The French revolutionaries grappled with debates regarding war and its discontents that speak directly to those faced by modern democratic societies, including the United States.

For the revolutionaries, these debates began in the spring of 1790, when deputies in the National Assembly contended with the king to decide which branch of government should have the power to declare war and peace. This debate, which is summarized in English most effectively by David Bell (99) and is easily accessible in primary-source form from the *Archives parlementaires*, offers perspective on the challenges that modern generations of Americans face when the executive power initiates conflicts without legislative authorization. Jean-François Rewbell's remark in 1790 before the National Assembly that affording the king, as France's executive authority, the power both to declare and to oversee wars ran the risk of "combining will with action, law with execution, conflating all the powers" (*Archives* 15: 564) might as easily have been a criticism of decisions by recent American presidential administrations to deploy American forces to Libya or Syria, or drones to Pakistan, without congressional authorization.

The parallels between past and present continue when France went to war in 1792. The National Convention's decree of 10 October 1793, which declared France "revolutionary until the peace," officially (if ambiguously) stated that constitutional government would be suspended so long as the country remained at war. This suspension was not unlike efforts by authorities in France, the United States, and other democratic societies today to scale back civil liberties in the name of national defense, even if the threat today takes the form of terrorism rather than a foreign or rebel army. Similarly, the Jacobin regime's obsession with surveillance, reflected not only in the *comités de surveillance* that the regime instituted in 1793 but also in efforts to intercept private mail (*Recueil* 6: 165), share affinities with the surveillance of electronic communications that, according to whistle-blowers like Edward Snowden, the United States now pursues. The revolutionaries' experiments with ensuring civilian control over armies and generals by dispatching representatives to oversee them, which clearly failed in the case of ambitious generals such as Napoleon Bonaparte, resemble challenges faced by modern American administrations, such as Douglas MacArthur's attempts to defy the policies set by Harry Truman during the Korean War. Asking students to study and evaluate these issues in revolutionary France can lead naturally to discussion of how present-day democracies confront problems related to the military and national security.

Revolutionary debates regarding what to do with conquered territory and peoples also resonate today. Some French leaders argued that annexing territory was at odds with the democratic image that the state sought to cultivate. That is why Pétion de Villeneuve suggested during the debate about war powers in May 1790 that France should "expressly renounce all idea of aggrandizement and conquest" (*Archives* 15: 544). Yet the experience of war showed that things were not so simple. Surrendering territory that French troops had gained could damage the army's morale and place the army at a disadvantage as it continued to battle absolutist enemies, an anonymous writer informed the Committee of Public Safety in 1795 (*Recueil* 25: 151). Another warned that if the post-Terror government renounced territorial aggrandizement, as the Jacobins had done, the Thermidorian regime would undercut its legitimacy by failing to distinguish itself from the Montagnard dictatorship of Robespierre and Louis-Antoine de Saint-Just (548–50).

The revolutionaries split the difference by annexing some territory, especially in Belgium and the Rhineland, and establishing networks of nominally independent "sister republics" elsewhere (Harouel; Guyot 170). The sister republics resemble the governments that the United States has installed during recent conflicts in places such as Afghanistan and Iraq. Unable to execute fully the democratic mission with which they are charged, these regimes rule over client states continually in need of American financial and military support, just as the sister republics looked to Paris for their defense against foreign and domestic enemies.

The role of ethnic and religious minorities in the French revolutionary army proves similarly relevant to the present. The revolutionaries formed legions of black troops in part to reinforce policies regarding racial emancipation. In turn, all-black units became a liability for the state after Napoleon reintroduced slavery in 1802. Meanwhile, the experience of Jews in the army demonstrated the eagerness with which the revolutionaries and Napoleon alike encouraged a marginalized constituency to take up arms as a way of reinforcing its newfound integration into French society following the extension of citizenship to Jews early in the Revolution (Tozzi 198–216). The residents of formerly foreign territories underwent a similar process after the French annexed their homelands and sought to transform them into republican citizens or, under Napoleon, into imperial subjects. Each of these topics offers a foundation for studying the relation between race, religion, and national origin on the one hand and social and political identity on the other.

Note

Translations from the French are mine, unless otherwise indicated.

Works Cited

Archives parlementaires de 1787 à 1860: Recueil complet des débats législatifs et politiques des Chambres françaises, première série (1787–1799). 82 vols., edited by M. J. Mavidal and M. E. Laurent, Paul Dupont, 1879–1913.

Bell, David A. *The First Total War: Napoleon's Europe and the Birth of Warfare As We Know It.* Houghton Mifflin, 2007.

Bertaud, Jean-Paul. *La révolution armée: Les soldats citoyens et la Révolution française.* Robert Laffont, 1979.

Blanning, T. C. W. *The French Revolutionary Wars, 1787–1802.* Arnold, 1996.

Blaufarb, Rafe. *The French Army, 1750–1820: Careers, Talent, Merit.* Manchester UP, 2002.

Elias, Norbert. *The Civilizing Process.* Urizen Books, 1978.

Encyclopédie, ou dictionnaire raisonné des sciences, des arts et des métiers. 17 vols., edited by Denis Diderot and Jean le Rond d'Alembert, Briasson, 1751–65.

Ewers, Justin. "Why Don't More Colleges Teach Military History?" *US News*, 3 Apr. 2008, www.usnews.com/news/articles/2008/04/03/why-dont-colleges-teach-military-history.

Furet, François. *Interpreting the French Revolution.* Translated by Elborg Forster. Cambridge UP, 1981.

Guiomar, Jean-Yves. *L'invention de la guerre totale, XVIIIe–XXe siècle.* Éditions du Félin, 2004.

Guyot, Raymond. *Le Directoire et la paix de l'Europe: Des traités de Bâle à la deuxième coalition (1795–1799).* Alcan, 1912.

Harouel, Jean-Louis. *Les républiques soeurs.* PUF, 1997.

Joas, Hans. *War and Modernity.* Translated by Rodney Livingstone, Polity, 2003.

Lucas, Colin. "Nobles, Bourgeois, and the Origins of the French Revolution." *Past and Present*, vol. 60, 1973, pp. 84–126.

Lynn, John. *Bayonets of the Republic: Motivation and Tactics in the Army of Revolutionary France, 1791–94.* U of Chicago P, 1984.

———. "The Embattled Future of Academic Military History." *The Journal of Military History*, vol. 61, 1997, pp. 777–89.

Ozouf, Mona. "War and Terror in French Revolutionary Discourse, 1792–1794." *The Journal of Modern History*, vol. 56, 1984, pp. 579–97.

Recueil des actes du Comité de salut public: Avec la correspondance officielle des représentants en mission et le registre du Conseil exécutif provisoire. 28 vols., edited by Alphonse Aulard, Imprimerie Nationale, 1893–1955.

Roberts, Michael. "The Military Revolution, 1560–1660." *The Military Revolution Debate: Readings on the Military Transformation of Early Modern Europe*, edited by Cliff J. Rogers, Westview Press, 1995, pp. 13–36.

Schneid, Frederick C., editor. *European Armies of the French Revolution, 1789–1802.* U of Oklahoma P, 2015.

———. "The French Army." Schneid, *European Armies*, pp. 13–35.

———. Introduction. Schneid, *European Armies*, pp. 3–12.

Scott, Samuel. *The Response of the Royal Army to the French Revolution: The Role and Development of the Line Army, 1787–93.* Clarendon Press, 1978.

Tozzi, Christopher. *Nationalizing France's Army: Foreign, Black, and Jewish Troops in the French Military, 1715–1831.* U of Virginia P, 2016.

"Who Are Today's Student Veterans?" *VA Campus Toolkit*, 22 June 2016, www.mentalhealth.va.gov/studentveteran/studentvets.asp.

Séverine Rebourcet

Liberté, *Égalité*, *Fraternité*, and *Laïcité*: Frenchness, Islam, and French Hip-Hop

> *La France est une République indivisible, laïque, démocratique et sociale. Elle assure l'égalité devant la loi de tous les citoyens sans distinction d'origine, de race, ou de religion. Elle respecte toutes les croyances.*
>
> —Constitution, article premier
>
> *France is a republic that is indivisible, secular, democratic, and social. It ensures that all citizens are equal before the law irrespective of their religion or ethnic origins. It respects all religious beliefs.*

Laïcité ("secularism") is central to the foundation and essence of the French Republic. The laïc laws were enacted in the 1880s, and the vote on the separation of church and state took place in 1905. The secularization process itself started during the French Revolution, because the Revolution began the removal of the Church's power from the civil and political space, the removal of its role in the governance of France. Since 1905, *laïcité* officially defends the neutrality of the state, freedom of conscience, and pluralism (Baubérot, "Questions").

The neutrality of the state emphasizes the idea that all citizens are equal before the law. Their rights do not depend on race, background, or religious beliefs. All civil servants and state workers apply this neutrality in the performance of their duties. They must show no sign of religious affiliation. In the 2004 law on secularism, this rule applied to the students of public schools. Freedom of conscience supports freedom of religion, the separation of church and state, and freedom of expression. Finally, pluralism means that the state must protect religious freedom against discriminatory policies.

The French historians and sociologists of religion who define French secularism emphasize its different aspects.[1] Olivier Roy, for instance, focuses on religious visibility and the public space:

> *Laïcité* is explicit: it is political choice that defines the place of religion in an authoritarian, legal manner. *Laïcité* is decreed by the state, which then organizes public space (but it does not necessarily cast religion into the private sphere, contrary to a persistent legend; it rather defines, and this limits in every sense of the word, the visibility of religion in the public space). (8)

In his monographs and articles on the subject, Jean Baubérot gives a definition that echoes Roy's but stresses the notion of freedom and consensus. His approach reflects article 1 of the 1905 law, which stipulates, "La République assure la liberté de conscience. Elle garantit le libre exercice des cultes sous les seules restrictions édictées ci-après dans l'intérêt de l'ordre public" 'The Republic ensures freedom of conscience. It ensures the free practice of religion under the sole restrictions issued below in the interest of the public order' ("Article premier"). In his work on *laïcité,* Baubérot also responds to the misinterpretation of secularism.

In 2003–04 he participated in the Stasi Commission, whose report led to the 2004 law against signs of religion in schools. This commission was set up by President Jacques Chirac in 2003 in order to discuss *laïcité* and the ways it is enforced in France. During the final vote, Baubérot opposed the law, because, he argued, it targeted only the Muslim community. He explained his decision in an article underlining the fact that the law was passed during the national debate about the Muslim head scarf. He criticized the politicians (and the media) for their misconceptions based on the idea that the veil signifies feminine submission or Islamist allegiance or both. Baubérot insisted that the secular law did not prohibit the wearing of religious signs unless it disturbed school curricula or school discipline or unless it was employed to proselytize inside the school limits ("Commission stasi" 137). Patrick Weil, also a member of the commision, backed

Baubérot's arguments on what the veil meant for Muslim women. He stressed the importance of equality to France's diverse religious communities and warned that the Muslim community, which "is the largest and most recent in mainland France," must be protected. Weil emphasized that "[the] commission demanded that the French state respect fully the freedom of building mosques, performing funerary rites, and observing culinary customs" (147). Both Baubérot and Weil foresaw the negative attention that would be given to the Muslim population by the media and conservative politicians and the discrimination that the Muslims would suffer. This community is the target of damaging perceptions.

Current tensions in Europe related to terrorist threats from groups such as the Islamic State and the growing animosity toward the waves of migrants have changed the way Islam is perceived. In France, the religion is a relative newcomer in what some right-wing politicians have called a long-standing Judeo-Christian society. The complaint that Muslims have trouble assimilating or adjusting to societal customs can be frequently heard in the nationalist and conservative discourses in France. But voices from the outskirts of major cities are defying such ideas about Islam and questioning the validity of secular ideology when it endorses intolerance toward a community that is both ethnically and religiously defined. Several hip-hop artists who are strongly bound to their religious background are questioning the uniform perception of national identity, of Frenchness, and of *laïcité* in the twenty-first century. Lara Dotson-Renta explains:

> The [hip-hop] artists' avowed distance from a sense of unified identity is intricately intervowen with French colonial history, as well as the construction of *laïcité* and its careful delineation of religious subject. The fissures of *laïcité* and the ways in which its implementation may be viewed as racialized and spatialized are particularly evident in the *banlieue*, where Islam is highly visible. (355)

French hip-hop artists like Médine and Kery James epitomize issues related to identity, religion, and colonial heritage, and in their texts they capture a new concept of Muslimness.

In this essay, I explore how popular culture emerging from the periphery increasingly criticizes the abuses that have resulted from the conservative interpretation of secularism and national identity. Hip-hop not only offers a way into a discussion of contemporary issues but also plays out in real time what is at stake in the battle of symbols, both religious and political. The value of these texts, songs, and other art forms is twofold: first, they are all available online; second, they characterize, in a media familiar to students, the conflicts taking place in society now. Music is an effective way of grounding a sensitive and difficult topic. For any course that examines secularism, the legacy of the French Revolution, and religions today, an understanding of the importance of religious and political symbols is essential.

The French Revolution and the War of Symbols

The history of France and the history of Roman Catholicism are so closely connected that in the fourteenth century, in the midst of the Crusades, the papacy was at Avignon instead of at the Vatican. French conceptions of national identity cannot be detached from the Catholic Church: France is often called the eldest daughter of the Church. The first French monarch's conversion to Christianity is "widely regarded as the founding act of the French nation-state" (Hargreaves and McKinney 13). "Catholicism legitimized the monarchy and sacralized key moments of the life of both individuals and communities" (Kselman 66). It was incorporated into life at many levels. For instance, it kept official registers of births through baptism, of weddings, and of deaths. It played an essential role in art and culture. It is inscribed in France's landscape, architecture (cathedrals, famous pilgrimage sanctuaries), and daily life—calendars bear the names of saints' feast days, and streets and cities are named after holy people or events.

The Enlightenment and the French Revolution, however, weakened the general influence of Catholicism and secularized public record keeping of individual lives (Furet and Ozouf 31). A republican calendar was created. Royal subjects became citizens, and their duties became social and civic (Hunt 35). The Revolution and the ensuing First Republic changed the political and religious landscape: the secular left opposed the right wing, which was strongly associated with Christian values. Religious signs or references were erased from politics, and national rhetoric was cleansed of religious allusions. A clean break was sought from the monarchic past and heritage: "Although it was enunciated with religious fervor, revolutionary language was nonetheless resolutely secular in content. . . . The new social contract needed no analogy to Biblical Covenants: it was grounded in reason and the natural right of man" (28). The purge of religious signs meant the removal of royal symbols, since the religious and the royal were tied in essence. This focus on symbols was a counterreaction to their omnipresence under the Bourbons, who "had succeeded in making power virtually coterminous with the symbolic apparatus of monarchy, especially the monarch's person" (55). Since the body of the king had been likened to the body of Christ, "power was measured by the proximity" to it (58). Symbols, emblems, and allegories often captured "the virtues and the force of the divine power [*pouvoir divin*] of the nation or of the king to whom or to which subjects or citizens must submit" (Laurent 363). Therefore citizens, to assert themselves, had to sever this connection with the king's body. Yet "the rhetorical matrix of revolutionary politics also enhanced the import of symbolic forms" (Hunt 55), such as liberty trees, clothes in the colors of the nation, and earthenware dishes bearing revolutionary symbols.

In 1792, year 1, a "woman [with] her hand on fasces and holding a spear, with a Phrygian cap" stood as the chosen representation of the First Republic. Marianne, a symbol of liberty, was a direct borrowing from Greco-Roman iconography. This choice directly challenged the hold of Catholicism, as "Liberty was secular and easily associated with Reason (both were represented iconographically as female figures) and opposable to the central female figure of Catholicism, the Virgin Mary" (Hunt 65). Michel Vovelle, who offers a rich analysis of the evolution of Marianne, indicates that her posture or headdress varied during the French Revolution, because attributes related to *fraternité* (uncovered breasts) and *égalité* needed to be added. Baubérot summarizes the semiotic subversion that occurred during the Revolution:

> Sous la Révolution, la laïcisation progresse avec la proclamation explicite de la liberté de culte par la Constitution de 1791, la laïcisation de l'état civil, la création du mariage civil. . . . Mais, en même temps, des mesures affirment l'émergence d'une religion civile avec son calendrier républicain, ses martyrs, sa déesse Liberté, sa déesse Raison. ("Questions")

> During the French Revolution, secularization moves forward with the explicit proclamation of the freedom of religion in the 1791 Constitution, the secularization of the civil registry, the creation of civil marriage. . . . In the meantime, measures state the emergence of a civil religion with its republican calendar, its martyrs, its goddess Liberty, its goddess Reason.

The Revolution overturned royal and religious (Catholic) symbols in order to create a breach between the church and state in the civil, political landscape and, more generally, in the public sphere.

The Third Republic (1870–1940) explicitly included *laïcité* among its republican principles and inaugurated Marianne as a national emblem, officially selecting "La Marseillaise" as the national anthem and the fourteenth of July as the national day. The ideology behind *laïcité* was simply to force all religious practices out of the public sphere and allow them to be observed only in the private sphere. Schools were secularized and public prayer forbidden. The Third Republic sought to unite a country that past revolutions, wars, and other national crises had divided. This unity was to cover every aspect of life: everyone had to use the French language, and everyone had to attend school until sixteen years of age. The notion of fatherland was "mediated between the private society (family) and the official society (the nation)" (Weber 96).

France is proud and protective of its republican values and of their emblems, because they are ideal expressions of the nation. Disrespect is not tolerated. In the early 2000s, during soccer games (between France and Algeria or, in the national league, when Bastia and Lorient were playing), supporters hissed and booed as the French national anthem was played, because Corsica is a stronghold of separatist militants. Chirac, exasperated by such insolence, interrupted a game and made a public address on national television: "Quelques irresponsables ont cru devoir siffler 'la Marseillaise' . . . . C'est inadmissible et inacceptable. . . . Je ne tolèrerai pas et n'accepterai pas que soit porté atteinte aux valeurs essentielles de la République et à ceux qui les expriment" 'Some reckless individuals felt the need to boo "La Marseillaise". . . . It is impermissible and unacceptable. . . . I will not tolerate and not accept that the essential values of the Republic be violated as well as those who express them' (Dhers). The French Republic (and its essential attributes: the tricolor flag, the anthem, Marianne) must not be dishonored. Nonetheless, the twentieth and twenty-first centuries have witnessed new tensions in the concept of Frenchness and French citizenship. What does it mean to be French?

"La République Métissée": Questioning the Symbols and the Ideals

The 1998 French victory at the soccer World Cup introduced the image that France is a *république métissée*—a multicultural and a multiracial republic (Dubois): the blue-white-and-red (the colors of the French flag) team proudly became the *black-blanc*-and-*beur* team. *Black* refers to the Caribbean and West African diaspora, epitomized by players such as Marcel Desailly and Lilian Thuram; *blanc* signifies white France; and *beur* alludes to the northern African community, with Zinedine Zidane, among others.[2] Many in the former colonies felt that this new motto meant a true integration, but some considered it hypocritical, because the French Republic did not apologize for the abuses of its colonial history, a history that led to the existence of certain ethnic and religious groups in France. The subject is controversial in contemporary politics. Immigration brings forward the notion of racial equality and inequality and is constantly linked with the colonial heritage of France in the Caribbean islands and other former colonies. "During the 1790s, and again during the important French imperial expansion under the Third Republic, the principle of universal inclusion became layered with practices of racial exclusion" (23). The universalist idea of the French Republic revealed itself to be less egalitarian than as espoused in the process of colonization (Conklin). The exclusionary practices of colonization tainting the republican discourse of equality came under fire and were denounced by hip-hop artists who were the sons and grandsons of colonial subjects.

After the independence of the colonies, former colonial subjects immigrated to France in the hope of having better lives. Most of them took up residence on the outskirts of metropolitan areas, in *bidonvilles* ("slums"). The state ordered the destruction of the *bidonvilles* in order to build housing projects as new urban planning developments. These spaces remain peripheral, marginal. The postcolonial immigration "embodies the exception to the universality of the Republic" (Boubeker 185), revealing the politics of sociocultural exclusion especially after the 2005 and 2007 riots in Villiers-Le-Bel and other suburban cities. Suburban youth felt it had no future, not being integrated into French society. Unfortunately, at that time, the French president and other right-wing politicians employed rhetoric in which the other was not a foreigner from abroad but rather came from within (Boubeker). This amalgam of despair and fear was exacerbated by the 2012 and 2015 terrorist attacks in France, in which the perpetrators claimed their allegiance to Islamist groups:

> The Specter that was thought to have been exorcised in the dark days after the Dreyfus Affair and Action Française once again haunted the public sphere. The image of the "enemy within" was now associated with an Islamist polygamist, living off the state and whose children were left loafing on the streets. (191)

The other was marked both ethnically and religiously.

Up until the 1980s, the Muslim community was better integrated within French society, because being a "secular citizen means abstracting one's *Muslimness* and rendering it invisible from the public" (Fernando, *Republic* 36). This notion of religious invisibility resonates with the performativity of citizenship and shows compliance with the universalist values of the French Republic. In the 1980s–1990s, the *beur* generation regarded "their relationship to Islamic tradition as cultural attachment rather than [a] religious or ethical one" (38), and their religion belonged to the private, not the public, sphere. They were purposefully secular, considering their religion only an ethnocultural identity. But in the 2000s a generational shift occurred, and invisible Muslimness was no longer acceptable. The head scarves affair was the first sign of this change. In 1989, when three Muslim girls refused to take off their head scarves at school, the religious signs that were once obliterated from the public space moved to the forefront of cultural and political discussion. The burka, a full-face veil covering all but the eyes, was prohibited, and the burkini, a modest swimsuit, was a topic of heated discussion.

The concern was not limited to the national landscape but also affected the Muslim community, whose new generation wanted their religion to relocate the Islamic tradition to the public space. They asserted their identity as Muslim rather than *beur* and accused the *beur* generation of lacking piety and of feeling ashamed of their religious identity as something "backward, demonized, retrograde, not adapted to the West." Despite the state's attempts to intervene, Islam was politically underrepresented "at the table of the Republic" (Fernando, "Republic's Second Religion" 40). This generational divergence on the practice of the faith demonstrated clearly the heterogeneity and diversity of the community and the difficulty to establish an "Islam of France." This internal shift had an explosive effect in the Muslim community. The challenge was to become visible and claim a voice and a strong religious identity without disavowing secularity and Frenchness.

The twenty-first-century hip-hop scene has seen the emergence of artists who openly praise their Muslim faith as French citizens. They redefine their Frenchness as nurtured by cosmopolitanism—an example is Abd Al Malik, a slam poet. They claim to belong to multicultural France, *la France métissée*. Their message is in response to the undeniable growth of the nationalist and extreme right parties not only in France but also in Europe. The nationalist and populist political movements declare that multiculturalism and Islam work hand in hand to corrupt national identity.

These movements feed the French population's anxiety that the Muslims are a threat to French identity and values. Médine Zaouiche, known as Médine, a rapper from Le Havre whose parents came from Algeria, is a practicing Muslim who uses rap as a testimony of the oppressed and underrepresented minorities in France. He notes:

> People like me—the descendants of immigrants, whether Arab, Black or Asian—are turning to our roots and embracing our heritage, just the opposite of what our parents did when they arrived. . . . But people of my generation are not shy about embracing their heritage, and, far from seeking invisibility, we're standing up to denounce the prejudice and injustice we face. In my case, Islam is an enormous part of who I am, just as being French is. The two aren't in opposition or even mutually exclusive. Yet when you hear the debate in France today, you'd swear they must be.

His brutal rap texts reflect the inner struggle that Muslim minorities experience on a daily basis. The feeling of not belonging that the suburban youth and minorities read in the eyes of French society crushes the appreciation they feel toward their country. In their love-hate relation with France, they often express hatred for French society as a static monolithic entity turned to past glory but show attachment to France as an evolving dynamic body open to the future. Dotson-Renta encapsulates the true motive behind Muslim rappers' intentions: "Through lyrics that acknowledge marginalization while frequently referencing Islam [a visible marker of banlieue space] such artists alternatively choose to mediate and reaffirm a designed French identity while undertaking a redeployment of French ideals."

These artists seek to defy *laïcité* as a misused and therefore useless notion, and their commentary questions the French republican model and its relation to minorities (especially to those living on the outskirts of major French cities). Dotson-Renta adds:

> By challenging *laïcité* as the only legitimate avenue to Frenchness [and insisting on quotidian urban *banlieue* narrative], French rap artists have constructed an alternative discourse in which elements of society viewed as an/other within France are reimagined as simultaneously disruptive and fundamentally constitutive of French identity. (356)

The concerns of hip-hop artists focus on how political parties and government officials try to reshape the basic subjectivities and epistemological claims of religion and secularism in relation to the notion of national identity (Asad).

French, Rapper, Muslim, *Banlieusard*, and *Fier de l'être*: Médine and Kery

Médine's approach to the French republican model and *laïcité* unfolds as a diatribe; it involves whip lashing and castigating. As a Muslim artist, Médine was affected by the negative media coverage after the 9/11 attacks and later by the consequences of the Charlie Hebdo attacks. In his lyrics he often refers to the colonial history of France. He considers that one must know the injustices of that history in order to situate oneself in the present time. His message also echoes African American history and the resistance of the civil rights movement. He attacks institutions that ignore racism and injustice. The strong beats in his music are sporadically accompanied by harangues, shotgun reports, the voices of journalists reporting tragic events, and lamentations. The violence and ambiguity of his lyrics limited the broadcasting of his work on TV and radio. The titles of his albums—*11 September* (2004), *Jihad, le plus grand combat contre soi-même* (2005; "Jihad, the Biggest Battle against Oneself"), *Table d'écoute* (2006 and 2011; "Wiretap"), *Don't Panik Tape* (2008), *Arabian Panther* (2008), *Made in* (2012), *Protest Song* (2013), *Le démineur* (2015; "The Bomb-Disposal Expert")—are confusing. In addition, he coauthored a book with the sociologist Pascal Boniface entitled *Don't Panik: "N'ayez pas peur"* (2012; "Do Not Be Scared").

A song from Médine's album *Le démineur* illustrates his protest against a certain type of *laïcité*. In the essay-interview with Boniface, the rapper explains, "I am a bomb disposal expert who is taken for a bomber" (Boniface and Zaouiche 18). He is stigmatized by a religious identity that he proudly embraces. On his theme "Don't panik," he elaborates, "[The] slogan makes sense because it is pronounced by someone who physically epitomizes France's fantasy. I am a rapper, a *banlieusard*, a Muslim, an Algerian immigrant, and I have a beard" (17). "Don't laïk," the title of the song, deals with some of the negative aspects of secularist ideology in France. The title and the beat are inspired by "I Don't Like," by the American rapper Chief Keef. The lyrics and visuals can easily be misinterpreted as religious proselytism. Clearly Médine bases his work on controversy.

"Don't Laïk" mixes French and English—"don't like / *laïque*"—with a phonetic play on words that emphasizes the fear of some activists of *laïcité*.

The lyrics of the song refer to current affairs, such as the teacher in the Baby Loup daycare center who refused to take off her veil in the workplace and was dismissed; the many accusations of rape against the politician and director of the International Monetary Fund, Dominique Strauss-Kahn; and the racist insinuations by the right-wing politicians Nadine Morano and Jean-François Copé (see Lambert; Chrisafis). These references should be explained in the classroom, since they give an overall idea of the tensions present in France in the early twenty-first century. Médine especially targets social and religious inequalities. In this song it becomes rapidly clear that he insists on the difference between *laïque* and *laïcard*. *Laïque* for him means one who respects the actual doctrine or institution of secularism; a *laïcard*, on the other hand, is one who demonizes, stigmatizes, and pays lip service to secularism. The refrain is revealing:

> Ta barbe, rebeu, dans ce pays c'est Don't Laïk
> Ton voile, ma sœur, dans ce pays c'est Don't Laïk
> Ta foi nigga dans ce pays c'est Don't Laïk
>
> Your beard, Arab bro, in this country, it's "don't like"
> Your veil, my sista, in this country, it's "don't like"
> Your faith, nigga, in this country, it's "don't like"

At the first reading, the play of stereotypical images of traditional practicing Muslims (the beard, the veil) or the "proto-image of the violent Islamist" (Jouilli 69) is obvious. Earlier, Médine wrote "Code Barbe," an ironic song about the Muslim beard mistaken for an Islamist sign. In his music video *Don't Laïk* he displays the Islamic symbols but also presents republican signs (such as Marianne). Jeanette S. Jouilli notes that "Médine wants his performance of a Muslim identity to be primarily understood as a strategy to expose the anxiety around Islam reflected in many public and political discourses" (69). Both his lyrics and his videos use mirroring to respond to anxieties about Islam (which in Médine's message is the "nigga" or racially marked faith).

With weighty sarcasm and double entendre, the refrain validates the Muslim faith as a solid fellowship in contrast to the French politicians, who further their personal ambitions by creating discord among the French population. He indicts the politicians for poisoning and degrading the values of the French Republic by exploiting the public's fears. According to him, Marianne has changed into a member of the Femen, the feminist activist group from Ukraine that campaigns against both sexism and religious institutions (see Meredith). Médine notes the intolerance of the

Femen activists and stresses the antireligious and brutal turn of their secularist practices. He points to the hypocrisy of politicians who set themselves up as defenders of moral values but cannot produce righteousness:

> Le polygame vaut bien mieux que l'ami Strauss-Kahn . . .
> Au croisement entre le voyou et le révérend
> Si j'te flingue dans mes rêves j'te demande pardon en me réveillant
> En me référant toujours dans le Saint-Coran . . .
>
> The polygamist man is worth more than dear friend Strauss-Kahn . . .
> Between the scum and the reverend
> If I shoot you in my dreams, when I wake up, I ask you for your forgiveness,
> Following the principles of the Holy Coran. . . .

The rapper condemns the difference between divine justice and judicial decision:

> Religion pour les francs-maçons, catéchisme pour les athées
> La laïcité n'est plus qu'une ombre entre l'éclairé et l'illuminé
> Nous sommes l'épouvantail de la République
> Les élites sont les prosélytes des propagandistes ultra laïcs
>
> Religion for the Freemasons, catechism for the atheists
> Secularism is only a shadow between the enlightened and the demented
> We are the bogeyman of the Republic
> The elites are the disciples of ultrasecular propagandists

He regrets that identity-related secularism has overthrown universalist doctrine. Identity-related secularism, or what Baubérot calls *laïcité identitaire* (*Sept laïcités* 103), refers to religions that participate in the construction of the nation and are tolerated and included in the definition of the national identity. But this tolerance goes with a prejudice against other religions. Such a protectionist ideology targets Islam in particular. *Laïcité identitaire*, revolving around an exclusionist, nationalist paradigm, therefore implicitly justifies racism, inequality, and discrimination. It favors only the religion of the majority and thereby corrupts the French republican model.

In his song Médine employs a religious metaphor in which the Republic and *laïcité* are bodies under the spell of diabolic forces:

> Pour la dernière fois ô démons, annoncez-vous ou disparaissez de notre chère valeur
> je vous chasse de ce corps et vous condamne à l'exil pour l'éternité
> Vade retro satanas.

For the last time, Demons, let us know your presence or disappear from
our dear value
I cast you out from this body and condemn you to eternal exile
Vade retro satanas

The music video of the song explicitly shows the subversion of the republican symbols. What might be perceived as a desacralization of the emblem of the French Republic reveals in fact the profound disenchantment of suburban youth about the French political establishment that has demonized them socially, culturally, and religiously. They do not support ethnic or religious factionalism; they are not opposed to integration—they are, after all, French by birth and cherish their Frenchness. They attack the politicians' exclusionist misinterpretation of republican ideology.

Kery James, a Muslim rapper from Orly, released "Lettre à la République" 'Letter to the Republic' in 2012, in which he revised the national narrative, "positing that French ideals were built upon and are in fact contingent upon the '2ème France' that it now rejects" (Dotson-Renta 357). James disparages the national and nationalist misperceptions of France's minority communities and exhorts France to accept those communities into the national imagined community. In a sepia-colored video staged on a black set, he displays a bellicose Republic. Like Médine, he accuses the politicians—*les dirigeants* ("the leaders")—of perpetrating hate speech along with hypocrisy, malevolence, and dishonesty:

En pleine crise économique, il faut un coupable
Et c'est en direction des musulmans que tous vos coups partent
J'n'ai pas peur de l'écrire : La France est islamophobe
D'ailleurs plus personne ne s'en cache dans la France des xénophobes

In the middle of the economic crisis, we need a scapegoat
And your blows are directed at Muslims
I am not afraid to write about it: France is Islamophobic
By the way, nobody hides it anymore in the France of xenophobes

James "questions the foundations of the République and the discourse of assimilation, implying that it was always doomed to fracture" (Dotson-Renta 358). The politics of assimilation and integration occupies the center of Médine's and James's messages. Both rappers declare the absolute validity of their Frenchness but face constant interrogation about their national allegiance because of their religious and racial difference:

Mon respect s'fait violer au pays dit des Droits de l'Homme
Parce que moi je suis Noir, musulman, banlieusard et fier de l'être

> Quand tu m'vois tu mets un visage sur c'que l'autre France déteste
> Ce sont les mêmes hypocrites qui nous parlent de diversité
>
> The respect due to me is violated in the country of the Rights of Man
> Because I am black, Muslim, a suburbanite, and proud of it,
> When you see me, you put a face on what the other France hates
> Those are the same hypocrites who tell us about diversity

James, like Médine, recognizes that the Republic has been taken hostage by leaders who are the ones responsible for the desacralization. Whereas he employs militant lyrics, Médine provokes by playing subversively with images. For instance, his video shows Marianne eating a blue-white-and-red cake with white frosting that spells *Halal.*

These images and lyrics are chosen to provoke and perhaps scandalize viewers. The result of such provocation was greater than Médine expected. In June 2018, right-wing and extreme right politicians asked that his scheduled concert in the Bataclan in October 2018 be canceled because of his negative comments about French secularism expressed in *Don't Laïk* and because of the 2015 attacks (Dagorn). The artist countered, "[P]asser de la provocation à la dédramatisation satirique n'a qu'un but: Rassembler" 'Going from provoking to satirically dedramatizing aims only at uniting people' and "impulser une dynamique de réforme des mentalités" 'creating a dynamic impulse for reforming mentalities' requires a double discourse (Boniface and Zaouiche 17, 44). Although their methods of rap differ, Médine and James both wish to unify and rally after the 2015 attacks in Paris and 2016 in Nice.

Médine defines the rap as "un moyen de s'opposer intelligemment à des décisions politiques ou idéologiques injustes . . . nous transformons ces situations d'injustices en art" 'a means to object intelligently to political decisions that are ideologically unjust . . . through it we change these situations of injustices into art' (43–44). He favors unity, because French *laïcité* hinges profoundly on a national unity "that is sustained by a community of sentiments epitomized notably through the principle of fraternity" (Jouili 74). His French identity is connected to being revolutionary: he seeks "to promote the desired change . . . through republican loyalty and spiritual renewal or through radical critique and change in power relations" (75). His main concern is religious tolerance. He urges the politicians and the state to be more inclusive, as the universalist model of 1789 demands. Despite his provocative manners, he pleads for unity, advocates *vivre-ensemble* ("living together"), and, most important, argues for the compatibility between true Islamic belief and practice and the *laïque.*

French rappers pursue the legacy of the French Revolution, portraying themselves as revolutionary against the exclusionist, conservative constructions of French identity. The French Revolution contested and overthrew the power of the Catholic Church and the monarchy, which led to the creation of the First French Republic, a political system that favored the rights of its citizens under the motto *liberté, égalité, fraternité*. French Muslim hip-hop artists value each principle of this motto and take pride in their French citizenship. They deny the frequent contention that their religion, Islam, is incompatible with Frenchness. They aim to demonstrate to French society that despite their religious piety they believe in *laïcité*. Secularism as understood originally is not antireligious; it is "intended to guarantee French citizens' freedoms of conscience and worship as opposed to suppressing them . . . *laïcité* is linked to Republicanism, which by principle aims to integrate all citizens regardless of their cultural, ethnic, and religious backgrounds" (Date). But xenophobia and protectionist ideas have turned *laïcité* into a shield against Islam. In opposition, the rappers employ varied tactics and styles: Médine opts for provocation and James for a strong and direct condemnation. But both claim France as their nation.

Teaching Suggestions

The iconography of the French Republic and of Marianne abounds, and the Internet offers great teaching materials for them. A first activity for students in a unit examining contemporary discussions of Frenchness, contemporary society, and French contemporary music might be to study "La Marseillaise" and its lyrics. French rappers, criticized for their violent texts, often point out that the French national anthem has a brutal message. One way to approach the subject of revolutionary speech, which includes politics, history, and music, is to show Jean Renoir's film *La Marseillaise* (1938), which includes the creation of the anthem but also deals with the first popular theme song of the French Revolution, "Ça ira" (1790). The film *La faute à Voltaire* (2001; *Poetical Refugees*), by A. Kechiche, could also be included. A contemporary text written by Christiane Taubira, a political leader, might accompany the iconography of French symbols: *Paroles de liberté* (2014; "Words of Liberty").

Notes

All translations from the French are mine, unless otherwise indicated.

1.The nineteenth century and the late twentieth century have generated several interpretations of secularism, each highlighting the concerns of its period. Jean

Baubérot, a historian and sociologist of secularism in France, indicates that seven representations of secularism exist in France. The first four, *laïcité anti-religieuse* ("antireligious secularism"), *laïcité gallicane* ("Gallican tendency in secularism"), *laïcité individualiste stricte* ("strictly separatist secularism"), and *laïcité collective inclusive* ("inclusive-separatist secularism"), correspond to the disputes and concerns during the elaboration of the 1905 law on the separation of church and state. The subsequent three, *laïcité ouverte* ("secularism open to religious and spiritual aspirations"), *laïcité identitaire* ("identity-based secularism"), and *laïcité concordataire* ("secularism that builds on the experience of the concordat in Alsace-Moselle"), are related to more contemporary cultural, social, and political issues (Kelly 112).

2. *Beur* is a linguistic play on the word *arabe*, in that letters are inverted to go from one word to the other: *a-ra-be* → *be-ar* → *beur*. *Beur* often refers to French-born people who have Maghrebi origins.

Works Cited

"Article premier." *Constitution*, 1 Jan. 2015, www.conseil-constitutionnel.fr/conseil-constitutionnel/root/bank_mm/constitution/constitution.pdf.

Asad, Talal. *Formations of the Secular: Christianity, Islam, Modernity*. Stanford UP, 2003.

Baubérot, Jean. "La commission stasi vue par un de ses membres." *French Politics, Culture, and Society*, vol. 22, no. 3, Fall 2004, pp. 135–41.

———. "Questions à Jean Baubérot." La *Documentation française*, www.ladocumentationfrancaise.fr/dossiers/d000095-laicite-les-debats-100-ans-apres-la-loi-de-1905/questions-a-jean-bauberot.

———. *Les sept laïcités françaises: Le modèle français de laïcité n'existe pas*. Éditions de la MSH, 2015.

Boniface, Pascal, and Médine Zaouiche. *Don't Panik: "N'ayez pas peur."* Desclée de Brouwner, 2012.

Boubeker, Ahmed. "The Outskirts of Politics: The Struggles of the Descendants of Postcolonial Immigration in France." *French Cultural Studies*, vol. 24, no. 2, 2013, pp. 184–95.

Chrisafis, Angelique. "French Right Wing Hijacks the Pain au Chocolat." *The Guardian*, 11 Oct. 2012, www.theguardian.com/world/shortcuts/2012/oct/11/french-rightwing-pain-au-chocolat.

Conklin, Alice L. "Colonialism and Human Rights, a Contradiction in Terms? The Case of France and West Africa, 1895–1914." *The American Historical Review*, vol. 103, no. 2, 1998, pp. 419–42.

Dagorn, Gary. "Le rappeur Médine au Bataclan: La polémique en quatre questions." *Le monde*, 13 June 2018, www.lemonde.fr/politique/article/2018/06/12/le-rappeur-medine-au-bataclan-la-polemique-en-quatre-questions_5313815_823448.html.

Date, Kiyonobu. "*Laïcité* in the Late Ninetenth-Century France and Its Significance Today." Lecture given at the Santander International Summer School, Kyoto U, 16 Mar. 2015.

Dhers, Gilles. "Chirac: Zéro tolérance au Stade de France." *Libération*, 13 May 2002, www.liberation.fr/evenement/2002/05/13/chirac-zero-tolerance-au-stade-de-france_403300.

Dotson-Renta, Lara. "'On n'est pas condamné à l'échec': Hip-Hop and the Banlieue Narrative." *French Cultural Studies*, vol. 26, no. 3, 2015, pp. 354–67.

Dubois, Laurent. "La République Métissée: Citizenship, Colonialism, and the Borders of French History." *Cultural Studies*, vol. 14, no. 1, 2000, pp. 15–34.

Fernando, Mayanthi. "The Republic's Second Religion." *Middle East Report*, vol. 235, 2005, pp. 12–17.

———. *The Republic Unsettled: Muslim French and the Contradictions of Secularism*. Duke UP, 2014.

Furet, François, and Mona Ozouf, editors. *Critical Dictionary of the French Revolution*. Translated by Arthur Goldhammer. Harvard UP, 1989.

Hargreaves, Alec G., and Mark McKinney, editors. *Post-colonial Cultures in France*. Psychology Press, 1997.

Hunt, Lynn. *Politics, Culture, and Class in the French Revolution*. U of California P, 2004.

Jouili, Jeanette S. "Rapping the Republic: Utopia, Critique, and Muslim Role Models in Secular France." *French Politics, Culture, and Society*, vol. 31, no. 2, 2013, pp. 58–80.

Kechiche, Abdellatif, director. *La faute à Voltaire*. *YouTube*, 19 June 2012, www.youtube.com/watch?v=mCgFUhXADTk.

Kelly, Michael. "Laïcité and Atheism in France." *French Cultural Studies*, vol. 28, no. 1, 2017, pp. 111–22.

Kselman, Thomas. "State and Religion." *Shorter Oxford History of Modern France, 1780–1880*, edited by Malcolm Cook, Oxford UP, 2001, pp. 63–92.

Lambert, Élise. "Nadine Morano et la 'race blanche': La polémique en cinq actes." *Franceinfo*, 30 Sept. 2015, www.francetvinfo.fr/politique/ump/nadine-morano/nadine-morano-et-la-race-blanche-la-polemique-en-cinq-actes_1106339.html.

Laurent, Stéphane. "Les ornements de la République, un héritage décoratif." Monnier and Cohen, pp. 363–72.

Meredith, Rebecca. "Femen Are Brave Women—but Their Anti-Muslim Rhetoric Is Dangerous." *HuffPost*, 4 July 2013, www.huffingtonpost.co.uk/rebecca-meredith/femen-are-brave-women---b_b_3032961.html.

Monnier, Gérard, and Evelyn Cohen, editors. *La République et ses symboles, un territoire de signes*. Publications de la Sorbonne, 2013.

Renoir, Jean, director. *La Marseillaise*. 1938. *Vimeo*, vimeo.com/274252400.

Roy, Olivier. *Securalism Confronts Islam*. Columbia UP, 2009.

Taubira, Christiane. *Paroles de liberté*. Flammarion, 2014.

Vovelle, Michel. "La symbolique républicaine sous la Révolution française." Monnier and Cohen, pp. 31–40.

Weber, Eugen. *Peasants into Frenchmen, the Modernization of Rural France, 1870–1914*. Stanford UP, 1976.

Weil, Patrick. "Lifting the Veil." *French Politics, Culture, and Society*, vol. 22, no. 3, Fall 2004, pp. 142–49.

Zaouiche, Médine. "How Much More French Can I Be? *Time Magazine*, 6 Nov. 2005, www.time.com/time/magazine/article/0,9171,1126720,00.html#ixzz2UKDxhcN.G.

Part II

Rhetoric, Rights, and Revolution

Jeffrey Champlin

Rights, Revolution, Representation: Thinking through the Language of the French Revolution

Eminently universal in their announced jurisdiction, human rights have no proper location. Yet they are always received in a particular place and time, and, as both Edmund Burke and Thomas Paine say, this is where the problem—or the progress—starts. Teaching the Declaration of the Rights of Man and of the Citizen in an interdisciplinary and global setting, I have found that an attention to language, both thematically and in the practice of writing, gives students the opportunity to confront this tension between the ideal and its instantiation. Creative linguistic engagement both promotes critical reflection on the origin of rights and encourages students to see themselves in relation to the mutability of these rights.

Interdisciplinary study and global teaching compel reflections on pedagogy by pushing comfortable methods beyond their limits. I have taught this module at liberal arts schools in very different settings that pose intriguingly parallel challenges. At Middlebury College in Vermont, the class Thinking Revolution was cosponsored by the departments of Political Science and Philosophy. The course at Bard College's partnership with Al-Quds (Jerusalem) University in Palestine was titled Self and Society and was the third seminar in a four-year core sequence of great works of global literature and thought.

The units I present seek to impart the relevance and relatability of the debate over rights but not simply equate it with something that students think they already know. How can students see themselves today not as the ones who simply employ the language of rights but as cocreators of a continuing tradition that emerges in decisive ways from the French Revolution? How might this understanding contribute to their expanded sense of citizenship and civic engagement in a global age?

I begin with some remarks on the context of the classes in terms of the syllabi and background of my students, then move to units specifically on Jean-Jacques Rousseau, the Declaration of the Rights of Man and of the Citizen, and Burke. Drawing on adaptations of generative in-class writing in the tradition of Peter Elbow, we approach these texts through the performative potency of language. By encouraging writing that creates new ideas in the classroom instead of justifying pregiven positions, I seek to promote an emphasis on the students' own relation to the distant texts of the eighteenth century in Europe.[1] The goal for the students is then to use the new relations they have described to write a paper that contrasts the conceptual and figurative dimensions of a key line from the French Revolution or its legacy.

Revolution between the Disciplines

Enlightenment optimism reached a high point with the French Revolution, which at first promised a way out of monarchy and toward political equality. I highlight the interdisciplinary nature of studying this time period in the background I present in lecture format. This background includes context from history, political science, and French studies. For time lines, social context, and familiarity with historical personas, I use Georges Lefebvre's classic text *The Coming of the French Revolution*, especially chapters 11 and 12, which focus on the Declaration of the Rights of Man and of the Citizen. To open a wider span of development, I also briefly review important historical documents related to this document, such as the English Bill of Rights in 1689, the Declaration of Independence in 1776 and United States Bill of Rights in 1789, and the Universal Declaration of Human Rights of 1948.

I give this time line with 1789 as the hinge, focusing on the universal claim of the French Revolution.[2] How did this event develop from particular economic, social, and political forces but at the same time intervene in the history of ideas? At Middlebury, the class moved from the historical background of Lefebvre to Rousseau, Burke, Paine, and Arendt. The course in Palestine was part of a sequence that progressed from the ancient world (including Gilgamesh, Plato, and Ih-bin-Yaktzan) in the first year to modernity in the second. This specific second-year seminar was coming from *Paradise Lost* and John Locke's *A Letter concerning Toleration* and had *Frankenstein* on the horizon as the semester's closing text.[3] At Middlebury, we were on the path of a secularization of politics running into the Cold War; in Palestine, we tracked changing conceptions of the human in both its religious and rational casts.

In the historical and conceptual context of the classes, specific attention to linguistic multivalence offered a way to assume and shift the burdens of historical and philosophical traditions. This attention worked as a corrective to the tendency to anchor discussions of rights and revolution in a discipline such as political science or history. At the same time, taking the language of the texts first as a spur to creativity instead of immediately asserting canonical definitions allowed new reflections on the meanings of rights to enter the classroom. The goal was not to displace history, political science, or philosophy with an approach to rights circumscribed by literary methods but to open new perspectives and interdisciplinary orientations.

Generative Writing and the Practice of Rights

The specific prompts that follow seek to impart a critical sense of the meaning of *rights* that arises from students' seeing themselves as inheritors of, rather than simply subjects to, the tradition of human rights discourse. Students employ methods of close reading and generative writing to explicate intercultural interpretations of classic texts. In a previous class in Palestine, we covered Rousseau's key terms "general will" and "social contract." As homework, students read chapter 1 of *On the Social Contract* again and the Declaration of the Rights of Man and of the Citizen.

At the opening of this unit, I ask students to begin with a ten-minute period of focused freewriting. I modified this practice from Peter Elbow's work for my students, who are bilingual in Arabic and English or high-level ESL (English as a second language) students.[4] I ask them to write in English but give them permission to emphasize exploration over accuracy at first. Although these students are familiar with the method from past classes, I find that new students quickly come to appreciate the exploration and creativity of such responses.[5]

I announce the following question and write on the board, "What are human rights, and where do they come from?" I keep track of the time for five minutes, and the only requirement is that students keep their pen moving. I ask them to write for another five minutes in response to the opening of the first chapter of *On the Social Contract*: "Man is born free and everywhere he is in chains" (41). When they complete this writing exercise, I ask them to review their response and select, with brackets, a passage of their raw writing to share.

The responses of the Al-Quds Bard students raised three points that transferred to classes with students in other contexts. First, as bilingual and ESL students, they had a linguistic sensitivity that results from stumbling on language. With appropriate practice and reflection, infelicities often produce rhetorical insights. For example, students once insisted that we pause on the registers of birth in the Rousseau quote. ESL students have a tendency to read literally, which can serve as a corrective to unexamined metaphorical assertions. In this case, they might talk philosophically about where humans come from, but just as frequently students will tell stories of the young children in their families. An example is, "My son's not free, at two he still cannot do anything without me." Other students start to see a new principle of sovereignty developing from below in this optimistic vision of free children.

Second, the students' distinct cultural perspective teaches us to be wary of our own Enlightenment assumptions. Those students who strongly hold to Islamic faith offer a corrective to the Hegelian assumption that religion naturally tends toward secularization. Instead, we reexamine the question of modernity as rupture and grapple with the overlapping values of tradition and progress. As teachers in the United States know, this secularization can no longer be taken for granted. Instead, we are reexamining the question of modernity as a break with tradition. Classes grapple with the overlapping values of tradition and modernity. My students, of varying religious beliefs and modes of nonbelief, discussed "born" as "created." They asked to what extent rights in the Qur'an are attributed to all people and to what extent only to fellow believers.

Third, geographic awareness led us to think about the differences between the implementations of rights in France in 1789 as opposed to the United States now or Palestine after 1948. To one student, Rousseau's "everywhere in chains" drew the response "Just like Palestine!" These students have a concrete sense of the limits of freedom and consider rights declarations as active instruments of liberation. They inquired into the extent of this confinement and the potential of rights proclamations to counter it.

In philosophical terms, Rousseau's phrase puts forth a norm as a statement of fact. Yet historically the language of his appeal crossed directly into politics when revolutionaries drew on his text in 1789. We read aloud, together, the Declaration of the Rights of Man and of the Citizen in its entirety. In an ESL context especially, in-class reading offers students a structured opportunity to build their speaking skills. Often we read the text twice with a reminder to annotate while listening the second time around.

I draw the second focused writing prompt from the Declaration of the Rights of Man and of the Citizen: "Men are born and remain free and equal in rights. Social distinctions can be founded only on the common good."[6] Students respond to this quotation in writing in the context of the discussion already under way. They quickly focus on the key difference in the phrase "and remain free." This observation leads to a further discussion of history and the temporality of rights. Who guarantees them today? At some point I bring in the French original: "L'homme est né libre, et partout il est dans les fers," prompting a discussion of the two meanings of "est né." Does Rousseau assert that man *is* born free or that he *was* born free? We also discuss how the phrase "and equal in rights" changes the meaning of *free*. What kind of positive content does freedom gain in this phrasing?

We end with a reflective writing prompt: "How has your understanding of the origin of rights changed through studying these quotations?" For homework students are assigned to read the United Nations Universal Declaration of Human Rights. I ask for a two-to-three-page response to the first article: "All human beings are born free and equal in dignity and rights. They are endowed with reason and conscience and should act towards one another in a spirit of brotherhood." This unit concludes with a four-to-five-page close reading of a single passage that focuses on one concept. The paper must describe what the authors of the declarations themselves said and then integrate the student's own creative analysis.

Dialogue and the Future of Representation

The students in both classes had surprisingly similar goals. In what I have come to see as a mark of the millennial generation at liberal arts programs, they combined a reflective commitment with practical résumé-building activities. A number of them intended to pursue law degrees, and some in both classes had volunteered at NGOs, often with experience abroad. This background influenced their relation to questions of rights at the start of the class. For these students especially, reference to the United States Bill of Rights (at Middlebury) or the United Nations Declaration (in Palestine) offered an anchor for questions of rights that paralleled the temptation to seek a single disciplinary order for a mutating human rights landscape.

My students in North America were native speakers of English or fully bilingual speakers and inhabited a world where rights were assumed rather than objects of aspiration. Yet by employing generative writing, we brought something of a creative ESL approach to traditional close reading methods. Over twenty years ago, the renowned literary theorist J. Hillis Miller affirmed a connection between ESL and composition and urged a stronger connection between these programs in the university (Olson). He was attuned to the growing number of international students and second-generation immigrant students. Although Miller has been proved right that this trend and challenge is only increasing, in my view we can now draw a broader arc to connect composition, ESL, and literature in our departments. Students who learn to engage specific argumentative structures in exploratory writing often go beyond mere practical competency to develop a higher level of reflection and mental flexibility. They work more fluently between cultural expectations.[7] Through writing, my Middlebury students also moved in the direction of experiencing rights without guarantee, in need of institution, yet still open to expansion.

Thinking Revolution at Middlebury College employed a similar sequence from Rousseau to the French Revolution as the class in Palestine. The Middlebury course took Burke as the next text, and I describe one more method here to show how writing in the classroom can work.[8] This sequence leaves time for lecturing and more traditional seminar-style work as well. The reading for the first day is the first fifty pages of Burke's *Reflections on the Revolution in France* (1790). An opening short lecture describes how, in the theoretical history of political identification, Burke offered a unique intervention that asserts the organic stability of the body while at the same time wishing for malleability.

We then work together to examine how Burke offers a unique intervention in the concept of the body politic. This "dialogical notebook" exercise takes over forty-five minutes.[9] Students divide a few pages of their notebooks into three equal columns, then engage in a discussion in writing with a student next to them. Students respond to the prompt in the first column, then hand the notebook to their partner, who reads their response (talking only to clarify handwriting) and then writes out a reply to specific sentences or phrases. Finally the notebook is handed back to the original writer, who now replies to the reply and selects a chain of response from all three columns to share with the class.

In Burke, we read the paragraph from "This policy appears to me" to "and our altars" (33–34). It proposes a model of the state as a corpus that contains all ages of life and signals of death but itself does not change. I asked students to respond in writing through the dialogical notebook to the phrase "a permanent body composed of transitory parts." This phrase runs into Burke's argument that "by preserving the method of nature in the conduct of the state, in what we improve we are never wholly new; in what we retain we are never wholly obsolete" (34).

We discuss how Burke draws a system of logic from nature, abstracting its rules and transferring them to the sphere of government. Instead of lurching forward with progress, he repeats the limiting phrase "never wholly." Students ask what we are to make of this political body that is also in a sense never whole, and they even suggest examples from current United States politics that indicate a dangerous disunity, such as the Tea Party movement. We discuss what kind of limit Burke's organic figure puts on change and to what extent they can envision it succeeding as a heuristic device.

Both at Middlebury and at Al-Quds Bard, generative writing has served as complement to textual analysis, be it by combining with ESL work or reinvigorating standard close reading methodologies. These units offer students a chance to make their own sense of rights. Granted, rights usually come into being when challenged, as a legal perspective teaches us. On a global scale, such challenges lead in the extreme to the paradoxical requirement for what Hannah Arendt calls the "right to have rights" (*Origins* 296).[10] Students in Palestine are much closer to these lessons through experience. The units I propose seek to superimpose a literary path through rights on the objective, legal (and, from a different perspective, philosophical) approach. Through engaging the language of rights and tradition, students scribble and scramble their way between their roles as subjects *and* objects of rights.

Notes

1. As Thomas Keenan puts it in an analysis much closer to our time, the discourse of human rights is "not special pleading but general pleading, a plea on behalf of everyone, passing through someone in particular. . . . The paradox of

rights talk is that the claim is senseless if not universalizable but is only effective if rooted concretely" (1602).

2. Students have consistently drawn attention to the revolutionary context of our own historical moment, both in terms of the larger development of the Arab spring and, in a less direct way, through the widening distance between political parties in the United States and the extreme criticisms of government by the Tea Party and Occupy movement.

3. When we transitioned to literature, our class drew on Kerry Bystrom's work on the role of narratives of witnessing in delineating the functions and failures of power. Her critical synthesis of work on the topic offers a challenging yet accessible range of entry points into the scholarsip of the field. On *Frankenstein* and human rights in particular, see Cadava.

4. Elbow's classic definition of freewriting: "The idea is simply to write for 10 minutes (later on perhaps for fifteen or twenty). Don't stop for anything. Go quickly without rushing. Never stop to look back, to cross something out, to wonder how to spell something, to wonder what word or thought to use, or to think about what you are doing. If you can't think of a spelling, just use a squiggle or else write, 'I can't think of it.' Just put down something. The easiest thing is just to put down whatever is in your mind. If you get stuck it's fine to write 'I can't think of anything to say, I can't think of anything to say' as many times as you want; or repeat the last word you wrote over and over again; or anything else. The only requirement is that you never stop" (3).

5. When low-level ESL speakers predominate, I have found it better to start with short (three-minute) periods of writing, or occasionally say that after three minutes they can switch to their mother tongue if they wish.

6. I use the English text at the end of Lefebvre (219–21), though it is also easily accessible through online sources. The standard French can be found at *Déclaration*. I would like to thank Murray Dry of Middlebury College specifically for recommending Lefebvre as a resource and also for his broader guidance on the contours of the course. Martha Woodruff supported this interdisciplinary endeavor and generously shared her reflections regarding the philosophical dimension of the class.

7. "I see ESL as a frontier of composition" (Olson 322).

8. In Palestine, I follow up with Gouges rather than Burke. Students work with this first article: "Woman is born free and remains equal to man in rights. Social distinctions may be based only on the common welfare" (31).

9. See Bledsoe 95–118. I change the name of the technique from *dialectical* to *dialogical* so students have discussion in the forefront of their minds. Bledsoe's book, produced by Bard College's Institute for Writing and Thinking, is an excellent resource for scholars looking for further guidance on these techniques. I'd like to thank the recent faculty of Bard's Language and Thinking Program, especially Celia Bland, Bill Dixon, and Peg Peoples, for the many illuminating discussions and pedagogical training sessions over the years. Joan Retallack originally encouraged me to find a joy in in-class writing, a joy that I was later able to share with my students. I am also grateful for the guidance that Murray Dry and Martha Woodruff offered on the class at Middlebury College.

10. I guided students who wished to expand on this aspect of the legacy of the French Revolution in future work to Arendt's *On Revolution* and Avital Ronell's contemporary inquiry into authority in Arendt.

Works Cited

Arendt, Hannah. *On Revolution*. Penguin, 2006.

———. *The Origins of Totalitarianism*. Harcourt Books, 1994.

Bledsoe, Margaret Ranny. "Dialectical Notebooks." *Writing-Based Teaching: Essential Practices and Enduring Questions*, State U of New York P, 2009, pp. 95–118.

Burke, Edmund. *Reflections on the Revolution in France*. Oxford World's Classics, 1999.

Bystrom, Kerry. "Literature and Human Rights." *The Routledge Handbook of Human Rights*, edited by Thomas Cushman, Routledge, 2011, pp. 637–46.

Cadava, Eduardo. "The Monstrosity of Human Rights." *PMLA*, vol. 121, no. 5, 2006, pp. 1558–65.

Déclaration des Droits de l'Homme et du Citoyen de 1789. Conseil constitutionnel, www.conseil-constitutionnel.fr/conseil-constitutionnel/francais/page-d-accueil.1.html.

"Declaration of the Rights of Man and of the Citizen." Lefebvre, pp. 219–21.

Elbow, Peter. *Writing without Teachers*. Oxford UP, 1998.

Gouges, Olympe de. "The Rights of Woman." *Between the Queen and the Cabby: Olympe de Gouges's Rights of Woman*, by John Cole, McGill-Queen's Press, 27–42.

Keenan, Thomas. "'Where Are Human Rights . . . ?': Reading a Communiqué from Iraq." *PMLA*, vol. 121, no. 5, 2006, pp. 1597–607.

Lefebvre, Georges. *The Coming of the French Revolution*. Princeton Classics, 2005.

Olson, Gary A. "Rhetoric, Cultural Studies, and the Future of Critical Theory: A Conversation with J. Hillis Miller." *Philosophy, Rhetoric, Literary Criticism: (Inter)Views*, edited by Olson, Southern Illinois UP, 1994, pp. 317–45.

Paine, Thomas. Rights of Man, Common Sense, *and Other Political Writings*. Oxford UP, 2008.

Ronell, Avital. "What Was Authority?" *Loser Sons: Politics and Authority*, U of Illinois P, 2012, pp. 19–34.

Rousseau, Jean-Jacques. The Social Contract *and Other Later Political Writings*. Edited and translated by Victor Gourevitch, Cambridge UP, 1997.

Universal Declaration of Human Rights. United Nations, www.un.org/en/universal-declaration-human-rights/.

Pratima Prasad

Human Rights and Human Wrongs: Slavery and Colonialism in a Time of Revolution

The French Revolution haunts Romantic texts of the early nineteenth century. Alfred de Musset, the poet who is said to have given expression to the so-called existential malady of the French Romantics known as the *mal du siècle*, famously identified the events of 1793 as the original "wound" of the Romantic generation (20; my trans.). Unlike Musset, Victor Hugo evokes the Revolution in his writings as an empowering rather than a debilitating force: he associated the lyric innovations and the poetic disobedience of his peers with the insurgent symbolism of the Phrygian cap of the revolutionaries. Indeed, Romantic texts revisit the Revolution in myriad ways: in them, revolutionary events are mythologized, contested, and transformed.

In my classes, my students and I routinely grapple with the ways in which the French Revolution is represented in nineteenth-century texts. In addition, my courses engage with what has come to be termed as the global nineteenth century—that is, the disparate forces of capitalism and colonialism from the late eighteenth to the early twentieth century that reshaped both France and the world beyond its hexagonal borders. My course syllabi on Romanticism feature early-nineteenth-century texts by metropolitan French authors that offer varying representations of the

French Revolution at home while at the same time engaging with the French colonial empire abroad. Alongside Chateaubriand's *René* (1805), the quintessential novel about postrevolutionary Romantic malaise among young French men, my students encounter texts such as Hugo's *Bug-Jargal* (1826), which is set in Saint-Domingue during the slave revolt.

Reading these texts against the backdrop of the French Revolution, students are almost immediately confronted with a contradiction: just as the French state was beginning to espouse the values of equality and liberty at home, it upheld slavery in its colonial territories. French revolutionary principles are at odds with the goals of an expansionist French empire that during the eighteenth and nineteenth centuries was encroaching on the sovereignty of peoples in the Caribbean, the Indian Ocean, Africa, and North America. How, students ask, did the country that stirred the Western world with the notion of human rights (*les droits de l'homme*) simultaneously engage in stripping those rights from peoples across the globe?

This question resonates at my institution, the University of Massachusetts Boston. Part of the statewide university system, it is an urban campus with a diverse student body that is not dissimilar to the student population described in the essay by Habiba Boumlik and Robin Kietlinksi in this volume. In upper-level French courses, several of our students are of Haitian and francophone African origin, tracing their family histories to regions of the world colonized by the French. While some UMass Boston students attend college straight out of high school, most begin their university education during their twenties or later. Over half of them are the first in their family to attend college. Almost all students work during the school year in order to pay for their education and support themselves. Several students are army veterans. Given the personal experiences of my students and the ruthless social and economic inequalities of the Old Regime, the topic of the French Revolution holds both an intellectual and a visceral attraction for them.

Notwithstanding the particular socioeconomic milieu of my university, my methods and approaches are applicable in a variety of teaching contexts. First, like most literary critics, I approach the Revolution not as empirical truth but as a contested historical terrain. As Lauren Pinzka's essay in this volume contends, the study of literary and other artistic works can help illuminate how the historical past is memorialized, reappropriated, and mythologized in a particular culture. Second, the types of undergraduate courses I teach are typical at other universities: classes for French majors and minors in the French program, introductory general education classes or cross-disciplinary classes composed of both liberal arts and nonliberal arts majors, and classes in the honors program. Third, the interpretive methodology that I adopt in my classes is similar to that of most teachers of literature: close textual analysis of literary texts in their historical contexts. I assign novels as primary texts, with theoretical and critical readings serving as secondary sources. In this essay, I elucidate how the French Romantic novel can be exploited in the undergraduate classroom to understand and complicate revolutionary ideals such as equality, liberty, and citizenship in the context of French colonialism. I focus on Claire de Duras's *Ourika* (1823), a Romantic text that is at once accessibly short and rich with meaning and thus suitable for courses at various stages of an undergraduate curriculum, including introductory survey classes and advanced electives.

Ourika has several hallmarks of Romantic storytelling of early nineteenth-century France, such as a tale bearing the first name of its heroine, a psychological narrative told in the first person, and an alienated protagonist with a melancholic disposition. The novel tells the story of a Senegalese girl who is brought to France as a child and adopted by an aristocratic family during the years leading up to the Revolution. After a blissful childhood, Ourika overhears a conversation between her adoptive mother, Mme de B., and another aristocrat in which they speak of the complete impossibility of Ourika's integration into French society. Made cognizant for the first time of her racial difference and of the social isolation to which her identity condemns her, she becomes afflicted with chronic melancholy. When the reader first encounters her at the start of the tale, it is during the Napoleonic years; the heroine is living in a convent, suffering from an unspecified illness. There she is visited by a doctor—the narrator—to whom she tells the story of her life in flashback, recounting her psychological tribulations as she comes of age during the Revolution and its immediate aftermath.

As the novel is short, I ask students to read it in its entirety for our first class session (by contrast, most other nineteenth-century French novels that I teach tend to be long, calling for a serialized reading). I begin our discussion of *Ourika* with the allusions in the novel to eighteenth- and nineteenth-century historical events, because they are less immediately comprehensible to students than the heroine's psychological narrative. Since my pedagogy favors discussion over lecture, students are asked to come to the first class meeting having already researched specific moments in the text that contain references to historical occurrences: Ourika's many allusions to the events of the French Revolution, interspersed throughout her story, such as the seizure of émigré property, the king's death in 1793, and an offhand mention of the events of 20 June and 10 August; her early rescue from a slave ship in Senegal by a French colonial administrator; and her response to the massacre of white planters during the Haitian Revolution.

These references take students across historical terrain that is largely unfamiliar to them. They are exposed to revolutionary happenings that needed no explanation for readers of the novel in 1823 but that are often inscrutable for today's undergraduate student. My students also learn about France's eighteenth-century trading posts in West Africa, the role of Gorée and St. Louis, Senegal, as centers of slave trafficking, and some of the intricacies of the Haitian Revolution. During the first class session, they report on what they have researched and discovered; I offer clarifications and explanations as necessary. I sometimes supplement the discussion with a *PowerPoint* or multimedia presentation on key themes of the French Revolution and the state of the French colonial empire in the late eighteenth century. This initial focus on the historical underpinnings of the novel makes clear that the fortunes of revolutionary France were truly global. Having lost North America and India to the British, and faced with the revolt of Saint-Domingue, which would soon establish itself as a Haitian republic free from European hegemony, the French empire had its eyes on establishing trade and colonies in Africa. The finances of France were closely tied to those of its slave colonies in the Atlantic and the Indian oceans and to its trading posts elsewhere in the world. Moreover, there was a cross-pollination of the revolutionary ideals of liberty, equality, and fraternity between metropolitan France and its colonies in the Caribbean.

Once we have established these historical contexts, we begin a close reading of passages in which the turbulence of the Revolution mirrors the turbulence of Ourika's psyche. In preparation for close reading, I assign a secondary text: Naomi Schor's entry on universalism in *Columbia History of Twentieth-Century French Thought*, with accompanying comprehension questions.[1] We start with a two-page section in the novel, when an alienated and depressed Ourika describes the roller coaster of emotions that is triggered by the unfolding of the Revolution. At first, the talk of revolutionary reforms in Mme de B.'s circles raises the hopes that Ourika, as a black woman, may be integrated as an equal: "J'entrevis donc dans ce grand désordre, je pourrais trouver ma place; que *toutes les fortunes renversées, tous les rangs confondus, tous les préjugés évanouis*, amèneraient peut-être un état de choses où je serais moins étrangère" 'I sensed that at the end of this great chaos I might find my true place. When *personal destiny was turned upside down, all social caste overthrown, all prejudices had disappeared*, a state of affairs might one day come to pass where I would feel myself less exiled' (18–19; 19 [my emphasis in both the French and English]). Over time, hope turns to disillusionment with the realization that her inferior status will endure: "Bientôt leur fausse philanthropie cessa de m'abuser, et je renonçai à l'espérance, en voyant qu'il resterait encore assez de mépris pour moi au milieu de tant d'adversités" 'I soon stopped being the dupe of their false notion of fraternity. Realizing that people still found time, in all this adversity, to despise me, I gave up hope' (19; 20).

Although Ourika's language is expansively sentimental and not overtly political, I urge students to look beyond the face value of this passage and ponder what it can tell us about the political processes of revolutionary change as they related to France's disenfranchised and marginalized subjects: women, colonized peoples, slaves, or migrants like Ourika.[2] To get the discussion going, I invoke—by way of short excerpts that are read aloud in class—Rogers Brubaker's theorization of citizenship, a concept that went through a profound transformation in revolutionary political thought. The Old Regime's inegalitarian and privilege-based notion of citizenship, which granted the status to a wealthy minority of ruling elites, was substituted by common law, and a more inclusive and rights-based idea of citizenship was formulated (35–49). We delve into the nitty-gritty of Schor's essay, which explains how universalism is inherent in the revolutionary concept of the citizen as an "abstract, rights-bearing individual," "a neutral subject who must be divested of all particularities to access those rights" (345). The republican ideology of human rights viewed citizenship as all-encompassing and universal; it renounced the particularities of difference, such as race, gender, language, and ethnicity. Students can see how the events of the Revolution, and the many political and philosophical conversations that the heroine routinely imbibes in Mme de B.'s salon, hold out the promise of inclusiveness. Ourika hopes that her own racial difference, which she experiences as an oppressive burden, will be made irrelevant or neutralized in postrevolutionary France.

I then present the class with two cases of revolutionary legislation pertaining to persons of color. In 1791, the Constituent Assembly granted citizenship to black men born to free parents in the French colonies, but not to freedmen (*affranchis*) who had either been granted freedom or had purchased it. A year later, in 1792, the Republic granted full citizenship to the *gens de couleur*. *Gens de couleur* was a term that applied to free people of color in Saint-Domingue, specifically to a wealthy population of mixed French and African descent who were often both slave owners and owners of property. Although the French citizen was defined as an abstract and universal subject who must not in any way lay claim to racial or class status, these cases make clear that in practice citizenship in the French colonies was offered selectively: the particulars of identity—such as parental status, gender, or membership in a specific ethnic class—underwrote an individual's eligibility for equal rights.

Consideration of these cases brings Ourika's situation into sharper relief, raising the thorny question of how a black woman, who happens to be an African migrant adopted by a white aristocratic family, would be integrated into the postrevolutionary French body politic. We now can trace a political meaning in her sentimental language of dashed hopes. When she speaks bitterly of "fausse philanthropie" 'false . . . fraternity' (19; 20), she may as well be lamenting the fickle promise of the Revolution's grand abstraction. Schor's essay helps deepen the class conversation further. In addition to theorizing and historicizing universalism, it examines how France's strongly held belief in republican universalism was often at odds with the *parité* movement of the 1990s, which campaigned for women's increased inclusion in elected office, and also continues to have an uneasy relation with the cultural practices of French Muslims. Discussing Schor's essay alongside *Ourika*, students are animated by the contemporary relevance of the nineteenth-century novel. The essay typically triggers a spirited classroom dialogue on revolutionary principles, the relation of these principles to the assimilation of immigrants, and the accommodation of difference in French society.

We turn our attention to moments in the text when Ourika seems to be criticizing the Revolution from an entirely different perspective—namely, that of a royalist or legitimist. She alludes to certain revolutionary dates as "les affreuses journées" 'the terrible days' (20; 21), calls the king's decapitation a "grand crime" 'that outrage,' and refers to the confiscation of émigré property as a "désastre général" 'universal catastrophe' (21; 22). Her tendency to espouse the outlook of a privileged minority is repeated during the Haitian Revolution, when she appears to identify with the white plantocracy of Saint-Domingue, shunning the violence of Haitian revolutionaries while failing to recognize the profoundly devastating violence of slavery. Although her rejection of the legitimacy of the Haitian Revolution comes under vigorous—and at times disapproving—scrutiny by modern-day American undergraduates, her identification with the French nobility tends to be viewed by them as logical. She is, after all, an aristocrat herself and naturally empathizes with the suffering of the aristocrats through the Revolution and the Terror. When students have closely examined passages in which Ourika responds to the Revolution both as a black woman and as a noblewoman, I ask them to think further about her identity as a black aristocrat. By simultaneously adopting the point of view of both the most marginalized and the hyperprivileged of French society, does she represent a contradiction in terms, and does she risk becoming an unreliable narrator of revolutionary change? Or does the unique vantage point of a black aristocrat help shed light on the successes and failures of the Revolutions?

Ourika's status as a black aristocrat is worth pursuing in the classroom for another reason: it is a variation on a familiar trope in the literary tradition of European antislavery fiction. European abolitionist fiction dating back to the seventeenth century often adopted the topos of the noble Negro, a black protagonist who is exceptional in all respects: his extraordinary physical beauty is matched by his nobility and his refined demeanor. A "European aristocrat in blackface," as Laura Brown puts it, he is generally the son of an African chief and receives a superior early education before being tragically ensnared into slavery. Such a protagonist created a "sentimental identification" with the European reader, which helped form public opinion against the institution of slavery (37).

Placing *Ourika* in the context of the French antislavery movement of the Enlightenment tackles head-on what present-day students see as a fundamental contradiction: French slavery's stark opposition to liberty, the first of the Revolution's three grand ideals. We go through a quick historical overview, because *Ourika* straddles different stages of the French abolitionist movement. The heroine grows up during the time of high Enlightenment abolitionism. The antislavery thinking of some philosophes, and the work of the Société des Amis des Noirs (Society of Friends of Blacks), led to the Revolutionary Convention's decree abolishing slavery in French colonies in 1794. In 1793, slavery was abolished in Saint-Domingue, the most brutal of France's eighteenth-century slave colonies. When Ourika spends the second part of her life in a convent, slavery has been reinstated by Napoleon, a decision that was influenced in large part by slave owners' participation in the counterrevolution and the political influence of wealthy planters.

Duras wrote and published *Ourika* in 1823, during the conservative era of the Bourbon Restoration. At this time, the French abolitionist movement was still active—in the work of organizations such as the

Société de la Morale Chrétienne (Society of Christian Morality)—even if not as vigorous as during the Enlightenment. After situating the novel in this historical context, we examine how Ourika fits in with the long line of "noble Negroes" that populated European abolitionist fiction and abolitionist discourse. We discover Aphra Behn's *Oroonoko; or, The Royal Slave* (1688), one of the first noble Negro fictions, that tells the tragic story of an African enslaved in Surinam. Pierre Antoine de La Place's 1745 French translation and adaptation of Behn's original tale enjoyed a considerable vogue in France during the second half of the eighteenth century. Depending on the level of the class, we read *Oroonoko* (or the French translation) in its entirety or in excerpts.

We also explore how the figure of the noble Negro finds its way into the antislavery treatise *De la littérature des nègres* (1808), by Abbé Grégoire, one of the most prominent French abolitionists of the late eighteenth and early nineteenth centuries. The republicanism of this ardent Enlightenment thinker went hand in hand with his antislavery activism. Grégoire's text, which highlights the cultural and literary achievements of blacks, contains a brief biographical sketch of an African named Angelo Soliman who lived and worked amid the Austrian and Liechtensteinian aristocratic societies during the eighteenth century. I ask students to read the whole text of this supposed real-life story, which bears an uncanny similarity to the tale of *Ourika*.

In Grégoire's telling, Soliman is the son of an African prince who lives an idyllic life until he is captured and sold to whites in the slave market. After being passed from one European master to another, he is gifted to a European noblewoman, receives a European education, and spends his life in the midst of European nobility. Angelo's story, like *Ourika*, is an inflection of the standard plot of noble Negro fictions. Instead of being governed by the simple binary of liberty and servitude, as their literary predecessors were, the lives of Ourika and Soliman are marked by the comforts of an aristocratic lifestyle; yet their rights and freedoms are in no way guaranteed to them by the European legal, economic, and political system. A triangulated reading of *Oroonoko, De la littérature des nègres,* and *Ourika* produces good results in the classroom. Among other things, I ask students to take a position on whether *Ourika* functions effectively as an abolitionist text when read alongside these other two overt antislavery texts. Student opinions are wide-ranging in this regard and make for an energetic final debate, which serves to bring to a close our encounter with the text.

It is tempting to read and to teach early-nineteenth-century French Romantic texts like *Ourika* in ahistorical terms, because they evoke in detail the ennui, melancholy, and exaltations of the self (*le moi*) of their primary characters. But the works of Romantics were also produced under precise cultural-historical circumstances, and therefore they chronicle, in their own idiosyncratic ways, the twists and turns of history. Arriving as it did on the heels of the French Revolution, literary Romanticism has a great deal to teach us and our students about one of the most momentous events in French history.

Notes

1. In advanced classes, students read the longer version of Schor's essay, entitled "The Crisis of French Universalism."

2. A scholarly analysis of some of the ideas that follow can be found in chapter 4 of my book *Colonialism, Race, and the French Romantic Imagination*. Here I propose how these ideas may be parsed out in the classroom, using a student-centered and participatory approach.

Works Cited

Behn, Aphra. *Oroonoko: or, The Royal Slave*. *Internet Archive*, 26 Aug. 2009, archive.org/details/oroonoko_0908_librivox.

Brown, Laura. *Ends of Empire: Women and Ideology in Early Eighteenth-Century English Literature*. Cornell UP, 1993.

Brubaker, Rogers. *Citizenship and Nationhood in France and Germany*. Harvard UP, 1992.

Duras, Claire de. Ourika*: An English Translation*. Translated by John Fowles, Modern Language Association of America, 1994.

———. Ourika: *The Original French Text*. Edited by Joan DeJean, Modern Language Association, of America 1994.

Grégoire, H. *De la littérature des nègres*. *Project Gutenberg*, 26 May 2005, www.gutenberg.org/files/15907/15907-h/15907-h.htm

Musset, Alfred de. *La confession d'un enfant du siècle*. Garnier Frères, 1968.

Prasad, Pratima. *Colonialism, Race, and the French Romantic Imagination*. Routledge, 2009.

Schor, Naomi. "The Crisis of French Universalism." *Yale French Studies*, vol. 100, 2001, pp. 43–64.

———. "Universalism." *Columbia History of Twentieth-Century French Thought*, edited by Lawrence D. Kritzman, Columbia UP, 2005, pp. 344–48.

Habiba Boumlik and Robin Kietlinski

Teaching the French Revolution at a Community College: Challenges and Benefits

Revolution is a term that may feel foreign to many college students. While it gets thrown around loosely in twenty-first-century political campaigns and is used rhetorically by the media, many traditional college-age students likely have little understanding of the historical or linguistic implications of the word. Does a revolution necessarily involve violence? Are class and political discontent always at the heart of a revolution? Is a social revolution the opposite of social evolution? How have the costs of revolutions measured up against the benefits that they have produced? Such questions are fundamental to an understanding of revolutions past and present. While these questions may feel theoretical and abstruse, in some cases they are anything but abstract. At LaGuardia Community College of the City University of New York, arguably one of the most diverse campuses in the country, we teach courses to a student body that hails from all corners of the world and that has a huge variety of life experiences. In teaching the French Revolution to such students, we have found that there have been a number of rewarding pedagogical experiences despite the often daunting hurdles that we face.

Our faculty members have a teaching load of four to five classes per semester, and the content knowledge, reading level, and English ability of our students are often not on par with that of their counterparts at four-year colleges and universities. This essay is a collaborative interdisciplinary endeavor by two professors at LaGuardia, a public institution with almost 50,000 students from over 150 different countries. The student body is diverse across a number of matrices: about 40% of students are Hispanic, 20% African American, 20% Asian, and 16% white. Students in the traditional seventeen-to-twenty-two-year age range compose about 50% of the student body, and the other half are students twenty-three and older. Well over half the student body comes from families in which the total family income is less than $25,000 a year (*Fast Facts*). As professors of both world history and French language and literature, the authors of this essay face challenges inherent to teaching such a diverse student body on top of the challenges of any introductory-level course: world history surveys cover such a broad amount of content that it is difficult to devote much time to any individual topic, and the level at which the French-language courses are offered generally does not enable students to engage deeply with the course content.

The benefits of teaching the French Revolution in a sometimes challenging environment, however, are greater than the difficulties. One of the key learning outcomes that this essay focuses on is the ability of our students to draw parallels between historical events and the ideals that current revolutionaries are fighting for. Our students are rarely withdrawn from world events, because they come from such a wide variety of countries and circumstances, often from parts of the world where revolutions have recently occurred or are currently taking place. For example, students from China, who have lived through the aftereffects of the cultural revolution there (and have parents who grew up during it), have perspectives on class difference and capitalism that can differ greatly from those of the American students. Others have fled recent turmoil in Eastern Europe, the Middle East, and Central Africa. Moreover, many participated in local class- and race-based protests that took place in New York City over the past five years. Our students bring to the classroom firsthand knowledge and valuable testimony from their life experiences. Discussions on the causes and the driving ideals behind the French Revolution can deepen their understanding of issues such as class injustice and therefore their engagement with the historical content. Learning this content furthers their French-language learning.

The classes we teach assume little to no prior knowledge of French history or world history. Both classes use a methodological approach that endeavors to get students from different levels of preparation, English ability, and educational backgrounds to end the semester with a solid grasp of the course content, with a particular emphasis on our college's core competency of "global learning" (*Outcomes Assessment*). This essay should therefore be of interest to anyone looking for new ideas about how to present the Revolution to a diverse student body as well as to instructors at community colleges who are looking to broaden their pedagogical approaches.

French-Language Class

LaGuardia's academic calendar consists of two twelve-week semesters, and students have the option of taking intensive six-week courses in the winter and summer (*Academic Calendar*). Language classes meet four hours per week (three classes are face-to-face, one is in the lab). So we have sixty hours of class contact with our students. Elementary French II, open to students who have previously taken only one semester of French, is taught partly in French and combines lecture, discussion, and oral reports by students. Students present orally and in writing on various assignments, which gives them the opportunity to express themselves in French in a situation where they have prepared their thoughts and formulated their expression in advance (sometimes they prepare with the Modern Language Lab tutors). No exam was given on the French Revolution project, but it made up ten percent of their total grade.

The goal of the assignments is to teach cultural content by exposing students to a variety of cultural mediums (painting, song, literature, film, and so on), giving them experience in the five C goal areas for foreign language learning elaborated by ACTFL, the American Council on the Teaching of Foreign Languages (*World Readiness Standards*). Students are encouraged to consider this project part of their intellectual development and an opportunity to make connections between the language course and other courses, as the ACTFL guidelines recommend. The intensive focus on the French Revolution reflects a model of integrated course design: its goals go beyond an understand-and-remember type of learning (Weimer 46–71).

Research has provided compelling evidence that language and culture are intricately connected (Kramsch; Moran; Hinkel; DeCapua). Language textbooks reflect the shift from grammar-focused instruction to an approach that is more balanced, taking culture into consideration (Dema and Moeller; Peterson and Coltrane; Byram and Grundy). But which aspects of culture are to be taught, and how? Can an instructor realistically incorporate culture in the course of no more than two semesters? Many instructors argue that students first need to acquire the rudiments of the language before being taught complex cultural facts. Gilberte Furstenberg defines culture as "a highly complex, elusive, multilayered notion that encompasses many different and overlapping areas and that inherently defies easy categorization and classification" (329). Yet language and culture are certainly integral to each other (Lange).

In our course, the ten assignments on the French Revolution replaced some culture-related activities included in the textbook. Incorporating this material had a noticeable effect on language acquisition. For instance, the session on Eugène Delacroix's painting fulfilled two language objectives: description and prepositions in addition to expanding the basic vocabulary of painting and gaining cultural knowledge about symbols of the Revolution. Furthermore, this vocabulary and cultural knowledge were integrated with specific language acquisition goals. Reading an excerpt in French from Stefan Zweig's biography of Marie-Antoinette not only introduced students to a literary piece that second-semester students are not typically exposed to but also was tied to the use of the *passé composé* and the *imparfait* in narration and enriched their vocabulary for clothing.

The revolutionary song "La Carmagnole" alerted students to the French phonemes /i/ and /e/ and liaison in French. When the various readings expected from students grew longer and more complex, students were divided into groups, each in charge of searching for vocabulary and presenting for the group. Owning their parts and acting as experts of their small section motivated students, and they showed pride in accomplishing their task. Questions and statements (assigned as homework) were both revised three times before students rehearsed in preparation for the debate in class.

ACTFL has advocated and proved not only that teaching culture should go hand in hand with language instruction but also that they are both more effective when done in tandem: "Through the study of other languages, students gain a knowledge and understanding of the *cultures* that use that language and, in fact, cannot truly master the language until they have also mastered the cultural contexts in which the language occurs" (*World Readiness Standards*). To this end, we felt that the French class students would benefit linguistically from the deeper cultural context that a joint session with the world history course would provide.

World History Class

The course Global History from 1500 to the Present meets three hours per week for a total of thirty-six contact hours each semester. The course has only one prerequisite, English Composition I, and most students take Global History to fulfill a core curricular requirement and have little prior exposure to college-level history. The objective of the course, as spelled out in the syllabus, is "to understand global history from 1500 to the present day . . . with a focus on the origins and spread of global interdependence. Through exercises in critical reading and writing, we will learn to engage with the discipline of history while developing important skills in analytical thinking and communication." In other words, the purpose of the course is not for students to acquire historical data (as many assume at the beginning) but to learn transferable critical thinking skills along with a contextualization of processes of globalization that shape the world we live in today.

To that end, the inclusion of the French Revolution material was part of a three-week unit on the American, French, and Haitian Revolutions, along with the Industrial Revolution. This unit was designed to help students think critically about both the causes and the outcomes of revolutions. For the French Revolution, students read a selection from an English translation of Jean-Jacques Rousseau's *The Social Contract* (originally published in 1762) in addition to the Declaration of the Rights of Man and of the Citizen.

We analyzed two articles from the Declaration of the Rights of Man: article 1, "Men are born and remain free and equal in rights. Social distinctions may be founded only upon the general good," and article 11, "The free communication of ideas and opinions is one of the most precious of the rights of man. Every citizen may, accordingly, speak, write, and print with freedom, but shall be responsible for such abuses of this freedom as shall be defined by law" (*Declaration*). We chose to focus on this primary document for a number of reasons: the ideas contained in it are universally applicable and relevant to contemporary global society; the declaration itself was a foundational document that highlights how revolutionary ideas were both influenced by and had an influence on other movements around the globe; the Enlightenment ideals addressed in the declaration, such as equality and freedom or freedoms, are relevant to our students' lived experiences; and document-based analysis is a key skill that college-level history courses seek to develop. After this assignment, students were required to watch *La Révolution française: Les années lumière* ("The Years of Light") before the joint class meeting with the French class.

Collaborative French Revolution Project

The research for this project was based on data collected from assignments that span two semesters, during which the teaching of the French Revolution was independently incorporated into the syllabi for both courses. The assignments for the Revolution unit in the French course were based on the premise that "one cannot separate the two [culture and language] without losing the significance of either" (Brown 189–90). The French instructor integrated nine written activities and one oral presentation.[1] The history professor assigned the two primary document readings mentioned above (Rousseau and the declaration) in addition to a chapter from a world history textbook (Bentley et al., ch. 25 ["Revolutions and National States in the Atlantic World"]) and the *Révolution française* film to provide background information and contextualization.

Given that the French course targets students who have taken only one semester of French, the first assignment about the Revolution was done in English. The goal was to provide students with a historical foundation that would allow them to engage with assignments on various aspects of the Revolution. In the first week of the semester, they were asked to watch a video documentary and summarize it in English (in one page). They were encouraged to prepare to discuss in French the remaining assignments, albeit with a limited vocabulary.

Students were asked to complete their work before coming to class in order to engage meaningfully in class discussion about the content. Each assignment had a guiding set of questions. The use of French was mandatory; students had to ask for permission to use English. For a basic historical foundation about the French Revolution, they were referred to a twelve-minute *YouTube* video, about which they wrote a one-page summary (*French Revolution*). The first written assignment consisted of two short texts about the Terror and the nationalistic song "La Carmagnole."

Students searched the vocabulary of the lyrics of the song, listened to it in class, and discussed its content in relation to the previous text on the Terror. The third activity was based on the Delacroix painting *La Liberté guidant le peuple* (*Liberty Leading the People*): students had to discuss some of the symbols of the Revolution used in the painting. The fifth assignment was to watch the first part of the film (with English subtitles)

La Révolution française, which was produced in 1989 to celebrate the two-hundredth anniversary of the Revolution. Students were introduced to film vocabulary to write a film critique.[2]

After the film screening, which was scheduled to coincide with the Revolution unit in the history course, both classes met to discuss the film in English; they interacted, exchanging opinions about what they had learned through both the film and their respective classes. The French and history students drew parallels between Revolution-era France and contemporary United States society. The professors, who jointly led the discussion, asked such questions as "Who had power in prerevolutionary France, and what problems existed because of the differences between classes?" and "Who has power in the United States today, and what problems exist because of the differences between classes?"

Students responded well to these discussion prompts, and their comments suggest that they made new connections between their present and eighteenth-century France. The joint discussion took place 12 April 2016, which happened to be exactly one week before the United States presidential primary election in New York, a time when political campaigning between Hillary Clinton and Bernie Sanders was at a fever pitch. One student brought up Sanders's criticism of economic inequity and his call for a "political revolution" (see berniesanders.com/revolution/). Some students brought up their personal experiences living in and fleeing from revolutions around the globe (e.g., from Serbia and Tunisia). After the session, students from both classes were asked to write reflections.

One student wrote, "The history professor asked what it took for a revolution to take place. Did it mean we had to wait until we were starving to fight back?" Another wrote, "What I found surprising was the fact that we [the history students and the French students] were on the same page, even though [the French Revolution] was taught in different courses." A history student wrote, "I felt that having the French class come over was a good way to ignite our attention towards certain facts of the [Revolution] that seemed unfamiliar, . . . [and it] provided different perspectives." A student summarized the joint discussion: "As a class, we agreed that due to the power structure of the time and the fact that people were starving, it was logical that the people would rebel. Also, that such rebellions and revolutions always will be violent because people do not just give up power."

The French students followed the joint class session with a debate of their own. One side argued that the gap between the poor and the palace was so great and the lavish life so irresponsible that revolution was inevitable. The other side focused on the taxation inequity and the influence of the Enlightenment. One student dismissed Marie-Antoinette's cause of the people's revolt: "A mon avis, Marie-Antoinette était trop jeune pour avoir les responsabilités qu'elle avait. Elle était une jeune-fille égoïste qui cherchait à simplement avoir du plaisir" 'In my opinion, Marie-Antoinette was too young to assume the responsibilities that were put upon her. She was a self-centered young lady who was simply looking to have fun.' Then the students pretended to be French citizens and wrote letters of protest to the queen.[3] In their class presentations at the end of the unit, they spoke on topics that highlighted the wide range of historical and social issues that had been covered and that proved interesting to them.[4]

A questionnaire was distributed to students at the end of the fall and spring semesters. Students responded enthusiastically and made specific connection between the French language and the French Revolution. A few French-language students reported liking the project because it allowed them to learn content (history, literature, painting, song) without having to worry so much about grammar and mechanics. Some students complained about not having enough time to discuss the Revolution.

Challenges and Benefits

The time factor indeed posed a problem: we would have liked to linger over some aspects of and documents about the Revolution for more than a few class sessions. One history student lamented, "I feel that if my class [had gone] more into depth on the [Revolution] before combining the classes, I would have been more engaged and certain of my outlook on [it]!" As the instructors, we intend to have students from both classes spend more time in the joint-class format in the future. For example, they could watch selections from the film together in class and build a common experience through it, which would open more lines of communication between them.

Overall, our interdisciplinary collaboration on the French Revolution unit was a success: our new pedagogical approach was well received by our students. At a school as socioeconomically, racially, and nationally diverse as LaGuardia, our classrooms are especially good places to discuss revolutions past and present. In exploring innovative ways to foster communication and critical thinking, we believe that students will not only come away from their classes with a firmer grasp on the course content but also be able to use that knowledge in meaningful ways moving forward.

Notes

1. The assignments were varied, including one song ("La Carmagnole"), one painting (*La Liberté guidant le peuple*), one excerpt from a literary piece (Zweig's biography of Marie-Antoinette), a document on the symbols of the French Revolution, a debate on how the life at Versailles and the life of ordinary people differed, a class presentation on a topic related to the Revolution, and a short composition that took a form of a letter sent by the students to Marie-Antoinette.

2. Reading excerpts from the biography Zweig wrote about Marie-Antoinette and a text describing the harsh life conditions of the people in order to contrast it with her life led to the next assignment: writing a letter of protest to Marie-Antoinette in which students complained about their difficult living conditions. The next assignment consisted of a debate about the luxury in Versailles and the misery of most of the French people and how this difference led to the Revolution. For the last assignment, students gave three-to-four-minute individual class presentations in French.

3. Among the themes in these letters were the queen's egoism, her expensive clothes, people's sickness, people's poverty, the need for the reduction of taxes, and the American Revolutionary War. In one of the letters, a student wrote, "Nous n'avons pas besoin d'une reine rococo, mais d'une reine responsable qui nous aidera à surmonter et affronter nos problèmes" 'We don't need a rococo queen, we need a responsible queen who will help us overcome our problems.'

4. Among the final presentation topics were women's involvement in the French Revolution (e.g., the march of women to Versailles on 5 October 1789, the feminists in Societé des Citoyennes Républicaines Révolutionnaires), the novel *Les misérables*, the Bastille, the marriage of Marie-Antoinette and Louis XVI, the Declaration of Human Rights, the guillotine, social classes in prerevolutionary France, rococo, Marie-Antoinette's biography, and the celebration of Bastille Day today.

Works Cited

Academic Calendar. LaGuardia Community College, www.laguardia.edu/Academics/Academic-Calendar/.

Bentley, Jerry, et al. *From 1500 to the Present.* 3rd. ed., McGraw-Hill Education, 2014. Vol. 2 of *Traditions and Encounters: A Brief Global History.*

Brown, H. Douglas. *Principles of Language Learning and Teaching.* 6th ed., Pearson Education, 2014.

Byram, Michael, and Peter Grundy. *Context and Culture in Language Teaching and Learning.* Multilingual Matters, 2003.

DeCapua, Andrea. *Crossing Cultures in the Language Classroom.* U of Michigan P, 2004.

Declaration of the Rights of Man. The Avalon Project, avalon.law.yale.edu/18th_century/rightsof.asp.

Dema, Oxana and Aleidine Kramer Moeller. "Teaching Culture in the Twenty-First-Century Language Classroom." *Faculty Publications: Department of Teaching, Learning, and Teacher Education*, 2012, digitalcommons.unl.edu/teachlearnfacpub/181. Paper 181.

Fast Facts. LaGuardia Community College, www.laguardia.edu/About/Fast-Facts/.

The French Revolution: Crash Course World History #2. YouTube, 10 Aug. 2012, www.youtube.com/watch?v=lTTvKwCylFY.

Furstenberg, Gilberte. "Making Culture the Core of the Language Class: Can It Be Done?" *Modern Language Journal*, vol. 94, no. 2, 2010, pp. 329–32.

Hinkel, Eli. *Culture in Second Language Teaching and Learning*. Cambridge UP, 1999.

Kramsch, Claire. *Context and Culture in Language Teaching*. Oxford UP, 1993.

Lange, Dale L. "The Teaching of Culture in Foreign Language Courses." *Modules for the Professional Preparation of Teaching Assistants in Foreign Languages*, edited by Grace Stovall Burkart, Center for Applied Linguistics, 1998, www.nclrc.org/essentials/culture/cuindex.htm

Moran, Patrick. *Teaching Culture: Perspectives in Practice*. Heinle, 2001.

Outcomes Assessment. LaGuardia Community College, www.laguardia.edu/Assessment/Resources/.

Peterson, Elizabeth, and Bronwyn Coltrane. "Culture in Second Language Teaching." *Online Resources: Digests*, 2003, www.cal.org/resources/Digest/0309peterson.html.

La Révolution française. Part 1, directed by Robert Enrico, TFI Video. Disc 1.

Weimer, Maryellen. *Learner-Centered Teaching: Five Key Changes to Practice*. 2nd ed., Jossey-Bass, 2013.

World Readiness Standards for Learning Languages. ACTFL, www.actfl.org/publications/all/world-readiness-standards-learning-languages.

Zweig, Stefan. *Marie-Antoinette*. Translated by Alzir Hella, Livre de Poche, 1999.

Melanie Conroy

Teaching Republican Culture through Caricature: The Scandal of *Charlie Hebdo*

The Provocation of French Republicanism

In 2006, the French Ministry of Culture and the newspaper *Le point* held a banquet to celebrate the achievements of French political caricaturists, including Cabu, Wolinksy, Charb, and Luz of *Charlie Hebdo* ("SOS caricatures"). At that dinner the caricaturists and writers of *Charlie Hebdo* were feted as an exemplar of the French republican satirical tradition. The true history of caricature in the French Republic has been rather more complicated. The French state, including the Republic, has often condemned caricatures as libelous when they mock the powerful. Indeed, one of the most hard-fought rights for caricaturists in France has been the right to caricature recognizable political figures, a right that is still not recognized in French law. French political caricatures have run afoul of the prohibition on insulting public officials, including the head of state—from Daumier's caricatures of Louis-Philippe to Nadar's of Louis-Napoléon to Cabu's of Charles de Gaulle. Caricatures have also been denounced for satirizing religious leaders, newspaper editors, and even celebrities. It is in this context that we must see *Charlie Hebdo*'s claim to the right to depict the Prophet and other Islamic religious authorities, if we are to understand the importance of religious and political provocation for the satirical magazine.

One of the challenges of teaching the French Revolution is revealing the extent to which republican culture remains a living force in French and francophone cultural life. *Charlie Hebdo*'s reinterpretation of traditional republican tropes and themes provides a powerful example of the continuity and renewal of political satire. Republican culture has, from the first years of the First Republic, articulated not a set of comfortable symbols but discourses that trouble contemporary norms. *Charlie Hebdo* draws on established traditions of French political satire, in which the right to mock powerful individuals is fundamental. Yet this right is not now, nor has it been since 1881, recognized legally. The French state has, in the words of Manus McGrogan, "rhetorically assimilated the paper, its writers, and artists to an expansive republican ideal" (168) without granting true legal freedom to artists. Ever the troublemaker, *Charlie Hebdo* stands out in the number of court cases that have been filed, the brutality of the attacks on the magazine's staff, and the frequency of the attacks. *Charlie Hebdo* has tested—and continues to test—the limits of political speech in France, all while staying within discourses legible as part of the French republican tradition.

It is hard to give students a sense of how controversial and offensive caricatures from the revolutionary period were to conservative Catholics, monarchists, and other partisans of the Old Regime. Much of the imagery of the First Republic, such as the tricolor and the figure of Marianne, have been co-opted by establishment figures to symbolize the more moderate version of France espoused by the Fifth Republic (Kidd and Reynolds 160–62). These symbols are so familiar to students around the world as symbols of French liberal democracy that it may be unthinkable that they were once truly revolutionary—that is, hostile to the existing political order. Other imagery from the First Republic, such as attacks on the clergy, nuns, aristocrats, and non-French Europeans—are so removed from contemporary political discourses that they may appear apolitical or obscure. In this essay, I consider how select caricatures from recent issues of *Charlie Hebdo* can be used in a course on the French Revolution to reactivate the controversial political content of the First Republic caricatures. I also examine the ways in which the republican ideology of *Charlie Hebdo* diverges from the politics of the First Republic and the ways in which *Charlie Hebdo* is not useful in teaching republican culture. Finally, I revisit *Charlie Hebdo*'s provocation of Muslim readers and how the magazine's treatment of Muslim religious leadership has skirted racism and religious bigotry.

The weekly magazine *Charlie Hebdo* has been a fixture of French politics since its founding in 1970, after its predecessor, *Hara-Kari Hebdo*, was banned for satirizing the funeral of Charles de Gaulle (McGrogan 169). Despite having no consistent editorial line over the forty years, *Charlie Hebdo* has consistently courted controversy and frequently been accused of obscenity, sexism, racism, and bigotry (173). Frequent targets of the magazine include political figures like Nicolas Sarkozy, the former French president; celebrities; and religious figures, primarily representatives of the Catholic Church, Judaism, and Islam. *Charlie Hebdo* has maintained a far-left, or even left anarchist, sensibility and is known for attacking famous figures using scurrilous, incoherent, or sexually charged rhetoric. While it is easy to paint *Charlie Hebdo* as an extremist publication, especially given the magazine's low circulation throughout most of its history, it is important to note that French political caricature, from the revolutionary period onward, has frequently occupied this marginal territory in French culture, flouting laws and courting controversy (Goldstein 94). *Charlie Hebdo*'s provocative use of republican ideologies and symbols inherited from the revolutionary era shows that French republicanism is a living, changing ideology in which a range of views is possible, including some that may be shocking to students, especially without adequate context. The story of how *Charlie Hebdo* weathered four decades of controversy and mastered walking the line between legal and illegal political speech is the story of modern French republicanism with its divisions between left and far left, secularism and moderation.

Teaching through Caricature

I teach French Civilization, a course that primarily looks at variations in ideas of the Republic and of revolutions from 1789 to the present day. Starting with revolutionary caricature and ending with *Charlie Hebdo*, I integrate caricature and graphic novels into the course as the predominant example of cultural continuity. Whereas styles in painting, literature, music, and architecture are unpredictable, French political caricature remains remarkably similar in its codes and symbolism, both of which come out of the combative culture of the First Republic.

Using caricatures in classroom discussions can prompt more active conversation than texts do, in part because this course is taught entirely in French and students may be more comfortable moving from image to speech than from a complicated written text to oral production. So long as we remember that images are actively constructed and first interpreted in their cultures of origin, they can open up another means of seeing similarities and differences between French and American culture. "Images serve not only to *represent* various realities and imaginaries," writes Erin Kearney, "but also to *engage us* in the social and cultural construction, interpretation and negotiation of our worlds" (37).

The extreme liberty in the production and circulation of caricatures was an essential part of the culture of the First Republic. Indeed, the period from 1789 to 1799 saw, according to Robert Justin Goldstein, "a massive wave of satirical drawings which flooded the country after the effective collapse of censorship controls amidst the revolutionary agitation of that year" (93). Thanks to the vast increase in online archives of French caricature, the most difficult task in using caricatures in a course on modern France is selecting the images. The largest collection of revolutionary-era images is *Images of the French Revolution*, an online database created by the Bibliothèque Nationale de France (BNF) and Stanford University Libraries. The collection contains 14,000 digital images, which can be browsed by document type, artist, genre, date, and more. From the revolutionary period alone, there are hundreds of caricatures available on dozens of themes.

The types of revolutionary caricatures are often unfamiliar to students, so discussing them is a window into the social classes of the Old Regime, as well as into the new regime's perspective on these various types. In my course, we examine and classify caricatures of priests, nobles, soldiers, and Jacobins. Students review the images one by one and guess the ideological orientation of the artist. I then reveal to the students who created the caricature and what that person's attitude was toward the French Revolution. What emerges is the strongly polarized politics of the era, in which priests and aristocrats or Jacobins and the urban poor are coded according to the ideology of the artist. I use our discussion of revolutionary-era images as a way of introducing the ideas and tropes, both revolutionary and counterrevolutionary, that will be recycled and reworked in later caricatures.

Many of these late-eighteenth-century caricatures are surprisingly vulgar. One common trope is relating a political or sociocultural enemy to the act of defecation. In the first years of the Revolution, this trope is reserved for enemies of the Revolution, notably financiers. By 1793, it is being used against the Jacobins themselves. One such caricature, a watercolor from 1793, depicts a man, probably noble, finely dressed in a wig, cravat, and cuffed swallowtail blue coat. Strain is evident in his furrowed eyebrows as he looks back over one shoulder, crouching, a black cocked hat under one arm, his breeches pulled down, bottom bared, defecating on the ground. From his buttocks trails a ribbon carrying script, of the sort that usually trails from mouths, signifying speech. The words on the ribbon, "Fi, le vilain jacobin!" 'Fie, the nasty Jacobin,' suggest that the sound of this man's defecation constitutes a curse on a hated enemy. Another common trope is the depiction of a political opponent in profile with the face composed of sexualized nude figures of women. One such image constructs the profile of the vicomte de Mirabeau from overlapping images of a wine barrel, an upturned bottle, and, at different scales, reclining nude women stimulating disembodied erect phalli (*Reconnoissez*); the "noble works" of the vicomte are thus reduced to drunken orgy. Other such images target the Abbé Mauri, M. de Polignac, and Cazalès. Eight examples produced in 1791 can be found under the category "La politique au boudoir" 'Politics in the Boudoir' in the *French Revolution Digital Archive* (frda.stanford.edu).

The scatological nature of these images is often surprising to students who, familiar with the historical consequences of the French Revolution, expect the political discourse to be less coarse. When it becomes apparent that mocking political enemies in vulgar ways was common during the revolutionary period, it is easier to see how later French political satire continues this tradition of childish mockery of elite political figures. At the end of the course, after discussing the work of Honoré Daumier, Nadar, Charles Léandre, and others, I often come back to these first caricatures, to show students how much more legible these revolutionary and counterrevolutionary discourses are now that they have seen more modern examples of satirical political caricatures.

After our examination of earlier French political caricature, I show students a collection of *Charlie Hebdo* images, classed by type: French presidents, foreign political figures, religious authorities, and celebrities. We try to discern the political and ideological commitments of the cartoonists. By building on our previous discussion of political caricature, we can avoid the simplistic transfer of ideological paradigms from the United States context. We can also see *Charlie Hebdo*'s unique contribution to the French republican discourses. This comparison gives students a window onto French political culture today and the current republican commitments of many in France, including the writers and cartoonists of *Charlie Hebdo*.

Teaching *Charlie Hebdo*

Although *Charlie Hebdo* has been widely known in France since the 1970s, the satirical weekly gained global fame only after the January 2015 attacks on its offices. The attacks on *Charlie Hebdo* united the French public and much of the world in defense of free speech and against political violence. In the months that followed, there was a national and global movement of solidarity, in which advocates of free speech, secular humanists, moderate Muslims, and people of all nationalities and religious backgrounds came together to denounce terrorism. This movement deployed French republican imagery (primarily the tricolor) alongside art and language inspired by *Charlie Hebdo* (Versieux and Delesalle-Stolper). The repurposing of French republican imagery in the service of a worldwide movement speaks to the continuing power of images drawn from the revolutionary era. But this contemporary use of republican symbols to signify solidarity also obscures differences from historical French republicanism, notably the current nationalistic discourses against Muslims and non-European immigrants.

The coverage of *Charlie* also elides significant differences in the French public before the attacks. This attack effectively put an end to many of the scandals that *Charlie Hebdo* had generated in prior decades, including more than fifty lawsuits against the paper. Before January 2015, *Charlie Hebdo* was a relatively minor publication, generating more negative press than regular readers. Afterward, it was a worldwide symbol of free speech and political bravery. Nothing better reveals the changed attitudes toward the paper than the jump in average weekly sales from 30,000 in 2014 to more than 200,000 regular subscribers in February 2015 (Cohen). News coverage of the 2015 marches and vigils can be used alongside cartoons to give students an idea of the degree to which French citizens of all backgrounds rallied around the surviving artists. Images from the vigils and marches in 2015 are further evidence for the contemporary relevance of republican imagery.

In the United States, there is no equivalent to the French magazine. In terms of scatological humor, *Charlie Hebdo* fits with comics like *Cracked* and *Mad Magazine*, which are aimed at the youth market. In terms of its political weight and substance, it is closer to influential television satire, such as *The Daily Show*. The combination of shocking imagery and serious political content is not easily found in American political satire. In order to help students make sense of *Charlie Hebdo*'s humor, teachers may assign *C'est dur d'être aimé par des cons*, a documentary by Daniel Leconte (2007; "It's Hard Being Loved by Jerks") as background. The film serves as an introduction to the group's legal problems and the reception of the magazine. It has the benefit of being entirely recorded and edited before the attacks of 2011 and 2015. The documentary shows the wide variance in opinion about *Charlie Hebdo* in France—from acceptance of the magazine as offensive but ultimately humorous to rejection of it as racist and bigoted against Muslims and Islam. The range of attitudes toward censorship and the defense of minority groups and religions in this film well portrays the range of republican views in France today, from reformist to hard-line. When showing this film, it is important to remind students that the film was produced before the attacks and that many of those interviewed opposing *Charlie Hebdo*'s portrayal of Muslims condemned the killing of *Charlie Hebdo*'s staff members.

The film shows that *Charlie Hebdo* had a vibrant culture of self-criticism and self-censorship before 2007. Despite the magazine's reputation for courting controversy by making jokes in poor taste, the editor (Philippe Val), the artists, and the writers are seen having lively debates about meaning and the social acceptability of their work, rejecting drawings for being crude or offensive, even those that were arguably funny. In one case, Val is choosing between two covers, saying, "*Ça*, c'est un scandale. . . . *Ça*, ça dépend . . ." 'That, now that's a scandal. . . . That, could go either way' before eventually letting the group's lawyer, Richard Malka, pick a third option (Leconte [19:45–20:18]). This self-censorship was in fact a long-standing practice for *Charlie Hebdo* and, before that, for *Hara-Kiri*. We can see the types of drawings that were rejected—generally personal attacks on celebrities, mixed with macabre references to tragedies like the AIDS epidemic, drug deaths, car crashes, plane crashes, and cancer—in the 265 drawings that Cabu published in 1991 as *Les interdits de Cabu* ("Banned Drawings by Cabu"). These drawings are similar to Cabu's recent work for *Charlie Hebdo* except that they often mock the innocent, such as the victims of colonization, political violence, and poverty.

These rejected drawings reveal that Cabu—like other artists associated with *Charlie Hebdo*—at times created caricatures in such questionable taste that they were unusable. Some smack of racism or religious bigotry. One section, "Mort aux pauvres!" 'Death to the Poor!,' is particularly difficult reading, as it contains many drawings that depict African victims of colonization and famine. The Africans in these drawings are depicted as emaciated and dehumanized in degrading ways. Other caricatures target rich countries' indifference to global poverty and exploitation of the poor, such as Benetton's 1980s advertising campaigns. It is important to bear in mind that many of these drawings, which could be interpreted as attacking the victims of poverty, violence, and misfortune, were rejected from mainstream publications. Whether or not instructors choose to show examples of such offensive drawings to students, with sufficient caveats, it is useful to remember that these instances of excessive provocation exist. By introducing students to the legal issues around political satire in France and to the ways in which publications self-censor, it is possible to have a more nuanced discussion about how *Charlie Hebdo*'s artists and editors provoked the public with the drawings that they chose to publish.

Part of the anarchic effect of an issue of *Charlie Hebdo* comes from the lack of a consistent editorial policy. Not only has the magazine had two distinct incarnations, the first from 1970 to 1981 and the second from 1992 to the present day, it also has had a series of editors. Therefore there is no one ideological view but rather a range of views, from anarchist to Marxist, all of which are a part of French republicanism today. The aesthetic of *Charlie Hebdo* is a constant clash of cheap, puerile jokes and highbrow topics like world politics, religion, and even wonkish domestic policy. That said, there is little doubt that the magazine is primarily political. Shortly after the attacks on its offices, the sociologists Jean-François Mignot and Céline Goffette published a study of the topics of *Charlie Hebdo* covers from 2005 to 2015 in *Le monde*. Mignot and Goffette found that 336 of 523 covers focused on political topics; only 38 covers commented on religion; of those, only 7 were concerned with Islam. The few covers that did become so controversial were presented in the context of satire of political figures, as an occasional digression into religious topics.

Charlie Hebdo's criticism of authority can be off-putting because it is so relentless. Three cover images provide an example. One caricature from 2013, *Il revient!* ("He is come!") is an excellent example of how religious and sacrilegious tropes are used to political ends. In this cover image, Sarkozy is depicted as Christ resurrected, ringed by a throng of elderly women feebly thrusting cash, envelopes, and purses at him (Charb). The artist and an editor, Charb, mocks both Sarkozy and his disproportionately elderly supporters. The occasion for the cartoon was the return of Sarkozy to the world of active politics. The figure is ridiculous: although he wears the crown of thorns and has the stigmata and halo of the resurrected Christ, his face is dopey, his body babyish (hairy legs notwithstanding), and his loincloth looks like a diaper. Despite the sacrilegious image and use of a famous quote from the Bible ("Come to me, all you who are weary" [Matt. 11.28, New Intl. Vers.]), the real joke here turns on a pun: the dubious, ridiculous Messiah accepts the enthusiastic approach (and financial support) of a group of elderly "faibles d'esprit" who are less "poor in spirit" than "feebleminded." Left unclear is the question of whom the cartoonist holds in less regard, the foolish, uncritical, easily manipulated donors or the silver-tongued politician who recognizes their frailty while accepting their cash. What is clear is that the cartoon makes no real religious or theological statement but rather is using religious discourse to lampoon the supposed alliance between Sarkozy and his elderly supporters. Despite the evident religious themes, the thrust is political.

Some of *Charlie Hebdo*'s famous covers that do feature religion and religious figures are more concerned with religious politics and authority than with theological matters. A cover from 2007, by Cabu, shows representatives of the three Abrahamic religions (Judaism, Christianity, and Islam) marching uniformly and calling for the censorship of *Charlie Hebdo* (*Il faut voiler* Charlie Hebdo ["Charlie Hebdo *must be censored*"]). In many ways, this image is the classic expression of *laïcité*, secularism, which in a French context means treating all religions with suspicion. This image shows that, although *Charlie Hebdo*'s most publicized religious criticism involves Islam, the magazine's criticism of religion is comprehensive. While the debate over the wearing of religious veils in public spaces left many Muslims feeling ostracized and victimized by non-Muslim French society, *Charlie Hebdo*, in this cover, sees itself as the victim of conservative religious hostility of all denominations. The imam, far from being ostracized, is part of the crowd, as he marches in lockstep, arm in arm with his Christian and Jewish counterparts, indistinguishable in posture and expression: all three are shouting with the same outraged, disgusted mouth and rage-filled eyes; all three are demanding the "veiling" of the satirical magazine's sacrilegious, offensive political speech.

Charlie Hebdo has most frequently been accused of racism and Islamophobia not when it comments on religious authorities but when current events and its thoroughgoing criticism of religious authority meet in the same cartoon. One prime example is a cover that appeared in 2013, after protestors attacked the Muslim Brotherhood's headquarters in Cairo. In this cover, Riss depicts a Muslim man trying to stop a terrorist attack using the Qur'an as a shield. The image is titled "Tuerie en Egypte" 'Massacre in Egypt.' The ironic caption "Le Coran c'est de la merde. . . . Ça n'arrête pas les balles" 'The Qur'an is crap. . . . It doesn't stop bullets' appears to the left of the shocked man. As we have already seen, many of Cabu's *interdits* were commentaries on recent tragedies that were considered newsworthy but not fair game for humorous drawings. In this cover, Riss combines the attack in Egypt—and perhaps the Arab spring in general—with the criticism of Islamic extremism that we find elsewhere in the pages of *Charlie Hebdo.* His satire of the Muslim Brotherhood is an example of a cartoon that perhaps does not belong in a classroom discussion of French republicanism. His anti-Muslim sentiment might be explained as a reaction to Islamic extremism, but it is arguably a form of secular extremism. The ridiculing of the man's religious beliefs might be characteristic of French *laïcité*, but the man's features are exaggerated in ways that suggest racism.

This image also courts victim-blaming by attributing delusional beliefs to the Muslim man, who is the object of political violence. For the secular reader, or anyone else looking through the lens of *laïcité* and a generalized condemnation of religion and religious authorities, the image might appear as an attack on superstition. Reading the image charitably through a theological lens, the reader might conceivably smile at the reminder that religious beliefs are no defense against violence and that no religion, including Islam, has solved the problem of mortality. But if we think about what Riss is saying about the victim, it is harder to justify this mockery of the victim's behavior and beliefs. What, after all, is the object of satire here? Against whom is Riss arguing? Do any Muslims actually believe the Qur'an can stop bullets? In the absence of a salient political or cultural message, cartoons like this one become susceptible to the charge of outright racism, of ridiculing a stereotypically bearded and dressed Middle Eastern Muslim man simply for being Muslim. In the classroom, such an image could be reasonably discussed as a reflection on political violence or on the relations between the French Republic and Islam.

The caricatures of *Charlie Hebdo* are meant to provoke—laughter, offense, grim assent, or outrage. But in the classroom, they can lead to valuable discussions on race, religion, political violence, and French secularism, after care has been taken to give students the appropriate scaffolding: the necessary cultural and political concepts. With the groundwork laid, students can respond to charged caricatures through the lens of historical context, which will minimize their personal feelings. The discussion of such emotional, controversial materials in class can be very fruitful, given the strong and diverse opinions held about secularism and multiculturalism in the French-speaking world today. The difficulty of these debates—

over the universality of French republicanism and the role of culture and religion in politics—mirrors the polarizing debates that were held under the First Republic. It is in this sense that *Charlie Hebdo*, for all its changing ideology and inconsistent subject matter, is a living embodiment of French republicanism.

Works Cited

Cabu. *Il faut voiler* Charlie Hebdo. *Charlie Hebdo*, no. 764, 7 Feb. 2007, p. 1.

———. *Les interdits de Cabu: 265 dessins presents par Jérôme Duhamel.* Seuil, 1991. Points Actuels.

Charb. *Il revient! Charlie Hebdo*, no. 1084, 27 Mar. 2013, p. 1.

Cohen, Patrick. Interview by Riss. *Le 7/9*, 24 Feb. 2015, www.franceinter.fr/emissions/le-7-9/le-7-9-24-fevrier-2015. France Inter radio show.

Fi, le vilain jacobin! 1793. *Stanford Digital Repository*, purl.stanford.edu/zb026jv1225. Stamp.

Goldstein, Robert Justin. *Censorship of Political Caricature in Nineteenth-Century France.* Kent State UP, 1989.

Kearney, Erin. "Images as a Resource for Culture Learning in the Foreign Language Classroom." *Practical Approaches to Foreign Language Teaching and Learning*, Peter Lang, 2009, pp. 33–66.

Kidd, William, and Sian Reynolds. *Contemporary French Cultural Studies.* Routledge, 2014.

Leconte, Daniel. *C'est dur d'être aimé par des cons.* Pyramide Video, 2009. DVD.

McGrogan, Manus. "The Politics of Provocation: *Charlie Hebdo*, Then and Now." *Contemporary French Civilization*, vol. 41, no 2, 2016, pp. 167–95.

Mignot, François, and Céline Goffette. "Non, *Charlie Hebdo* n'est pas obsédé par l'islam." *Le Monde*, 24 Feb. 2015, www.lemonde.fr/idees/article/2015/02/24/non-charlie-hebdo-n-est-pas-obsede-par-l-islam_4582419_3232.html.

Reconnoissez les nobles travaux du vicomte de Mirabeau. 1791. *Stanford Digital Repository*, purl.stanford.edu/bf954rz9987. Stamp.

Riss. *Le Coran c'est de la merde, ça n'arrête pas les balles. Charlie Hebdo*, no. 1099, 10 July 2013, p. 1.

"SOS caricatures." *Le Point*, 23 Mar. 2006, www.lepoint.fr/actualites-politique/2007-01-17/sos-caricatures/917/0/27509.

Versieux, Nathalie and Sonia Delesalle-Stolper. "A l'étranger, on est Charlie aussi." *Libération,* 11 Jan. 2015. www.liberation.fr/planete/2015/01/11/a-l-etranger-on-est-charlie-aussi_1178542.

Part III

Writing the Revolution

Editors' Choice: Essential Texts of the French Revolution

Le loup philosophe (1789), presented by Julia Douthwaite Viglione

Having taught courses on the French Revolution in the United States for about a decade, I can attest to only one sure thing: it is hard! So many names, dates, and events to get straight, so many terms that change meanings and people who switch camps, not to mention all the newspapers, book publishers, and clubs that seem to burst on the scene and lead public opinion for a week, a month, or more . . . only to disappear, go out of business, or fold overnight. Given the difficulty, students may rightly wonder, "Why bother?"

One of my main goals in teaching the Revolution, then, is to make students realize why it matters and the personal stake they have as Americans in sustaining the ideals of 1789. They may catch that spark in three ways, two of which I describe below. First, reading works published during the 1790s helps them identify some of the resentments and hopes that drove events. Second, by studying alternative versions of the same materials published before or after the Revolution, they notice how social problems take on different senses of urgency over time, just as solutions remain difficult to attain. Finally, by trying their hands at rewriting a revolutionary tract or story for their own audience, they realize how difficult it is to recreate the irony and double meanings that characterize political prose. (Some "altered books" created by former students can be seen at revolutioninfiction.wordpress.com.) Hopefully students will also realize how many of the issues that irked French people of various ranks during the 1790s—unfair practices of taxation that benefited the wealthy to the detriment of the poor and middling ranks, uneven access to education, an unwieldy judicial system, and provincial rivalries for state resources—remain a thorn in our side today. As noted elsewhere in this volume, France is not the only modern democracy that continues to legislate discrimination; the United States is also plagued by inconsistent attitudes toward people's equality before the law, some 240 years since its founding.

Before teachers delve into the literature of the Revolution, I recommend that they have students spend one or two classes imagining what it was like to live as a working person—a peasant, tradesman, or artisan—in eighteenth-century Paris. The costume melodramas unfolding in the first minutes of films like D. W. Griffith's *Orphans of the Storm* and W. S. Van Dyke's *Marie-Antoinette* may prompt laughter, but they also assault viewers with some harsh realities that ordinary people would have confronted under the Old Regime. Seeing a child killed by a fast-moving carriage owned by an indifferent aristocrat, hearing a mocking anthem sung by foreign mercenaries protecting the royal family from the rabble—such scenes stirred the resentment that ignited violent acts against the privileged in the summer of 1789.[1]

I recommend teaching the Revolution through short narratives that can be considered either stories or political parables. My favorites include an oriental allegory of 1789 about a king whose head is sliced off and replaced with others (*L'histoire véritable de Gingigolo* ["The True History of Gingigolo"]); a dialogue among fishwives and a public writer, who debate the guilt of King Louis XVI from their stalls in a Parisian market (*Le falot du peuple* [1793; "The People's Lantern"]); and a detective tale that captures the angst felt by Catholic witnesses to the king's execution, by Honoré de Balzac (*Un épisode sous la Terreur* [1831; "An Episode under the Terror"]). In order to lead students to appreciate the political lessons in these tales, one could pair them with scenes from Charles Dickens's *Tale of Two Cities* (1859), Victor Hugo's *Les Misérables* (1862), or even L. Frank Baum's *Marvelous Land of Oz* (1902), as I've explained elsewhere.[2]

A similar approach could be used with the eight-page philosophical dialogue by a little-known pamphleteer, *Le loup philosophe* (1789; "The Wolf Philosopher"), whose subtitle warns, "The dumbest one is not who you think."[3] It begins as an encounter between a stag, a symbol of the nobility, and a wolf, a symbol of the peasantry. The stag hails "brother wolf" with bonhomie, asks about his family, and exults over news coming from Paris, declaring, "Do you enjoy reading in your free time? Do you subscribe to the *Journal de Paris*? Have you seen *Le mercure*? Do you practice politics?" (La Roche 3). In a humorous dig at the night of 4 August 1789, when noble deputies spectacularly abandoned their inherited privileges for public display (Meaux), the stag switches between praise for equality, on the one hand, and warnings, on the other hand, against the rabble (*les vilains*) who dare to hunt on his grounds. When the wolf admits having no time to read newspapers, given his constant pursuit of food for his family, the stag exclaims, "You break my tender heart! My child, you are lucky to enjoy the 'graces of your estate' (*des grâces d'État*); you should praise Heaven! You endure hunger; that is a virtue that brings you honor!" (4). This play on words puts the fable's tension in full sight: the stag confuses the blandishments of privilege with traditional wisdom regarding other people's suffering. For a nobleman, enjoying the "graces of one's estate" meant taking advantage of an inherited position—to extract payments from sharecroppers, to maintain the family's standing at court, and so forth. For the less fortunate, it meant having the satisfaction that comes from long habit, such as the loss of hunger experienced by the undernourished ("Grâce" [def. A1]).

Once students unpack the linguistic and political connotations behind this text, they begin to see why the political schism dividing the French exploded in summer-fall 1789 and how traditional religious rhetoric justified the suffering of the poor while allowing immunity from guilt for the well-to-do. The notion of a stag's having confidence in a predator and seeking him out for reasoned conversation should make students uneasy. Switching to an American context might be interesting: one could discuss what defines a social predator and debate the pros and cons of blocking voting rights for rehabilitated felons. One might also ask if the stag's philosophy includes any concern for the lowborn *vilains* whom the stag ridicules. This question could lead to a discussion of the widespread acceptance of inequality even among the most enlightened of the philosophers and of their complicity in the slave trade.[4]

The stark differences of voice between the stag and the wolf could make this text a fun basis for a class skit or debate. One side could represent the sarcasm and latent hostility of the wolf, who congratulates the stag for his "good works" and looks forward to the day when he too may become a philosopher. The other could display the stag's blithe jollity and brush aside the wolf's knowledge of tax codes as well as the double meanings behind his sly remarks, such as, "Poor people have no friends" and "Sire, only the wealthy fear death; find help for that in your philosophy" (La Roche 7). After noting how plump the stag has become from eating seven days a week (unlike the poor, who dine only on Sundays), the wolf ends this dialogue: "You will surely not die, Sire; Heaven knows, the decrees of fate are always admirable" (8). Given that this text was published when the National Assembly had begun issuing decrees nonstop to undermine the power of traditional authorities, this homage to "the decrees of fate" (*les décrets du Destin*) sounds ironic.

Analyzing this fable alongside earlier wolf fables from the court of King Louis XIV might help a class explore how social attitudes toward rank, money, and status changed from the 1660s to the 1780s. In his *Fables*, Jean de La Fontaine (1668–94) invariably presents wolves as strong, successful predators who exist beyond the pale of civilization. Even if they are sometimes disarmed before they pounce, as in "The Wolf Turned Shepherd," where the wolf's failed disguise symbolizes the dangers of hypocrisy, the wolf invariably emerges as a killer. His bad reputation may be chalked up to prejudice, as in "The Wolf and the Lamb," where the wolf complains, "Sheep, men, and dogs of every nation, / Are wont to stab my reputation," yet his conduct proves consistently immune to morality (book 1, fable 10). One cannot reason with a wolf.

In *Le loup philosophe*, however, the stag tries to do exactly that, and his attempt prompts his traditional enemy to articulate some facts about life among the poor. The consequences of dialoguing with the enemy are not immediately apparent here, as they are in La Fontaine's "The Wolf and the Lamb," where the wolf devours the chatty, innocent sheep. At the end of *Le loup*, the status quo remains intact, and there is no indication that the stag's comfortable existence is soon to come under assault. Whether he dies at the hand of lowborn huntsmen breaking noble covenants or by the fangs of a hungry family of wolves that lives nearby, both outcomes reveal the folly of philosophizing.

*Les visites par mademoiselle D***K**** (1792), presented by Antoinette Sol

*Les visites par mademoiselle D***K****, by Marie Françoise Kéralio (née Abeille), is a brief, little-known epistolary novel published a short time before the Terror. Kéralio chose a narrative form for *Les visites* that falls somewhere between a journal and a social column recounting the conditions and events of the time as seen through the eyes of the aristocratic salon. After 1793, it reminds one a bit of the story of Nero fiddling while Rome burned. The text is versatile and can be used to accompany history, literature, or theater courses on the Revolution or the late eighteenth century. It is short enough to be used in a variety of situations. The author states that the work was written in 1791 and published in 1792. She orchestrates these visits in a loose monophonic epistolary structure, which at first seems to present an unbiased view of events in Paris, because both Amélie d'Orvillars, the letter writer, and the person to whom she is writing are from the provinces and therefore should have the distance to judge events impartially. But Kéralio's antirevolutionary bias is clear in the first letter, "For the past five days, I have been in town, once so brilliant and that is now a place of injustice and crime" (2). Nostalgia is one of the markers of antirevolutionary rhetoric, so its purpose here is not to set the tone of the text, which is ironic, witty, acerbic, and sometimes sentimental, but to signal the narrator's political orientation to the eighteenth-century reader, who therefore knows what is to come.

Kéralio gives the reader the aristocratic take on revolutionary politics, embedding her commentary, her criticism, in a sentimental narrative of friendship and social education. She plays with duplicity on many levels. The subtext of revolutionary rhetoric underlies seemingly transparent signs of loyalty in words and deeds, calling authenticity into question. The relation between signifier and signified, between symbol and meaning, is corrupted and broken. Dissimulation is the order of the day. Kéralio takes on the spectacle of revolutionary culture, comparing it with the artifice of the theater. In opposition to that culture, which aims for a false transparency, she disguises her criticism in a roman à clef. Her identity, as well as that of her characters, is hidden under easily decipherable semi-anonymous initials, so her hidden truth, like that of the revolutionaries, is not really a secret.

The story tells of the provincial Amélie's introduction into Parisian society. Her education, both social and political, is undertaken by a friend, Madame de Verseuil, who represents the best of Old Regime society: scatterbrained but intelligent, witty but sensitive, a pragmatist but generous and selfless. Amélie begins to understand the complexity and art of society through her visits to her mentor's apartments, while the artifice of revolutionary society is revealed. Literature, art, poetry, religion, and politics are seamlessly integrated into Amélie's social initiation in this rarefied atmosphere of salon society. Amélie takes care to separate her private sentimental discourse, which is communicated in letters, not available to the reader, to another female friend remaining at home, from her more public take on revolutionary politics in its social context. Her intention is to amuse her friend, who stayed at home, and she declares that "only truth will guide my pen" (6). The duty of the reader, who stands with the friend in the place of the recipient of the correspondence, is not only to be amused but also to hear the truth.

The young women's first salon evening is a model for all the others to follow, and Kéralio's first volley is to draw attention to the spectacular aspect of the political by a condemnation of the politicization of theater (14). Once the political-theatrical connection is established, it is a short step to the condemnation of the theatricalization of the political. When Amélie is asked if she has been to the National Assembly and says no, her interlocutor feigns astonishment: "[W]hat? Not even to the National Assembly? They are really excellent actors; their talents will soon be out of price range. Nothing is more astonishing than their ease at playing all their roles; they are good patriots, vile agents, legislators, evil subjects; the only role that they have trouble with is that of an honest man" (17). Fictional characters take the stage, in this novel, with real people who are either singled out for praise (such as the abbé de Mouhy, in a passage where Amélie actually does visit the assembly) or whose sex lives are open season for the salon culture. Witty, vicious commentaries on contemporaries such as Madame de Staël are sown throughout the text and give truth to the statement that if revolutionary politics created the image of public man, participation in the same arena turned women into *filles publiques* ("public women"; Outram 127). The notion of equality both social and political is transferred to a sexual register for women, whose favors are shared liberally and democratically. Another woman's behavior is a topic for discussion: "It appears that you know her well; admit that she has moments of amiability.—yes, and is 'easy' as well" (Kéralio 105). Men, on the other hand, are taken to task for their stupidity or greed.

Specific actions of the revolutionary government are targeted, such as the decree of 19 June 1790, which abolished hereditary nobility, while in this text all the characters openly use their titles, and their servants wear livery. Certain nobles who have subscribed at least on the surface to the renunciation of titles, the soberness of the revolutionary dress, or to wearing the revolutionary colors are sharply criticized and shown to be hypocritical: "That is prince Charles de Roch——t, one of those princes who appeared to give up their title, with the hope to better preserve it; and who, while claiming equality with the common man, really had the hubris to want to be the equal of kings" (38). Amélie finds out that sporting tricolor clothes doesn't necessarily mean one is a revolutionary beneath the surface and that some nobles are "democrats by design," if not by stupidity, and "nothing is as it seems" (128). On the other hand, the danger of appearing exactly what one is, is apparent in an incident when a group of the *salonniers* decide to go for a promenade in the Bois de Boulogne. In a chilling scene, Amélie describes their splendid turnout and the liveried footmen who "guided us in great pomp though the democratic crowd, who in astonishment of our splendor, took revenge on us by crying out against the aristocracy" (114).

Dorinda Outram points out that the act of seeing was powerful and associated increasingly with the *sensible* (sensitivity) during the redefinition of gender roles of this period (42). Women's emotional capacity allowed women to see into things more deeply than men, who were concentrated on a "remorseless control over body and emotion" (84). It will not be lost on students that Kéralio's reading of revolutionary culture takes place in an epistolary exchange among women, in a female-hosted space, the salon. This reading or seeing, then, is coded as feminine and sensitive, revealing the stupidity, greed, and hypocrisy of revolutionary politics. The accusation that politics was determined by private interests is shown to be just as true for the new government as for the old when two women leaving the National Assembly overhear two men speaking about a new law forbidding dueling as "a crime against nature, an inhuman act" (Kéralio 31). The older woman laughs and tells the young woman of this particular representative's reputation for cowardice. The comment shows how private interests and desires still regulate public policy. The work of interpretation, of perception, has an effect on the *sensible* body as well, when Amélie informs her friend that she suffers from "[a] horrible headache, a common consequence of the unbearable banging in the senate, where our modern Lycurgus and Solon, et cetera preside" (31).

The physical aspect of the revolutionaries reflects their baseness and sets them apart from other, well-meaning citizens (27). Amélie points out the gap between the revolutionaries and the people of France when to her shock and dismay she sees the assembly in action. She complains that "if the provinces were witness to the atrocities committed by their representatives . . . to the division between them . . . [they] would be ashamed to have given over their power to such mercenary hands" (29). The pervasiveness of the revolutionary fervor and rhetoric is underlined in settings both public and private. In contrast to revolutionary ideology and hypocrisy (and even fashion) are accounts of the generosity and sensibility of the nobility, who help the needy, to which the revolutionaries are insensible. When military pensions for disabled war veterans are cut by the assembly, which results in real suffering, private aristocrats come to the rescue. Revolutionary rhetoric about *sensibilité*, equality, merit, family, and service to the nation is shown to be empty of meaning when used by the revolutionaries but true when speaking of the nobility. Each party shows its true colors (25). Even the most important revolutionary figures are shown to be duplicitous and working toward their own ends. In the last conversation between Brissot and one of the deputies, where they are discussing the state of the revolution, we overhear "learn from us how to seduce the people and to lead them to injustices upon injustices" (151) and "where would we be if truth ripped error's veil and revealed to French eyes the abuse, our secret plots?" (147).

Standing in for the intended reader and having the same political and social education as Amélie, we are flattered to be let in on all the latest gossip, to be included in this select circle. The educative factor extends to not only telling the reader what is considered good form (Rousseau, Voltaire, Racine), what is amusing (the comic hero Faublas), and what is considered bad form (Laclos and anyone attached to Philippe d'Orleans) but also what to read to keep up-to-date after the book is done, the journal *De la cour et de la ville*, which has "charming things, full of finesse and gaiety" (102). The *Visites* has taught the reader how to see beneath the surface of revolutionary rhetoric, has exposed falsehoods, has seduced the reader with the salon culture, while Kéralio has rendered transparent the new political system and all its signs, symbols, and rhetoric.

The novel serves as an example of partisan politics and can be used in a literature course on the late-eighteenth-century novel or the theater as well as in a history course on the French Revolution. Students can be asked to identify signs of the author's bias that point to royalist politics, such as the revelation of unbecoming behavior of the politicians or the blatant hypocrisy of aristocratic liberals like Madame de Staël. Pairing the novel with political revolutionary pamphlets targeting aristocrats and other political figures is a powerful way to demonstrate the oppositional ideologies at stake. Anonymously published pamphlets such as *Vie politique de Jérôme Pétion, ci-devant maire de Paris, ex-député à la Convention-nationale, et traître à la République française* (1793; "The Political Life of Jérôme Pétion, Former Mayor of Paris, ex–National Convention Representative, and Traitor to the French Republic") or *Portraits exécrables, du traître Robespierre et ses complices* (1794; "Execrable Portraits of the Traitor Robespierre and His Accomplices") demonstrate the political use of calumny to take down and diminish the power of political opponents or opposing revolutionary factions.

In using revolutionary pamphlets with undergraduate students, one has to be aware of the common use of pornography as a political weapon. Whereas one reads sexual insinuations against political figures in *Les visites,* the authors of these two pamphlets use calumny, with accusations of cowardice, hypocrisy, duplicity, treachery, and avarice, rather than pornography against their targets. The pamphlet war that was waged during the last years of the eighteenth century spills over into a sentimental novel to create a hybrid. Students can be challenged to identify rhetorical strategies found in sentimental novels and those that are taken from satirical political publications.

The digital archives of the French National Library (*Gallica*), the *Internet Archive*, and Stanford's *French Revolution Digital Archive* offer a resource for an interesting project for students to read political and cultural columns in newspapers from 1791 and 1792 to compare similarities of rhetoric and subject matter. *L'ami du peuple* (1789–93), published by Jean-Paul Marat; the radical *Le père Duchesne* (1790–94), published by Jacques Hébert; or the *Gazette nationale ou Le moniteur universel* (1789-1810), published by Charles-Joseph Panckoucke, reported both domestic and international news. Pamphlets, newspapers, and broadsides all demonstrate how the rhetoric of disparagement of political figures and false revolutionaries entered daily life and even ostensibly nonpolitical literature.

Comparing the issue of false news facing us today with the revolutionary press's production of propaganda can teach students not only how to judge authenticity but also how to put into perspective our contemporary discussion of truth, falsehood, and integrity. Students can be asked to identify elements of intentional authorial irony that butt up against unintentional historical irony, given the events that directly followed the publication of *Les visites*—in other words, the Terror.

Delphine (1802), presented by Catriona Seth

Germaine de Staël's works offer unparalleled teaching material for anyone interested in the French Revolution. They cover a wide field in terms of genre and period. Some were written in the heat of the moment; others, which deal with France's historic upheavals, were left unfinished at her death in 1817. An advanced class in French could be invited to reflect on the differing impact of a discourse on current events in the 1793 *Réflexions sur le procès de la Reine* ("Reflections on the Queen's Trial"), which was written to stop Marie-Antoinette being put on trial, and an overarching work that benefits from hindsight, like the posthumous *Considérations sur la Révolution française* ("Considerations on the French Revolution"). It could also ask why a writer might choose revolutionary Paris and Switzerland as the backdrop for a novel (*Delphine*). These different texts prompt us to consider what literature can and cannot do and its imbrication with current affairs and the writing of history.

A brief biographical sketch of Staël will make students aware of her close connections to political life before and after the French Revolution. She was the daughter of one of the most famous statesmen of the Old Regime, Jacques Necker. Her lover, Louis-Marie de Narbonne, the father of her sons, was a minister of war during the Revolution. Benjamin Constant, the father of her daughter, was heavily involved in postrevolutionary politics. She acted as an unofficial counselor to these three public figures and, through them, although she was a woman in a world that excluded her sex from direct participation in policy making, had greater access than most of her contemporaries to the centers of power and influence.

Delphine, which exists in a modern English-language translation for those who are not fluent in French, is a must read. It is a novel with a sentimental plot: the young widowed Delphine d'Albémar and Léonce de Mondoville, who is a bachelor, fall in love. There is no happy end. The text is mainly in epistolary form, which offers a great occasion for reflecting with students on how we convey information: the medium shapes the message to a certain degree and entails other problems—letters do not always reach their addressee. News did not circulate in revolutionary Paris as it does now in our time of constant *Twitter* feeds and headline updates. The story unfolds between 12 April 1790 and late 1792. Two of the main characters get married on 13 July 1790. Cue for a reflection on the Fête de la Fédération ("Festival of the Federation") the very next day? Actually no, the festival does not even get a mention. That such major events are ironed out of the narrative is a reminder that we tend to live according to our personal calendar and not by national events. Students can be invited to work out how the Revolution and the love story are intermingled: there are references to the new right to divorce, the abolition of monastic vows, laws on émigré fighters, and so on. These important developments come up when they affect the characters instead of being dry dates on a time line, which means we become more involved with them.

The title page of *Delphine* is a good place to begin: show students a photograph of one of the early editions of this 1802 novel, and the first thing to note is the double date.[5] The unusual "an XI" 'year 11' refers to the revolutionary calendar, which is computed from a secular event, the September 1792 abolition of the monarchy and proclamation of the Republic. Year 11 of the "République une et indivisible" 'One and Indivisible Republic' ran from 23 September 1802 to 22 September 1803. This separate calendar was meant to mark a new era, and many, like Staël herself, hoped that it would usher in a fairer and more democratic regime.

Another thing worth noting on the page is the epigraph, drawn from the writings of Staël's mother, which says that a man should stand up to public opinion, but a woman should submit to it ("Un homme doit savoir braver l'opinion, une femme s'y soumettre"). There are twists and turns in the novel relating to this idea. That several characters are clearly the victims of rumor and prejudice makes us reflect on public opinion as a force in the revolutionary context. One might also look at the numerous caricatures that flourished then—for example, Marie-Antoinette was the subject of scurrilous pamphlets and pornographic sketches.[6]

Staël claims that her subject is the destiny of women, seen from various points of view (*Correspondance* 322), and in *Delphine* she gives us a varied cast of more-or-less sympathetic mothers and daughters, wives and widows, sisters and aunts. Women often had their reputation as their sole (or most important) possession, and there was no option for them to display military heroism in the way men could—or even to defend themselves by denouncing their adversaries. The novel gives a stark indication that in the society of the Revolution happiness could be acquired only at a price; if one slipped the bonds of society, one had to accept a marginal existence. When writing her novel, Staël was conscious of her position as something of a social outcast. She was wealthy but born of Swiss parents and seen as a promoter of republican ideals that were fast going out of fashion. As a woman, she was expected to remain on the sidelines, not to express opinions on serious matters, and she was often the victim of xenophobic and misogynistic attacks.

Staël famously promised that there would be not a word of politics in her book despite its revolutionary setting ("Il n'y aura pas un mot de politique, quoiqu'il se passe dans les dernières années de la Révolution" [*Correspondance* 326]), and yet she dedicated the book to "la France silencieuse," the silent majority whom she hoped would rise up to condemn the shift toward autocracy. She also gave some characters clear political views, like Henri de Lebensei, whose words probably echo those of Staël's immediate circle:

> Cette révolution que beaucoup d'attentats ont malheureusement souillée, sera jugée dans la postérité par la liberté qu'elle assurera à la France; s'il n'en devait résulter que diverses formes d'esclavage, ce serait la période de l'histoire la plus honteuse; mais si la liberté en doit sortir, le Bonheur, la gloire, la vertu, tout ce qu'il y a de noble dans l'espèce humaine est si intimement uni à la liberté, que les siècles ont toujours fait grâce aux événements qui l'ont amenée. (*Delphine* 284)
>
> This revolution, which has unfortunately been sullied by many attacks, will be judged by posterity according to the liberty that it guarantees to France. Should only diverse forms of slavery result from it, it will have been the most shameful period of history, but if liberty is to come from it, Happiness, glory, virtue, all that is noble in the human species, are so intimately tied to liberty that centuries have always shown mercy to the events that brought them about.

This is fighting talk indeed and can be read on two different levels, referring to the moment when the fictional character makes the pronouncement and to history's judgment. The question of the extent to which the Revolution led to freedom is still being debated, and it could be worth dividing the class in two, giving each half the brief of arguing for or against the achievements of the Revolution.

Delphine is marked by the circumstances of its composition, the political context and prejudice of its time, which Staël was trying to resist, but it also transcends that time: the heroes' struggle between desire and duty is one to which we can all relate. In addition, the author does not judge her characters: she lets her readers into their lives. We are free to decide whether they were right or wrong to behave as they did. A final reason to include *Delphine* on any syllabus is that it is a great read!

Notes

Translations from the French are ours unless otherwise indicated.

1. Railing against the privileged, as Abbé Sieyès famously does in *Qu'est-ce que le tiers état?* (1789; "What Is the Third Estate?") is a handy yet disingenuous strategy for stoking popular anger against the wealthy of Old Regime France. To understand the many kinds of privileges that were associated with trades and venal offices, see Behrens 46–75.

2. To see how *Gingigolo* and *Le falot* relate the October 1789 march on Versailles as part of the *poissard* ("fishwife") tradition leading to L. Frank Baum's *Oz* books, see Douthwaite, *Frankenstein* 17–35, 48–58. For connections among Balzac's story, the Terror, and *A Tale of Two Cities*, see 218–24. For ideas on teaching scenes from *Les Misérables* as pendants to these stories, see Viglione, "*Les Misérables*."

3. Since the literary quality of *Le loup* and the other literary sources quoted is less important than their political commentary, this essay provides citations in translation only.

4. For references to quotes by Voltaire, Diderot, and other Enlightenment philosophers on the slave trade, see Curran.

5. The novel came out in December 1802 but bears 1803 on the title page of the first edition. Photographs of this interesting title page are easily found on the Internet.

6. Staël herself was no stranger to such attacks, but the material necessary to study them is less accessible (and far less plentiful) than those aimed at the queen.

Works Cited

Behrens, C. B. A. *The Ancien Régime*. 1967. Harcourt Brace Jovanovich, 1979.

Curran, Andrew W. *The Anatomy of Blackness: Science and Slavery in an Age of Enlightenment*. Johns Hopkins UP, 2011.

Douthwaite, Julia Viglione (*see also* Viglione, Julia Douthwaite). *The Frankenstein of 1790 and Other Lost Chapters from Revolutionary France*. U of Chicago P, 2012.

"Grâce." *Ortolang*, www.cnrtl.fr/definition/grace.

Kéralio, Marie Françoise. *Les visites par mademoiselle D***K****. 1792. *Google Books*.

La Fontaine, Jean de. *Fables*. Translated by Elizur Wright, Jr., 1841.

La Roche, A.-C.-N. de Closquinet de [Chevalier de La Roche]. *Le loup philosophe, à bon chat bon rat, ou le plus bête[s] des deux n'est pas celui qu'on pense: Conte moral*. Imprimerie de Valleyre aîné, 1789.

Meaux, Nicolas. "4 août 1789: La Folle nuit de l'abandon des privilèges." *L'agenda en révolution, 1989*, Éditions du Chêne, 1988.

Outram, Dorinda. *The Body and the French Revolution: Sex, Class, and Political Culture*. Yale UP, 1989.

Sieyès, Emmanuel-Joseph. *Qu'est-ce que le tiers état? Internet Archive*, 12 May 2008, archive.org/details/questcequeletie01sieygoog.

Staël, Germaine de. *Correspondance générale*. Edited by Beatrice W. Jasinski, vol. 6, Pauvert, 1976.

———. *Delphine*. *Œuvres*, edited by Catriona Seth, Gallimard, 2017, pp. 305–1002. Bibliothèque de la Pléiade.

———. *Delphine*. Translated by Avriel Goldberger, Northern Illinois UP, 1995.

Viglione, Julia Douthwaite (*see also* Douthwaite, Julia Viglione). "*Les Misérables* and the French Revolution: How to Keep That 'Unfamiliar Light' Aflame." *Approaches to Teaching Hugo's* Les Misérables, edited by Michal P. Ginsburg and Bradley Stephens, Modern Language Association, 2018, pp. 129–35.

Logan J. Connors

Teaching the Revolution's Theater as Cultural History

> *Tout citoyen pourra élever un théâtre public et y faire représenter des pièces de tous les genres.*
>
> —Article 1, Le Chapelier Law, 13 January 1791
>
> *Any citizen may establish a public theater and perform there any genre of play.*

An extremely productive and innovative period in the history of theater is absent from most of our classrooms. First, the facts: the number of plays penned during the French Revolution was matched only by an equally impressive thirst for public performances. During the revolutionary decade, the period from 1789 to 1799, Parisians enjoyed over 40,000 performances and 855 new theater productions (Kennedy et al. 6–7). Readers across France had over 1600 new published plays at their fingertips, constituting a powerful literary market for drama and indicating that plays at the time were literary works to be bought, read, and sold.[1] When the country's emerging citizens took the Bastille on 14 July 1789, Paris had twelve theaters; less than two years later, and thanks to the provision of article 1 of the Le Chapelier Law (*Loi*), there were thirty-five. No decade to that point in French history had ever enjoyed such a vast and varied dramatic landscape; the difference from previous eras is astonishing. For example, there were twelve new theatrical productions in Paris during the 1700–01 season; in 1789–90, Parisian theaters staged 255 new plays by dozens of different dramatists.[2]

Dramatic authors during the French Revolution were not only prolific but also dramaturgically bold. The period was witness to the birth of new genres, such as the *mélodrame* and the *vaudeville*, literary forms that would later dominate the nineteenth- and twentieth-century stages. Writers at the time expanded on and altered genres from the twilight of the Old Regime, such as the *drame bourgeois*, national (or patriotic) tragedy, and the satirical *pièce de circonstance* ("ephemeral play"). The period established new theories of exactly who constituted the public and of what determined a spectacle. It was during the Revolution that artistic directors, actors, and everyday citizens came together for public festivals and other collective politico-aesthetic events. All in all, it would not be an exaggeration to call the Revolution one of the most important epochs in the history of French theater. So what happened? Why don't we teach the Revolution's drama or its unique theatrical practices?

The most obvious answer lies in methodology, in the pedagogical resources we have for our surveys and seminars. French literature anthologies on both sides of the Atlantic ignore the Revolution's diverse theatrical legacy. Often the literary output of the period is eclipsed by a reductive political take on revolutionary cultures. In the French tradition (Lagarde and Michard; Boursin; Décote and Sabbah; Collet) and in anthologies geared toward anglophone students (Leggewie; St. Onge et al.; Berg and Leroy), the theater history presented to students, whether implicitly or explicitly, repeats the post-Romantic narrative that French drama went to sleep after Beaumarchais's *Marriage of Figaro* (1784) only to wake up again with Victor Hugo's and Alfred de Musset's renovations to the stage during the 1830s. Aside from the occasional reference to Beaumarchais's *La mère coupable* (1792; "The Guilty Mother") or to the period's ephemeral current events theater, there is virtually no reference to the Revolution's drama in French literature anthologies, both past and present.

Most anthologies treat the Revolution as a cataclysmic moment of political seriousness that has little time for the literature of a defunct Old Regime. The Revolution is not ignored entirely, of course; anthologies include excerpts from political tracts and speeches, such as Count Mirabeau's *Sur les finances et la banqueroute* ("On Finances and Bankruptcy"), Georges Danton's "De l'audace" ("Some Audacity"), Rouget de Lisle's famous "La Marseillaise," and of course the Declaration of the Rights of Man and of the Citizen. More recently, Olympe de Gouges's *Declaration on the Rights of Woman and of the Female Citizen* has made its way into several anthologies—no doubt thanks to important revisionist studies on de Gouges and on the role of women during the Revolution. Though ideologically innovative, from a generic point of view, de Gouges's *Declaration* maintains the image of a solemn Revolution with no time for literature.[3] Several anthologies include an ode or two by André Chénier, and others are illustrated with a few paintings by Jacques-Louis David (e.g., *The Death of Marat*). A few anthologies provide eyewitness reports of violence during the Terror or of the royal family's execution. Only in the anthology by Christian Biet, Jean-Paul Brighelli, and Jean-Luc Rispail do students get a glimpse of the many plays from the Revolution (probably because Biet is a renowned early modern theater expert). This volume, however, covers literature only from the seventeenth and eighteenth centuries; it seems that when one tacks on excerpts from the medieval or the modern periods—when a literature course becomes a literature survey—the Revolution loses its plays, novels, and (most of its) poems.

If revolutionary theater is indeed an opportunity to show students a "different cultural model" (Frantz and Marchand 507), a conceptual bridge between the cultural practices of the Old Regime and market-driven modernity, a "paradigm shift" (Poirson 14) in the relation between public consumption and artistic production, and a "new cultural politics" (Frantz 10), then instructors of French literature and history need to start teaching students about the Revolution's unique drama and intense theatermania. In this essay I propose several ways of presenting French dramatic literature and theatrical culture from the Revolution to students, using two different undergraduate courses I have taught as examples: a survey on French-language literature from the medieval period to 1800 and a practicum seminar on French theater.

In both courses, French drama and theater history from the Revolution help me achieve a few of my learning objectives. From the perspective of theater history, students learn about a moment in time when the dramatic arts played an essential role in the formation of new political cultures. In terms of the history of literature, the Revolution's drama renders more complex students' notions of how political events and literary artifacts intertwine. When students investigate the Revolution's diverse theatrical corpus, they begin to question the seemingly intuitive but ultimately simplistic idea of literature as a naturalistic mirror. They learn that, contrary to the dominant critical opinion portraying the French Revolution's theater as little more than political pamphleteering,[4] the period was actually characterized by dramaturgical innovation and new, ambiguous relations between political identities and theatrical practices. They realize that debates about history and literature are not settled but, rather, ongoing and ever-changing discussions in which they can now—armed with this knowledge—begin to participate.

Teaching Drama of the Revolution in a Survey Course on French Literature

A survey course on French-language literature from the medieval period to 1800 presents several challenges to any instructor. First, it covers over nine centuries but not the most recent two, thus spanning a period that many students have never studied at the college level. Second, students are asked to read dozens of works—medieval lais, seventeenth-century novels, Enlightenment political treatises, and other sources—when they have only an intermediate to intermediate-high knowledge of French. Third, it takes significant class time to help students understand the basic historical and political background that undergirds each period's literary works (the reign of Louis XIV, the Wars of Religion, the Hundred Years' War, the Regency, and more); this pressure to cover a vast chunk of European history limits the time we can spend on the literary works themselves. Despite these difficulties, students come away from this survey with broad knowledge of French literature and history, several tools for analyzing literary works and other cultural materials, and their first experience with research methods in humanistic studies, including a series of methods sessions—taught in English and with the help of university research librarians—on historiography, the evaluation of secondary sources, and proper citation.

Given the chronological sweep of the survey, we study the Revolution at the end of the course. By this time, students should have an admirable set of intellectual skills for analyzing complex primary and secondary sources. But in one semester I cannot devote several weeks to the Revolution. I am also constrained by limited access to the Revolution's plays—an ongoing problem that James Gilroy first noted over twenty-five years ago in an article on teaching the Revolution's literature (565). With few to no passages of revolutionary literature in the course anthology (Berg and Leroy; Leggewie), one must favor a quick reading of "La Marseillaise," an eyewitness report of Louis XVI's execution, or the Declaration of the

Rights of Man over any rigorous interrogation of the period's literary works or theatrical culture.

Thanks to the recent publication of a new resource book on eighteenth-century French theater (Frantz and Marchand), instructors and students have short yet focused passages from about a dozen plays composed during the revolutionary period (and many others from before 1789).[5] Moreover, the volume includes critical essays geared to university students on various topics, ranging from the idea of heroism in revolutionary drama to sociological analyses of the period's complex cultural politics and theatergoing practices.

With this anthology, students are able to take in the diversity of revolutionary drama, which puts into question the myth that plays from the period were merely "vehicles of political indoctrination" (Gilroy 565). Students do read excerpts from several overtly indoctrinating plays, such as Dorvigny's Jacobin *La parfaite égalité, ou Les tu et toi* (1793; "The Perfect Equality; or, The 'Tu' and 'Toi'") and Charles-Pierre Ducancel's Thermidorian *L'intérieur des comités révolutionnaires* (1795; "The Interior of Revolutionary Committees"). But they also read excerpts from Chénier's *Charles IX ou L'école des rois* (1789; "Charles IX; or, The School for Kings") and from Beaumarchais's *The Guilty Mother*—plays that belie the claim that all French revolutionary drama is based solely on current events, poetic codes of derision, and overt political quarrel. With the critical essays, students engage with terms like *Jacobin*, *counterrevolutionary*, and *Thermidorian*, as well as with the precise political cultures that marked the period's dramatic output and theatrical institutions. Lastly, Pierre Frantz and Sophie Marchand include production notes from twentieth- and twenty-first-century dramaturgs and stage directors who have produced the plays from the Revolution in the anthology. Students can thus follow the historical arc of a play from its origins to its ongoing status as a cultural artifact in contemporary (or recent) France. For example, we read excerpts from Sylvain Maréchal's *Le jugement dernier des rois* (1793; "The Final Judgment of Kings") with an essay on theater during the Revolution and the Terror by Frantz and a sample from Jean-Louis Martin-Barbaz's production notes when he staged Maréchal's play at the Théâtre de la Cité Internationale Universitaire in 1989 (Frantz and Marchand 519–21, 507–15, and 521–22, respectively).

Frantz and Marchand's anthology gives students a holistic image of theater during the Revolution in a short amount of time (approximately two 75-minute class sessions). After this lesson, they realize the importance of the Revolution in the overall history of French theater;[6] they gain more knowledge of revolutionary literature than they would with typical anthologies; and, perhaps most important, when they read the reviews and director's notes from contemporary productions, they come to understand that people nowadays (and not just their instructor) still care about the period's dramatic legacy. This unit furthers students' analytic skill sets and prepares students for more rigorous inquiry of cultural artifacts in advanced undergraduate seminars. They analyze primary source material, come to grips with secondary opinions about those sources, and learn to synthesize various types of texts in order to better write about and discuss theater as a social and political institution, a literature, and a unique cultural experience.

Teaching Drama of the Revolution in a Practicum Seminar on French Theater

The experience of the performing arts is the focus of my practicum seminar on French theater. In this course, taught in French but with specialized dramaturgy workshops and performance components in English, students analyze classical, modern, and contemporary plays from the French-speaking world, from Racinian tragedy to the contemporary works of the Lebanese Canadian writer Wajdi Mouawad. In addition, students learn how to write for, direct, and act in theater through a series of workshops, cotaught with my colleagues from the Department of English and the Department of Theatre Arts.[7] The semester culminates with a festival of short (5–7 minute) adaptation performances through which the students demonstrate their knowledge of the themes and tensions in the syllabus plays, expand their writing skills as dramatic authors, and engage with new creative and pedagogical processes through the corporeality of performance. Early in a unit on adaptation, they make a group production pitch, in which they justify, to a mock review board, their conception of how they would adapt one of the plays in the syllabus. They present on the dramaturgical and staging changes that would need to be made when adapting a play for a new audience, and they describe the casting, costuming, and staging of their adaptation. Students are required to budget their production and propose a series of venues (standard theaters or more innovative performance spaces) for their mock premiere. Some examples in the past include an adaptation of Racine's *Phaedra* set in antebellum Georgia, Molière's *The Learned Ladies* in New York City during the 1929 stock market crash, and Beckett's *Waiting for Godot* in a nondescript dentist's office. At the end of the semester, the student performances are significantly scaled-down versions (we all use the same venue, a multipurpose room on campus) of the production ideas they pitched during this activity.

This final project is ambitious and, quite frankly, not easy to pull off. Many of the students have never taken a theater course, and even fewer enroll in the class with previous knowledge of playwriting. The last time I taught the practicum seminar, I did not fully flesh out the formal mechanisms and intellectual stakes of theatrical adaptation, and a few students felt unprepared for the end-of-semester performance events. Although I showed the students various contemporary theatrical and filmic adaptations of Molière's and Shakespeare's comedies, they struggled to adapt texts to new contexts and were unsure to what extent they should incorporate lines from the original play. They were able to identify adaptations and discuss why certain textual changes worked in new environments, but conceptualizing and writing an adaptation of their own was challenging. But this struggle presents a pedagogical opportunity: next time I teach this course, I will address the students' concerns with adaptation by assigning a few excerpts of plays from the revolutionary years well before embarking upon the adaptation pitch and mini-adaptation performances at the end of the semester.

With titles such as *Sans-culotte Othello* (1793, by Jean-François Ducis, after William Shakespeare), *L'épreuve du républicain* (1793, by Marie Laugier, after Marivaux; "The Republican Tested"), and *La clubomanie* (1795, by Leprevost d'Iray, after Alexis Piron; "Clubmania"), dramatists during the Revolution engaged with the contemporary sociopolitical climate by adapting well-known plays and storylines. In anticipation of my production-pitch assignment, in the future I will couple readings of Molière's *The Learned Ladies* with an examination of Jean-Louis Laya's *L'ami des lois* (1793; "Friend to Laws"), an adaptation of Molière's play that retells this story of deceit and charlatanism through veiled jibes at the revolutionary leaders Jean-Paul Marat and Maximilien Robespierre. Until recently, Laya's play was just another intriguing yet inaccessible work from the Revolution: students and instructors lacked an affordable version of the play, let alone any sort of contextualization of the work for a university audience. Thanks to a new Anglo-French cooperation to bring plays from the French eighteenth century to a wider audience through low-cost critical editions, in 2011 Mark Darlow and Yann Robert published a comprehensive scholarly edition of Laya's *L'ami des lois,* which includes a rich explanatory introduction about both the play and the wider context of drama during the Revolution and Terror. This new resource helps students grasp the dramaturgical effort and deep knowledge of both form and context that are required for theatrical adaptation. Moreover, Darlow and Robert's introduction explains the complicated ways that performances are received by many different and sometimes competing types (and, during the Revolution, factions) of spectators and readers. The introduction provides students with detailed knowledge of Laya's technical reworking of Molière's play, including the specific references to political debates and personalities in 1793 through the author's manipulations of the original seventeenth-century play text.

The complex relation between past and present is an important theme in French drama of the Revolution; it is also the intellectual backbone of my practicum seminar on French theater. I hope to intrigue students by showing them the clever manipulations of classical theater during the tumultuous years of the Terror. By studying Laya's rewriting of Molière, they can understand better how adaptation operates, both mechanically ("What do you need to do to a text so that it works in a new context?") and symbolically ("What are the contextual characteristics that make this particular adaptation work?"). Students should in turn emerge as better prepared to make more rigorous and theoretically bold production pitches and mini-adaptations.

I have found that undergraduate students come to enjoy the vibrant and engaged drama of the Revolution and that many students are fascinated by the period's culture of the spectacle and theatergoing fervency. Theater was a powerful collective experience through which France's new citizens interrogated previous political and aesthetic regimes and established new ones. We need to start teaching about the period's drama and theatrical practices; otherwise we fail to provide students with one of the bases of modern French theater culture. Without reevaluating how we teach the French Revolution—perhaps the most important of Karl Marx's "locomotives of history" (110)—we are letting one of the most important moments in Western culture slip into oblivion.

Notes

Translations from the French are mine, unless otherwise indicated.

1. See Tissier for more information about the publication of dramatic works during the Revolution.

2. For more analysis on the quantity and diversity of published plays and

theatrical performances during the Revolution, see Poirson 30; see also the appendixes in Tissier.

3. This is even more unfortunate, given de Gouges's prolific literary output during the Revolution.

4. For a purely political take on the theater's merits during the Revolution, see Carlson; for a criticism of this approach, see Frantz; see also Feilla.

5. The Revolution's plays included in this anthology are Beaumarchais's *La mère coupable*; Lemierre's *Guillaume Tell*; Marie-Joseph Chénier's *Charles IX ou L'école des rois*, *Timoléon*, and *Fénélon*; Laya's *L'ami des lois*; Maréchal's *Le jugement dernier des rois*; Dorvigny's *La parfaite égalité ou Les tu et toi*; Mathelin's *Marat dans le souterrain des Cordeliers*; Ducancel's *L'intérieur des comités révolutionnaires*; and Monvel's *Les victimes cloîtrées*.

6. By this point in the semester, students have read complete or abridged dramatic works by Pierre Corneille, Molière, Racine, Marivaux, and Diderot.

7. I am particularly indebted to Robert Gainer, of the Department of Theater and Dance, and Joseph Scapellato, of the English Department at Bucknell University. Both led the acting and playwriting workshops for this course when it was first taught in 2014.

Works Cited

Berg, R. J., and Fabrice Leroy. *Littérature française: Textes et contextes*. Vol. 1, Harcourt, 1997.

Biet, Christian, et al., editors. *XVII*e*–XVIII*e *siècles: Collection textes et contextes*. Magnard, 1983.

Boursin, Jean-Louis. *Anthologie de la littérature française: Textes choisis du XI*e *au XXI*e *siècle*. Belin, 2007.

Carlson, Marvin. *The Theatre of the French Revolution*. Cornell UP, 1966.

Collet, Francis. *Les grands textes de la littérature française*. Ellipses, 2010.

Décote, Georges, and Hélène Sabbah, editors. *Histoire de la littérature française: XVIII*e *siècle*. Hatier, 1991. Itinéraires littéraires.

Feilla, Cecilia. *The Sentimental Theater of the French Revolution*. Ashgate, 2013.

Frantz, Pierre. "Les tréteaux de la Révolution (1789–1815)." *Le Théâtre en France 2: De la Révolution à nos jours*, edited by Jacqueline de Jomaron, 2nd ed., Armand Colin, 1992, pp. 9–36.

Frantz, Pierre, and Sophie Marchand, editors. *Le théâtre français du XVIII*e *siècle: Histoire; textes choisis; mises en scène*. L'avant scène, 2009.

Gilroy, James P. "Teaching a Literature Course on the French Revolution." *French Review*, vol. 66, no. 4, 1993, pp. 562–71.

Gouges, Olympe de. *Déclaration des droits de la femme et de la citoyenne*. *Wikisource*, fr.wikisource.org/wiki/Déclaration_des_droits_de_la_femme_et_de_la_citoyenne.

Kennedy, Emmet, et al. *Theatre, Opera, and Audiences in Revolutionary Paris: Analysis and Repertory*. Greenwood, 1996.

Lagarde, André, and Laurent Michard. *Littérature: XVII*e *et XVIII*e *siècles*. 1948. Bordas, 2003.

Laya, Jean-Louis. *L'ami des lois.* 1793. Edited by Mark Darlow and Yann Robert, MHRA, 2011.

Leggewie, Robert, editor. *Anthologie de la littérature française: Tome 1: Des origines à la fin du dix-huitième siècle.* Oxford UP, 1990.

Loi du 13 janvier 1791 relative aux spectacles. Legifrance, https://www.legifrance.gouv.fr.

Marx, Karl. *The Class Struggles in France, 1848–1850.* Progress, 1969.

Poirson, Martial, editor. *Le théâtre sous la Révolution: Politique du répertoire (1789–1799).* Desjonquères, 2008.

St. Onge, Ronald, et al. *La civilisation française en évolution I: Institutions et culture avant la 5e République.* Heinle, 1995.

Tissier, André. *Les spectacles à Paris pendant la Révolution: Repertoire analytique, chronologie et bibliographie.* Droz, 1991.

Amir Minsky

The French Revolution and the German Chimera: Theatricality, Emotions, and the Untransferability of Revolution in J. H. Campe's *Briefe aus Paris*

> *Si j'avais à imaginer un nouveau Robinson, je ne le placerais pas dans une île déserte, mais dans une ville de douze millions d'habitants, dont il ne saurait déchiffrer ni la parole ni l'écriture: ce serait là, je crois, la forme moderne du mythe.*
>
> —Roland Barthes, *Le bruissement de la langue*

> *If I had to imagine a new Robinson, I would not place him on a desert island but in a town of twelve million inhabitants, where he would be able to decipher neither speech nor writing; this would be, I believe, the modern form of the myth.*

Journeying to a foreign country in the throes of revolution to write a travel guide would seem no less an odd choice in the eighteenth century than it would today, yet this is what Joachim Heinrich Campe (1746–1818), a noted Prussian pedagogue and author of children's literature, did in the summer of 1789, shortly after the fall of the Bastille. *Briefe aus Paris während der französischen Revolution geschrieben* ("Letters from Paris, Written during the French Revolution"),[1] his travelogue documenting a three-week sojourn in revolutionary Paris, was among the first German eyewitness accounts of the Revolution, and it achieved almost overnight celebrity by capitalizing on a growing European literary market and on its readership's thirst for travel and exploration narratives.[2] Although this new genre of revolutionary travelogue often emulated the rhetorical devices and emotive repertory of the sentimental novels of previous decades, it promoted emotional identification with political actors and ideologies rather than with the suffering and travails of fictional characters.[3] Readers who vicariously immersed themselves in the unfolding drama of the French Revolution through the experiences of so-called freedom pilgrims—those foreigners who, like Campe, flocked to Paris to bask in the French people's reclaiming of egalitarian human rights—could ideally begin to anticipate overcoming the divisiveness of social status, class, and property in their own everyday lives, even if such changes took much longer to manifest as political reality.

The importance of introducing the *Briefe* to modern audiences therefore stems not only from its status as an example of the French Revolution's multilayered global reverberations but also because the Revolution generated what Northop Frye called "polysemous meaning" (72) in its activation of contemporary readers' identification with both its plot (*mythos*) and ideas (*dianoia*). Students can explore further polysemy in the apparent tensions of Campe's insider/outsider perspective—between the descriptive and quasi-documentary aspects of the letters, on the one hand, and their prescriptive, pedagogical, and propagandistic aspects, on the other. Furthermore, Campe's interpretation of the Revolution as a concrete event of both local and global significance is counterpoised by his assessment of its symbolic dimension (both aesthetic and moral) and its adaptability to cultural translation and transmission abroad.

Given that Campe was a pedagogue, teaching representations of the French Revolution to his readership was at the core of his concern in the *Briefe*. This essay explores interlocking issues in his dual utilization of the Revolution, both as an instructive model and as a cautionary tale, to serve as points of engagement for teaching this text: the problems associated with culturally translating *revolution* as an operative concept between its French and German meanings; Campe's deployment of theatrical metaphors in representing the French Revolution and its emotional topography; and the risks posed to German national self-identity by excessive assimilation to French revolutionary culture.

An Untranslatable Revolution

Campe's *Briefe* is first and foremost a prorevolutionary manifesto. However, faced with a situation of geopolitical fragmentation by the crumbling of the Holy Roman Empire, on the one hand, and the German educated middle classes' search for political agency and unity, on the other, the *Briefe* also testifies to Campe's subjection of the Revolution to intra-German cultural and political agendas. Despite the immense enthusiasm that the Revolution's inception elicited among the German liberal intelligentsia, the *Briefe* also percolated their concerns about revolutionary violence spilling across the Rhine. These concerns grew into widespread disillusionment once the Revolution's emancipatory goals transformed into expansionist encroachment on German turf in the course of the French Republic's continental wars from 1792, and the inception of the Terror regime in 1793. The Revolution thus features in the *Briefe* as the apogee of universal human emancipation but, at the same time, as a German cautionary tale.

This duality also shaped Campe's political stance, a far cry from revolutionary firebrands such as Anacharsis Cloots, Adam Lux, or Eulogius Schneider—German radicals whose involvement in French revolutionary politics ended in their execution during the Terror. In the *Briefe*'s preface, for instance, Campe extolled the freedom enjoyed under enlightened monarchs such as Friedrich II and his nephew, the duke of Braunschweig-Wolfenbüttel, Karl Wilhelm Ferdinand, who was Campe's patron. Although he was aware of the encroaching restrictions on freedom of the press in the German principalities, these paled, in his opinion, compared to the oppression perpetrated by French absolutism, whose crimes could be exposed only in hindsight: "only under the reign of Trajan could one scold, as did Pliny, the abominations and outrages carried out under Nero and Domitian" (iv).

Campe wished to label tyranny as a foreign phenomenon in both political and geographic terms to his German readership, but the notoriety the *Briefe* achieved soon after its publication may have shaken that belief. Having had a French honorary citizenship bestowed on him in August 1792 (along with other men of letters and political reformers, such as Johann Pestalozzi, Friedrich Schiller, Thomas Paine, and George Washington), he was subsequently vilified as a Jacobin and a traitor in the German conservative press. The further accusation of atheism made against him by Church authorities was cleared only through his patron's intervention and Campe's own public declaration of his steadfast German patriotism and call for political moderation. For Campe, as for other prominent German intellectuals of the time, such as Kant, avoiding political extremism was a way to disarm the "fermenting" passions unleashed by the French Revolution. Reaching an affective balance both in individual bodies and in the body politic was a goal that Campe pursued in his pedagogical works as well ("Von der nöthigen Sorge"). His own experience of persecution, moreover, accentuated his awareness of the unpreparedness of the German public for radical political change. If freedom of thought and of the press could be effectively curtailed by state censorship, and if the sole guarantee of personal security for writers was their dependence on princely patronage, what indeed were the prospects of implementation of the French Revolution's ideals on German soil?

The initial stumbling blocks, as Campe saw them, were conceptual and linguistic. In 1792, his prize-winning essay, submitted to a contest sponsored by the Prussian Academy of Sciences on the question "Is complete purity of language possible in general and for the German language in particular?," noted that after centuries of exposure, the Latin word *revolutio* remained a foreign element in the German language, resisting accurate translation. Reflecting on the aural texture of the various German synonyms to *revolution*, such as *Umschwung* or *Umwälzung*, Campe noted their sluggish, drawn-out semiosis, akin to the slow-changing German constitutions that lagged behind the French Revolution's "impossibly light and speedy motion" (*Ueber die Reinigung* 287). This foreignness of revolution to the German experience in both concept and reality was reflected in the divergent temporalities of the French and German political languages, which made the emulating of French radical political transformations undesirable from a German perspective. During the Napoleonic wars, the fear of French cultural influence was the background to Campe's linguistically purist dictionary project, which intended to rid the German language of its foreign contaminants (namely, French and Latin).[4]

These dynamics of German patriotic nationalism, interlaced with anti-French feelings, gained greater traction in the early 1800s and have been largely explained by the drive to demonstrate German spiritual superiority in the face of practical failure and by the search for linguistic and national purity in the absence of political unity or autonomy. Campe, however, was no Francophobe, and although the French Revolution did not provide a suitable model for German regime change, it spoke volumes to the emergent aesthetic and affective sensibilities he wished to promote among the German middle classes, by increasing their investment in projects of self-edification (*Bildung*). The cultural reform it afforded to his readership, so he hoped, would impel the German nation to foment new political institutions and absorb the Revolution's spiritual fruits without having to suffer its excesses.

Staging the Revolution

Given this obstacle to the Revolution's direct translation, the value of the Revolution for Campe was its instructive and symbolic power as an event of historical and global significance. His impressions of Paris in the *Briefe*, for instance, are expressed in two interchangeable ways. The city features as a tangible place, having topographic and demographic constituents: streets, plazas, landmarks, and inhabitants. At the same time, it is symbolically interpreted as a *theatrum mundi*, the world stage. Campe sometimes engages the theater as an art form that affects the spectator in a concrete, emotional way as well as pedagogically, given the robust contemporary debate that concerned the theatric medium's aesthetic and social functions (Wiles 110–11). More often than not, however, he sees revolutionary Paris as a vast laboratory where new social and political configurations and their symbolic representations are being put to the test for the instruction and benefit of humanity at large.

Campe's discussion of revolutionary theatrics can also be seen in the wider context of the redefinition of the work done by both political and dramatic actors after 1750. French dramatic actors were on the whole trained to portray their parts abstractly, in a manner that would seem realistic to their audience rather than experienced as real by the actors themselves (Friedland 6). With the coming of the Revolution, abstract representation became the defining characteristic of the French political sphere. In a break from the royal past, the National Assembly did not claim to be the nation but rather to speak on its behalf. The symbolic practices of revolutionary culture—the elaborate processions, festivals, and extensive pageantry—were also heavily scripted and theatrical events, meant to maximize emotional appeal to the masses and enhance their identification with the mythology of the Revolution's foundation (Reichardt and Kohle 13–34). French legislators were not oblivious to the power of the theater to generate images, ideas, and emotional identification. Worried that theatrical venues might be used to generate support for aristocratic plots, the revolutionary government published reports and passed several bills, beginning in the summer of

1789, to impede the possibility of theatrical spectacles becoming hotbeds of counterrevolutionary agitation (see, e.g., "Discours").

Campe's impressions of Paris were thus marked by an attempt to distinguish between realities and representations. Navigating surroundings rife with deceptive appearances and shifting political discourse, however, made applied sentimentality (*Empfindsamkeit*) his central interpretative tool in the *Briefe*. Moods and emotions are invoked in many anecdotes as his seismograph for deciphering the French public's emotional landscape and its responses to revolutionary situations—tensions threatening to turn violent are sometimes dispelled with a crude joke; a nobleman condemned by the popular justice of a lynch mob is pardoned by begging for his would-be executioners' mercy. Campe's descriptions of the Parisian mob also defy reader expectations, commenting frequently on its composure, inherent organization, and restraint even in the throes of rage over its hunger and deprivation. Such newly found republican sternness (which to Campe's mind seemed more befitting of the ancient Greeks and Romans) supports the theatrical master metaphor, yet Campe shows how his protagonists both assume and step out of perceived roles, in order to dispel national stereotypes:

> Are these really the people that we in Germany thought of as "French"? Were those whistling, warbling, skipping, and chattering dandies, the airy, dodgy, bloated, and mindless snobs who we used to see coming across the Rhine and who, once in Germany, turned a scornful nose at anything German; were all these laughable and disgusting French caricatures only bastards, only the residue and sputum of a nation, of which we could not detect until then a single one of its peers? Or has this nation's character been so completely knocked over since the inception of revolution fourteen days ago, that all that is good and noble, which lay at its foundation has abruptly surfaced, whereas all that is fatuous and laughable sank entirely to the bottom and vanished from sight? (17 [letter 1])

Campe wished to arrive in Paris early enough to "attend the funeral procession of French despotism," in the city that he defined as "the stage on which one of the greatest political performances the world has ever seen in modern times is now taking place" (3 [letter 1]). In decoding the Revolution as an unfolding drama, he simultaneously inscribes the French as this spectacle's actors (*Schauspieler*), whereas its German participants, among them himself, are cast as its spectators (*Zuschauer*). This dichotomy between active and passive roles that emphasize the moral fault line of scripted versus genuine emotion could harken back to a Rousseauist-type suspicion of the theater as a medium of make-believe and contrived emotion. Campe, however, despite venerating Rousseau, endorsed G. E. Lessing's dramaturgical theory as a guiding set of aesthetic principles to his deciphering of the Revolution (see Lessing et al.).[5]

In his aesthetic writings from the 1760s, Lessing charted his plan to transform the theatrical material available to the general public from mere entertainment to drama worthy of empathetic identification. In contrast to the baroque theater, which reflected the power structure of absolutism by designating the highbrow tragedies of historical significance to aristocratic audiences and the popular comedies (*Lustspiele*) to the general public, Lessing transformed the German national theater by valorizing the identificatory emotion of pity and minimizing the estrangement of admiration in the audience's response to tragic drama. Drama was detheatricalized by being removed from the spectacular context in which actors *played* their characters and being refashioned as a form of lived experience in which the actors *were* the characters on stage. The new drama aimed to position its audience in such a way as to reorganize their subjectivity, constituting it as an "affective inner psychical space" (Von Mücke 95–96, 105). Although aimed at individual spectators, this affective reorganization of subjectivity was intended to generate a community based on sentiments of humane sociability and national identity and espousing Enlightenment notions of rational dialogue, religious tolerance, and cosmopolitan humanitarianism.

Campe's understanding of the emotional impact of the Revolution on both actors and spectators thus charted its transformative effect in the reinvention of national character. Inasmuch as the French had shed off their much-maligned hypocritical and dandyish guise to become *citoyens* ("citizens"), their German spectators could also become morally transformed through emotional mimesis. As Campe wrote:

> One feels here even as a mere spectator, I do not know how, elevated in all of one's emotions, powers, and faculties and at the same time ennobled, and if I am not perceptive enough in my impressions and do not convey back to you the growth in communal spirit [*Gemeingeist*], courage, power, and drive of each action that requires altruism and self-sacrifice, then it is no fault of the school I currently find myself in. (30 [letter 2])

The Limits of Pedagogical Colonialism

The flipside of this moral schooling were the cultural boundaries set by Campe's interpretation of the Revolution. His belief in humanity's capacity for perfectibility, manifested in the French revolutionaries' increasing self-control through the cultivation of republican sentiments, optimistically conjectured a decrease in violence and coercive measures needed to consolidate the Revolution's achievements. The Revolution's violent excesses, which by Campe's estimate claimed more than 15,000 lives in Paris alone, paled next to the Old Regime's dispensation of state violence, orchestrated as a theater of cruelty: public executions were staged events conducted in the same locations where national festivals were celebrated and performed for a crowd cheering and applauding at the agonized death cries of the condemned. "It would seem," Campe wrote, "that [the executions] were performed there intentionally in order to deaden the people's feelings of compassion and pity and accustom them instead to wild Huron acts of barbarism and inhumanity" (58n [letter 2]). This characterization assumes greater significance in the context of his other pedagogical travel narratives (published in installments from the early 1780s to 1813) that recounted, among others, Columbus's discovery of America and the sixteenth-century Spanish and Portuguese conquests of the New World. Note that Campe's most commercially successful book to date was *Robinson der Jüngere* (1779–80), a German adaptation of Daniel Defoe's *Robinson Crusoe.* Such narratives distinctly represented a penchant for what one scholar called "colonial fantasies," in that they created in literary form the mental and ideological frameworks that were expedient for the later rise of German colonialism in the nineteenth century (Zantop, esp. 102–20).

In the *Briefe*, Campe's interpretation of the Revolution could be said to view the French in a similar cultural framework. Although the Revolution had humanized and refined the barbaric tendencies stoked by the Old Regime (pedagogically keyed to parallel the salvaging of Amerindians from their alleged cultural infancy by the conquests of Cortés and Pizarro), a moral ambiguity arises about the durability of such salutary changes. Despite the unprecedented situation of temperance in the midst of lawlessness and complete breakdown of civil society, the power vacuum created by the destruction of the old state constitution jeopardized newly won liberty. The Revolution was in danger, Campe thought, of being reshackled by the aristocracy or destroyed by a descent into anarchy. How long might peaceful tendencies persist "[when] even the greatest of bygone cultures could not protect itself for long under such circumstances of incessant turbulence and an endless moral decadence [*Verwilderung*] of national character?" (211–12 [letter 7]). Whereas the pedagogical colonialism applied in Campe's exploration and conquest narratives invariably culminated in the Amerindians' complete subjection to European culture, religion, and morals, a complementing fear of cultural annihilation arises in the *Briefe*, in this case concerning German assimilation to the French revolutionary model. While such aspirations to emulate the French may have seemed more feasible in the early years of the Revolution, the impact of the Revolutionary wars fought on German soil and the vicissitudes of enforced requisitions and military conscriptions again percolated anti-French national stereotypes.

The *Briefe* foreshadows this emotional turn. The opening letter of 4 August 1789 is marked by an overwhelming cosmopolitan sensation of the eradication of national and cultural barriers and the rebirth of the universal family of man—with Campe's quoting the Roman playwright Terence's motto, "I am human and consider nothing human alien to me"—but by the closing eighth letter of 26 August, cosmopolitanism has been reframed in an emphatically German, and providential, historical trajectory: "The more I see of it, the more profoundly convinced I am that the French Revolution is the greatest and most wholesale blessing vouchsafed by Providence to mankind since Luther; and all men, white and black, yellow and brown, ought to cry, 'Thank God for it'" (325). Campe thus seems to have returned to the opinion, popularized by German critics of the French Enlightenment, that Germany had achieved its own spiritual emancipation already with the Reformation and therefore did not need to dabble in French ideas any further. The linguistic and conceptual impasse that surfaced in his early attempts at representing the Revolution's novelty, when he reported, "I feel the impossibility to describe with German words this spectacle, never seen in Germany since the downfall of its primordial freedom, and so I abandon the attempt" (16 [letter 1]), had become a profound repudiation of cultural assimilation, as the French were by now too dissimilar to provide Germans with a salutary model for emotional identification and moral teachings. Germany would have to awaken from its feudal slumber by its own designs, or not at all.

What role did the *Briefe* ultimately play in its author's mind? As Campe admits in the preface, "One should not regard these letters as a history of the French Revolution, for which purpose they are by no means intended, but rather as a mere history of the feelings of a single human spectator who had the luck to be present at the most beautiful period of that great world [historical] event" (vii). Tellingly, it was this sentimental tone that irked Campe's conservative critics most. "A pedagogue of Campe's stature might have been expected to describe the unfolding drama of the French Revolution from the perspective of politics," one of them noted acerbically, "not in the manner that a weepy dame might view a sentimental tragedy" (Hoffman 66). For most educated German contemporaries, rational critique was as distant from irrational enthusiasm as enlightenment was from revolution. But although Campe saw revolution as the necessary outcome of enlightenment, he did not think that the French Revolution was a fitting political practice for German emulation. To his mind, it should have instead catalyzed a turn to *Bildung*: a quest for self-edification whereby moral reform is launched, and shared feelings of community and a joint purpose emerge to inspire the German educated classes in their task of launching national regeneration.

Teaching the *Briefe aus Paris* as a representative text of the French Revolution's German reception poses a significant challenge. Its liminal status, operating between the polarities of historiographic veracity and fictional verisimilitude, between prorevolutionary propaganda and cautionary moralism, makes it difficult to categorize or to tease out a consistent agenda from it. Moreover, although the overall tone of the *Briefe* is extremely enthusiastic, the work being a product of the Revolution's abrupt inception and the brief era of cosmopolitanism that followed, this sentimental disposition vanished from German public opinion with France's turn to continental expansion, conquest, and eventual imperialism in the 1790s and 1800s. Campe's taking the Revolution for a fait accompli a mere three weeks after it began is indicative of its tremendous acceleration of historical time in contemporaries' perceptions. It is also evident that Campe understood the Revolution at that point as a singular event rather than as a continual and evolving process.

The problems of revolutionary ideological transmission, as outlined in the teaching interventions suggested above, focus on Campe's perception of the Revolution as a cultural construct specific to its time and place. Notwithstanding the Revolution's robust global dissemination (both in its own time and by its later legacies), the difference in temperament between the French and the Germans determined, for Campe, different national expressions of revolutionary passion. Germany, for example, experienced its first democratic revolution only in the Spring of Nations of 1848. This explains Campe's reluctance to interpret the Revolution's main significance as political; instead, he saw the Revolution as a defining event in the realms of culture, aesthetics, and especially pedagogy. Despite his enthusiasm for its heralding a new era in world history, he preferred to see its ideas materialized in Germany by enlightened princes reigning over obedient and grateful subjects, not by social upheaval and popular sovereignty. In contriving his readership as a sentimental *Publikum*, he aimed to consolidate its self-identity as a prototype for the German nation to follow. The French Revolution, it could thus be argued, was transformed by his pen into the most influential work of fiction in German modern history.

Notes

1. The work first appeared as eight serialized letters in the *Braunschweigisches Journal*, from October 1789 to February 1790, addressed to Campe's friend and the coeditor of the journal, Ernst Christian Trapp. All translations are my own, unless otherwise noted.

2. On German travelers' accounts of revolutionary France, see Ruiz 229–51. On Campe's travels, see Schmitt 332–46; Fertig.

3. As Lynn Hunt has shown, emotional strategies acquired in the process of such reading often impelled audiences to become more sensitive to manifestations of suffering and pain in the world and thus contributed to the increased acceptance, in the second half of the eighteenth century, of the idea of inalienable human rights and the consequent expansion of the abolitionist movement in the Atlantic world (35–69).

4. Under the entry "Revolution" (*Wörterbuch* 556–57), Campe credits his *Briefe* with introducing the concept into German discourse, which at that point had been used in "a thousand or more publications." See also Schiewe.

5. Campe was part of Lessing's close circle in Hamburg and later in Wolfenbüttel, where Lessing spent his last years as librarian of the ducal library. See Lessing et al.

Works Cited

Campe, Joachim Heinrich. *Briefe aus Paris während der französischen Revolution geschrieben*. Braunschweig: im Schulbuchhandlung, 1790.

———. *Ueber die Reinigung und Bereicherung der deutschen Sprache: dritter Versuch, welcher den von dem Konigl. Preus. Gelehrtenverein zu Berlin ausgesetzten Preis erhalten hat*. Braunschweig: im Schulbuchhandlung, 1794.

———. "Von der nöthigen Sorge für die Erhaltung des Gleichgewichts unter den menschlichen Kräften: Besondere Warnung vor dem Modefehler die Empfindsamkeit zu überspannen." *Allgemeine Revision des gesamten Schul- und Erziehungswesens von einer Gesellschaft praktischer Erzieher*, vol. 3, edited by Campe, Hamburg, 1785, pp. 291–434.

———. *Worterbuch zur Erklärung und Verdeutschung der unserer Sprache aufgedrungenen fremden Ausdrücke. Ein Ergänzungsband zu Adelungs und Campe's Wörterbüchern*. Braunschweig: im Schulbuchhandlung, 1813.

"Discours et motions sur les spectacles." 22 Aug. 1789. Paris, Chez Denné.

Fertig, Ludwig. "Ein Pädagoge auf Reisen: Joachim Heinrich Campe 1785 in Braunschweig, Darmstadt, Karlsruhe und Laubach." *Archiv für hessische Geschichte und Altertumskunde*, vol. 69, 2011, pp. 151–72.

Friedland, Paul, *Political Actors. Representative Bodies and Theatricality in the Age of the French Revolution*. Cornell UP, 2002.

Frye, Northrop. *Anatomy of Criticism: Four Essays*. Princeton UP, 1957.

Hoffman, Leopold Aloys. "Ueber die politischen Angelegenheiten Frankreichs: In Briefen an der Herrn Educationsrath und Buchhändler J. H. Campe in Braunschweig." *Wiener Zeitschrift*, vol. 1, no. 1, 1792, pp. 54–84.

Hunt, Lynn. *The Invention of Human Rights: A History*. W. W. Norton, 2007.

Lessing, Gotthold Ephraim. "G. E. Lessings Briefwechsel mit Joachim Heinrich Campe: Von 1779 und 1780." *Gotthold Ephraim Lessings sämmtliche Schriften*, Vossische Buchhandlung, 1794, vol. 29, part 5, pp. 459–71.

Lessing, Gotthold Ephraim, et al. *Briefwechsel über das Trauerspiel*. Edited by Jochen Schulte-Sasse, Winkler, 1972.

Reichardt, Rolf, and Hubertus Kohle. *Visualizing the Revolution: Politics and the Pictorial Arts in Late Eighteenth-Century France*. Reaktion Books, 2008.

Ruiz, Alain. "Deutsche Reisebeschreibungen über Frankreich im Zeitalter der Französichen Revolution, 1789–1799: Ein Überblick." *Reiseberichte als Quellen europäischer Kulturgeschichte: Aufgaben und Möglichkeiten der historischen Reiseforschung*, edited by Anton Mączak and Hans J. Teuteberg, Wolfenbüttel, 1982, pp. 229–51.

Schiewe, Jürgen. *Sprachpurismus und Emanzipation: Joachim Heinrich Campes Verdeutschungsprogramm als Voraussetzung für Gesellschaftsveränderungen*. Olms, 1988.

Schmitt, Hanno. *Vernunft und Menschlichkeit: Studien zur philanthropischen Erziehungsbewegung*. Verlag Julius Klinkhardt, 2007.

Von Mücke, Dorothea E. *Virtue and the Veil of Illusion: Generic Innovation and the Pedagogical Project in Eighteenth-Century Literature*. Stanford UP, 1991.

Wiles, David. *Theatre and Citizenship: The History of a Practice*. Cambridge UP, 2011.

Zantop, Susanne. *Colonial Fantasies: Conquest, Family, and Nation in Precolonial Germany, 1770–1870*. Duke UP, 1997.

Erin A. Myers

The *Sans-culottides*: Learning Revolutionary-Era French Culture through Celebration and a Reading of Hugo's *Quatrevingt-treize*

The *sans-culottides* festival was conceived of by Fabre d'Eglantine, a Jacobin playwright and friend to Georges Danton, as a way to complete the republican calendar. Twelve months of thirty days each made 360 days; the remaining five days for the Earth's voyage around the sun were given over to five festivals: virtue (*vertu*), talent (*génie*), industry (*travail*), ideas (*opinion*), and heroic deeds (*récompenses*). As the first *sans-culottides* festival approached, the editors of republican rituals responded to the void of customs by publishing a manual, *Cérémonies à l'usage des fêtes nationales* ("Ceremonies for National Festivals"), containing instructions for ceremonies that could be performed under the auspices of individual municipalities. All the festivals are outlined, ranked in importance, and described.

The editors also expound a theory of celebration in the manual. The success of a festival depends on the degree to which the classical principle of unity of action is observed (8). The dual objective is the same—that is, to move and instruct the participant: "Varions nos fêtes. . . . Choisissons pour les plus solennelles celles qui paraissent les plus propres à produire des impressions fortes, et à tourner les cœurs vers la vertu, par les émotions vives des sens" 'Let us vary our festivals. . . . Let us select for the most solemn occasions festivities that seem the most apt to make a strong impression, and impel hearts to virtue by stimulating the senses' (10). These words summarize the power and appeal of revolutionary imagery, be it visual, intellectual, lyrical, or musical. They also provide insight into the spirit of the Revolution.

Students researched and planned a revolutionary festival in a third-year French course, Reading and Expression, that I developed and taught. Combining the reading of Victor Hugo's *Quatrevingt-treize* (1874; "Ninety-Three") with a class celebration of the *sans-culottides* made for a powerful experience of the forces at play in the French Revolution. Hugo's text offers the advantage of telling the history in a way that invites the novice reader into it, while raising questions about literature as a vehicle for the interpretation of historical events.

Fortunately for the English-speaking student of French literature and history, *Ninety-Three*, a recent English translation of Victor Hugo's last novel, is available as a free e-book on *Project Gutenberg*. Unfortunately, the translation often does not render the poetic turn of Hugo's prose. Regardless of language, readers complain about the novel's rants and lists of names (see for example the reviews on goodreads.com). But some prefer the novel to better-known works by Hugo, because of the difficulty of the subject—the year 1793 was the crucible for the newly declared French Republic—and the brilliance of Hugo's characters, whose psychological depth and sympathetic appeal turn this chronicle of the Revolution into a drama of human proportions without oversimplifying the complexity of the history of the period. That the text gives significance to things and people both great and small is apparent in its plurality of voices.

Students in my course read Hugo's *Quatrevingt-treize* in seven weeks, a pace that is challenging. The novel is divided into three parts, of four, three, and seven books, and students may be assigned one book per class meeting, twice per week. Resources to help them succeed include practice skimming texts for main ideas; precirculated discussion questions and illustrated lists of vocabulary; in-class plot review; games, discussion, and reading quizzes; an online forum for questions about the reading; and an optional one-hour weekly group read in the library. In this way, students become familiar with the persons, places, things, and events mythologized in Hugo's novel.

The culture of revolutionary France is particularly tangible in the chapter "Les rues de Paris dans ce temps-là" 'The Streets of Paris at That Time' (*Quatrevingt-treize* 143–51; *Ninety-Three* 123–32 [2.1.1]). This is a good place for students to start planning their own *sans-culottides* celebration.

By researching the cultural products and rituals of the Revolution—imagery, clothing, food, songs, games, the new calendar, and awards for civic virtues—and by organizing this knowledge into a commemoration of the *sans-culottides*, they gain insight into the enormity and paradox of the Revolution, which Hugo called an "abyss" (*Œuvres* 1: 139). Moreover, they can better understand later literary and historical interpretations of the age of Revolution, from Hugo's *Quatrevingt-treize* (published eighty years after the Terror) to echoes in contemporary revolutions. They develop research skills and digital-age information-sifting and collaboration savvy. They acquire vocabulary for thinking about literature and tools for reading and analyzing it when they encounter the language or languages of revolution in Hugo's text. Most important, perhaps, they confront the surging emotions of popular unrest and can begin to sympathize with multiple and conflicting viewpoints.

Students will encounter difficulties when researching the *sans-culottides:* spelling first, followed by the lack of hits for the term in contemporaneous texts searchable in databases such as the University of Chicago's *ARTFL-FRANTEXT* and *Project Gutenberg*. They will find *Portail: Révolution française* (fr.wikipedia.org/wiki/Portail:Révolution_française), which links to over seven thousand Wikipedia articles in French. Other Web pages contain information of varying degrees of accuracy and relevance. The best resources are *Gallica*, the Bibliothèque Nationale's digital online collection, which features images as well as texts, and librarians who can steer students to the stacks as well as to journals and online databases. The sheer number of volumes on the French Revolution in the library will be daunting, so it is important that students become familiar with some trusted scholars, perspectives, and studies. They should read the founding texts of the Revolution.

Three committees can be organized based on student interests: for food, festivities, and publicity. Group members may communicate by a digital platform that allows them to post messages, links, and files in a designated location accessible only to the group and the instructor. They should organize their research and planning efforts in order not only to prepare the venue, invitations, food and beverages, music, posters, games, and clothing but also to present their findings to the class.

The celebration should be held outdoors or in a chapel-like location, since the former churches of the Revolution were prescribed for the celebration of festivals during inclement weather. Ceremonies and theatrical performances should be rehearsed and performed in order to revive the great oratories of the past. Scenes from *Ninety-Three* could be prepared as short plays. Walls could be decorated with blue, white, and red festoons, posters, printed images of the female figures representing the months of the republican calendar year, and so forth. *PowerPoint* presentations could be used to display original illustrations from *Quatrevingt-treize* (available at www.gallica.bnf.fr), portraits of the three heads of Cerberus (Robespierre, Danton, and Marat), images (including cartoons) depicting the clergy, the sansculottes, the noblesse and the court and their clothing, and of course the *bonnet rouge* (Phrygian cap). Dance students might enjoy learning and teaching a *ronde*. Art students might make papier-mâché reproductions of the *trophées* (monuments more like a float or a plaster statue) displayed for certain festivals. *YouTube* videos play music of the Revolution: "La Marseillaise," "La Carmagnole," "Ça ira." Our festivities committee found and printed images of board games, along with the rules for play, which exercised students' gaming vocabulary.[1] Brochures, playing cards, calendars, posters, faux assignats, and the like might be produced and printed for distribution. Wherever possible, the iconography of the First Republic should be preserved, since iconoclasm played such an important role in the Republic's establishment. Clothing can help shift the mood from investigative to festive and uses the power of corporeal sensation to stimulate the imagination.[2]

An awards ceremony is a fun way to recognize student achievement in the course. A week ahead of time, the citizens may nominate their peers for awards for civic virtues: *le génie*, for the person who has contributed some of the most interesting or original thoughts to group or class discussions, on the online forum or in his or her oral presentation or poetry recitation; *le travail*, for the person who has worked the hardest to read and engage with ideas and is always ready with a reflection, a correction, or a question; and *les récompenses* (or *la vertu*), for the person who most contributes to the atmosphere in class by showing concern for classmates, using humor, or volunteering to answer questions, read, or perform.[3]

In this way, students may experience both pleasant and unpleasant republican sentiments: pride, for participating in something greater than oneself; dignity, for having one's opinion solicited and one's vote counted; admiration for classmates whose efforts and virtues are rewarded; envy, for the same reason; humility, either for receiving or for not receiving an award—in short, passions of all kinds.[4]

The *sans-culottides* would normally take place over six days as six separate festivals, some mirthful, some solemn. The celebration could begin as suggested by the editors of republican rituals, with the Humankind Festival (*la fête du Genre Humain*). Persons representing the regions of France and the nations of the world (perhaps from other sections or classes) would arrive sporting appropriate costumes. This assembly should have a spokesperson, the ambassador, who will announce, "The delegates from all the nations of the world are approaching the Commune, and their intention is to renew, in the very heart of the French Republic, the universal pact of brotherhood that must unite all the free peoples of the earth" (*Cérémonies* 53–54). Amid encouraging cheers of "Vive la liberté!" the mayor (emcee) will respond, "The happiest day of the Republic is that day on which it will harbor all the peoples of the earth in its bosom, to tighten the bonds of universal brotherhood and celebrate the triumph of liberty over all despots" (54). There may be embraces, but cannon fire should be omitted. Olive or oak sprigs may be carried by the celebrants, who will be invited to join in well-known (read: rehearsed ahead of time) songs and dances. The Declaration of the Rights of Man and of the Citizen may be read. Distribution of awards may be accompanied by acclamations from the crowd. For *le génie*, the good citizens might pronounce the admirable qualities of their classmate and say in response to the naming of the honoree for genius, "Vertueux!" ("Virtuous!") and "Vive la République!" For *le travail*, they might shout, "Honneur au travail! honte et mépris à la paresse!" 'Honor for those who labor! Down with sloth and indolence!' (83).

Our class celebration of the *sans-culottides* was scheduled for the day after the students finished reading *Quatrevingt-treize* in order to coincide with their achievement. Although the novel ends on a tragic note, its assertion of human bravery and dignity and its visual and aural surveys of the revolutionary quotidian celebrate, even while they condemn, the spirit of Revolution. Class celebration of the *sans-culottides* reveals how revolutionary artifacts can acquire affective meaning. Prepared in parallel with the reading of the novel, the celebration also highlights the ways in which language played a vital role in the Revolution.

In his *Citizens: A Chronicle of the French Revolution,* Simon Schama underscores the importance of what he calls "utterances" of the Revolution (xiv–xvi). Hugo's *Quatrevingt-treize* resounds with echoes of revolutionary utterances. Most spectacularly, the votes of the Haute-Garonne representatives to put Louis XVI to death are imagined, one after another, in what seems like a thousand repetitions of *la mort*: "Éternelle répercussion qui emplit toute l'histoire, et qui, depuis que la justice humaine existe, a toujours mis l'écho du sépulcre sur le mur du tribunal" 'eternal reverberation that fills all history since the birth of human justice has continued to send forth a funereal echo from the walls of the tribunal' (*Quatrevingt-treize* 209; *Ninety-Three* 206 [part 3, book 1, chapter 7]). If Hugo often monumentalizes the spoken and written word, he also emphasizes its fragility. From the first few pages, readers encounter phrases that disturb the association of language with reason, order, and progress. For instance, in the opening passages one reads, "Les oiseaux gazouillaient au-dessus des baïonnettes" 'The birds twittered above the bayonets' (47; 3). The novel is riddled with the words *gazouiller*, *jaser*, *balbutier*, *bégayer*, *murmurer*, *chuchoter*, *crier*, and their derivatives, and they are particularly salient in part 3, book 3, in which the three Fléchard children destroy a precious tome. Hugo problematizes language in his novel, and the narrative is often interrupted by commentaries on its use. Misunderstanding due to a language barrier takes place in the first chapter, when a Breton mother, Michelle Fléchard, encounters a republican battalion from Paris, which later adopts her and her children as wards of the newborn Republic, though the adopters and the wards share neither the same political geography nor the same native tongue. The Parisians find her hiding in a thicket like a terrified doe, but the narrator tells us that she perceives their speech as a sound more animal than human.

Hugo's reconstruction of revolutionary sights, sounds, tastes, and smells is found in "Les rues de Paris dans ce temps-là." Judith Wulf notes (Hugo, *Quatrevingt-treize* 143n1) that Hugo justifies digressions like this one in the chapter "L'année 1817" of *Les Misérables*: "L'histoire néglige presque toutes ces particularités, et ne peut faire autrement; l'infini l'envahirait" 'History neglects nearly all these particulars, and cannot do otherwise; the infinity would overwhelm it" (*Misérables* [ed. Gohin] 180; *Misérables* [trans. Hapgood]; part 1, book 3, chapter 1). The details to which he is referring include people at their tasks, supporting the revolutionary enterprise or seeking personal gain among the chaos; posters, playbills, paper money, objects for sale that used to adorn palaces; dancing in the crumbling cloisters; rumors; and above all words attributed to this person or that. The difficulty of the references to people, places, events, and things and the breathless rush of the description lead the reader to rely on the language itself. Words are repeated that draw the reader and narrator into the crowd, making them participants rather than observers: *on, tous, personne, la foule, le peuple, tout le monde*. Wulf wrote in her presentation to this edition: "la parole du peuple contamine celle du roman" 'the speech of the people contaminates the narration' (Hugo, *Quatrevingt-treize* 38; my trans.). Parts of speech become fluid; nouns, adjectives, and verbs meld together visually and aurally in phrases such as "les chanteurs ambulants pullulaient" 'Street singers swarmed' (145; 125). Many actions are expressed in the imperfect tense, as is fitting for past description. But the present participle, the passive voice, and occasionally the complete absence of a verb lend the impression of chaos, of a barely transcribable scene. Agency is eroded in a flood of objects that momentarily assume significance: "les suifs fondant sur les marchandises" 'tallow candles, which, melting, dripped upon the merchandise' (145; 125); "la rue Richelieu se nommait rue de la Loi" 'The Rue de Richelieu was called the Rue de la Loi' (145; 126); "le pain manquait, le charbon manquait, le savon manquait" 'Bread, coal, and soap were scarce' (147; 128).

This chapter in the French original is rich with literary figures, including anadiplosis, anaphora, asyndeton, and paradox.[5] In the last example above, an anaphora resounds in the repetition of the final *manquait*. One anadiplosis follows another, each toppling into an expression in the simple past: "Après le 9 thermidor, Paris fut gai, d'une gaieté égarée. Une joie malsaine déborda. À la frénésie de mourir succéda la frénésie de vivre, et la grandeur s'éclipsa" 'After the 9th Thermidor, Paris was like one gone mad with gayety. An unwholesome joy prevailed, exceeding all bounds. The frenzy of life followed the frenzy of death, and grandeur eclipsed itself' (149; 130). These figures of style are salient and accessible to students in quite a range of reading ability in French. The shape of these poetic phrases retraces the shape of other objects and their motion in the novel: the loose cannon, the scales, the pendulum, the guillotine. Excess marks every line.

The many literary figures offer opportunities for students of French language and literature to practice recognizing them and interpreting the text through close reading. This practice prepares them to understand Hugo's ambivalence toward the Revolution, the hot and cold reception of the novel by his contemporaries, and the way that the text is inscribed in the broader history of human struggles for self-determination. As E. Telle said in defense of the novel, "Vous, Hugo, vous avez placé la Révolution dans l'âme même de l'humanité" 'It is you, Hugo, who planted the Revolution in the very soul of humanity' (461; my trans. [*Dossier*]). The novel is an instrument of commemoration as well as criticism. When Hugo began to plan it, he had been living in exile for a dozen years. Writing about civil war in the Vendée allowed him to return, vicariously, to his mother's homeland and to the origin of the internal political conflict in his family. Family bonds and loyalty to ideals suffuse the third and final part of the novel and lift the dramatization of the struggle at the Tour Gauvain to its moving climax. Schama concurs that revolutionary history lives on in human language and celebration better than in stone: "Commemoration has been easiest when least monumental. Annual pyrotechnics and dancing on the fourteenth of July have served better than grandiose architectural projects. But it was the feat of the first generation of Romantic historians to celebrate the Revolution by lighting bonfires in their prose" (5).

Language and revolution are similar in that they both exist in the tension between the universal and the particular and they both work to articulate the flow of meaning between the two. Everything that has been said will be said again, and yet every iteration will mean something new, just as every revolution is and is not a recapitulation of prior revolutions. The progress of human beings toward self-determination consists in the creative-destructive power of both language and revolution. As for celebration, it carries momentum. The *sans-culottides* were still celebrated several years after the convention which created them. Although celebration is artificial, the creative energy needed to renew the memory revives part of the feeling inspired by the event or events being remembered. Moreover, feeling emerges in new subjects who can relate even to that which they have not experienced. Language, revolution, and celebration uphold one another against forgetting.

Notes

1. From Lacombe's *Dictionnaire des jeux* or Providence Public Library Special Collections (www.pplspc.org/play/).

2. Clothing suggestive of the period may be made from items found at home. For instance, an embroidered round or square table covering with a lace edge can be gathered with a ribbon and worn on the head. Together with a simple linen dress, a sash of gathered fabric, and some tall wool stockings, the makeshift mob cap may give the impression of Charlotte Corday as she is portrayed in the lithograph by François Séraphin Delpech. A jacket typical of the period, the Carmagnole, may be simulated by wearing an open, short-waist sport coat (possibly double-breasted) with a wide collar, brass buttons, or cuffed or three-quarter-length sleeves. Wide-striped pants and wooden clogs may be harder to come by.

3. Awards may be small cockades made from blue, white, and red striped crepe paper folded fan-like, tied at the center, ends glued together to form a circle and topped with a brass button.

4. Graded assessments of student achievement and understanding may include an essay in two drafts and reading quizzes. The essay allows students to hone

analysis and writing skills, and reading quizzes prepare them for the essay and the cultural research by presenting images and quotations from the novel to situate and illuminate, such as "un flamboiement" (216), "the Lady in white" (229), and "Lieu immense. Tous les types humains, inhumains, et surhumains étaient là" (describing the National Convention; 213). Ungraded responses about group member participation in researching and planning the event, announced at the beginning of the project, help ensure equal efforts.

5. Anaphora: "A rhetorical device involving the repetition of a word or group of words in successive clauses. It is often used in ballad and song, in oratory and sermon . . . , but it is common in many literary forms" (Cuddon 37). Anadiplosis: "The repetition of the last word of one clause at the beginning of the following clause to gain a special effect. . . . It is not uncommon in prose" (35–36).

Works Cited

Cérémonies à l'usage des fêtes nationales, décadaires et sans-culottides, de la République française, saisies dans leur but moral, combinées dans leurs rapports généraux, et rendues propres à être exécutées dans les moindres communes. 1793–94. *Bibliothèque Nationale de France*, catalogue.bnf.fr/ark:/12148/cb37245373r. Les Archives de la Révolution Française.

Cuddon, J. A. *Dictionary of Literary Terms and Literary Theory.* Revised by C. E. Preston, Penguin, 1999.

Hugo, Victor. *Les Misérables.* Edited by Yves Gohin, vol. 1, Gallimard, 1995.

———. *Les Misérables.* Translated by Isabel F. Hapgood, *Project Gutenberg*, 25 June 2018, www.gutenberg.org/files/135/135-h/135-h.htm.

———. *Ninety-Three.* Translated by Aline Delano, *Project Gutenberg*, 6 July 2015, www.gutenberg.org/files/49372/49372-h/49372-h.htm.

———. *Œuvres complètes de Victor Hugo.* Edited by Paul Meurice, 2 vols., Albin Michel, 1934–37.

———. *Quatrevingt-treize.* Edited by Judith Wulf, Flammarion, 2002.

Lacombe, Jacques. *Dictionnaire des jeux.* 1792. *Bibliothèque et Archives Nationales du Québec*, bibnum2.banq.qc.ca/bna/dicoJeux/index.html.

Schama, Simon. *Citizens: A Chronicle of the French Revolution.* Alfred A. Knopf, 1989.

Jennifer Gipson

Rethinking History: The "Marseillaise Noire" and Legacies of the Revolution in Creole New Orleans

Introducing legacies of the French Revolution in general education or humanities survey classes teaches not only history but also critical thinking about history: not only who writes it and how literary and artistic representations continually rework the past but also what voices history's dominant narratives silence. "La Marseillaise noire" 'The Black Marseillaise,' an 1867 poem published in *La tribune de la Nouvelle-Orléans* ("The New Orleans Tribune"), links these questions to themes of race and violence in the United States, some chillingly relevant today. It also introduces students to a little-known elite of color who wrote in French on American soil and helps place the Revolution in their Reconstruction-era poetry and political engagement. Subtitled "Chant de paix" 'Song of Peace,' this poem makes meanings through intertextual references: it follows the tune of "La Marseillaise" and appeals to egalitarian tenets of the Revolution while ultimately criticizing violent resistance and transforming images of war into a vision of a world that is at peace and free of racial division. Part of the poem's poignancy in the classroom today comes from our knowledge that the writer's dream will not be quickly realized.

That nothing is known of the poem's author, Camille Naudin (likely a pseudonym), is a reminder of the tenuous position of the French-speaking

Creoles of color behind the production of *La tribune de la Nouvelle-Orléans*, the radical newspaper in which these verses appear. In the antebellum South, they were *gens de couleur libres*, free people of color, a largely mixed-race group occupying an intermediary social position, not slave but not fully free. Some of them owned land; a smaller number owned slaves. Their revolutionary heritage was not an abstraction: many owed the presence of their families in Louisiana to the Haitian Revolution, and some claimed links to revolutionary France. They saw the French revolution of 1848 celebrated in New Orleans's French press (Bell 163–64). Their literacy rate surpassed that of the general population, and they published their own poetry anthology, *Les cenelles* ("The Holly Berries"), in 1845. Poetry and, more rarely, prose of some writers of color appeared in the columns of white newspapers in Louisiana. Overall, their antebellum literary production in Louisiana reads as an emulation of French Romanticism but conceals currents of resistance particular to their sociopolitical situation, a testament to both the constraints of this climate and the creativity of these writers.

The fall of New Orleans to Union forces in 1862 made possible the rise of Creoles of color in the periodic press but simultaneously brought new problems for these people, whose culture and loyalties were already ill-understood by outsiders. Shirley Thompson singles out newspapers as a means by which Creoles of color found their place in a new American nation and explained themselves and their past to others: the newspapers were vehicles of "translation," not simply for rendering a text in another language but making that which is culturally or politically foreign readily legible or acceptable (216–21). For example, one of the most pressing questions was how formerly free men would relate to recently freed slaves. Though not devoid of equivocation or paternalism, the writers of the *Tribune* favored a fairly consistent position of solidarity with the slave population, whose future now seemed inextricably intertwined with their own.

In its title, the "Marseillaise noire" (the text and translation are given in an appendix to this essay) raises this question of race from the start, linking it to a revolution. If French verse implicitly valorizes the literacy and heritage of former *gens de couleur libres*, the adjective *noire* obliterates these past distinctions and locates the poem's call to action in a new racial order. The subtitle qualifies this revolution and makes Rouget de Lisle's "Marseillaise" its point of reference. A quick scan of dominant lexical fields in this revolutionary hymn, now the French national anthem, points to its origins as a song of war whose refrain calls not just for bloodshed but also for the impure blood of enemies:

> Citizens, take up your arms!
> Form your battalions!
> Let us march, Let us march!
> That an impure blood
> May water our fields!

As a point of contrast, students might be asked to imagine what a writer during United States Reconstruction might use to evoke race, oppression, or liberation and then find examples in Naudin's poem like "fers" 'irons' and "fouet" 'whip.'[1] A closer look at the sentence-level context of such words would, however, reveal a rhetoric not of vengeance or victimization, for negative elements are ascribed to the past. Furthermore, the final stanza includes no such references, underscoring the poem's narrative of progress.

The first line of the "Marseillaise noire" undertakes this exploration of race and violence in earnest. By summoning "Fils d'Africains!' 'Sons of Africans' to forgive past crimes, presumably those of the antebellum South, and by proclaiming Jesus "*Fraternité*" 'Fraternity,' the poem says that all people are brothers and bloodshed must cease. If dissonant with the antireligious sentiment of 1789, Naudin's Christ seems to draw on the iconography of Christ as fraternity incarnate that surrounded the revolution of 1848 (Ozouf 94–97). It is important to note that, at a time when the boundaries of fraternity were being debated in relation to the formerly enslaved, the "Marseillaise noire" does not respond to the precise pragmatics of a black-white racial binary but questions the very relevance of racial categories. Whereas "Fils d'Africains" speaks of familial and geographic ties consistent with prevailing biologically determined notions of race, Naudin's Christ uses a language of universal kinship that supersedes ties of blood, making all war senseless. It is in this vision of race and kinship that Naudin locates his nonviolent revolution.

While easy to overlook today, the violence Naudin criticizes is not simply that of the French Revolution or of the American Civil War: Reconstruction in New Orleans had also proved bloody.[2] On 30 July 1866, white supremacists and city police fired on supporters of black suffrage who gathered as a constitutional convention reconvened at the Mechanics' Institute. In a different poem, Naudin terms this event the "Barthélémy des Noirs"—referencing the 1572 Saint Bartholomew Day's slaughter of French Huguenots—and tells of police instigating chaos, even shooting a priest raising a white handkerchief ("Ode" 92–93).[3] Whatever the riot's numerous and complex causes, it left at least forty-eight dead and two hundred wounded (Hollandsworth 3). The "Marseillaise noire" does not allude to these events. But readers, the trauma of 1866 still fresh in their minds, needed no prompting to see pleas for peace in this context and to understand the poem's evocations of oppression as not limited to slavery but encompassing their own recent experiences.

Allowing students to voice some of the obvious parallels between the problems of modern American society and the racially motivated violence and quashed political expression of Reconstruction can make the world of the poet seem more real, while at the same time highlighting the less familiar question of why and how Naudin responds through poetry. Ultimately, the answer lies not only in the chaos of Reconstruction but also in its promise. We know what will happen in coming years and realize that Jim Crow looms. This historical hindsight can obscure what poets of the *Tribune* believed could happen. The newspaper itself points to these fleeting dreams and a moment in which they did not seem ephemeral. On 21 July 1867, for example, the "Marseillaise noire" shares the front page of the *Tribune* with a platform statement for the Louisiana Radical Republican Party and a call for universal male suffrage entitled "Ayez Confiance" 'Have Confidence': "C'est nous désormais qui ferons les lois dans la Louisiane: il suffit pour cela de le vouloir" 'Henceforth, we are the ones who will make the law in Louisiana: to have this, it suffices to want it.'

This hope of drastic change brought about by force of belief and action captures the perennial appeal of the French Revolution as a matrix for envisioning liberation for peoples far from Old Regime France: the downfall of an old order, a turning point that relegates certain practices and hierarchies to a world that is no more and makes a different world possible. "The political premises of Reconstruction were revolutionary, and *imagining* a nation of equality was necessary to carry people's spirits through the violence and disappointment that lay ahead," Caroline Senter notes, suggesting that poetry in the *Tribune* was a site of this imagining and inspiration that ultimately challenged dominant paradigms of race and nation (278). Envisioning the future, however, can rely heavily on the past. Sometimes this reliance takes the obvious form of historical figures, like John Brown or Toussaint Louverture, who were freely allied to causes of radical Reconstruction. But poetry in the *Tribune* also allowed writers to insert themselves and their tumultuous present, marked by the events reported in the newspaper and the date stamped on it, into a larger scope of human events in an effort to change their course.[4] We might understand the work of the "Marseillaise noire" in this way: its author tried to separate the present from the past and called for action to realize the revolutionary potential of the moment.

From the first stanza, the only instance in the poem of the imperfect tense, "abrutissait" 'brutalized,' locates the effect of slavery and oppression in the past. This past gives way to the present with the imperatives "Pensons" 'Let us think' and "Embrassez-vous" 'Embrace each other.' The refrain lends urgency to a call for action, announcing that the time has come for workers to claim the fruits due them, whatever their color, a gesture to the apportionment of wages or goods pertinent to the downfall of the plantation economy. Repeated exclamations like "Assez longtemps!" 'Long enough!' or "Assez de fers! De honte, assez!" 'Enough chains! Shame, enough!' signal a breaking point of accumulated injustice.

The third stanza stages this transitory moment in a rite of succession in which "staggering despotism," a faltering holdout of the old, does not abdicate or die but, more meaningfully, actively acknowledges and crowns "*Liberté*." The next stanza casts the impact of this new order in a reversal of the biblical account of Cain and Abel, initiated by the white man who calls the black man his brother. The curse of Cain, a consequence of his murder of Abel and a historical justification for racism, disappears. Fraternity—which demands a more mutually participatory relationship than liberty or equality—replaces fratricide. As the stanza concisely concludes:

Plus de sang! L'impie ignorance,
Arme terrible du tyran
Aux peuples s'entredéchirant,
Ne dit plus: mort, sang et vengeance.

No more bloodshed! Ungodly ignorance,
Tyranny's horrific weapon,
To nations destroying each other,
No longer says: death, blood, and vengeance.

In a sense, the poem follows its own prescription: evocations of war and violence cease. In the last stanza, the "Sons of Africans" addressed at the start are replaced by "hommes de cœur" 'men of courage'—a formulation whose proximity to *hommes de couleur* ("men of color") underscores a progressive abandonment of racial categories: *cœur* reads as a shortening of *couleur*, as if *cœur* removed the extraneous to retain only the essence of human beings. The poem concludes with the ambitious wish that on the forehead of humanity there should be engraved the words ". . . en toi j'espère / Tu règneras, *Égalité*" '. . . in you I hope, / You will reign, *Equality*.' This direct address to *Égalité* uses the informal second-person pronoun. The verb stands out as the only future tense of the poem, projecting forward the hopes of the final line. It speaks of power and regime change, inseparable from revolutions and inseparable from Reconstruction, and makes equality a force that rules or governs.

More than a fantasy of social justice, this poem uses the Revolution to reflect on the human condition and its own moment's movements for change. In fact, the Mechanics' Institute massacre had helped sway the nation toward congressional Reconstruction. Senter rightly suggests that the poem is a reminder of these promising developments (290–91): for example, Naudin's "sainte alliance" 'sacred alliance' of white and black confidently facing the future corresponds to the Louisiana legislature, where many persons of color now sat. It bears noting, however, that Naudin makes such references legible without making them explicit—or exclusive. Was the *Tribune* itself not an alliance of persons of color and white sympathizers? More so than other genres in the newspaper's columns, poetry created multiple, simultaneous meanings. Furthermore, the poem, beyond commenting on its own day, might be read as a commentary on and consolidation of the rhetoric of revolution that regularly filled the columns of the *Tribune*. References to *liberté*, *égalité*, and *fraternité* abounded, indeed became synonymous with a vision of a racially egalitarian America. This poem draws on one of the most recognizable emblems of the French Revolution, "La Marseillaise," to align it with a notion of revolution that eschews bloodshed and questions the relevance of race in the future it imagines. The "Marseillaise noire" is not a *Marseillaise des noirs*, neither a Marseillaise of or for blacks nor a revolution constituted by a certain group but instead a revolution that obliterates human divisions and categories. By the end of the poem, the "noire" of Naudin's title is not blackness defined in biological terms or in opposition to whiteness but a different kind of kinship, one based on politics, philosophy, and religion.

Even in classes without time for a detailed study of poetic devices, this poem lends itself well to lessons in close reading, the slow systematic interrogation not simply of what a text means but also of how it makes meaning. More than decoding historical references, such interpretive work demands analysis of small or seemingly obvious details as a foundation for broader conclusions. For example, temporarily setting aside the revolutionary baggage of *liberté*, *égalité*, and *fraternité*, students may be asked to focus on how Naudin reworks these watchwords for his own revolution. That the words are capitalized suggests that they might function as proper nouns. In fact, each is, to some degree, personified.[5] They are also italicized, as if to indicate emphasis or a special sense. These concrete details help inexperienced readers of poetry formulate or answer more abstract questions. One might ask what parallel nontypographic means Naudin employs to set off these words. One word of the great revolutionary trinity appears in each odd-numbered stanza, for instance, and a complicated syntax places "*Égalité*" as the last word of the poem, affirming its primacy in the future the poet envisions. Finally, the poem's musical reference allows students to experience the limits of poetic translation and start to recognize its challenges for close reading. The tune of "La Marseillaise," which Naudin says his poem follows, conveys the intended rhythm, something that a translation simply cannot capture: the words in English, as students can try for themselves, will not conform to the tune or the rhyme scheme.

For the humanities survey course, this poem also serves as a way to encourage critical thinking about how meaning is made through intertextual references. To make this point concrete, we might ask how the poem would mean something different or make meaning differently with no mention of the title or tune of "La Marseillaise." How would that lack of reference change the subtitle? This question prompts students to recognize in "La Marseillaise" a cultural shorthand for revolution—one that a simple Internet search will reveal to be legible well beyond France and the nineteenth century and could serve as a springboard for studying other rewritings of "La Marseillaise." In Naudin's day, "La Marseillaise" already carried the baggage of adaptations and rewritings.[6] Naudin acknowledges this in a note, denying any link between his poem and the "Marseillaise noire" of the great Romantic Alphonse de Lamartine's play *Toussaint Louverture*—though the note only calls attention to the play and could ultimately align the work of the *Tribune* poets with revolution elsewhere or point out the gap between what Haiti and Louisiana had accomplished.

However, if we think of the *Tribune*'s larger function of explaining the identity and loyalties of French-speaking Creoles of color to the American nation in the 1860s, Lamartine was probably less relevant than several southern versions of "La Marseillaise," "one of the Confederacy's most popular songs," whose tune became so synonymous with the Confederate cause that French actors in New York were "jailed as southern sympathizers for singing it" (Faust 12–13). That "La Marseillaise" was totally divorced from its French revolutionary origins seems unlikely: "The Southern Marseillaise" (1862) included the French tricolor and French lyrics along with a Confederate battle flag and its own words calling for southern liberty in the face of federal tyranny. Did Naudin have these rewritings of "La Marseillaise" in mind? We will likely never know. But what seems certain is that, for some of his readers at least, his poem represented not just a rewriting but also a symbolic recuperation of revolutionary legacies for Reconstruction, a compelling example of interconnected layers of meaning in writers' and artists' reworkings of history for their own present.

Our own historical distance can obscure such contexts and references—for example, this "Southern Marseillaise." Therefore, it can be useful, to return to the question of how this very distance gives the poem other meanings in our present, to allow students to trace the evolution of their own thinking in response to this question and to ask again how Naudin's dreams and aspirations—far from being realized in his own day—live on. Concluding discussions might return more broadly to the French-speaking Creoles of color behind this revolutionary vision of Reconstruction and their place in history. The existence of this little-known linguistic, racial, and political minority points to the propensity of dominant historical narratives to silence voices that are not easily categorized or recognized. Since no course or syllabus could ever encompass all such marginalized histories, thinking critically about the past becomes all the more important. Indeed, part of what this poem fosters is a realization that history is not inconsequential for the present and that we must filter our understandings of its narratives, its politics, and even its poetry through an awareness of its multiplicities and invisibilities.

Notes

Unless otherwise indicated, all translations of titles or quotations from French are my own.

1. All quotations of the "Marseillaise noire" are from the *Tribune*.

2. It is worth noting that Naudin works against established narratives linking the American Civil War to the Haitian Revolution—for example, narratives that support violent abolitionism, most notably John Brown's at Harpers Ferry, and later the arming of black soldiers in the Civil War. See Clavin, esp. 33–54, 77–97.

3. Naudin's "Ode" was originally printed in the *Tribune*, 30 July 1867.

4. This sense of simultaneity that links events reported in the paper and readers who read them in a common time is central to Benedict Anderson's notions of how newspapers create "imagined communities" (33).

5. Personification is a frequent rhetorical strategy in representations of the Revolution. The nineteenth-century French historian Jules Michelet's accounts of the Revolution provide a case, including his proclamation that the Bastille, driven beyond reason by her "mauvaise conscience" 'guilty conscience,' was not taken but "se livra" 'gave herself up' (203).

6. For a summary of the vast scholarship on "La Marseillaise," its inception, controversies, adaptations, and path to becoming France's national anthem, see Vovelle 72–74. Modern adaptations abound online, including an interpretation of Naudin's poem by a French-speaking singer in Madagascar, Edgar Ravahatra, which edits out the religious references so central to nineteenth-century New Orleans.

Works Cited

Anderson, Benedict. *Imagined Communities: Reflections on the Origin and Spread of Nationalism.* Verso, 2006.

Bell, Caryn Cossé. *Revolution, Romanticism, and the Afro-Creole Protest Tradition in Louisiana, 1718–1868.* Lousiana State UP, 1997.

Clavin, Matthew J. *Toussaint Louverture and the American Civil War: The Promise and Peril of a Second Haitian Revolution.* U of Pennsylvania P, 2010.

Faust, Drew. *The Creation of Confederate Nationalism: Ideology and Identity in the Civil War South.* Louisiana State UP, 1989.

Hollandsworth, James G. *An Absolute Massacre: The New Orleans Race Riot of July 30, 1866.* Louisiana State UP, 2001.

Michelet, Jules. *Histoire de la Révolution française.* Vol. 1, A. Lacroix, 1877.

Naudin, Camille. "La Marseillaise noire." *La tribune de la Nouvelle-Orléans*, vol. 7, no. 889, 21 July 1867, p. 1.

———. "Ode aux Martyrs." *La Marseillaise noire et autres poèmes français des Créoles de couleur de la Nouvelle-Orléans (1862–1869)*, edited by James L. Cowan, Éditions du cosmogone, 2001, pp. 92–94.

Nora, Pierre, and Lawrence D. Kritzman, editors. *Realms of Memory: The Construction of the French Past.* Translated by Arthur Goldhammer, vol. 3, Columbia UP, 1998.

Ozouf, Mona. "Liberty, Equality, Fraternity." Nora and Kritzman, pp. 77–116.

Ravahatra, Edgar. "La Marseillaise noire / Edgard Ravahatra: Camille Naudin." *YouTube*, uploaded by Tsokaina, 20 Oct. 2010, www.youtube.com/watch?v=XcTYX2vCD3w.

Senter, Caroline. "Creole Poets on the Verge of a Nation." *Creole: The History and Legacy of Louisiana's Free People of Color*, edited by Sybil Kein, Louisiana State UP, 2000, pp. 276–94.

Thompson, Shirley. *Exiles at Home: The Struggle to Become American in Creole New Orleans.* Harvard UP, 2009.

Vovelle, Michel. "La Marseillaise: War or Peace." Nora and Kritzman, pp. 29–76.

Appendix: Text and Translation

"La Marseillaise Noire: Chant de paix"
Air: "La Marseillaise"

Fils d'Africains! Tristes victimes,
Qu'un joug absurde abrutissait.
De monstres oubliant les crimes,
Pensons à Jésus qui disait: (bis)
"Peuples, plus de sang, plus de guerre
"Qui font rougir l'humanité
"Moi je suis la *Fraternité*,
"Embrassez-vous, vous êtes frères."

Debout! L'heure est venue, à chaque travailleur
Le pain (bis) qu'il a gagné, qu'importe sa couleur.

Assez longtemps! le fouet infâme
De ses sillons nous a brisés,
Sans nom, sans patrie et sans âme;
Assez de fers! De honte, assez! (bis)
Que dans une sainte alliance
Les noirs et les blancs confondus
À la mort des anciens abus,
Marchent tous pleins de confiance,

Debout!, etc.

Debout! C'est l'heure solennelle!
Où sur le vieux monde écroulé
Le despotisme qui chancelle
Vient couronner la *Liberté*,
La discorde reprend sa pomme,
La raison humaine grandit;
C'est l'intelligence et l'esprit
Et non plus la peau qui fait l'homme.

Debout!, etc.

Plus d'ombre! partout la lumière,
C'est l'Évangile qui paraît;
Le Blanc dit au Noir: mon frère,
À jamais Caïn disparaît
Plus de sang! L'impie ignorance,
Arme terrible du tyran
Aux peuples s'entredéchirant,
Ne dit plus: mort, sang et vengeance.

"The Black Marseillaise: Song of Peace"
Tune: "La Marseillaise"

Sons of Africa! Sad victims,
Brutalized by an absurd yoke
Forgetting the crimes of monsters,
Let us think of Jesus who said: (repeat)
"Peoples, no more blood, no more war
That make humanity blush with humiliation,
Brotherhood am I;
Embrace each other, you are brothers."

Arise! The time is here, to each worker
The bread (repeat) he has earned, whatever his color.

Long enough! the infamous whip
Has crushed us with its lashes,
Deprived of name, fatherland, and soul;
Enough chains! Shame, enough! (repeat)
In a sacred alliance, may
Blacks and whites together
Towards the death of past abuses,
Go forward, brimming with confidence.

Arise!, etc.

Arise! The solemn hour has come!
When, upon the collapsed and ancient order,
Staggering despotism
Comes to crown *Liberty*,
Discord rescinds its apple,
Human reason grows;
Now it is intelligence and mind
And no longer skin that makes a man.

Arise!, etc.

No more shadow! Light everywhere!
It is the Gospel that appears
The White calls the Black "my brother,"
Cain vanishes forevermore
No more bloodshed! Ungodly ignorance,
Tyranny's horrific weapon,
To nations destroying each other,
No longer says: death, blood, and vengeance.

Debout, etc. etc.

Allons! malgré votre race,
Hommes de cœur, unissez-vous;

Ici bas chacun a sa place,
Car le soleil luit pour tous.
Que chaque peuple heureux, prospère,
Au fronton de l'humanité,
Grave ces mots: en toi j'espère,
Tu règneras, *Égalité*.

Camille Naudin

Nouvelle-Orléans, 17 juin 1867

Arise!, etc.

Let us go forth! Regardless of your race,
Men of courage, unite.

Here below, there is a place for everyone,
For the sun shines upon all.
May each happy prosperous nation
On the forehead of humanity
Etch these words: in you I hope,
You will reign, *Equality*.

Camille Naudin

New Orleans, 17 June 1867

Matthew Lau

Writing to Appreciate the Enigmas of *Danton's Death* and *Monsieur Toussaint* at the Community College

Things take indeed a wondrous turn
When learned men do stoop to learn.

—Bertolt Brecht, *Life of Galileo*

"What Would Happen If We Had a Revolution in This Classroom?"

In a striking metaphor, Walter Benjamin argues that an important work of literature is "a burning funeral pyre" (298). While philological commentary examines the wood and the ashes, critique explores the enigma of the work's living, still burning flame. Approaching literatures of the French and Haitian Revolutions, students and instructors, I argue in this essay, do both. Through studying and writing about representations of the revolutions, they heap new interpretations onto the fire and examine what they do to the flames. The goal of this approach is to promote student interest in and understanding of what is both historically valuable and still alive in these fundamental modern events through close interpretations of key literary exemplars. Like Benjamin, when I introduce literary texts and these revolutions to students who may be encountering both for the first time, my own accent as an instructor often falls on questions of critique. How can students relate the revolutions and the literary texts to their own daily lives in modern America? What metaphors and similes can they add to the enigmatic, living flame of the literary works read in the course? How can a professor foster an appreciation for enigmas when students are so often looking for the right answer and fixated on what their grade will be?

The goal of having students value enigmas instead of correct answers and good grades can be accomplished when professors make way for their voices and strive to learn from them. Such an approach is especially vital at a community college, where there are many student levels and backgrounds, where collectively the students' backgrounds and life experiences form a knowledge base more diverse and therefore richer than any one instructor's, no matter how educated and cosmopolitan the instructor may be. Queensborough Community College, where I teach composition and literature courses, is both a representative and extreme example of the diversity of the community college classroom. The college's *Fact Book* notes with pride:

> Our students come from 139 countries and speak 87 different languages. Twenty-five percent were born outside the USA. They come from every corner of the globe including Asia, North and South America, Africa, Europe, and Australia. The top five non-English native languages are Spanish, Chinese, Korean, Bengali, and Urdu. (18)

Additionally, several hundred students at Queensborough are military veterans on the GI Bill. The fuller potential of this diversity of perspectives is in no small part activated when students assume control of their educational destiny.

How can one help them assume control? One answer is the Socratic method: the venerable search for truth through continual questioning to expose contradictions. The catch with the Socratic method is that it more often than not ends in uncertainty (aporias) rather than certainty. But such a result is ideal if the goal of the instructor is for students to appreciate questions more than answers. Low-stakes in-class writing, followed by pairing and sharing, is another method. One can combine these two methods, the ancient and the modern. For example: one might begin day 1 of a month of discussion, reading, and writing about the plays *Danton's Death*, by Georg Büchner, and *Monsieur Toussaint*, by Édouard Glissant, with the following question: "What would happen if we had a revolution in this classroom?" Students in my experience often respond with alacrity, "We would get rid of you!" "We would throw you out the window!" Such spontaneous responses set the table for a low-stakes, think-write-share, in-class writing prompt: "Write three or four sentences about the potential consequences for your education of overthrowing your professor and how you might overcome any negative consequences."

As with many low-stakes, open-ended prompts, students' answers to this prompt vary widely but tend to reveal astute understandings, in this case of the difficulties that begin to mount in a revolution and its aftermath. Some think that the class could work well without a professor. Others worry that it would be too much responsibility to organize themselves to make decisions about curriculum and writing assignments. "Who would grade us?" they wonder aloud after writing and sharing. "How would we learn from ourselves?" In order to learn from them à la Bertolt Brecht, one must delay answering their questions by falling back on restrained responses like "Well, what do you think?" and "Can someone else answer that?" for as long as possible. Even if not every student joins the entire-class discussion, their low-stakes writings and partner shares permit even the most reticent students to engage in the dialogue with their pen.

"It Is Too Soon to Tell" about the Revolutions and Their Dramatic Exemplars

From the point of view of Benjaminian critique's appreciation for enigmas, a useful anecdote for students is an apocryphal one that purportedly occurred almost two centuries after the French Revolution. When asked by a journalist what he thought of the French Revolution, the Chinese prime minister Zhou Enlai reportedly quipped, "It is too soon to tell" (McGregor). Even if this story has now been widely debunked as a simple misunderstanding (apparently Zhou thought he was being asked about the protests and general strike in France in May of 1968), it is still a meaningful tale, and not just because it has become fashionable in Western Marxism to praise Zhou's prescience about the exaggerated claims of "the end of history" after 1989 (Žižek). Pedagogically, this story is useful because it builds a bridge between the past and the present that Benjamin has in mind in his still-living flame of critique. It demonstrates in a vivid way that students' critiques are still needed. Perhaps a student can finally tell us what the Revolution means. It also allows one to frame the basic facts about the Revolution in the light of their enduring relevance to contemporary life. Consider the fact that the terms *left* and *right* in politics originate from the seating arrangements in the National Assembly during 1789 (Gauchet 242–44). Consider that the stereotype of Haiti as the quintessential underdeveloped nation dates from the retaliation in the aftermath of its daring and successful rebellion (1791–1804) against the French empire. There are several excellent documentaries about Haiti that convey the overall sense of the complicated history and legacy of the Revolution well for students by connecting it to the present-day reality of Haiti (*Égalité*; *In Haiti*).

The ironic time lag in Zhou's apocryphal quip can also set up a general theme. It is too soon to tell about the French and Haitian Revolutions in two senses: they were ahead of their time (their significances were difficult to ascertain in the moment), and in a way neither ever fully ended (the processes they started continue). Both these time gaps and lags apply to two major plays that students can both read and partially act out. *Danton's Death* (1835) represents the essential elements of the works of the playwright Büchner: frank depictions of sexuality, violence, and working-class life, which all made his work groundbreaking and also impossible to perform during his lifetime and for many decades after. Glissant's *Monsieur Toussaint* (1961) was written before there was really anything like a national theater tradition in Martinique (Glissant 13). Indeed, the play arguably did not receive its proper premiere until 2004, when it was performed where it is set, in the very prison at Fort de Joux where Toussaint L'Ouverture, the leader of the Haitian Revolution until his capture by Napoleonic forces in 1802, died two hundred years before (11).

Büchner's play traffics in several fundamental ironies one can emphasize to show both the distinction between aesthetic realism and historical reality and the enigmas of each. The first irony is that the play itself is a triumph of realism, up to and including its use of dialogue transcribed directly from Büchner's historical sources. Yet the play's detailed representation of Danton's guilty conscience and resignation to his fate are Büchner's invention. The play is faithful to history to the point of quotation from speeches given at the Jacobin Club and before the Revolutionary Tribunal, yet it undermines and surpasses historical reality to represent psychological interiority in a way that would become fashionable decades later in the German expressionist movement, which lionized Büchner. The Jacobin-led Committee of Public Safety held France together by defeating the other European powers bent on destroying the Revolution. Yet the Jacobin government also liberated slaves throughout the empire and thereby provided a turning point in the Haitian Revolution, the moment when black and mulatto rebel forces, led by Toussaint, realigned themselves with the French Republic and defeated the opportunistic Spanish and British forces with whom they had been temporarily allied. The Terror, begun by the Jacobins, was the moment when the Revolution, as Büchner's play emphasizes, began to devour its own children Saturn-like. Yet it, as Büchner quotes Robespierre, was also "an emanation of virtue" (14).

Looking at the Terror through Büchner's vivid rendering, students easily identify Robespierre as an extremist and sympathize with the more relatable Danton. The difficulty in teaching the play is to get them to view Danton and Robespierre's flaws not just as moral but also as political, to encourage them to see the moral conflict between the left factions as a problem of the practical exercise of political power. One way to help students grasp the significance of the internecine struggles that overcame the left is to broaden the conversation by bringing in figures from the Revolution outside the play. Stephen Jay Gould's essay "The Passion of Antoine Lavoisier" serves this purpose well. Lavoisier was a moderate supporter of the Revolution and, as a renowned chemist and eminent government minister, an important figure in its early years. His gunpowder, for instance, gave French forces a crucial advantage against the foreign powers arrayed against them (Gould 360).

In Gould's reading, Lavoisier provides a moderate foil not just to Robespierre but to Danton as well. Unlike Danton, Lavoisier was never a proponent of the regicide and the ensuing Terror and therefore is a more uncomplicated example of a victim of the Terror. The ultimate victim of Lavoisier's murder, Gould argues, was the cause of scientific knowledge. "It took them only an instant to cut off that head," Joseph Louis Lagrange, a mathematician and friend of Lavoisier, noted, "but France may not produce another like it in a century" (qtd. in Gould 355). The theme of Gould's essay, "the tragic asymmetry of creation and destruction," serves as a pedagogical foil for the Revolution. "Centuries are needed to nurture the tree of science and make it grow," observes Lavoisier's contemporary, the zoologist Bernard-Germain Lacépède, "but one blow from the hatchet of destruction cuts it down" (358). This message cautions against the zealotry of revolutionaries. For students, Gould's perspective on the life of Lavoisier provides a counterpoint to the events depicted in Büchner's play.

Women's Diamonds, Violent Roses, and Other Useful Enigmas

The first scene of *Danton's Death* is representative of many of the enigmas in Büchner's depiction of the Revolution. Büchner renders Danton's existential angst in a double entendre that announces the play's frankness about sexual matters as well: "She shows her heart to husband . . . and her 'diamond' to her lover" (5). The duplicity of lovers in a libertine culture leads Danton to wonder how anyone can really know anyone. His own character is an example of the opacity his question implies. He alternates throughout the play between different moods and attitudes, by turns playful and morose, enervated and enthusiastic, often in a single moment of dialogue. The complexity of the first scene's staging is also worth dwelling on. At the back of the stage is a card game, which suggests the contingencies of chance and luck, but this is a destiny play, where the outcome is foretold by the very title. Danton has been playing the house, the French state, and the house always wins. Meeting at the front of the stage, he and Julie express their ennui in a melancholy conversation on the futility of love, communication, and even action. The best way to render such a scene in the student read-through is to ask students to prepare for it in advance. They need not memorize lines, simply study the scene. Bringing the play to life in this way enhances the discussion that follows. Students begin almost immediately to ask questions for which one cannot provide simple answers. Why is Danton in such a mood? Who is this Swiss watchmaker (Rousseau) they are talking about, and why does he matter? How does the card game relate to the overall problem of trying to rein in the state terror that Danton and his allies have created?

This process of getting students to raise complex questions can continue when we study Glissant's *Monsieur Toussaint.* Because the staging is even more complicated than Büchner's, acting scenes from the play becomes even more vital for comprehension. Toussaint remains in his cell throughout the play as the action shifts from his humiliating present circumstance to memories of his past glory. Like Büchner, Glissant raises questions about the life of his protagonist instead of trying to answer them. He cites two competing influences on his play, the work of C. L. R. James (see his *Black Jacobins*) and that of Aimé Césaire. For Glissant, James sees Toussaint's loss of power as rooted in his losing touch with the people. From Césaire, Glissant derives the idea that Toussaint was aware of that problem and sacrificed himself to give the Revolution the unifying martyr it needed (15). Introducing the play by presenting the conflict between these two perspectives gives students an enigma as their starting point, so that they are positioned less as seekers of information from experts and more as detectives working a case. The question of Toussaint's knowing or unknowing sacrifice can be revisited throughout discussions of the play, especially in scenes or dialogue with his double-crossing aide-de-camp.

Another benefit of seeing the play through this question is that it gives students a concrete example of the idea that a historical process is greater than any one individual. The beginning of act 4 is especially revealing. His wife accuses Toussaint of being too trusting of the French generals who asked him to meet with them. It is clear to her that something is wrong with their request. But for Toussaint, not to meet with them would be a danger as well. "They will suspect me of intrigue," he tells her, "they will be convinced that I am plotting against the public order." He then tells his wife cryptically in front of his General Dessalines: "You go down to your garden and take care of your flowers. (*to Dessalines*): Is that not a great delight, General? I love roses, there is violence in them. (*turning to Madame Toussaint*): Prepare a bouquet for my return" (103). As many students remark, bouquets have a dual purpose: celebrations and funerals. Perhaps it is both here: Toussaint will die, but Haiti will be born from his sacrifice. One of my more perceptive students several semesters ago said that Toussaint had to sacrifice himself to fulfill his duty as a leader. The student knew something about leadership in warfare: like many students at Queensborough and other community colleges throughout the country, he was veteran of combat operations in Iraq and Afghanistan.

The Enigma of Writing about the Revolutions

It is a good idea to remind students that their daily low-stakes writings could be the beginning of a longer essay and that they should think about writing an essay in general as a way to explore a text, topic, or theme that interests them. My main assignment for the second half of the semester is for them to write an essay that provides a close reading of a passage that they have chosen. In a format borrowed from the organization of each chapter of Erich Auerbach's *Mimesis*, the passage is an epigraph followed by three titled sections of several paragraphs each: "Summary of Context and Paraphrase," "Analysis of Text," and "Commentary." Although one may acknowledge to students that these activities overlap, the point of this essay and its structure is to make them conscious of the differences among these activities of critical writing. The structure they are given is meant to stimulate them creatively (Bean 126). A different but still guiding structure defines their first essay, in which they are asked to pick a side of an argument suggested to them regarding either Brecht's *Life of Galileo* or Büchner's *Danton's Death*. The prompt for the essay on *Danton's Death* asks that they argue for or against the idea that the leaders of the Revolution learn their movement is in trouble when they lose touch with the ordinary people who support them. They are also asked to refer to Gould's Lavoisier essay.

Many students in the course of their argument provide commentaries critical of the Terror, but one should remind them that it is still too soon to tell, that the enigma persists. As much as the Jacobins can be criticized for the bloodletting of the Terror, their government held France together against enemies plotting within and foreign powers aligned against them abroad (Hobsbawm 67–69). More saliently for modern sensibilities, the Jacobins also freed the slaves and welcomed visiting black citizens from Haiti as equals in the National Assembly (*Égalité*). Perhaps when one day Haiti controls its own destiny, we will finally know what both these Revolutions and the Jacobin-led Terror mean.

Works Cited

Auerbach, Erich. *Mimesis: The Representation of Reality in Western Literature*. Translated by Willard Trask. Princeton UP, 2013.

Bean, John C. *Engaging Ideas: The Professor's Guide to Integrating Writing, Critical Thinking, and Active Learning in the Classroom*. Jossey-Bass, 2001.

Benjamin, Walter. "Goethe's Elective Affinities." *Selected Writings: Volume 1: 1913–1926*. Translated by Stanley Corngold, edited by Marcus Bullock and Michael Jennings, Harvard UP, 1996, pp. 297–360.

Brecht, Bertolt. *Life of Galileo*. Translated and edited by John Willet, Penguin, 2008.

Büchner, Georg. *Danton's Death. Complete Plays,* Lenz, *and Other Writings*, translated and edited by John Reddick, Penguin, 1993, pp. 209–37.

Égalité for All: Toussaint L'Ouverture and the Haitian Revolution. YouTube, uploaded by Uptown Flava, 19 Dec. 2012, www.youtube.com/watch?v=IOGVgQYX6SU.

Fact Book, 2014-2015. Queensborough Community College, www.qc.cuny.edu/About/Research/Documents/Fact_Book_2014-2015_Final.pdf

Gauchet, Marcel. "Right and Left." *Realms of Memory: Conflicts and Divisions*, edited by Pierre Nora and Lawrence D. Kritzman, translated by Arthur Goldhammer, Columbia UP, 1997, 241–300.

Glissant, Édouard. *Monsieur Toussaint*. Translated by J. Michael Dash and Glissant, Three Continents Press, 2005.

Gould, Stephen Jay. "The Passion of Antoine Lavoisier." *Bully for Brontosaurus: Reflections in Natural History*, W. W. Norton, 1991, 354–66.

Hobsbawm, Eric. *The Age of Revolution, 1798–1848.* Vintage, 1996.

In Haiti: A Roadtrip Documentary. YouTube, 6 Sept. 2013, www.youtube.com/watch?v=FoZ2DTeUCO8.

James, C. L. R. *The Black Jacobins: Toussaint L'Ouverture and the San Domingo Revolution.* Vintage, 1989.

McGregor, Richard. "Zhou Enlai's Caution Lost in Translation." *China Digital Times CDT*, chinadigitaltimes.net/2011/06/zhou-enlais-caution-lost-in-translation/.

Žižek, Slavoj. "Robespierre; or, The 'Divine Violence' of Terror." *Lacan.com*, www.lacan.com/zizrobes.htm.

Part IV

The Revolution in Art and Mass Media

Beth S. Wright

"Speaking to All the Senses at Once": The French Revolution through the Visual Arts

Visual works and experiences played a central role in the French Revolution. The Committee of Public Instruction considered paintings, prints, civic festivals, and funeral ceremonies to be instruments of the "kindly, seductive, enchanting" education of patriots that would regenerate the nation through a "revolution in heads and hearts" (Baczko 296, 298).[1] The artist Jacques-Louis David, elected a deputy for Paris to the National Convention in September 1792 with Marat and Robespierre, served as a member of its Committee of Public Instruction between October 1792 and October 1795.[2] The rich storehouse of visual material that exists offers many possibilities for class discussion and student research.

Representations ranging from paintings to prints to pottery can be used not simply to illustrate events and protagonists but also to demonstrate ways of thinking about the French Revolution in courses in history, literature, cultural studies, aesthetics, and art history. The same examples may be used to achieve different pedagogical goals. Students comparing engravings of the same event published in France or in Great Britain will discover that compositional arrangements and figural poses reflect political viewpoints. David's organization of the funeral display of Lepelletier de

Saint-Fargeau's corpse in 1792 could be compared with those he dedicated to Marat in 1793 in aesthetic terms by art history students or as reflections of Girondin and Jacobin viewpoints by history students.

Today we are reminded of the importance of visual markers in forming national convictions. Statues commemorating heroes of the Confederacy are being moved from public sites to historical museums, as occurred for nationalized art relics in 1791 when Alexandre Lenoir formed his Museum of French Monuments.[3] In 1794 the National Convention asked David to design clothing appropriate for "the republican way of life and to the character of the Revolution." His designs included robes for legislators emblazoned with the virtues of liberty and equality (Schnapper 144–46; David's *The Representative of the People on Duty,* a colored drawing, is at the Musée Carnavalet in Paris). Modern laws by the French government to regulate a national, republican community through clothing (prohibiting Muslim girls from wearing head scarves to school and Muslim women to wear burkas in public) are rooted in efforts that began during the French Revolution (Douthwaite 129–30). Eighteenth-century theorists gave primacy to visual engagement because it requires substantial metacognitive activity to express sensory perceptions in words and because our emotions as well as our thoughts are deeply affected by the experiences of viewing, discussing, and remembering an image. Teaching the French Revolution through visual representations enables our students to enter into the experience of the original participants, who were invited to regenerate the nation.

Contemporary Events as Eternal History

In October 1790 David was commissioned to depict the oath taken on 20 June 1789 at Versailles's tennis court in a work to be placed on permanent view at the National Assembly (see Bordes; Johnson 77–90; Weston, "Witnessing"). David intended this monumental painting (30′ x 19′) to teach all humanity "present and future" that they had a right to be free.[4] He faced many challenges. His visual rhetoric needed to be lucid and inspirational, avoiding both traditional historical painting's erudite allegories and the flat emotional affect of the *Tableaux historiques de la Révolution Française* (the first edition of 144 prints was issued 1791–96), which documented architectural landmarks where events had taken place. It soon became evident that several participants in the oath would need to be excluded for political reasons. Like many other commissions in this period, it was never completed.

We know David's *Oath of the Tennis Court* through a pen-and-sepia compositional drawing and an unfinished painting in oil on canvas with black and white chalk and brown ink with portrait heads of Edmond-Louis-Alexis Dubois-Crancé, Michel Gérard, Honoré-Gabriel Riquetti, comte de Mirabeau, and Antoine-Pierre-Joseph-Marie Barnave at the right of the composition (both drawing and painting were begun in 1791; they belong to the Musée du Louvre, Paris, and are on view at the Musée National de Versailles). In the lower half of the scene, one action unifies the deputies: they are committing themselves as individuals. Repeated diagonals of gesturing arms carry our eyes across the room from both sides, reaching the apex at Jean-Sylvain Bailly's arm as Bailly administers the oath. Below him is a smaller pyramid formed by three religious representatives. Martin Dauch, the only dissenter, is marginalized at the extreme right. He holds his arms crossed against his chest, refusing to swear an oath not sanctioned by the king. The balance of a smaller equilateral triangle within a larger one provides stability for the dynamic figural responses on the ground and the irregular angles and arcs in the upper area, where representatives of the French nation and humanity gaze through the windows and where curtains blow in the wind. When the large preparatory drawing was shown to friends and colleagues in David's studio in June 1791 and to the Parisian public in the exhibition at the Salon du Louvre in September 1791, spectators felt that they themselves were present at the scene, taking the oath.[5]

The French People Demanding the Overthrow of the Tyrant on the Tenth of August 1792, by François Gérard, David's student (the drawing is in the Musée du Louvre, Cabinet des Dessins) was submitted in 1794 to the Committee of Public Safety's competition to immortalize "deeds that are the work of the entire people" (Olander, "French Painting" 36–37). Gérard's composition recalled David's *Oath of the Tennis Court* in its proposed monumental scale (25′ x 30′) for exhibition in a public site and its invocation of the spectator's participation. But here we see the National Assembly's thoughtful deliberations disrupted by the sudden arrival of sansculottes whose patience has been exhausted, as Nicolas de Condorcet described the original event (Perovic 94).[6] Instead of symmetrically balanced figures in the lower region, the movement of Gérard's sansculottes rushing into the scene from the left overwhelms the spatial field. Like David's *Oath*, Gérard's *Tenth of August 1792* was never completed.

In a New Space: Festivals and Funerals

Scenarios of festivals and state funerals, voted on by the National Assembly, were published and disseminated throughout the nation. These events, like our modern Olympic opening ceremonies, were multimedia spectacles that lasted for hours and included thousands of people who were "simultaneously actor and spectator" (Perovic 158).[7] Processions incorporated music, choreography, temporary architectural and sculptural works, costumes, and slogans on banners. Graphic representations provided more information than would have been available even to eyewitnesses. These ephemeral experiences of nationhood could have a lasting influence.

David's Festival of Unity and Indivisibility of the Republic on 10 August 1793 took place at five Parisian sites (Schnapper 138; see also Weston, "Witnessing" 126).[8] At the site of the former Bastille, delegates of France's eighty-six departments drank water gushing from the breasts of a statue of Isis, the symbol of regeneration and nature. On the Boulevard Poissonnière, honor was given to the market women who had brought the royal family back to Paris in October 1789. On the Place de la Révolution (now Place de la Concorde), the site of Louis XVI's execution, a bonfire consumed attributes of "feudalism." On the Place des Invalides, a colossal plaster statue of Hercules with his club represented the power of the people defeating federalism. Finally, on the Champ de Mars, the crowd decorated the altar of the fatherland with the fruits of their labors and swore loyalty to the second Constitution of the Year 1. Jacques Blanchard, Villeneuve, and other engravers were able to contain in one graphic work a day-long experience throughout the city of Paris.

The Committee of Public Instruction asked David to organize the state funerals and commemorative art works representing two martyrs to liberty: Lepelletier de Saint-Fargeau (murdered in January 1793 for voting for Louis XVI's execution) and Jean-Paul Marat (murdered in July 1793 by Charlotte Corday, a Girondin). The sight of mortal wounds and bloodstained objects would inspire patriots to avenge their death. Marie-Joseph Chénier's proposal for Lepelletier's funeral display and cortege specified the inclusion of bloodstained clothing and sword, "sanctified by the blood of a patriot" (Simon 463).[9] David's painting of Lepelletier (which he created without a commission) was destroyed by Lepelletier's royalist daughter in 1826 after she purchased it from David's death sale. We know its composition through a drawing by A. Devosge, David's student (the drawing is in the Musée des Beaux-Arts in Dijon) and an engraving by P.-A. Tardieu (see Simon; Weston, "Witnessing" 123; Johnson 94–100). David's paintings *Michel Le Pelletier de Saint-Fargeau on His Deathbed* and *Marat at His Last Breath* (1793; Musées Royaux des Beaux-Arts in Brussels) were exhibited for six weeks in a funerary crypt at the Louvre, then sent to the National Convention's Assembly Hall (Salle des Séances), where they hung behind the speaker's rostrum for more than a year. David promised members of the National Convention, "Your gazes, traveling over the livid and bloody features of Marat, will recall to you the virtues that must never cease being yours" (Baecque 294n37 [*Archives parlementaires*, vol. 79, p. 211]).

For Marat's funerary display and painting, David represented his friend as he had seen him the day before his murder, in a bathtub with a vinegar-soaked cloth on his head to alleviate his skin condition: "Near him he had a block of wood on which ink and paper were placed, and, with his hand emerging from the bathtub, he was writing his final thoughts for the good of the people" (Johnson 102; Wildenstein and Wildenstein 55).[10] Marat's objects of martyrdom (bathtub, inkstand, bloodstained shirt) played a prominent role in his funeral display, as we see in Fougea's painting *The Funeral of Marat in the Former Cordeliers Church* (1794; the painting is in the Musée Carnavalet in Paris). In 1792, David's state funeral for Lepelletier displayed his draped corpse on the bare high pedestal that had once held an equestrian statue of Louis XIV in the Place des Piques (now Place Vendôme). In 1793, Marat's nude corpse, covered with flowers and crowned with oak leaves, could be approached by mourners. The crowd carried the bathtub, inkstand, and bloodstained shirt behind the corpse through Paris in a torchlit funeral procession, returning to the Cordeliers, where Marat was buried in the garden. On 18 August 1793, a wooden obelisk was erected "Aux mânes de Marat" 'To the Spirit of Marat' on the Place de la Réunion, with a bust of Marat and the bathtub, chair, table, inkwell, quill pens, and papers (Weston, "Corday-Marat Affair" 146).

David's *Marat at His Last Breath* is a deliberately disturbing work. Its color range recalls blood and putrefaction. Its compressed space seems too shallow to hold the body in its tub in the foreground plane (Johnson 105). Corday is excised from our view: she has no place in the eternity into which Marat is entering through his agony.

Erasing and Remaking: Iconoclasm and Phantasmagoria

The destruction of monuments could edify, like the spectacle of a traitor's execution, or be seen as vandalism (a term invented in 1793).[11] In August 1792, the National Assembly decreed, "It is the manifest will of the people that no public monument should any longer exist that recalls the reign of despotism" (Clay 176 [citing *Actes et décrets rendus par l'Assemblée nationale, depuis le 10 août 1792*]). The destruction of sculptures on the portal of the Cathedral of Notre Dame was described as "decapitation" of "the kings of stone" (Clay 217; "décapiter . . . ces rois de pierre").[12] The denuded pedestal, where Edmé Bouchardon's statue of Louis XV in the Place des Victoires had stood until August 1792, was a prominent feature of prints and drawings representing Louis XVI's execution on 21 January 1793. In July 1793, Bertrand Barère urged that the anniversary of the people's uprising on 10 August 1792 be celebrated by the destruction of the royal mausoleum at Saint-Denis (Lindsay 476). Excavations began the next month; the Bourbon tombs were destroyed 12–16 October 1793, while Marie-Antoinette's trial and execution were taking place.

Rubble could be rededicated to the Revolution. In November 1793, David proposed to the Committee of Public Safety that there be a competition to use the remnants of royal monuments ("piled-up debris of the idols of ignorance and superstition") to construct a statue of the French people, replacing Giambologna's statue of Henri IV (1614) on the Pont Neuf, which had been pulled down in August 1792 (Clay 220n59 [citing Guillaume, vol. 2, p. 806]). David's prize-winning design for *Triumph of the People* was a colossal male figure holding Hercules's club and allegorical figures of Liberty and Equality and bearing the inscriptions "Light" on its forehead, "Strength" on its arms, "Work" on its hands, and "Nature and Truth" on its chest. The National Convention ordered its construction in bronze, even though bronze was urgently needed by the military. A colossal model in plaster was placed on the esplanade of the Invalides, but the sculpture was never completed.[13]

While patriots were edified by the sight of symbolic destruction, monarchists were consoled by hallucinatory reappearance. Graphic works such as *Un sans-culotte . . .* (1794) or Pierre Crussaire's *The Mysterious Urn* (1794) incorporated silhouette profiles of the royal family by reversing the figure-ground relation.[14] In Crussaire's print, phantom profiles of

Louis XVI and Marie-Antoinette form the sides of an urn above a tomb; those of the king's sister, son, and daughter appear in a weeping willow.[15] In Robertson's phantasmagoria of 1798, a magic lantern show in which optical illusions were supported by ventriloquism, music, and sound effects, the ghost of Robespierre appeared, only to be decapitated and explode into pieces (Wright, *Painting* 51–53; O'Rourke 33–34).

"Speaking to All the Senses at Once"

On the day of Louis XVI's execution, the National Convention decreed that educational matters should be permanently on the agenda (Leith, "French Republican Pedagogy" and "Allegory"). Like John Locke and Jean-Jacques Rousseau, they believed that an education that relied on sensory engagement and open-ended discovery would forge patriots who could think for themselves. In his *Essai sur l'instruction publique* (1793; "Essay on Public Education"), P.-C.-F. Daunou insisted that "to teach is not to dictate what must be thought . . . not to reveal to a pupil what has been done before him but to lead him to conduct his own research" (322). In visual works such as ABC manuals and pedagogical games, rebus images and letters in "deliberate disorder" as well as symbols, people, and events of the Revolution could be manipulated, decoded, discussed.[16]

A different visual approach supported the government's desire that the people emulate patriotic actions after seeing illustrations of physical courage or war wounds. These demonstrations were to be imitated, not decoded or debated. The National Convention ordered 150,000 copies of Léonard Bourdon de la Croisnière and Antoine-Claire Thibaudeau's *Recueil des actions héroïques et civiques des Républicains Français* (1793–94) to be sent to municipalities, armies, and schools (Olander, "Pour transmettre" 312–13; Baecque 287). Six representations of its "heroine of Saint-Milhier," a mother ready to use pistols and dynamite to protect her family from royalist brigands in the Vendée, were submitted to the 1794 art competition.

Grasset de Saint-Sauveur promised in his *Fastes du peuple français en tableaux raisonnés de toutes les actions héroïques et civiques du soldat et du citoyen français* (1796; "Annals of the French People Portrayed through Descriptive Images of All the Heroic and Civic Actions of French Soldiers and Citizens"), "His mother, his friend, his wife will say: There he is! It's really him! How honorable is his wound! How wonderful it is to see him, missing an arm, a leg, an eye." Men would rush to enlist in the army. "This is how, through speaking to all the senses at once, one electrifies the soul and one sows the seeds of a nation of heroes."

Visual works and experiences were potent means of informing and inspiring the people who were working to regenerate the French nation.

Notes

All translations are mine except where otherwise indicated.

1. The quotations are from Rabaut Saint-Étienne (21 Dec. 1792).

2. After Robespierre's arrest on 27 July 1794 David was arrested and imprisoned twice before his release 3 August 1795. Only after the general amnesty of 4 Brumaire in year 4 (26 Oct. 1795) was his liberty ensured.

3. On Lenoir's Museum of French Monuments, see most recently Stara.

4. Johnson 81–82, quoting from David's letter to the president of the Assemblée Nationale of 5 February 1792; also cited in Bordes 165.

5. "On croit assister et prendre part à cette scène immortelle qui a préparé le triomphe de la liberté française" (Bordes 163; Johnson 284). The quotation comes from *Supplément au Journal de Paris*, 10 June 1791.

6. "[L]a patience du peuple était épuisée: tout à coup, il a paru tout entier réuni dans un même but et dans une même volonté" (13 Aug. 1792, in *Archives parlementaires*, vol. 48, p. 97).

7. "Il faut que chacun se trouve acteur & spectateur tout en même temps," wrote Marie-Joseph Lequinio in *Des fêtes nationales* (16 Nivôse III / 5 Jan. 1795).

8. Schnapper cites David's preliminary report of 11 July 1793 (138).

9. Chenier's address, given in the January séance, was cited in the *Moniteur*, vol. 15, p. 267. See Wildenstein and Wildenstein 71 (document 675).

10. The document cited is in *Procès-verbaux de la Convention*, vol.16, p. 183. See Vaughan and Weston, Introduction 3; Weston, "Corday-Marat Affair."

11. The first recorded use of the term *vandalism* was by Joseph Lakanal on 4 June 1793, when he addressed the National Convention on the nation's patrimony. Abbé Grégoire presented three reports on *vandalisme* to the National Convention between 31 August 1793 and 14 December 1794. See Clay 268.

12. Clay quotes from Chaumette's "Signes de la royauté effacer" in Prudhomme's *Révolutions de Paris*, 20–27 July 1793.

13. Schlanger 387–88. See Schnapper 142; Clay 220–21; Weston, "Witnessing" 126.

14. The artist of *Un sans-culotte instrument des crimes dansant au milieu des horreurs* is unknown. See Clay 269; frda.stanford.edu/en/catalog/sb757tp0548. The text states that although a sansculotte dances on a list of crimes including murder and vandalism, Louis XVI's ghost will prevail.

15. Wright, *Painting* 50–52 and notes 41–42. Similar prints with phantom profiles appeared in the Musée Carnavalet's exhibition catalog (Trogan and

Forray-Carlier): for example, catalog 115: *Urnes et saules pleureurs*, de Vinck 5924-5926 (Coll. Liesville, Musée Carnavalet Hist. PC 27D). Other examples are de Vinck 5222, de Vinck 5513, de Vinck 5931, Hennin 12284.

16. Wright, "'That Other Historian'" and "'L'éducation'"; Reichardt and Kohle; Taws.

Works Cited

Baczko, Bronislaw. *Une éducation pour la démocratie: Textes et projets de l'époque révolutionnaire*. Garnier, 1982.

Baecque, Antoine de. *The Body Politic: Corporeal Metaphor in Revolutionary France, 1770–1800*. Translated by Charlotte Mandell, Stanford UP, 1997.

Bordes, Philippe. *Le* Serment du jeu de paume *de Jacques-Louis David: Le peintre, son milieu et son temps de 1789 à 1792*. Éditions de la réunion des musées nationaux, 1983.

Clay, Richard. *Iconoclasm in Revolutionary Paris: The Transformation of Signs*. Voltaire Foundation / SVEC, 2012.

Daunou, P.-C.-F. "Essai sur l'instruction publique." Baczko, pp. 303–44.

Douthwaite, Julia. "Martyrdom, Terrorism, and the Rhetoric of Sacrifice: The Cases of Marat, Robespierre, and Loiserolles." *Martyrdom and Terrorism*, edited by Dominic Janes and Alex Houen, Oxford UP, 2014, pp. 109–30.

Grasset de Saint-Sauveur, Jacques. *Fastes du peuple français en tableaux raisonnés de toutes les actions héroïques et civiques du soldat et du citoyen français: Ouvrage orné des gravures, représentant les belles actions, traits de courage, de bienfaisance, de patriotisme et d'humanité qui ont illustré la nation française*. Deroy, 1796.

Guillaume, James, editor. *Procès-verbaux du Comité d'instruction publique de la Convention nationale*. 7 vols. Paris, 1893.

Johnson, Dorothy. *Jacques-Louis David: Art in Metamorphosis*. Princeton UP, 1993.

Leith, James A. "Allegory and Symbol in the French Revolution." *Images of the French Revolution*, by Claudette Hould, Musée du Québec, 1989, pp. 95–123.

———. "French Republican Pedagogy in the Year II." *Canadian Journal of History / Annales canadiennes d'histoire*, vol. 3, 1968, pp. 52–67.

Lindsay, Suzanne Glover. "Mummies and Tombs: Turenne, Napoleon, and Death Ritual." *Art Bulletin*, vol. 82, no. 3, Sept. 2000, pp. 476–502.

Olander, William. "French Painting and Politics in 1794: The Great *Concours de l'an II*." *1789: French Art during the Revolution*, edited by Alan Wintermute, Colnaghi, 1989, pp. 29–45.

———. "Pour transmettre à la postérité: French Painting and Revolution, 1774–1795." 1983. New York U, dissertation.

O'Rourke, Stephanie. "Beholder, Beheaded: Theatrics of the Guillotine and the Spectacle of Rupture." *Visual Culture and the Revolutionary and Napoleonic Wars*, edited by Satish Padiyar et al., Routledge Press, 2017, pp. 25–39.

Perovic, Sanja. *The Calendar in Revolutionary France*. Cambridge UP, 2012.

Rabaut Saint-Étienne, Jean-Paul. "Projet d'éducation nationale présenté à la Convention nationale." Baczko, pp. 296–301.

Reichardt, Rolf, and Hubertus Kohle. *Visualizing the Revolution: Politics and Pictorial Arts in Late-Eighteenth-Century France.* Translated from the German by Corinne Attwood and from the French by Felicity Baker, Reaktion Books, 2008.

Schlanger, Judith. "Le peuple au front gravé 1793." *Les fêtes de la Révolution: Colloque de Clermont-Ferrand (juin 1974)*, edited by Jean Ehrard and Paul Viallaneix, Société des Études Robespierristes, 1977, pp. 387–95.

Schnapper, Antoine. *David.* Translated by Helga Harrison, Alpine Fine Arts Collection, 1982.

Simon, Robert. "David's Martyr-Portrait of Le Peletier de Saint-Farbeau and the Conundrums of Revolutionary Representation." *Art History*, vol. 14, no. 4, Dec. 1991, pp. 459–87.

Stara, Alexandra. *The Museum of French Monuments, 1795-1816: "Killing Art to Make History."* Ashgate, 2013.

Taws, Richard. *The Politics of the Provisional: Art and Ephemera in Revolutionary France.* Pennsylvania State UP, 2013.

Trogan, Rosine, and Anne Forray-Carlier. *La famille royale à Paris: De l'histoire à la légende.* Paris-Musées, 1993.

Vaughan, William, and Helen Weston. Introduction. Vaughan and Weston, pp. 1–33.

———, editors. *Jacques-Louis David's* The Death of Marat, Cambridge UP, 2000. Masterpieces of Western Painting Series.

Weston, Helen. "The Corday-Marat Affair: No Place for a Woman." Vaughan and Weston, pp. 128–52.

———. "Witnessing Revolution." *Jacques-Louis David: New Perspectives*, edited by Dorothy Johnson, U of Delaware P, 2006, pp. 119–30.

Wildenstein, Daniel, and Guy Wildenstein. *Documents complémentaires au catalogue de l'œuvre de Louis David.* Fondation Wildenstein, 1973.

Wright, Beth S. "'L'éducation par les yeux': Texte et image à la fin du XVIIIe siècle." *Cahiers de l'Association des Études Françaises*, no. 57, May 2005, pp. 153–71.

———. *Painting and History during the French Restoration: Abandoned by the Past.* Cambridge UP, 1997.

———. "'That Other Historian, the Illustrator': Voices and Vignettes in Mid-Nineteenth-Century France." *Oxford Art Journal*, vol. 23, no.1, Spring 2000, pp. 113–36.

Amaya Martin and José A. Martin-Pereda

The French Revolution and the Beginning of Modern Communications

Science and Technology in the French Revolution

The French Revolution marked an inflection point in the development of science and technology, in France and in Europe in general. Concepts and institutions that are extremely familiar today, such as the metric system and the École Polytechnique, have their roots in the period of the French Revolution. Scientists' public profiles also became more elevated during this period, whether through teaching in new educational institutions or through participating directly in politics, as did the astronomer Pierre-Simon Laplace, the mathematician and physicist Joseph Fourier, and the chemist Antoine Lavoisier.

The French Revolution promoted the sciences—both their teaching and their practical applications in society. It also was critical for the development of certain technologies, such as new forms of long-distance communications. The quick transmission of information without a physical document—so common today that we take it for granted—has its origins in the ingenious and practical solutions of the revolutionary government to defend and administer territory beyond the range of a day's journey.

Menaced by powerful enemies, the new authorities had to know the current situation both inside the country and at its borders and exert control. The entire revolutionary enterprise would fail without a communication system that covered the whole territory and transmitted information quickly and accurately. This communication system, ideally, would link all provinces with Paris and allow the rapid exchange of messages with distant places.

Such a system was in fact developed and installed all over France, and it helped the First French Republic survive. In 1793, Claude Chappe's optical telegraph represented the dawn of modern communication systems.

Background

Chappe's optical telegraph was technically not the world's first means of communicating over long distances by visual line of sight, but it was such an advance over earlier systems and its influence is so enduring that it can be considered the beginning of modern communications. Ancient Persians, Greeks, and Romans had their methods: reports of the use of torches go back to the twelfth century BCE, and mirrors and flags were used in Greece in the fifth century BCE. Trajan's column in Rome depicts a communication system based on torches. Similar optical systems, together with acoustic systems and other, more traditional systems to transmit information, such as pigeons, runners, or horseback messengers, were also used during the Middle Ages and until the modern period. In most of these cases, both sender and receiver knew ahead of time the kind of information to be transmitted, and new information could not be added to a previously agreed code. For example, two flares or the sound of two cannon was agreed to mean that the king had had a son, and one flare or the sound of one cannon would mean that the king had had a daughter.

A more complex approach was proposed in England in 1684. The physicist Robert Hooke presented in his lecture "On Showing a Way How to Communicate One's Mind at Great Distances" what is considered to be the first system to transmit information that did not fit a previously established code. He was the first to design an optical transmission system that incorporated control codes in two-way communications, allowing operators to signal acknowledgment or error conditions. The apparatus itself was a frame and several panels; the letters of the alphabet were encoded through arbitrary mappings of the panels. Because there was no urgent need at the time for such a device, the system was never implemented, but the design became known, and it probably inspired later devices.

Chappe's optical telegraph, then, did not represent an original idea per se; it is doubtful whether it would have been implemented in less troublesome times. What triggered its use and gave it the importance that it has today was the French Revolution, in which quick transmission of information became essential for the survival of a new political order in the face of powerful military and ideological enemies. Chappe was not the first to create a long-distance communication system, but he undertook his work at a time when his country depended on communication to survive.

Influence of the French Revolution on the Development and Success of Chappe's Optical Telegraph

Neighboring monarchies and domestic counterrevolutionaries who abhorred the Revolution's ideology and felt threatened by its new political institutions threatened France in 1792. Wars broke out at the borders between the new French Republic and England, Holland, Prussia, Spain, the Italian states, Hanover, and Hesse. Internally, many revolts erupted, trying either to bring back the Old Regime or to change the orientation of the current government.

In the face of these enemies, the new authorities had to exert strong control both inside the country and at its borders. There was an urgent need for a communication system that could cover the whole territory and transmit information quickly. The centralization of the government during the Jacobin period (Sept. 1792–July 1794) only increased this need. An ideal communication system would link all provinces with Paris and allow the rapid exchange of messages with distant places.

Claude Chappe

Claude Chappe, the second of seven children, was born into an influential family on Christmas Day of 1763 at Brûlon, a town about two hundred kilometers southwest of Paris. His grandfather was a baron, and his father was *directeur des domaines* ("state property administrator") of the French king in Rouen. Raised for the church, Chappe studied to become *abbé commendataire* ("commendatory abbot"). When he graduated from the seminary around 1783, he obtained two religious benefices, which gave him generous funds and few obligations. During his religious training, he showed a strong interest in science and published several papers on physics.

As a result of the Revolution, Chappe lost his religious benefices in November 1789 and had to return to Brûlon, unemployed. Along with his four brothers, he spent the winter of 1790–91 experimenting with telegraph designs, as many others were doing at the time. In March 1791 they were ready for a first public demonstration. Luckily for Claude, his elder brother, Ignace, was elected to the new Legislative Assembly in Paris in October 1791. Ignace influenced the assembly to study his brother Claude's proposal.

In 1792 the National Convention approved the adoption of Chappe's telegraph for national communications and assigned the Committee of Public Safety to plan suitable telegraph routes. Beginning in August 1793, members of the National Assembly, such as Georges Couthon, Bertrand Barère, Marie-Jean Hérault, Louis-Antoine de Saint-Just, Jacques-Alexis Thuriot, and Maximilien Robespierre, signed decrees for immediate extensions of Chappe's system. Chappe was authorized to place his machines in any belfries, towers, or situations of his choosing. He also had the power to cut down trees that might interfere with the line of vision between the machines, and the government made general provisions for expediting the project. On 24 September 1793, Chappe was given the title of *ingénieur télégraphe* and was granted the benefits of an engineering lieutenant, which included, among others, a salary and government housing. Less than a year later, by mid-August, he had installed an optical telegraph line with fifteen stations between Montmartre, Paris, and Lille.

Chappe transmitted a first test telegram from Lille to Montmartre on 15 August 1794, and just over two weeks later he telegraphed the first official message: military news that Condé had been recovered: *Condé être restituer à la Republique. Reddition avoir eu lieu ce matin à six heures* ("Condé is restored to the Republic: Surrender took place this morning at six o'clock").

At the end of 1804, he fell ill during an inspection tour of lines that were under construction. When he returned to Paris after a sickness of several months, he fell into a depression from which he did not recover. On 23 January 1805, he committed suicide by jumping into a well outside the Telegraph Administration at the Hôtel Villeroy in Paris.

Description of the Optical Telegraph

A detailed description of the optical telegraph can be found in many works.[1] The basic mechanical structure of Chappe's telegraph was a semaphore composed of iron columns 4.55 meters high with a movable wooden regulator attached to the top. At the end of the regulator were two movable indicators counterbalanced with lead weights and steel rods. A control handle at the bottom of the column moved the regulator and the indicators. Specific positions of the regulator and indicators could be a letter, a word, or even the name of a city. The meaning of these positions was changed from time to time to prevent interception and manipulation by people whom today we would call hackers.

Other systems transmitted only letters, simplifying the code but slowing the transmission speed. An example of the letter-only method is the telegraph developed in Britain in 1796 by Lord George Murray (1761–1803), in which the regulator and the indicators were replaced by panels in horizontal or vertical positions. The need for higher speed caused the simplification of the words. Today's social media and text message abbreviations—*rsvp*, *lol*, and the like—have their ancestors in the optical telegraph, which sought to transmit as many words as possible in the fewest letters. In Britain, one transmitted message read, RSOV ANCHOR SPITD YESDA SAIL PLYTH TMRO, which meant, H.M.S. ROYAL SOVEREIGN ANCHORED AT SPITHEAD YESTERDAY SAILING FOR PLYMOUTH TOMORROW.

The system developed by Murray in England is only one of many optical telegraphs that emerged in Europe after Chappe's system demonstrably enabled the success of the French Revolution. For example, one of Chappe's assistants, Pierre-Jacques Chatau, traveled to Russia and built a similar system in the early 1820s, with its first line, between Warsaw and St. Petersburg, operating from 1824 to 1855. In Britain, the Royal Navy commander Home Riggs Popham (1762–1820) supplemented Murray's system in 1824 with a simplified land telegraph whose lines covered the south of England. Agustín de Betancourt (1758–1824) and José María Mathé (1788–1868), Spanish military engineers, implemented their own systems in Spain. Although Betancourt's first line, erected in 1797, did not cover much territory, Mathé's telegraph linked the north and south of the Iberian Peninsula with a line that, from 1845 on, connected Cádiz with Irún, a distance of over a thousand kilometers. The optical telegraph's importance was appreciated in Sweden too, where Abraham Niclas Clewberg-Edelcrantz (1754–1821), a poet, diplomat, and inventor, in 1796 wrote a comprehensive treatise on an optical telegraph of his own design.[2]

Echoes of Chappe's Optical Telegraph in Today's World

Chappe's optical telegraph continued to be used for decades, until Samuel Morse's electrical telegraph spread broadly and replaced it in the second half of the nineteenth century. Even so, today's communication systems retain traits of Chappe's optical telegraph system and can be seen as a continuation of the communications methods developed by the Frenchman.

In present-day communication systems, information, after being digitalized, is divided and transmitted in packets. Each packet has a header, which contains information about the source and characteristics of the packet (length, destination, and so forth), along with a body of data. Packets travel along different possible paths but are reassembled at the final destination according to the information provided in their headers.

This header-and-packet construct is similar to the one employed by Chappe. The first signals transmitted through Chappe's semaphore were similar to today's header. They provided information about the final destination, the urgency of the message for its receiver, and its priority in the network—messages coming from or going to Paris, for example, always had priority over other destinations. It is interesting that the basic routes of Chappe's net of telegraphic lines in France were maintained in future communication systems, such as the electrical telegraph and the telephone.

Accounts of Chappe's Optical Telegraph in French and Foreign Literature

Chappe's system left a mark on the French society of its time, and numerous authors depicted the telegraph in illustrations and literary works. There are no particularly famous paintings that include Chappe's optical telegraph, but it was commonly illustrated in its time.[3] We know what the optical telegraph looked like and how it was situated in locations throughout France from a number of nineteenth-century art works, such as Charles Norry's 1799 *Vue de l'intérieur du Louvre d'après nature l'an 4eme* ("View of the Interior of the Louvre in the Fourth Year, Life Drawing"), and Antoine-Louis Goblain's *Télégraphe de Montmartre*, about 1815, which can be found today on the Internet.

Many of France's most prominent writers noted the importance of Chappe's optical telegraph. The feelings of Victor Hugo toward the device changed over time. At first he termed it the "cursed telegraph," but he later conceded that it had its usefulness in society. In his satire entitled "Le télégraphe," published in 1819 in Paris, when he was seventeen, he wrote:

> Ce maudit télégraphe enfin va-t-il cesser
> D'importuner mes yeux qu'il commence à lasser ?
> Là, devant ma lucarne ! il est bien ridicule
> Qu'on place un télégraphe auprès de ma cellule !
> Il s'élève, il s'abaisse . . . et mon esprit distrait
> Dans ces vains mouvements cherche quelque secret. . . . (407)

> This accursed telegraph . . . Will it finally stop
> Disturbing my eyes that it begins to tire?
> There, in front of my window! It is ridiculous
> For a telegraph to be placed right next to my cell!
> It rises, it falls . . . and my distracted mind
> Seeks some secret in these vain movements. . . .

Chappe's optical telegraph made a significant impression on both French and foreign authors. Accounts written in the first half of the nineteenth century have special interest because his telegraph was still in use, and contemporary impressions, admiration, and even envy come through unfiltered. Among French authors, Alexandre Dumas, Stendhal, and François-René de Chateaubriand alluded to the optical telegraph in their works (Fortunato 150–57). Dumas, for example, mentioned Chappe's telegraph in *The Count of Monte Cristo*, in the chapter entitled "How a Gardener May Get Rid of the Dormice That Eat His Peaches," in which the main character, Edmond Dantes, bribes a telegraph employee to send false financial information in the line between Paris and Spain to provoke the ruin of the banker Danglars. Dantes succeeds, and the receipt of incorrect information is attributed to fog. Among non-French authors, Thomas Carlyle, a Scotsman, referred to the optical telegraph in *The French Revolution: A History*, first published in 1837. In book 5, "Terror the Order of the Day," and chapter 7, "Flame-Picture," he writes:

> What, for example, is this that Engineer Chappe is doing, in the Park of Vincennes? In the Park of Vincennes; and onwards, they say, in the Park of Lepelletier Saint-Fargeau the assassinated Deputy; and still onwards on the Heights of Ecouen and further, he has scaffolding set up, has post driven in; wooden arms with elbow joints are jerking and flying in the air, in the most rapid mysterious manner! Citoyens ran up, suspicious. Yes, O Citoyens, we are signaling: it is a device this, worthy of the Republic; a thing for what we will call *Far-writing* without

> the aid of postbags; in Greek it shall be named Telegraph.—*Télégraphe sacré!* Answers Citoyenism: For writing to Traitors, to Austria?—and tears it down. Chappe had to escape, and get a new Legislative Decree. Nevertheless he has accomplished it, the indefatigable Chappe: this Far-writer, with its wooden arms and elbows-joints, can intelligibly signal; and lines of them are set up, to the North Frontiers and elsewhere. On an Autumn evening of the Year Two, Far-writer having just written that Condé Town has surrendered to us, we send from the Tuileries Convention-Hall this response in the shape of Decree: "The name Condé is changed to *Nord-Libre*, North-Free. The Army of the North ceases not to merit well of the country."—To the admiration of men! For lo, in some half hour, while the Convention yet debates, there arrives this new answer: "I inform thee, je t'annonce, Citizen President, that the Decree of Convention, ordering change of the name Condé into North-Free; and the other, declaring that the Army of the North ceases not to merit well of the country; are transmitted and acknowledged by Telegraph. I have instructed my Office at Lille to forward them to North-Free by express. Signed, CHAPPE." (665)

Classroom Implementation

A teaching module devoted to Chappe's optical telegraph can provoke thought about the meaning of modernity and the nature of communication problems that seem modern, such as speed, privacy, and accuracy. We can draw out lessons for students of science and engineering, among other disciplines, by comparing Chappe's optical telegraph with Morse's electrical telegraph, Bell's wired telephone, Marconi's wireless radio, and today's cell phones and the Internet.

Professors can inspire discussion with the following guiding questions.

Questions exploring the historical circumstances of technological advancement

Why was there a need to change the preexisting system? Could it occur only in a period of turmoil? For example, the Internet evolved from ARPANET, developed by the United States Department of Defense during the Cold War. Is government the indispensable technology incubator?

What similarities do we see in the development of new systems?

What examples from art and literature can we recall that portray communications technology? What factors does the artist or author use to make the portrayal positive or negative?

Questions comparing the advantages and shortcomings of communication systems

What are the advantages and disadvantages of each system (Chappe, Morse, Bell, Marconi, Internet)?

Which system would today's privacy advocates prefer and why? Which would hackers prefer?

How robust is each system against jamming (intentional disruption) and interference (unintentional disruption)? In the Chappe system, for example, fog and darkness would be interference, while smoky fire deliberately set between two stations would be jamming.

Can wireless communication today (omnidirectional, radiomagnetic), be truly considered superior to Chappe's visual point-to-point system?

Questions examining design considerations

Is a communications system complete without encryption? Was Morse's standardized electrical telegraph code truly superior to Chappe's encrypted optical semaphore?

How critical is redundancy? What is the responsibility of network developers to identify critical nodes and reveal these to the information consumer?

If we consider today's cell phone a communications device, is portability a necessity or only a convenience? Although Chappe's optical telegraph could never be pocket-sized, the French army carried a portable optical telegraph that could be set up in a matter of minutes, and semaphore is used to this day on ships and boats of all sizes.

Is the single limiting factor ease of operations? Did wireless voice devices supplant wireless optical devices simply because everyone knows how to dial and talk in plain language but it takes a trained signalman fluent in symbols and codes to operate in a visual medium?

We conclude this essay just as we propose concluding our teaching module, by underscoring the opportunity to draw general lessons for the present from particular cases and insights in history. We are confident that thoughtful students in many disciplines will benefit from knowledge of Chappe's optical telegraph, and that technology critical to the French Revolution offers a rich and eye-opening perspective on today's information age.

Notes

1. For a particularly clear description, see Holzmann and Pehrson 79–90; in French, see Gachot. A depiction of Chappe's optical semaphore appears in Ternant 12 (see gallica.bnf.fr).

2. A full translation of the treatise is given in Holzmann and Pehrson, ch. 4.

3. The way the optical telegraph is portrayed in paintings is analyzed by Taws.

Works Cited

Carlyle, Thomas. *The French Revolution: A History.* Random House, 1955.

Dumas, Alexandre. *The Count of Monte Cristo.* 1844. *The Literature Page*, www.literaturepage.com/read/countofmontecristo.html.

Fortunato, Valerie. "Le télégraphe optique et la littérature au XIX siècle." *Les cahiers de la FNARH*, no. 116, 2010, pp. 150–57.

Gachot, Henri. *Le télégraphe optique de Claude Chappe.* Imprimerie et Édition Savernoises, 1967.

Holzmann, Gerard, and Björn Pehrson. *The Early History of Data Networks.* IEEE Computer Society Press, 1995.

Hugo, Victor. *Œuvres complètes.* Le Club Français du Livre, 1967.

Taws, Richard. "Telegraphic Images in Post-revolutionary France." *Art History*, vol. 2, Apr. 2016, pp. 400–21.

Ternant, Alcide-Ludovic. *Les télégraphes.* Hachette, 1881.

Giulia Pacini

Ideas on the Table: Teaching with the *Faïences Révolutionnaires*

The French Revolution was a heavily mediatized event in which competing ideas and political positions were staked out in print, oratory, songs, images, and a wide variety of objects. Historians have long shown how official seals, symbols, even articles of clothing (e.g., images of Marianne, liberty trees, the tricolor cockade, the Phrygian cap) played important roles in the construction of the Republic and the performance of its citizenry. Similarly, in the early 1790s, architectural projects were designed to publicize republican values through "talking" facades, which were covered with political mottos and governmental decrees.[1]

More discreet talking objects from this period were the *faïences révolutionnaires* ("revolutionary faiences"), household ceramics that were produced mainly around the city of Nevers and featured a broad variety of political emblems and written slogans.[2] A study of this tin-glazed, painted earthenware contributes to our understanding of the communicative and performative aspects of revolutionary culture, revealing how private individuals were able to navigate political tensions and to articulate a range of different claims for themselves. These domestic objects serve as an intriguing pendant to more usual academic discussions of the cultural initiatives of the Committee of Public Safety, for the plates' production and circulation were driven by consumer choice and shifting costs rather than by central governmental doctrine. The faiences also offer evidence of bourgeois tastes, ideas, and economic conditions in rural parts of France, just as they speak to the ambiguities of the revolutionary period, exposing the gap between political intentions and popular practices in everyday life.

I present these materials in French in an undergraduate seminar on the history of the Revolution and find that the accompanying images often stimulate discussion more easily than the verbal texts on my syllabus. Just as, in the eighteenth century, the faiences could speak even to the barely literate, so these ceramics now allow even intermediate-level language students to engage in debate in a topically focused, discussion-intensive seminar. The ceramics readily spark cross-cultural analyses of the political value of signs and material objects in both French revolutionary and today's (American) cultures. This unit therefore culminates with my asking students to identify other communities built or at least reinforced through the sharing or opposing of specific signs and practices (pins, T-shirts, flags, the contested French *arbres de la laïcité*, etc.). As students transpose their conclusions to a contemporary context, they actively engage these materials and recognize their ongoing relevance.

I divide my class into small discussion groups for many of the following exercises in order to maximize participation and to give language students a better opportunity to practice their communication skills. Activities are initially rather structured: students describe and classify photographs of this dishware, then analyze the plates' potential meanings and try to give an approximate date range for each object. We move on to more open-ended discussions as we assess both the significance of these ceramics for French revolutionary history and the value of visual signs of political participation today. Since my students can understand French, I require advance reading of an extract of Edith Mannoni's richly illustrated *Les faïences révolutionnaires.* I also distribute a vocabulary list that enables everyone to describe the given symbols in detail. For an anglophone class, the following introduction should allow teachers to place this dishware in context, to produce a legend identifying the meaning of each symbol, and therefore to work with these materials in English.

Until the eighteenth century, faience was the most popular kind of ceramic produced in France. This art came to France from Italy, in particular from the city of Faenza (known as Fayence in French) where a tradition of tin-glazed and painted earthenware had flourished since the Renaissance. In the sixteenth century, the duke of Nevers, Ludovico Gonzaga, brought numerous Italian artists to his court, including members of the Conrade family, who founded Nevers's first ceramic factory in 1580. Eleven more were established thereafter. Nevers' potters first worked with floral or geometric elements but soon turned to more figurative designs. Personalized faience—objects of all kinds, painted with an individual's name and patron saint or with the tools of a trade—became a highly popular gift to commemorate special occasions. These objects were therefore made to order: a peddler would present various models to his client, and together they would decide on a particular design.

Ceramic production intensified around the turn of the eighteenth century, and many historians have explained this phenomenon by referring to Louis XIV's sumptuary laws, notably his edicts of 1689, 1699 and 1709, which decreed that silver and gold furniture and tableware be given to the royal treasury to assuage the kingdom's financial difficulties. As a result, if one chooses to believe Louis de Rouvroy, duke de Saint-Simon: "[T]out ce qu'il y eut de grand et de considérable se mit en huit jours en faïence" 'In eight days all those who were grand and important took up ceramics' (576). In reality, however, these edicts had little effect, and the reasons for ceramic's exceptional development at the end of the seventeenth century were both economic and social: new nobles in search of recognition needed original coats of arms and emblazoned tableware for their families, and these commissions spurred the ceramic industry throughout the country (Rosen 57). Many factories were established across the Loire region, as earthenware could circulate by boat up and down the river and along secondary canals, reaching as far as Nantes to the west, Auxerre and the Morvan to the east, and Paris and Rouen to the north.

These factories had to compete with Chinese porcelain arriving through France's East India trading company, the Compagnie Française des Indes, but in the eighteenth century the production and circulation of French ceramics was nonetheless boosted by the country's economic prosperity, a broad fiscal deregulation, and a burgeoning consumer culture. A rural élite of well-off farmers, artisan entrepreneurs, lawyers, notaries, and low-ranking clergy members could then afford to spend two to four sols on essentially decorative objects.[3] To put this in perspective: workmen typically earned about forty sols per day (Brenot 189). Yet the ceramic industry slowed down again after 1786, when a treaty with England simplified the importation of whiter, lighter, and cheaper English porcelain. The rising costs of wood, necessary to fire the furnaces, similarly contributed to this crisis and ultimately forced many manufacturers to close.

Six of the twelve factories at Nevers were able to survive because they were well positioned on the Loire River and in the center of the country, at a good distance from British porcelain's ports of entry. They also managed to reinvent themselves strategically by creating new lines of ware decorated with rapidly changing references to current events. Having already introduced a military design to celebrate the soldiers returning from the War of Austrian Succession and the Seven Years War, in the late 1780s the factories started producing memorabilia celebrating the meeting of the Estates General and the ideal of unity that emerged from their cooperation. This new line of patriotic ceramics benefited from some state support and from the convention's blocking of English imports in 1792. Thousands of pieces were produced during the first three years of the Revolution, before the economic crisis hit the industry, causing prices to rise and individuals' purchasing power to fall. At that point even two to four sols became expensive, and the status of these objects became more and more that of a luxury item. Between 1794 and 1800 the industry was further hit by increasing social tensions and difficult salary negotiations between the directors of the Nevers manufactures and their dependents; it also struggled with outdated technology and inflexible organizational structures (Rosen 320–26, 359).

This line of patriotic ware ended under the empire and was more or less forgotten until the late nineteenth century, when collectors such as Jules-François-Félix Husson, better known as Champfleury, rediscovered these ceramic objects in the Loire valley, in the Morvan, around Beauvais and Amiens, and in Normandy. Champfleury became the curator of the porcelain museum in Sèvres, and his collection and book *Histoire des faïences patriotiques sous la Révolution* (1867; "History of the Patriotic Faiences during the Revolution") renewed the public's interest and unwittingly stimulated the production of many fakes. These ceramics found a new heyday in conjunction with the recent celebrations of the bicentennial of the Revolution. Numerous exhibits were put together to showcase these objects, and current research on the faiences was to a great extent produced at this time.[4]

My lesson opens with this brief lecture and a *PowerPoint* presentation showing photographs of a wide selection of ceramics. Students then do a short written exercise, which gets them to describe and classify the dishware's different designs. As the class shares its answers, my first goal is to observe that the faiences do not offer an exact chronicle of the Revolution. We note that the dishware is generally not dated and that it presents relatively few references to specific events—the main exceptions being the convocation of the Estates General, the fall of the Bastille, the Civil Constitution of the Clergy, the Festival of the Federation, and the new Constitution of 1791.[5] Despite their popularity in other revolutionary media, the attack on the Tuileries, the royal executions, or other bloody moments generally were not reproduced on these essentially decorative objects. When new military decors appeared in 1792, after the outbreak of war, they focused on abstract notions of defense and vigilance, drawing on Nevers's traditional flag decor and sometimes including generic fortresses, canons, or roosters. In similar fashion, only rarely did these ceramics refer to particular individuals (e.g., Honoré-Gabriel Riqueti de Mirabeau, Camille Desmoulins).

Students will also observe that these ceramics mainly spoke of abstract ideals through emblematic or otherwise symbolic images. Objects celebrating the unity of the three estates constituted the most popular genre, not only because of the general enthusiasm provoked by this event, but also—most probably—because they were produced during the first few years of the Revolution, before French purchasing power and consequent production plummeted because of inflation and war-related economic constraints. This series generally displayed a crown or fleur-de-lis accompanied by various symbols of the three estates (a cross or crosier, a sword, and a spade or other agricultural tool). Later pieces replaced the first and second estates with symbols of liberty, such as the Phrygian cap, a bird freed from a cage, or a tree of liberty, often decorated with patriotic ribbons. On some ceramics, a sly counterrevolutionary fox threatened the bird's flight. Other pieces memorialized the nation or the Republic, as well as the notion of fidelity.

As with any sign, these emblems were—and still are—open to multiple readings: the spade representing the third estate certainly pointed to the agricultural work of the serfs, but it could also be read as a vindication of their freedom from feudal dues (Tixier 7); additionally, to the intellectual élite, the spade may have been read as a reference to current physiocratic thought, an eighteenth-century school of economics that glorified rural life and believed that land, not trade, was the source of the nation's wealth. Conversely, the same concept could be represented in different ways, depending on the ceramics' intended clientele: Liberty, for instance, could be imagined as a classical deity on pieces made for a bourgeois Jacobin, but she more typically appeared as a bird fleeing from a cage on plates destined for rural farmers (Ajalbert and Bonnet 115).

Ceramics that expressed skepticism about current affairs were relatively rare, but a good example can be found at the Musée Carnavalet, where a plate shows images of a clergyman and a noble united by the slogan "Le malheur nous réunit" 'Misfortune unites us.' More common were ambiguous plates, often produced by the Petit factory in Nevers, which conveniently passed as gallant discourse even when mottos such as "Le Tiers ment" 'The Third Estate Lies' or "Le Tiers nuit" 'The Third Estate Is Harmful' could be intended as more critical discourse. At least they reflected the reactionary feelings of the Petit brothers, one of whom emigrated at the beginning of the Revolution. The risk of heavy fines or worse was likewise curtailed by the adoption of vague or equivocal wording such as "Si les choses ne changent de face, nous serons bientôt à la besace" 'If things don't change, we will soon be beggars' or the rebus "IL [image of a sickle, called *faux* in French] CD," which could be read as either "il faut s'aider" or "il faut céder" 'We must help each other out' or 'We must cede': in French, both variants sound the same as reading the letters *CD* (Brenot 201). This ambiguity was apparently necessary, for judicial records tell the story of a Petit salad bowl whose counterrevolutionary motto "VV les émigrés français" 'Long live the French emigrés' was sufficient reason for confiscation by the justice of peace of Tonnerre on 23 February 1792; the ensuing inquiry sparked the flight of the other Petit brother shortly thereafter (Rosen 329).

Challenging a class to interpret these ambiguous mottos can be a fun and thought-provoking exercise. Ultimately students will realize that the faiences of the revolutionary period represented a variety of positions and that their designs sometimes make them difficult to date or fully understand. Most striking are perhaps the ceramics' ideological ambiguities, which speak to the cultural continuities, contradictions, and appropriations of the revolutionary period. Liberal support for the new citizen-subject and a conservative resistance to dechristianization could coexist, in fact, on the same piece. A salad bowl at the Musée Carnavalet bears the inscription "Jean Duc 1793 citoyen" 'Jean Duc 1793 citizen' under the image of Jean's patron saint, a freedom tree, and a compass. A plate in the Heitschel collection is marked "Anne Chérot Bonne Citoyenne 1793" 'Anne Chérot Good Citizen 1793' under two women with halos.

Ongoing material concerns, and not only consumer tastes and ideology, affected the design process and complicated these ceramics' meanings. Surplus plates from a previous line of production (e.g., objects with

Louis XV-style garlands, rocaille elements, or gallant-themed earthenware that had accumulated in Nevers's warehouses after 1786, the date of the signing of the treaty with England) were cleverly updated and upcycled into revolutionary memorabilia. Conversely, the disappearance of an image was not necessarily due to ideological reasons and could precede a political event that would otherwise seem to be related to it, further complicating its dating. For instance, royal and noble iconography was certainly removed after the fall of the monarchy, but the crown's gradual disappearance even before 1791 may also been linked to its excessively labor-intensive and therefore costly design (Ajalbert and Bonnet 84–85). Along the same lines, anomalies in composition may have been due to formal or aesthetic considerations; they were not necessarily ideological choices (Delthe 240).

Overall, therefore, the significance of these objects is still open to debate. According to the historian Thierry Delthe, the ceramics indicate how little imagination the revolutionaries actually had: their images were mainly copied from preexistent political caricatures or other commemorative objects (engravings, medallions, and so forth)—the one exception being, perhaps, the design of a bird fleeing from a cage (239–40). These objects probably did not always express the opinions of their painters, who could be fined for politically incorrect work. The various decors spoke essentially to consumer tastes, but their political importance remains unclear, because we cannot assess in a quantifiable way the popularity of one decorative style over another. Faience collectors have the best sense of these numbers, but they also have their own financial reasons not to want to divulge this information (Delthe 240; Ajalbert and Bonnet 210).

When I ask my students to attribute a logical date range to select examples of this earthenware, my objective at first is simply to review the political debates and shifts that characterized the first years of the Revolution (1788–94). The presence or absence of insignia referring to the first and second estates, the increasing importance of the third estate, and the appearance of signs of war are all telling elements. This is an exciting exercise for students who have not yet thought about how a historian, working in an archive, discovers something new and must figure out what a given emblem means and when it was created. I underscore that at best the meaning and date range of a plate are only possibilities. This exercise obliges students to recognize the ambiguities that limit our interpretation of symbolic and material objects. It also encourages them to come to terms with the intentional equivocality of counterrevolutionary slogans. Because of these difficulties—not despite them—these objects offer both a valuable perspective on the material and visual culture of the revolutionary period and an interesting methodological lesson.

If time permits, I ask students to research other revolutionary media featuring the same symbols or mottos. This comparison allows for an informed assessment of Delthe's thesis that what these ceramics really demonstrate is that the Revolution was ultimately lacking in imagination (240). Alternatively, I might ask students to design and curate a catalog of these ceramic objects or to investigate the historical realities behind some of their most popular symbols, such as the planting (and occasional uprooting) of liberty trees or the adoption of the Phrygian cap.

Above all, it is important to open up discussion so that students have an opportunity to think critically about the multiple functions of these talking objects. If they have read Lynn Hunt's essay "Symbolic Forms of Political Practice" (*Politics* 52–86), they will appreciate how these plates, like the more famous Phrygian caps and tricolor cockades, helped create and transmit new feelings of nationalism. Hunt insists in fact that the adoption of these symbolic objects "made adherence, opposition, and indifference possible" and that their use "constituted a field of political struggle." My students tend to be particularly interested in the argument that "such symbols did not simply express political opinions; they were the means by which people became aware of their positions" (53). As individuals chose between ceramics with different slogans (e.g., "Hors de la constitution point de salut" versus "Hors de l'Église point de salut" 'Outside of the constitution no salvation' versus 'Outside of the Church no salvation'), they positioned themselves in the larger revolutionary debates.

The specific interest of the faiences stems from the fact that they were never meant to be public, didactic, and therefore unequivocal signs like the Phrygian cap, the republican cockade, or even the civil uniforms that Jacques-Louis David designed for the Committee of Public Safety. They were objects freely purchased and kept in the relative privacy of one's home; they represented a range of possible political positions, and their value was sometimes linked to their ability to defy clear interpretation—and thereby to escape censorship. In France's particularly vociferous revolutionary culture, where the voice of the nation was repeatedly announced and constrained by a powerful class of political orators, these discreet talking plates may ultimately have allowed private individuals the satisfaction of articulating some more nuanced claims for themselves.

Notes

1. Nineteenth-century critics coined the term *talking architecture* to describe revolutionary buildings whose geometries and inscriptions could "speak to the eyes" (Molok 43).

2. Large collections of these ceramics can be viewed in the Musée Carnavalet in Paris, in the Musée de la Faïence in Nevers, and in the Musée de la Révolution Française at the Château de Vizille. Students can visualize hundreds of these objects through parismuseescollections.paris.fr/ by searching for "céramique révolution française" at the Musée Carnavalet. One can also use the French national museums' database *Joconde* (www2.culture.gouv.fr/documentation/joconde/fr/pres.htm) and search for "faiences révolutionnaires" and "faiences patriotiques."

3. Boat inventories show that people used plain white plates for domestic use (Nicoud).

4. For scholarly purposes, the most comprehensive book on the topic is the third volume of Jean Rosen's *La faïence de Nevers, 1585–1900.*

5. Plates featuring the death of Louis XVI are late-nineteenth-century creations (Rosen 356).

Works Cited

Ajalbert, René, and Claude Bonnet, editors. *Les faïences révolutionnaires de la collection Louis Heitschel.* Arts Expo, 1985. Catalog of an exhibit at the seventeenth Salon des Antiquaires, 7–16 Dec. 1985.

Brenot, Anne-Marie. "Symbolique et imaginaire dans la faïence patriotique nivernaise du musée Carnavalet." *Historiens et géographes,* vol. 322, Mar.–Apr. 1989, pp. 185–201.

Delthe, Thierry. "La Révolution française et les faïences populaires." *Les images de la Révolution*, edited by Michel Vovelle, Publications de la Sorbonne, 1988, pp. 237–40.

Faïences nivernaises parlantes (faïences patronymiques, bachiques, grivoises et revolutionnaires). Catalog for an exhibit at the Musée Frédéric-Blandin 14 July–30 September 1965. Nevers: Chapelle Sainte-Marie, 1965.

Hunt, Lynn. *Politics, Culture, and Class in the French Revolution.* U of California P, 1984.

Mannoni, Edith. *Les faïences révolutionnaires.* Ch. Massin, 1989.

Molok, Nicolas. "'L'architecture parlante,' ou Ledoux vu par les romantiques." *Romantisme*, vol. 92, 1996, pp. 43–53. *Persée*, www.persee.fr/doc/roman_0048-8593_1996_num_26_92_4264.

Nicoud, Monique. Introduction. *Faïences,* p. 13.

Rosen, Jean. *La faïence de Nevers, 1585–1900.* Vol. 3. Faton, 2011.

Rouvroy, Louis de, duc de Saint-Simon. *Mémoires: Anthologie.* Edited by François Raviez, Le Livre de Poche, 2007.

Tixier, Louis. "Les faïences parlantes nivernaises avant, pendant, après la Révolution." *Faïences*, pp. 5–12.

Melissa A. Deininger

The French Revolution and Modern Propaganda

In many ways, our perceptions of the French Revolution are directly linked to the success of the propaganda used to bolster or defame political ideals and personalities. Theorists like Benedict Anderson, Pierre Nora, and Gilles Deleuze show us the importance of group identity and the use of history to inform society. Combating these cultural tropes can sometimes be a daunting task if the eighteenth-century imagery has proved strong enough to survive into modern perceptions of events. However, once students learn to consider newssheets and the visual arts with a critical and historically informed eye, they are much more likely to understand the many influences that act in the creation of our revolutionary myths.

With its focus on group dynamics rather than on the limited influence of a privileged few, the French Revolution marks the birth of modern propaganda. According to the *Oxford English Dictionary*, propaganda is "[t]he systematic dissemination of information, especially in a biased or misleading way, in order to promote a political cause or point of view" (definition 3). The term also refers to the information disseminated in this way and the means or media used to spread this information. This essay focuses on the use of propaganda as a political tool during and after the Revolution as well as on how the original intent of these ideals and images has been reappropriated today in order to evoke emotions and sell products.

Propaganda was not invented in the eighteenth century, of course, but it was only during the Revolution that public opinion campaigns were consciously directed at the masses. As Robert Darnton notes, "the eighteenth-century French 'public' did not exist in any coherent form; and insofar as it did exist, it was excluded from direct participation in government" (*Literary Underground* 33). Because the people were removed from their government, the libels and caricatures they encountered rarely had hidden or abstract messages; the works tended to attack rather than propose solutions. In contrast, the Revolution promoted what Bertrand Taithe and Tim Thornton call "thick" propaganda: a multilayered approach that emanates "from various outlets which may or may not belong formally to the state" (15). Propaganda evolved during the long nineteenth century from targeted campaigns waged by revolutionaries against the monarchy and the Church into Napoleon's broader approach that used established, shared values like liberty and equality to reinforce the glory of imperial France. This wide-reaching approach is what allows French cultural references to be grafted onto modern beliefs and advertising campaigns.

The popular press was a significant medium from the early days of the Revolution, providing one important conduit for influencing public opinion. The success and proliferation of newspapers at this time are easily linked to the extraordinarily high literacy rates, particularly in Paris. Hugh Gough estimates that as much as ninety percent of men and eighty percent of women in Paris could read well enough to follow basic newssheets by 1789 (195). This literacy, combined with the typically self-explanatory images used in caricatures and libels, meant that most of the large population centers were receiving antiregime propaganda with alarming frequency. As Jeremy Popkin demonstrates, the French public relied on the spreading press to explain and interpret the life-altering events taking place; the coverage became "the almost obligatory diet of daily conversation" (3). Because of the clandestine publication and dispersal of these newssheets, it was nearly impossible for the crown to combat their influence.

By the time of the great *Encyclopédie* project, art was easily recognized as a means to spread ideas. In his article on painting, Jaucourt notes the value of the arts in promulgating political and social messages; however, he finds art's greatest value to be in communicating long-lasting sentiments. This way of looking at art demonstrates that the French public was fully prepared for the use of propaganda during the Revolution. Intellectual salons and gatherings late in the Old Regime tended to favor progressive ideas of freedom and more liberal forms of government; as a result, many politicians and artists were already indoctrinated with these ideals as they began their work.

Another reason for the widespread success of revolutionary propaganda was the consistency of the message presented. Numerous libelers and caricaturists created propaganda critical of the leaders of the time, and one would expect to see a large variety of commentary. In reality, there are only a few themes: the monarchy is a bloated and avaricious monster, the Jacobin leaders were at first incorruptible but turned into crazed demagogues, and true wisdom comes from the common sense of the poor. It is rare to find sources that deviate from any of these themes. Even the opponents of the Revolution, counterattacking, focused on the same messages: pains are taken to show Marie-Antoinette as a devoted mother, revolutionary leaders are seen as hellish figures devouring souls, and, particularly in foreign journals, the peasants are depicted as bloodthirsty oafs who mindlessly follow rhetoric. No matter which side is chosen, the social perceptions are consistent.

Marie-Antoinette

Previous uses of propaganda were typically directed for or against a specific group, principally religious sects. Education of the subject-citizen became of primary importance, as regimes struggled to win over the population. The monarchy tried to rally popular support but had waited too long to woo the people. A prime example of this belated media spin is the case of Marie-Antoinette. Arguably the most reviled figure of the Revolution, the queen was portrayed in countless libels and caricatures as a hedonistic, sexualized monster who was devouring the country. According to Darnton, the mountain of defamation leveled against her during the Revolution has "no parallel in the history of vilification" (*Devil* 397). Attacking the foreign-born queen on a personal level was seen as safer and more acceptable than launching a direct attack on the French king and monarchy. Although libels had been used successfully in France during the Wars of Religion and the Fronde, revolutionary pamphlets were intended for a much wider audience and attacked not only individual figures but the monarchy as a whole. Marie-Antoinette remained the favored target, but it is clear that the pamphlets were very critical of her husband, who was unable to control her, and of the system that allowed her appetites to run unchecked.

In order to fight the devastating effect of the libels and caricatures, the palace began to put out its own counterpropaganda. Marie-Antoinette was frequently portrayed in pornographic libels as a controlling and insatiable woman whose base desires for material goods and sex was ruining the country. To combat these negative images, a favorite court painter, Élisabeth Vigée Le Brun, was engaged to create paintings showing the queen as a devoted and virtuous mother. The most famous of the many official portraits done of the queen is her *Marie-Antoinette and Her Children* (1787), in which the queen is shown surrounded by her children as the family mourns the passing of the youngest princess. The gentle lighting and rich jewel tones of the painting give the impression of a mother presenting her true treasures, her children. This message is reinforced by the absence of jewelry: the children sport noble sashes, but their mother is in a rich but simple gown. Unfortunately, despite the powerful message presented in this and other official portraits, Versailles had waited too long to enter the propaganda war. The libels and caricatures were easily and cheaply reproduced for the public at large, while the official portraits were shown primarily in limited settings to those already in power. The sheer magnitude of negative press made it impossible to recuperate the image of the queen, and she proved to be one of the most vulnerable targets for the Revolution's propaganda arsenal.

The Terror and Its Architects

A main goal of the French Revolution was to create national unity from disparate regions, religions, and languages. Perhaps learning from the mistakes of the monarchy, the revolutionaries quickly turned to art and newssheets to influence fellow citizens. The early years of the Revolution saw some attempts to use art as a propagandist tool, but as James Leith observes, "Only after the Revolution entered its most extreme phase was the pressure on artists really intensified in an attempt to conscript the fine arts in support of Revolutionary ideals" (104). As those in power changed from the oppressed subject to the empowered ruler, different propagandist messages had to be adopted. Philip M. Taylor notes, "[T]he very existence of a Committee of Public Instruction bears witness to the central role the French Revolutionaries ascribed to propaganda" (149). It quickly became clear to the revolutionary leaders that public opinion would have to be courted in order for the movement to survive and thrive as the power vacuum from changing regimes threatened all they had achieved thus far.

Once the monarchy was eliminated, the country needed a new focus for national pride. The Committee of Public Safety worked with artists, musicians, and writers to create public festivals celebrating the innate virtues of the French people. Relying heavily on classical references, artists like Jacques-Louis David created tangible links between virtuous societies and the newly freed French nation. Ideals like sacrifice for the greater good, patriotism (of the revolutionary variety), and an egalitarian society were seen everywhere, from large paintings to pamphlets to public worship of the state. Positive references to the aristocracy were virtually annihilated as churches became civic centers, streets were renamed, and even fashions proclaimed allegiance to the new nation. Students are intrigued by the idea of rewriting culture and enjoy seeing images of old street names carved into buildings side by side with modern street plaques (e.g., Paris's Rue St. Louis became Rue de Turenne). In small groups they may compare an old map of Paris with a new one to discover the changes, which then leads to discussion on why a name would have been seen as objectionable. Students may also consider fashions, looking at images provided of revolutionary garb (cockades, sansculottes pants, inclusion of the blue, white, and red color scheme). An excellent source for revolutionary clothing as propaganda is found in David's costume designs for the legislature, where he specifies dress based on civic service.

As Marie-Hélène Huet's admirable work shows, when the Terror turned on its creators, Maximilien Robespierre and his cohorts went from venerable leaders to reviled monsters. Nineteenth-century historians describe the terrorist leader as a diabolical puppet master and frequently compare him and his cohorts to ferocious wild animals. Huet follows Jules Michelet's interpretation and notes that "like monsters of Antiquity, Robespierre was thus constructed as a composite, mythical beast" (154). We have likely all seen the caricatures of the Revolution as a hellish monster devouring its own people, and these images seem to have been used increasingly by later French leaders as a way to distance the country from the insatiable violence of the Terror. Before the Thermidorian reaction, official imagery of the Revolution is that of a benevolent but stern leadership doing what must be done to purge France of its monarchical past. This representation changes radically after the fall of the Committee of Public Safety, when these same leaders are held responsible for all of

France's current suffering. A member of the immediate post-Revolution generation, Charles Nodier calls Robespierre "the Revolution incarnate" (191), and after his fall the Jacobin is consistently portrayed as preying on the French public. A prime example of antiterrorist artwork is Nicolas-Antoine Taunay's *Le triomphe de la guillotine* ("The Triumph of the Guillotine"), which depicts the Revolution as a horrifying and chaotic scene, in which even demons flee Robespierre and Louis-Antoine de Saint-Just, the newest residents of hell. A select few of the most virulent terrorists were chosen to carry the historical weight of a regime that had outlived its sustainability. After their executions, the search for a new and more positive focus created an opening for someone who understood the power of controlling public opinion.

Napoleon Bonaparte

Napoleon Bonaparte was considered by many a master of the art of revolutionary propaganda. His stylized military dispatches during foreign campaigns showed that he saw the importance of winning public opinion to his cause. In order to combat his detractors and improve his image, he established or controlled no less than six journals, some of which were popular with the general public (Hanley 74). Unlike most propagandist journals, his newssheets were frequently printed on high-quality paper and used various typefaces to underscore the ideas in the articles (80), leading readers to believe that they were receiving superior information. The journals served the stated purpose of communicating with the troops, but they also provided Napoleon with a platform from which to isolate his critics and facilitate his rise to power.

Napoleon also famously made use of artists to further his reputation. Masters including Antoine-Jean Gros, Jean-Auguste-Dominique Ingres, and David were quickly brought into the Napoleonic machine, and they created an ever-evolving image of the future emperor. Early in his career, Napoleon and his wife, Joséphine, crafted the image of a victorious general spreading the Revolution's ideals throughout the world. Among the paintings from this period are *Napoleon Crossing the Alps* (1800), by David, and *Bonaparte at the Pont d'Arcole* (1796), by Gros. In both works, we see a noble warrior who faithfully serves his country, while claiming his place among the greats of history. This image of service continues as Napoleon returns to take up the mantle of leadership. Two of the most famous Napoleonic paintings bookend his career as a leader. David's *Coronation of Napoleon* (1807) reestablishes the grandeur that the revolutionary regime lacked, something the people of France craved after the dark years of continuous struggle. Well into the empire, we have David's *The Emperor Napoleon in His Study at the Tuileries* (1812). This painting shows a man who continues to sacrifice himself for his country, putting his own comfort aside as he works for France's well-being.

A continuous thread throughout Napoleonic propaganda is the image of a calm and stable leader, willing to do whatever is necessary to serve his country. This concept of sacrificing for the nation was the basis for the cult of Napoleon, nurtured by the exiled emperor himself as he wrote his memoirs to solidify his myth. This legend continued to influence France for the next century, leading to the Second Empire and numerous societal and legal changes, all supported by the power of Napoleonic propaganda.

The Revolution in Use Today

When students today consider the Revolution, they generally fixate on the extreme violence of the Terror and see the ideology as a dichotomy of haves versus have-nots in French society. The corrupt aristocrat is juxtaposed with the poor peasant, with rarely a thought for the middle class. This juxtaposition leads to two key representations of the Revolution: downtrodden peasants who will eventually emerge as victors, playing to the popular triumph-of-the-little-guy trope, and identification with a wealthy, almost otherworldly existence associated with the French court before the Revolution. These representations have become such an ingrained part of our cultural history that they are now reflected in merchandising. Many advertised products reference the opulence of court life, even though everyone is aware that this lifestyle is shown just before its spectacular collapse.

Because propaganda serves as a substitute for the actual presence of leaders or ideology, the Revolution was able to insert itself and its beliefs into everyday life through newssheets, libels, and caricatures. Its values became accepted and were applied at all levels of society. As time passed and these representations were widely accepted, popular culture began to use propaganda in the place of historical facts. A product like Marie-Antoinette bath gel, an incongruent item from the perspective of history, in the popular view conveys the message of luxury and decadence for the prospective buyer.

The French Revolution continues to send contradictory messages today, as we are surrounded by references to both sides of the war. In museums, we are presented with exhibits showcasing Marie-Antoinette as a mother figure surrounded by the gentle wealth of the monarchy. But on Halloween we see costumes portraying the queen as a sexy vixen. Recent movies play into this dichotomy by showing the queen's suffering while casting questions on the parentage of her children.

The same ambiguity surrounds Napoleon. He is portrayed as a conquering hero in many textbooks, but we also see him as a bumbling narcissist in popular films. A romanticized figure in most media, he is a ruthless tyrant in Regency novels or a bloodthirsty general in video games. It is not surprising that students often come to class with strong preconceived notions of these historical figures, given the eighteenth- and nineteenth-century propaganda that still informs the images that flow into our modern perception of the past.

It is important for us to allow students to work through the process of identifying and responding to propaganda. Any course dealing with the French Revolution has a plethora of sources for students to analyze. For example, in a discussion of Marie-Antoinette, my students are asked to brainstorm how the queen of France has been represented throughout history. Typically, this knowledge is limited to pop culture references, but as we work through official portraits, political pamphlets, and caricatures, students begin to see very contradictory images of the queen emerge.[1] The same is true for Napoleon; most students know of him only through an occasional painting or a passing reference in a video game. After we work through a series of paintings and some of his letters and political dispatches, like the *Bulletins de l'armée*, the class begins to understand just how savvy the future emperor and empress were in controlling public opinion. To wrap up our understanding of revolutionary propaganda and its influence on society, I ask students to choose a modern image and relate it back to the eighteenth century. Because they actively participate in reading the images and propagandist messages, they become quite involved in the historic and contemporary meanings of those images. This passion facilitates other learning opportunities, including emphasis on historical events, improving lexical knowledge, and using the information as the basis for writing assignments.

The birth of modern propaganda took place as France underwent radical change in the late eighteenth century, a very short period. Darnton notes the rapid shift of public opinion about Marie-Antoinette, from her arrival at court to the monarchy's downfall: "In the first libels, she appeared in the court of Louis XV like a fairy princess in a bawdy tale. . . . In the last, she had become transmogrified into a satanic superwoman, the supreme conspirator and ultimate nemesis of the French Revolution" (*Devil* 421). Abrupt changes in how individuals and policies were perceived were common in the later days of the Revolution. As libels and caricatures helped create a new counterculture, the Revolution was easily able to spread its ideals to the French public, which had become much more united and politically savvy than previous generations. Propaganda was essential to the birth and success of the Revolution as a movement; without their understanding of the importance of controlling public opinion, the revolutionary leaders would never have achieved the wide support needed to establish a new society in France.

Propaganda of the Revolution was successful partly because it was self-perpetuating. Once a critical image became established though publication in the popular press, it often assumed a mythical status that maintained a life of its own, well beyond the intended target audience. We have only to consider David's *La mort de Marat* (1793; "The Death of Marat") or the ongoing characterization of Marie-Antoinette as a frivolous party girl to see that enduring myths from revolutionary propaganda still influence our perceptions of the Revolution more than two hundred years later.

Note

1. An excellent resource for these various images is Hunt.

Works Cited

Anderson, Benedict. *Imagined Communities: Reflections on the Origins and Spread of Nationalism*. Revised ed., Verso, 1983.

Darnton, Robert. *The Devil in the Holy Water; or, The Art of Slander from Louis XIV to Napoleon*. U of Pennsylvania P, 2010.

———. *The Literary Underground of the Old Regime*. Harvard UP, 1982.

Deleuze, Gilles. *Difference and Repetition*. Translated by Paul Patton, Columbia UP, 1994.

Gough, Hugh. *The Newspaper Press in the French Revolution*. Routledge, 1988.

Hanley, Wayne. *The Genesis of Napoleonic Propaganda, 1796–1799*. Columbia UP, 2005.

Huet, Marie-Hélène. *Mourning Glory: The Will of the French Revolution*. U of Pennsylvania P, 1997.

Hunt, Lynn. "The Many Bodies of Marie-Antoinette: Political Pornography and the Problem of the Feminine in the French Revolution." *Marie-Antoinette: Writings on the Body of a Queen*, edited by Dena Goodman, Routledge, 2003, pp. 117–38.

Jaucourt, Louis de. "Peinture." 1751. *Wikisource*, fr.wikisource.org/wiki/L'Encyclopédie/1re_édition/PEINTURE.

Leith, James A. *The Idea of Art as Propaganda in France, 1750–1799: A Study in the History of Ideas.* U of Toronto P, 1965.

Nodier, Charles. *Portraits de la Révolution et de l'empire.* Vol. 1., edited by Jean-Luc Steinmetz, Tallandier, 1988.

Nora, Pierre. *Les lieux de mémoire.* Gallimard, 1997.

Popkin, Jeremy. *Revolutionary News: The Press in France, 1789–1799.* Duke UP, 1990.

"Propaganda." *OED Online*, www.oed.com/view/Entry/152605?rskey=jAjqyY&result=1#eid.

Taithe, Bertrand, and Tim Thornton, editors. *Propaganda: Political Rhetoric and Identity, 1300–2000.* Sutton Publishing, 1999.

Taunay, Nicolas-Antoine. *Trimph of the Guillotine.* 1795. State Hermitage Museum, www.hermitagemuseum.org/wps/portal/hermitage/digital-collection/01.+Paintings/37479.

Taylor, Philip M. *Munitions of the Mind: A History of Propaganda from the Ancient World to the Present Day.* 3rd ed. Manchester UP, 2003.

Vigée Le Brun, Élisabeth Louise. *Marie-Antoinette and Her Children.* 1787. *Google Arts and Culture*, artsandculture.google.com/.

Dominica Chang

French Revolutionary Women: A Century of Media Representation

The prominence of interdisciplinary cultural studies, along with our ever-expanding digital capacities, has resulted in an explosion of exciting and novel ways to imagine, experience, access, and teach great events and the historical figures who participated in them. Thanks moreover to the work of recent scholars of popular political culture, our understanding of the French Revolution has deepened through the recognition and analyses of powerful symbols, cultural practices, and texts as varied as pornographic pamphlets, political caricatures, songs, clothing, accessories, and even cookware.[1] The proliferation during the Revolution of public venues (cafés, reading rooms, town squares) in which to exchange opinions on current events, combined with new liberties of expression and technological advances in printing, allowed for the mass production, circulation, and consumption of ideas on an unprecedented scale.[2] During this tumultuous period, information and power flowed more quickly, more democratically, and often with greater consequences than ever before in France. For all these reasons, the French revolutionary experience should be considered among the first mass-mediatized events, moments of historical acceleration during which competing interests sought to influence public opinion and political outcomes through mediated representations of events, people, and ideas.

In this essay I share primary sources and pedagogical objectives curated and developed over multiple iterations of teaching an advanced undergraduate French-language, literature, and cultural studies course entitled Media and French Revolutions.[3] My interdisciplinary approach privileges engagement with diverse primary source material as the principal means of interpretation and encourages students to think deeply about how mediated representations of events, ideas, and people—especially the representation of women—influence the interpretation and judgment not only of the past but also of our present. Among our guiding questions are, What are the major revolutionary events that took place in France from 1789 to 1880? How were revolutionary events and actors represented? How did these mediated representations shape understanding of these events? What material conditions influenced the production and consumption of these images? How do the media shape understanding of our world today? To what extent does the information disseminated through fictionalized filmic and novelistic accounts influence public opinion and historical memory? What roles do ideology, societal norms, identity affiliation, gender expectations, and censorship play in this process? How might this influence of media be complicated during moments of intensified social or political turmoil? These questions are already familiar and compelling to many of our students in the context of their hypermediatized twenty-first-century lives; consequently, I have found that they often respond with enthusiasm when asked to consider the past through a similar critical perspective.

This essay limits the discussion to a sample of representations of women between 1774 and 1880.[4] During this period, women's participation in the public sphere was often represented in dramatically opposing ways: sometimes as a maternal, courageous force for justice, sometimes as a sexualized, irrational, and violent threat to the existing rational, patriarchal order. The task of selecting representations that are sufficiently diverse is facilitated by the wealth of multimedia primary source material that is now accessible in the public domain: digitized sources such as the Bibliothèque Nationale de France's *Gallica* (the French National Library's electronic catalog, from which facsimiles of original texts may be viewed or downloaded), meticulously curated clearinghouse Web sites such as *Liberty, Equality, Fraternity: Exploring the French Revolution* (a collaboration between the Roy Rosenzweig Center for History and New Media and the American Social History Project, with over six hundred primary source documents), and *The French Revolution Digital Archive* (an online collaboration between the Stanford University Libraries and the Bibliothèque Nationale de France).[5] In my experience, these thought-provoking texts allow students to conceptualize and understand the complicated politics of gender representation and misrepresentation in ways that are new and intellectually stimulating for them.

I begin the course with an introductory unit that has three objectives. First, it is crucial to discuss the basics of media literacy, since these will provide the critical and theoretical framework to be used throughout the term. What do we mean by *media text*? What must we keep in mind when we analyze any given representation? Of course, the level of analytical sophistication will depend on the instructor, but at the very least students should keep in mind essential considerations and questions for each representation they examine—for example, Who produced this text? Who benefits from it? Who is the intended audience? What material conditions facilitate or hinder the production, circulation, and consumption of these images? What are the advantages or disadvantages of this particular form? What are the primary and secondary messages communicated? Which discursive or semiotic strategies are deployed to make the intended messages more convincing? Which points of view are omitted?

Second, a discussion of the emergence of the political public sphere will help students appreciate the magnitude of this sociopolitical transformation, particularly in regard to the unprecedented democratization of ideas that took place before and during the French Revolution. Third, an overview of the major events and actors of the French Revolution provides necessary historical context and offers additional opportunities to practice media literacy skills. Our study of the Revolution is heavily grounded in the examination of, for example, caricatures such as *Ça n'durra pas toujour*, a 1789 print illustrating the gross socioeconomic inequities of the Old Regime, the July 1789 *Révolutions de Paris* newspaper article reporting the fall of the Bastille, officially commissioned portraits of revolutionary leaders, Phrygian caps, tricolor cockades, and popular songs such as "La Carmagnole."[6] As each text is examined, students broaden their knowledge of revolutionary history and iconography almost exclusively through direct contact with primary resources while simultaneously becoming more confident media analysts.

Marie-Antoinette

The resurgence in both scholarly and popular interest in Marie-Antoinette over the past quarter century indicates that she remains an object of fascination. In addition to the recent spate of books, biographies, documentaries, and feature films about her life, a quick *Google* search reminds us that she is one of our most recognizable pop cultural icons. Whether in advertisements or as a Halloween costume, as a kitsch figurine with detachable head, or even as a persona adopted by Madonna, Beyoncé, or a Chanel runway model, her image is one that is immediately associated with excess, decadence, sexuality, heartless indifference toward the suffering of her subjects, and the guillotine.

Because Marie-Antoinette seems so familiar to them, students sometimes feel that there is nothing more that they need to learn about her. This assumption is one of the reasons that her example works so well for a discussion on gender in the media studies classroom. Students are surprised to learn that she almost certainly never uttered the callous words that have come to define her: "Let them eat cake." The more they learn about her, they more they see her as one of the first political casualties of media-fueled negative public opinion. They begin to think more carefully about how widespread condemnation of "the wicked queen"[7] was based on narratives born of misogyny, xenophobia, or the patriarchal impulse to control the bodies, behavior, and authority of women in the public sphere.

Teaching eighteenth-century representations of Marie-Antoinette can be a delicate matter, because many of the portrayals that best serve our objectives rely on pornographic images or descriptions. It is up to the instructor's discretion what is appropriate content for any given classroom, depending on institutional norms and the level of student maturity.[8] Adequate contextualization helps both to justify the inclusion of even the most graphic examples and to inspire mature discussion of them. The books by Dena Goodman and by Chantal Thomas (*Reine*) serve as excellent preparatory reading for students: they present the topic in such a complete and sensitive manner that they could stand alone for instructors or students who prefer to forgo direct engagement with texts deemed unsuitable for particular audiences.[9] Goodman and Thomas also provide a wealth of examples of arresting visual representations of Marie-Antoinette that would be appropriate for any classroom. One effective approach is to ask students to compare early, more positive official portraits of the queen, such as Élisabeth Vigée Le Brun's portrait of her, *Erzherzogin Marie-Antoinette, Könignin von Frankreich*, with the later explosion of more widely circulated and virulently negative caricatures of her as, for example, a monstrous and bloodthirsty harpy. The contrast is striking and strongly suggests a dramatic shift in public opinion and the politics of representation.

For those who choose to incorporate pornographic libel literature into their discussion, *L'Autrichienne en goguettes, ou l'orgie royale* ("The Tipsy Autrichienne; or, The Royal Orgy") is richly representative of the most common and influential tropes used to denigrate Marie-Antoinette specifically (identified in the title through her otherness as "l'Autrichienne" [the word means "Austrian woman" but also plays on *autre* and *chienne*, the French words for "other" and "bitch," respectively]) and to delegitimize or desacralize the monarchy more generally. In this spoof opera, we adopt the subject position of royal guards, witnesses to a drunken orgy involving Marie-Antoinette, the duchess of Polignac, and the count of Artois. The guards suggest that this is a regular occurrence for the trio, and their crude descriptions leave nothing to the imagination. The count of Artois, for example, promises to "be careful" during their sexual escapade lest his "brother [the king] . . . have another son tonight," immediately revealing the illegitimacy of the dauphin.[10] When the tryst is interrupted by the arrival of Louis XVI, Marie-Antoinette speaks to him disdainfully, telling him to drink and not worry about his cabinet meeting the following morning, since his advisers never listen to him anyway. "Your council will do as they please, as usual," she reminds him, an obvious jab at his lack of authority. The king proceeds to drink himself into a stupor while the queen sings, "Let us laugh, let us feast / let us make the most of our power / let's squander the riches / of the good Parisians." When Louis eventually passes out, the aroused threesome cannot resist the temptation to engage in sexual acts on the body of the snoring monarch. It does not matter if he wakes, Marie-Antoinette argues, since she is sure of her ability to manipulate the gullible king into believing whatever she says: "I am certain that if he woke now, I would convince him that he's wrong. It takes so little to persuade him to do what I wish!" It is not difficult for students to recognize the discursive power of a pamphlet like this. In just a few short, simply written, and easily reproducible pages, "The Tipsy Autrichienne" manages to titillate its audience with raunchy language and illicit images, giving imaginative, damning shape to existing rumors of the queen's homosexuality, infidelity, unbridled sexual depravity, contempt for the masses, and clear abuse of power over the king.

One of the most valuable objectives for a media studies approach is to encourage students to apply their new critical perspectives on the past to develop a more sophisticated understanding of how mediated representations function in the present. After discussing eighteenth-century depictions of Marie-Antoinette, students are often keen to discuss filmic versions of her life. There are at least three feature-length adaptations to consider. First, MGM's 1938 lavish production of *Marie-Antoinette* stars Norma Shearer and remains of interest to us today, perhaps not so much for its aesthetic value as for the fact that it is one of the first Anglo-American mass-mediatized representations of the French Revolution and its ill-fated queen.[11] Second, Kirsten Dunst plays the title role in Sofia Coppola's 2006 film *Marie-Antoinette*, a version that is particularly accessible to students because of Coppola's modern visual aesthetic, her casting of young Hollywood A-list actors, and her emphasis on an unmistakably contemporary pop soundtrack. Third, Benoît Jacquot's 2012 *Les adieux à la reine* (*Farewell, My Queen*), based on Chantal Thomas's 2002 novel of the same name, takes a unique approach, not only by allowing the audience to observe the courtly intrigues of Marie-Antoinette (Diane Kruger) through the eyes of her lower-class servant (Léa Seydoux) but also by suggesting that there was a sexual relationship between the queen and the duchess of Polignac. One assignment possibility is to ask students to select at least one of these films and present a written or oral analysis that revisits key media and gender studies concepts and reflects on the role that these modern retellings play in elucidating, distorting, or complicating our current understanding of history.

Beyond Marie-Antoinette: Additional Suggestions

Marie-Antoinette is not the only woman from the revolutionary era of interest to us. Students may be asked to research, present, and analyze representations of other, lesser-known women from the French Revolution. For instance, Charlotte Corday, the young woman who assassinated the Jacobin journalist Jean-Paul Marat, provides a fascinating case study of a revolutionary figure who was represented, depending on the artist or author's position vis-à-vis the Revolution, either as a courageous saint and martyr or as a murderous enemy of the people. Corday also provides a fitting opening for a more formal analysis of Jacques-Louis David's iconic *La mort de Marat* (1793; *The Death of Marat*), one of the Revolution's most famous images.[12]

A powerful myth of the French Revolution is that of the fierce and destructive revolutionary woman. Often represented as a hardened, unattractive wife or mother who is radicalized by the need to feed and protect her family, she is unafraid to risk her life to defend the Revolution through whatever means necessary. Some students will be familiar with the more bloodthirsty version of this trope, the *tricoteuse* ("knitter"), most famously embodied by Charles Dickens's Madame Defarge. I have used the remarkable 1789 illustration *Journées révolutionnaires des 5 et 6 octobre 1789* ("The Revolutionary Days of 5–6 October 1789"), an image that memorializes the women's march on Versailles,[13] to inspire fruitful classroom discussion about the origins and perpetuation of these stereotypes. Students generally agree on the interpretation of discrete symbols in the image (cannon, aged faces, pikes, shovels) but have difficulty determining whether we are meant to admire or fear these women. Of course, the answer is both, and this ambiguity paves the way for a more nuanced conversation about how the same image can be used to glorify or condemn women's participation in the public sphere.[14]

I cannot leave the eighteenth century without our examining the myriad representations of Marianne, the national symbol of the French Republic. She is, in fact, a media symbol par excellence. Instructors might introduce her history in part through secondary material (see Agulhon; Landes, *Visualizing* and *Women*) or more exclusively through presentation of the vast diversity of her incarnations: as painting, caricature, bust, currency, calendar decoration, or even as the lead role in a village play meant to inculcate republican values. Discussion questions here get to the core of media, gender, and cultural studies issues. Why must the first symbol of the Republic be a woman? How did she become known as Marianne? What are the cultural politics and history of a name with such obvious Catholic origins, particularly for a regime that wished to break with the religious past? If she is meant to represent the common people, should she be plain or ravishing? chaste or sexualized? maternal or bellicose?

Marianne, who has represented every French Republic from the 1789 Revolution to this day, is an ideal guide for our media studies journey from the eighteenth through the twenty-first century, as we discuss the 1830, 1832, and 1848 revolutions along the way.[15] We examine how each government refashioned her image according to the values it wished to instill—ask students to compare, for example, Eugène Delacroix's 1830 painting *La Liberté guidant le peuple* ("Liberty Guiding the People") with Daumier's 1848 *La République*—and also speculate on how such symbols contribute to collective national identity or how they might evolve to serve specific political agendas like the "civilizing mission" of colonial expansion.

A striking example of the use of the Marianne image is the 19 November 1911 cover of *Le petit journal* (*France*). After emerging victorious against Germany in a conflict over Moroccan territories, France began to formalize its colonial intentions toward Morocco, ultimately making the country a protectorate in 1912. On this cover, Marianne appears as a radiant, towering figure on the shores of Morocco; she bears a cornucopia overflowing with gold; at her feet, Moroccans bow down to kiss her robes and to marvel at the books she has brought with her. The caption reads "La France va pouvoir porter librement au Maroc la civilisation la richesse et la paix" 'France will be able to bring civilization, wealth, and peace freely to Morocco.' Finally, few topics inspire more animated discussion than debates over the modern-day Marianne. Students are intrigued to learn that modern likenesses are modeled after celebrities such as Brigitte Bardot and Catherine Deneuve, and they express strong opinions about how France, struggling now perhaps more than ever with challenges to its sense of national identity, should embrace a Marianne that more accurately and more inclusively reflects its present multicultural reality.

The Paris Commune of 1871

For nearly a century and a half, scholars of French history have debated the legitimacy as well as the accomplishments and failures of the Paris Commune of 1871, the final major French revolution of the nineteenth century. Was it the realization—if only for nine weeks—of a truly proletarian government working for the interests of the common people? Or, as anti-Commune conservatives maintained, was it merely an outrageous attack on social order, led by a band of drunken insurgents? What is clear and incontestable is that from 28 March to 21 May 1871, the Communards governed themselves, instituting several socialistic reforms: the death penalty was abolished; schools were made free, secular, and obligatory; worker reforms were implemented (e.g., the shortening of the working day and the prohibition of nighttime baking); the separation of church and state was declared; and the previous moratorium on rents was reestablished. Many of these social reforms proved to be short-lived, if successfully implemented at all. In the end, continued internal disputes coupled with the complications of dealing with the immediate threat of attack from antirevolutionary forces were to blame not only for the ineffectuality of the reforms but also for the ultimate defeat of the Commune. On 21 May 1871, the experiment of the Paris Commune came to a violent end as opposition forces succeeded in overtaking several military outposts on the western periphery of the capital. This marked the beginning of the two-month conflict's final *semaine sanglante* ("Bloody Week"), a seven-day battle during which approximately twenty-five thousand real or suspected Communards were killed in battle or summarily executed in the streets of Paris. To gain a sense of the one-sided nature of this final conflict, we need only consider that in comparison with the number of Communards killed, the antirevolutionary army lost fewer than a thousand men (Edwards 346).[16]

Despite the undeniable political importance of the event, as well as the astonishing death toll that occurred in the crushing of this revolution, few students have ever heard of the Paris Commune of 1871. This gap in historical knowledge merits reflection. The surprising dearth of images from 1871 is one of the reasons that the Paris Commune is such an appropriate event to examine toward the end of a course on mediated representations of revolution. It is definitely worthwhile to have students consider how the lack of representation of a particular revolution may be an important factor in why it is unknown to the general public.[17]

Some representations of the 1871 Paris Commune exist. These images are overwhelmingly negative, portraying the Communards as drunken, violent communists who wished only to relive the 1793 Reign of Terror, execute the bourgeoisie, and destroy French society. Arguably the most striking myth to come out of the Commune is that of *pétroleuses*, women Communards who, after campaigning actively for women's rights during the uprising, unleashed their fury during the Bloody Week, setting fire to Paris and destroying everything in their path. Representations of these women are terrifying: although a few are depicted in a threateningly sexualized manner, most resemble hideous old hags, their eyes wild and their hair disheveled.[18] In these virulently misogynistic images, there is often a powerful intensification and intermingling of tropes encountered all throughout the term—another reason why the *pétroleuses* make good objects of study at the end of the course.

For example, one caricature from 1880 combines every imaginable revolutionary horror in order to criticize the Third Republic for its selection of 14 July, the anniversary of the storming of the Bastille, as France's national holiday. In the *Royalist and Catholic Poster Rejecting the Celebration of the Quatorze Juillet*, we see a crazed medusa stomping on a crucifix. She wears a torn red dress decorated with skulls; in one hand she wields a dagger, in the other a fiery torch. Behind her, Paris burns while the guillotine stands at the ready. This image suggests that because these women revolutionaries so gravely threatened everything that bourgeois society held dear, the use of state violence against the Communards in 1871 was justified.

Could positive and negative representations have influenced how history has remembered or forgotten French revolutionary women throughout the eighteenth and nineteenth centuries? And today, even during less politically tumultuous times, how are women represented who behave in any way outside traditional gender expectations? How do these representations affect how we judge all women (or any marginalized group, for that matter), how we view their worth, or how we protect their rights? I remain optimistic that helping students make better sense of the media images that surround them will increase their ability to respond intelligently and humanely to the revolutions—both large and small—in their own lives.

Notes

1. In my own work on this topic, and for my thoughts putting together this course, I am especially indebted to the work of Lynn Hunt, Joan Landes (*Visualizing* and *Women*), and Laura Mason ("Adieux," *Singing*, and "We're Just Little People").

2. On the emergence of the public sphere in eighteenth-century Europe, see Habermas.

3. Although I have taught this course only in French, it could be taught in English with no change to the pedagogical suggestions given in this essay.

4. In 1774, Marie-Antoinette became queen of France. In 1880, exiled Paris Communards were amnestied and allowed to return to France. Both these events delineate a period of remarkably rich representations of women who participated in the revolutionary public sphere.

5. All cited images and texts are available in the public domain. The most complete list of sources that I am aware of can be found on the H-Net Web site (h-france.net/professionalresources.html). To this list I would add the online collections of the Musée Carnavalet in Paris (www.carnavalet.paris.fr) and the Musée de la Révolution Française in Vizille (www.domaine-vizille.fr).

6. Online versions of song performances are readily available. The *Liberty, Equality, and Fraternity* Web site provides an English translation and an audio file (chnm.gmu.edu/revolution/d/624).

7. A translation of the French "la reine scélérate."

8. The instructor must decide what to do if a student requests to be excused from exposure to such texts. In over a decade of teaching the course, I had one student who did not wish to engage with this material.

9. I would recommend, in particular, Goodman's edited volume *Marie-Antoinette: Writings on the Body of a Queen*, which includes the Thomas essay that I assign in my classes: "The Heroine of the Crime."

10. All translations mine unless otherwise indicated.

11. For more on these filmic versions of Marie-Antoinette's life, see Mason, "'We're Just Little People'" and "Adieux"; Milam.

12. For more on Charlotte Corday and *The Death of Marat*, I recommend Mazeau.

13. Several versions of this image—many of them very similar to each other—on the Internet. Those of the best quality come from the Bibliothèque Nationale de France.

14. For many more examples of representations of women during the French Revolution, see Godineau; Landes, *Visualizing* and *Women*; and Levy et al.

15. In this essay, and in my class, I focus on representations from the French Revolution of 1789 and the Paris Commune of 1871, partly because of space limitation and partly because primary sources for these eighteenth and nineteenth-century revolutions are much more accessible than for the revolutions of 1830 or 1848.

16. Edwards's *The Paris Commune, 1871* remains an excellent account of the event.

17. On the lack of representation of the Paris Commune of 1871, not only in America but also in France, see Lidsky; Boime.

18. For excellent discussions of women's participation in the Paris Commune and of the myth of the *pétroleuse*, see Gullickson; Eichner.

Works Cited

Agulhon, Maurice. *Marianne au combat: L'imagerie et la symbolique républicaines de 1789 à 1880*. Flammarion, 1979.

L'Autrichienne en goguettes, ou l'orgie royale. 1789. *Gallica*, gallica.bnf.fr/ark:/12148/bpt6k42704k.texteImage.

Boime, Albert. *Art and the Paris Commune: Imagining Paris after War and Revolution*. Princeton UP, 1997.

Edwards, Stewart. *The Paris Commune, 1871*. Quadrangle Books, 1971.

Eichner, Carolyn J. *Surmounting the Barricades: Women in the Paris Commune*. Indiana UP, 2004.

La France va pouvoir porter librement au Maroc la civilisation la richesse et la paix. 1911. *Gallica*, llica.bnf.fr/ark:/12148/bpt6k7169830.image.

Godineau, Dominique. *The Women of Paris and Their French Revolution*. U of California P, 1988.

Goodman, Dena, editor. *Marie-Antoinette: Writings on the Body of a Queen*. Routledge, 2003.

Gullickson, Gay L. *Unruly Women of Paris: Images of the Commune*. Cornell UP, 1996.

Habermas, Jürgen. *The Structural Transformation of the Public Sphere: An Inquiry into a Category of Bourgeois Society*. MIT P, 1989.

Hunt, Lynn. *Politics, Culture, and Class in the French Revolution*. U of California P, 1984.
Landes, Joan B. *Visualizing the Nation: Gender, Representation, and Revolution in Eighteenth-Century France*. Cornell UP, 2001.
———. *Women and the Public Sphere in the Age of the French Revolution*. Cornell UP, 1988.
Levy, Darline Gay, et al., editors. *Women in Revolutionary Paris, 1789–1795: Selected Documents, Translated with Notes and Commentary*. U of Illinois P, 1979.
Lidsky, Paul. *Les écrivains contre la Commune*. La Découverte, 2010.
Mason, Laura. "Les adieux à la reine / Farewell, My Queen." *Fiction and Film for French Historians*, h-france.net/fffh/the-buzz/les-adieux-a-la-reine-farewell-my-queen/.
———. *Singing the French Revolution: Popular Culture and Politics, 1787–1799*. Cornell UP, 1996.
———. "'We're Just Little People, Louis': Marie-Antoinette on Film." Goodman, pp. 239–52.
Mazeau, Guillaume. *Corday contre Marat: Deux siècles d'images*. Éditions Artlys, 2009.
Milam, Jennifer. "Imagining Marie-Antoinette: Cultural Memory, Coolness, and the Deconstruction of History in Cinema." *H-France*, www.h-france.net/rude/rudevoliv/MilamVol4.pdf.
Royalist and Catholic Poster Rejecting the Celebration of the Quatorze Juillet. 1880. *Bridgeman Images*, www.bridgemanimages.com.
Thomas, Chantal. "The Heroine of the Crime: Marie-Antoinette in Pamphlets." Goodman, pp. 99–116.
———. *La reine scélérate: Marie-Antoinette dans les pamphlets*. Le Seuil, 1989.

Artworks Referred to in Essay

Ça n'durra pas toujour. 1789. Collection de la Bibliothèque Nationale de France, Paris.
Daumier, Honoré. *La République*. 1848. Musée d'Orsay, Paris.
Delacroix, Eugène. *La Liberté guidant le peuple* ("Liberty Guiding the People"). 1830. Musée du Louvre, Paris.
La France va pouvoir porter librement au Maroc la civilisation, la richesse et la paix. Le Petit journal, 1911, Collection de la Bibliothèque Nationale de France, Paris.
Journées révolutionnaires des 5 et 6 octobre 1789. Collection de la Bibliothèque Nationale de France, Paris.
Vigée Le Brun, Élisabeth. *Erzherzogin Marie-Antoinette, Königin von Frankreich*. 1778. Kunsthistorisches Museum, Vienna.

Katherine Astbury

Engaging Students in Research: Stop-Motion Videos, Strip Cartoons, and the Waddesdon Manor Collection of Prints

One of the enduring difficulties in widening access to primary material of the French Revolution is the language barrier. For those without French, the choice has traditionally been somewhat limited, but the online collection of prints from Waddesdon Manor, an English stately home, has radically changed how the French Revolution can be taught, both to undergraduates and to primary- and secondary-school students. As Jack Censer and Lynn Hunt remind us in the seminal online discussion *Imaging the French Revolution*, "[H]istorians now treat images seriously as sources in their own right. . . . Things could be 'said' in the visual media that could not be expressed verbally" ("Picturing"). This essay outlines how caricatures from the revolutionary decade can be used to investigate the ambiguities of the Revolution, to grapple with issues of as much relevance today as then, such as equality, intolerance, and democracy, and even be put to creative use as the starting point for the students' own engagement with the Revolution through modern media.

Waddesdon Manor, built by Baron Ferdinand de Rothschild in the nineteenth century, houses a glittering collection of eighteenth-century art. Rothschild belonged to the Austrian branch of the famous Jewish banking family, but his mother was from the English branch. He was born in Paris and grew up in Frankfurt and Vienna before moving to Britain after his mother's death. Widowed when his wife and son died in childbirth, he poured his energies into collecting. In 1874 he inherited his father's wealth and spent millions recreating a French Renaissance château in the English countryside and filling it primarily with French furniture and porcelain, which were shown off at weekend house parties. He also became a member of Parliament for the Liberal party (and spoke in the houses of Parliament about the French Revolution [Hall 153]),[1] was a trustee of the British Museum, and an accomplished writer. He even tried his hand at lecturing—delivering talks on historical topics to the locals of Waddesdon, which were subsequently published as *Village Lectures*.

In 1889, around the time of the centenary of the French Revolution, Rothschild acquired a large collection of revolutionary prints and ephemera (passports, membership cards, assignats, entrance tickets), which were bound together in four large volumes as *Tableaux de la Révolution française* ("Tableaux of the French Revolution"). Some of them came from the French architect and collector Gabriel-Hippolyte Destailleur (1822–1893), who designed Waddesdon Manor. They were bound probably by Rothschild's Parisian book dealer, Damascène Morgand (active 1875–1912), since the volumes used French eighteenth-century boards and gold tooling.[2] The prints are loosely grouped together thematically and chronologically—for instance, many depict the royal family and are ordered from prerevolutionary official portraits to the satirical caricatures of the revolutionary decade. The large number of colored prints suggests that they were collected as much for their beauty as for their historical significance.

Rothschild was fascinated by the Revolution and critical of the Old Regime. Broadly speaking, he can be seen as someone who supported what we would now consider to be the principles of 1789 but who recoiled from the radicalization of the Terror. In a volume entitled *Personal Characteristics from French History* (1896), he outlined the key events of the Revolution and provided anecdotes about and character sketches of some of the protagonists. His view is clear: "It may be asked whether the condition of France and the temper of her people did not make the Revolution unavoidable at the time it occurred. . . . The Revolution apparently brought to the people of France the realisation of their most ardent dreams and desires." He repeatedly condoned the violence of the Revolution, even of the most ardent Jacobins, "for the benefits it brought to the French nation" (186). The royal family were prominent in his assessment of the Revolution, and he carefully weighed the political careers of Louis XVI and Marie-Antoinette as well as those of the revolutionaries who opposed them. He concluded, for instance, that Louis XVI's "private character is worthy of unstinted admiration" (155) and that there were two Marie-Antoinettes: "There was the Marie-Antoinette of the early and palmy days, who . . . flirted and gambled. . . . Then there was the Marie-Antoinette of later years, the devoted mother and consort" (161–62).

In his account of the Revolution, Rothschild included a number of women, including Madame de Fontenay, whose role in inspiring Jean-Lambert Tallien to effect the Thermidorian plot is described in detail. Just as he liked to have paintings of dazzling women on the walls of Waddesdon Manor, his writings on history also make space for renowned beauty. Although not every anecdote on the Revolution included in his *Personal Characteristics from French History* has a corresponding print in the four volumes of the *Tableaux*, the way in which the prints were bound and Rothschild's retelling of the Revolution are similar, and it is not hard to imagine him leafing through the *Tableaux* when writing the *Personal Characteristics*. In his collecting memoir, "Bric-a-Brac," he wrote, "Old works of art are not . . . desirable only for their rarity or beauty, but for their associations, for the memories they evoke, the trains of thought to which they lead, and the many ways they stimulate the imagination and realise our ideals."

As a historian Rothschild was attracted to works of art that gave access to the lived experience of the past, and the prints encompass different perspectives on the events of the Revolution. As he wrote in "Bric-a-Brac," "Art is a small factor in history, perhaps only an incident in it, yet it follows history in all its stages." Although many of the prints are prorevolutionary in general terms, critical views are also present, and a good number of the prints are overtly counterrevolutionary. There is therefore some tension between Rothschild's personal political standpoint and the rhetoric espoused by some of the prints.

The four volumes of Rothschild's prints and ephemera have been digitized and made freely available online as the result of collaboration between Waddesdon Manor and two British universities, the University of Warwick and Queen Mary, University of London. The project was funded by the United Kingdom's Arts and Humanities Research Council through a collaborative doctoral award scheme that provides money for projects between higher education institutions and non–higher education partners. Two PhD students, one at each institution, were given the task of cataloging the prints in the four volumes alongside the writing of doctoral theses on the collection.[3] Rothschild, who was aware of the ironies of being a wealthy collector keeping material of historical significance for personal pleasure, would undoubtedly have approved of the project. In "Bric-a-Brac" he wrote that "it should be a source of gratification to the public that most fine works of art drift slowly but surely into museums and public galleries. In private hands they can afford delight only to a small number of persons." Digitization, of course, widens access still further than can a museum or gallery. The prints, taken from their private collection, are no longer rare objects to show to visitors to Waddesdon. The context of origin that Susan Stewart sees as destroyed by the nature of a collection is, if not restored by digitization, now less removed, because we as Web users can decide which prints to look at and in which order (164).

The prints and ephemera, now publically available for the first time, are ideal for use as source material for those teaching the French Revolution, especially because translations into English are provided alongside a transcription of any French text found on the objects, thereby resolving one of the traditional difficulties of using online reproductions of revolutionary prints (see Censer and Hunt, "Introduction"). The advantage of using the Waddesdon material in teaching is twofold: the visual images produce a striking and immediate effect on an audience, and the translations given alongside the French texts ensure that there is no language barrier to engaging with the material. The collection is rich in its range of revolutionary themes covered—1789, the principles put forth during the early phase of the Revolution, and the increasingly hostile depiction of the monarchy are particularly well represented (though it should be noted that Rothschild's sympathy for Marie-Antoinette means that none of the pornographic images of the queen were purchased, so the collection is suitable for use with students of all ages). Fifty-four of the prints have detailed written commentaries (produced by the two PhD students) in addition to a brief physical description; these provide contextual information about individuals, events, and symbolism, helping those with a limited knowledge of the period to make sense of the prints.

The dramatic increase in the number of revolutionary prints online through *Gallica* (gallica.bnf.fr/), *Waddesdon* (www.waddesdon.org.uk/collection/special-projects/french-revolution), the *French Revolution Digital Archive* (frda.stanford.edu/en/images), and other sites means that an unprecedented range of primary material is now available not just for research but also for teaching purposes. As Censer and Hunt remind us, prints are now included "more systematically in interpretations and explanations of the French Revolution" by historians ("Picturing"). But because the prints "offer a different perspective on historical knowledge" (Cameron), they are also ideal teaching tools. They do far more than enliven lecture *PowerPoint* or *Prezi* presentations; they can serve to explore fundamental historical issues relating to reliability of sources and allow the students to pursue themed research of their own choosing. Using searches of the Waddesdon material by keyword, event, theme, or person (waddesdon.org.uk/the-collection/advanced-search/?collection=28), students can select their material for analysis and extend their engagement with primary sources well beyond the traditional handful of revolutionary prints available before the advent of mass digitization projects. The sheer variety of prints also means that they can be used for a wide range of audiences. Some images are relatively simple (a female sansculotte brandishing a sword [Waddesdon accession number 4232.2.43.74] is decipherable even without much knowledge of the Revolution); others require detailed examination and contextualization (many of the prints need to be accompanied by a key to the people alluded to).

My approach to using the prints is underpinned by the pioneering work of the *Imaging the French Revolution* project (chnm.gmu.edu/revolution/imaging/home.html), which provides a framework for using prints for historical purposes and reflects on their limitations. Censer and Hunt talk of how images can allow readers "to enter into the debate, rather than watching specialists from the sidelines" ("Introduction"), and my experience of using the prints with students of a variety of ages bears this out. Many of the secondary-school students I have worked with have strong visual literacy but are less enthusiastic engagers with written texts; images have an immediacy that allows everyone in the class to become involved in the process of interpretation.

One of the first things any group of students has to do is learn how to read a print. I demonstrate the process with an iconic and often reproduced image of the Revolution, a print from 1791 showing Louis XVI and Marie-Antoinette as a two-headed monster, entitled "Les deux n'ont font qu'un" 'The Two Make But One' (4232.1.13.26). We work our way clockwise around the print, describing what we can see, including any objects that might have a representative focus, and thinking about the print's title and message. The students then work in groups to put this process into practice for themselves with two or three more prints, describing what they see, guessing which events are referred to, looking for allegory or allusion, and finally making their interpretation.[4]

The richness of collections like the Waddesdon material means that many different themed workshops and study days can be created.[5] For students interested in a career in law, I focus on the imagery of the Declaration of the Rights of Man and of the Citizen and use prints connected to the notion of citizenship. For politics students, the focus might be revolutionary symbolism and how it can be traced through to the present day. The burkini ban on French beaches during the summer of 2016, for instance, prompted a series of cartoons on social media exploring how clothing is linked to republican ideals, and the Waddesdon prints permit fruitful comparisons with the imposition—or banning—of certain items of clothing in the 1790s. For English literature students studying Jane Austen's novels, I used revolutionary prints that allowed us to discuss the representation of women in France in the 1790s as a point of comparison and contrast with the situation in Britain at the time. For younger students to whom the Revolution is entirely new, it is easier to focus on the principles of 1789, the attempt to make France a fairer place, and the storming of the Bastille. Three-estate prints work particularly well here. With a print such as "Cette fois-ci, la justice est du côté du plus fort" 'This Time Justice Is on the Side of the Strongest,' which shows the three estates and Justice on a seesaw, with Justice and the member of the third estate low on one side of the seesaw and the nobleman and clergyman, representing the first two orders, high (4232.1.79.162), the interpretation is unambiguous even to quite young students. A print such as the one commonly known by a title absent from the Waddesdon copy, "Palsangué Messieurs v'la le coup" 'Uds-Bud, Sirs, See How It's Cast,' where the three estates are playing dice on a drum decorated with the royal coat of arms, opens up greater scope for discussion (4232.1.25.50). The member of the third estate may have just thrown a winning dice score, but inherent in the nature of dice throwing is that next time the dice may fall differently. The print's suggestion that the reunion of the three estates may not last contrasts with the messages of more celebratory prints.

For undergraduates taking courses on French literature and culture who spend a whole term looking at the Revolution, the focus can be multiple: we might use silhouette prints dating from after the executions of the king and queen to look at the notion of trauma in the Revolution,[6] or we might focus on the changing representation of the monarchy, comparing written pamphlet material with the images. The students are often more creative than I am and use the full range of prints as source material on a wide variety of essay topics. Although the prints pepper my *PowerPoint* slides and student essays, they do not serve just as illustrations. We spend one of the ten weeks focusing on them explicitly as source material, as cultural artifacts, evidence of how people responded to and felt about the Revolution. The advantage of working with students who have a good grounding in the events of the Revolution and its key issues is that more complex prints can be explored and a much more nuanced discussion about the target audience can be had. The students are encouraged to see prints as having multiple layers, as being "ambiguous, interactive and complex creations that can teach us much about the cultural production of the French Revolution" (Trévien, *Satire* 2).

Often the layers are created through literary or theatrical intertextuality. The references might be to classical sources (e.g., Marie-Antoinette with snakes for hair in the two-headed monster print mentioned above); to well-known texts, such as La Fontaine's fables;[7] or to more recent works, as in the gloriously hand-painted "La mort du patriote Marat" 'The Death of Patriot Marat,' where the moment in which Charlotte Corday stabs Marat in his bath is accompanied by a song set to an air made a hit by Beaumarchais's *Marriage of Figaro*, "Cœurs sensibles, cœurs fidèles" 'Sensitive hearts, faithful hearts' (4232.2.41.71).[8] Cultural references such as these show that printmakers were combining visual elements that anyone could understand with elements that required a certain level of education to be understood—allegories derived from classical sources, textual references. Above all, the allusions to literary or theatrical texts destabilize the interpretation of the prints, which is largely what makes them such interesting teaching tools. One of the most visually striking prints in the Waddesdon collection, "Marche du Dom Quichotte moderne" 'The March of the Modern Don Quixote' (4232.2.13.23), shows the prince of Condé as Don Quixote, leading counterrevolutionaries to defend the crown. That it is an impressive 459 x 580mm in size indicates that it was not produced for the cheaper end of the market, and the familiarity it assumes that people have with Cervantes's novel confirms that this is a print aimed at the educated. Tracing in more detail literary and theatrical references, as well as cross-references to English prints of the same period, would allow us intriguing angles on a decades-old debate on high culture versus lowbrow material.[9] Prints complicate this apparent dichotomy but enable us to better understand notions of shared culture during the revolutionary decade.

The caricatures and satirical cartoons of the revolutionary decade can be used in the classroom to great effect, but the ease with which they can be accessed online makes it possible for students to develop their own research projects. Armed with an overview of the Revolution and a session on how to come up with and refine a research question on a topic of interest, they can work alone or in groups over a period of weeks. This research can work at any level and for any age.

In 2013 and 2014, primary- and secondary-school children from local schools came to the University of Warwick to learn about the French Revolution. They then engaged in follow-up activities in their schools and at home to produce their own independent research project, which they presented in front of their parents back at the university at the end of the school year. Some were asked to run sessions to share what they had learned. This program was an effective way of raising their aspirations, because they were not just coming to campus for a day of activities but were also continuing to reflect on what they had learned and communicating it to their peers.

To date, dozens of research projects have been created based on the Waddesdon material. The projects have varied considerably, and this variety reflects the richness of the source material. The effort that the students put into their work indicates a high level of enthusiasm for a topic that was entirely new to them—and outside the school curriculum—but that had inspired them to find out more. How the monarchy is increasingly portrayed as monstrous and an object of ridicule intrigues British students particularly—which is ironic, given Rothschild's sympathies for the royal family. Representations of violence and the principles of 1789 have consistently attracted interest too.

The younger students were the most creative, though their projects often required considerable attention from their teachers. Some of the most effective projects transposed the prints to modern media. Students produced mock newspaper front pages (suitably stained with tea for an authentic old look) about the downfall of the monarchy; they made story boards on the role of the queen, using some of the Waddesdon images as inspiration and with visual echoes of the prints in their work. Groups created stop-motion animations of the fall of the Bastille (*Stop Motion*), and they dramatized in a puppet theater the start of the Revolution.

This essay has outlined how revolutionary prints have been used as source material not only by instructors but also by students. Prints make the Revolution accessible in a way in which text does not. Because many of the prints are satirical, they can be used to explore issues surrounding bias; because they are representations of events, they can be used to help us consider questions of authenticity. Revolutionary symbolism continues to be found in modern political cartoons and official campaigns (De Gaulle's call to vote yes in the 1958 referendum is a classic example: www.lelivrescolaire.fr/#!manuel/62/histoire-geographie-education-civique-3e/chapitre/804/de-gaulle-et-le-nouveau-systeme-republicain-1958-1969/page/694175/la-presidence-de-charles-de-gaulle-fondateur-de-la-ve-republique/lecon/document/716020). The Phrygian cap, the tricolor cockade, and the guillotine are frequent accoutrements, but sometimes a print from the revolutionary decade can be more explicit. In 2014, the news magazine *Marianne* updated the iconic image of the third estate weighed down by the nobility and clergy, in an issue devoted to twenty-first-century lists of grievances: a French worker struggling under the weight of the president and prime minister ("Cahiers"). A print can be used in the classroom to improve visual literacy, support historical analysis and interpretation, and encourage students to see that studying languages is not just about grammar but also about understanding the culture, history, and politics of the foreign country. Visual material from Waddesdon Manor's online collection of revolutionary prints brings the Revolution and some of its underpinning principles and issues to life in creative, thought-provoking ways. The only limit on the uses to which the prints can be put is the imagination of those responding to them. *Aux crayons, citoyens!*

Notes

1. Commons Sitting of 28 May 1889, *Nineteenth-Century House of Commons Hansard Sessional Papers*, third series, vol. 336. I am grateful to Phillippa Plock for the reference.

2. For more on Rothschild's collections of ephemera, see Plock.

3. The thesis of Claire Trévien (of Warwick) was "Revolutionary Prints as Spectacle"; the thesis of Paul Davidson (of Queen Mary) was "Capturing the Whirlwind: Paris Depicted through the Medium of Revolutionary Prints." A revised version of Trévien's thesis was published as *Satire, Prints and Theatricality in the French Revolution.*

4. Todd Finley in his article on visual literacy strategies has excellent advice on teaching activities to encourage pupils to observe and assess images.

5. A teaching pack of resources and exercises designed for post-16 students by Andy Holland, an experienced teacher, in conjunction with the author, is available at www2.warwick.ac.uk/fac/arts/modernlanguages/research/french/previousprojects/revolutionaryprints/teaching/.

6. Pupils respond enthusiastically to the puzzle prints that hide the faces of the royal family. Waddesdon has three: a German print of the guillotine (4232.2.35.60), a print of Humanity weeping at the sansculottes' crimes (4232.2.32.54), and a tobacco box lid print of assignats (4232.2.33.55).

7. An example is "Louis as Gluttonous Pig" (4232.1.14.29).

8. For more on the Marat print and examples of others that draw on plays of the period, see Trévien, "Revolutionary Prints."

9. For more on the highbrow/lowbrow debate, see Levine.

Works Cited

"Les cahiers de doléances des Français." *Marianne*, 28 Aug. 2014, www.marianne.net/politique/les-cahiers-de-doleances-des-francais.

Cameron, Vivian P. "Reflections on Violence and the Crowd in the Images of the French Revolution." *Imaging the French Revolution*, chnm.gmu.edu/revolution/imaging/essays/cameron1.html.

Censer, Jack, and Lynn Hunt. "Introduction: Imaging the French Revolution: Depictions of the Revolutionary Crowd." *Imaging the French Revolution*, chnm.gmu.edu/revolution/imaging/essays/introessay.html.

———. "Picturing Violence: Limitations of the Medium and the Makers." *Imaging the French Revolution*, chnm.gmu.edu/revolution/imaging/essays/censerhunt4.html.

Davidson, P. S. "Capturing the Whirlwind: Paris Depicted through the Medium of Revolutionary Prints." U of London, 2013. Doctoral dissertation.

Finley, Todd. "Common Core in Action: Ten Visual Literacy Strategies." *Edutopia*, 19 Feb. 2014, www.edutopia.org/blog/ccia-10-visual-literacy-strategies-todd-finley.

Hall, Michael. *Waddesdon Manor: The Heritage of a Rothschild House*. Revised ed., Scala Publishers, 2009.

Levine, Lawrence W. *Highbrow/Lowbrow: The Emergence of Cultural Hierarchy in America*. Harvard UP, 1990.

Plock, Phillippa. ""Le comble de la folie": Ferdinand de Rothschild, collectionneur de cartes-adresses." *Le vieux papier*, vol. 38, Oct. 2009, pp. 529–37.

Rothschild, Ferdinand de. "Bric-a-Brac: A Rothschild's Memoir of Collecting." *The Free Library*, www.thefreelibrary.com/Bric-a-Brac%3A+a+Rothchild's+memoir+of+collecting%3A+in+1897+the+creator...-a0166750878.

———. *Personal Characteristics from French History*. MacMillan, 1896.

Stewart, Susan. *On Longing: Narratives of the Miniature, the Gigantic, the Souvenir, the Collection*. Johns Hopkins UP, 1984.

Stop Motion. Video for All, videoforall.eu/34-stop-motion/.

Trévien, Claire. "Revolutionary Prints as Spectacle." U of Warwick, 2012. Doctoral dissertation.

———. *Satire, Prints and Theatricality in the French Revolution*. Voltaire Foundation, 2016. Oxford University Studies in the Enlightenment 10.

Part V

Global Reverberations

J. B. Mertz

Teaching the Revolution Debate: Edmund Burke, His Radical Respondents, and William Blake

The British response to the French Revolution has been of continuing interest in literary scholarship. Because the French Revolution was a national conflict with significance for foreign observers (particularly in Britain, with its lively culture of radicalism), it provoked a substantial body of English-language commentary, beginning in 1789 with Richard Price's *Discourse on the Love of Our Country*. In what was perhaps the first global reverberation of the fall of France's Old Regime, British authors engaged in a spoken and written debate concerning—to name only a few themes—their own history, the origin and nature of their monarchy, the constitution, and the rights of man and woman, in many cases responding to arguments in Edmund Burke's *Reflections on the Revolution in France* (1790).[1] The Revolution Debate ultimately comprised hundreds of different titles (Pendleton 65–66) and concluded late in 1795, when the administration of William Pitt halted the progress of radicalism with the Treason Act and Seditious Meetings Act (Butler 1, 3; Claeys 1: xviii, xlvi–xlvii). Amid the welter of conflicting accounts of events in France produced by British authors and journalists during the 1790s, the modern reader will recognize analogies to present-day news reporting, propaganda and misinformation,[2] and the contest to fix meanings on a rapidly evolving political situation.

Over the past several decades, editors have produced excerpted collections of works from the Revolution Debate, showing a perennial interest in making this complex body of material relevant and accessible to students: Alfred Cobban's *The Debate on the French Revolution, 1789–1800*, Marilyn Butler's *Burke, Paine, Godwin, and the Revolution Controversy*, and Jon Mee and David Fallon's *Romanticism and Revolution: A Reader* are three notable examples. Because of its importance for an understanding of British Romantic writing, the Revolution Debate is commonly taught in the early weeks of university literature courses, but students first encountering it can be daunted by the volume of material, the different genres and media used by its participants, the number of different voices, and conflicting representations of the Revolution. Editors also face challenges in balancing considerations of space with selecting the most important and representative texts from the debate. In this regard, the *Norton Anthology of English Literature* I used for a survey course (9th ed., 2012) contains a twenty-five-page section titled "The Revolution Controversy and the Spirit of the Age," but the selections are too slender to give students anything more than a basic familiarity with the debate. I understand that nothing more than basic familiarity may be the goal of a literature survey course, but the Revolution Debate invites substantial investigation and comprises more than enough material to build a full-semester graduate or upper-division undergraduate course. For example, during the fourteen-month period between 1 November 1790 (when Burke's *Reflections* was published) and the end of 1791, British authors published over forty responses to Burke (Tyson 122; Pendleton 79–103). As Butler observes in the introduction to her collection, the Revolution Debate "represents in its totality not discrete texts . . . but a single series of works which depend for their meaning upon one another, [and] upon the historical situation which gave them birth" (2).

Design

If you are planning a course on the Revolution Debate, giving your students a comprehensive overview of the core texts should be the first objective. In a typical sixteen-week term that includes a week of holiday, the first reading assignments should be the excellent introductory essays in Butler's collection and Mee and Fallon's reader, followed by lecture and class discussion during weeks 1–5 of Price's *Discourse*, Burke's *Reflections*, Mary Wollstonecraft's *A Vindication of the Rights of Men*, Thomas Paine's

Rights of Man, Wollstonecraft's *A Vindication of the Rights of Woman*, Paine's *Rights of Man* (part 2), and William Godwin's *An Enquiry concerning Political Justice.* Given time constraints and the lengths of most of the core texts, I recommend taking all readings from *Romanticism and Revolution*, which provides key selections with annotation and some helpful cross-references. If class size and the frequency of meetings allow, it may be useful to have one or two students present introductions to the daily readings (or aspects of them), so that every student is responsible for at least one presentation. I also recommend that the students work together in building their own list of key terms from the core texts, with basic descriptions for each term, including the author, the work in which it appears, year of publication, connotations of the term, and political orientation of the author or his or her argument. During each class, time should be taken to discuss whether new readings contain terms that need to be added to this list and also to note how writers and speakers sometimes use the same term to mean opposite things. At the end of the fifth week, I would administer a written, in-class examination that helps consolidate the students' understanding of the chronology of the core texts, their major themes, important historical background, and the dialogic nature of the Revolution Debate.

You might utilize, in addition to the prose of the 1790s, the products of contemporary visual culture, such as the political caricatures and graphic satire of James Gillray, Thomas Rowlandson, and Isaac Cruikshank, which provide variety in instructional media and additional historical context.[3] To give students some relief after the examination, use the sixth week to study contemporary visual culture. An outside lecturer from a department in one's institution or from a local museum may save you the effort of developing this module. A lecturer with expertise in eighteenth-century prints and caricatures can help students build on their understanding of the language of the Revolution Debate, see analogies between the core texts and visual culture (especially if caricatures of Price, Burke, Paine, Joseph Priestley, John Bull, and others are used to put faces to names), and navigate both printed and digital sources, such as M. Dorothy George's *Catalogue of Political and Personal Satires* and the British Museum online catalog. This week's work will also be useful if you wish students to incorporate contemporary visual material into their final essays.

In the seventh week, students begin to take a larger view of the Revolution Debate. The assigned reading of the introduction to Gregory Claeys's *Political Writings of the 1790s* and Gayle Trusdel Pendleton's "Towards a

Bibliography of the *Reflections* and *Rights of Man* Controversy," with lecture and class discussion, should show students how the Revolution Debate unfolds in its various phases. Some authors still grapple with themes first raised by Price, Burke, Wollstonecraft, and Paine, but new topics arise, and the tone of the debate changes under pressure from the government response to radical writing and events such as Britain's declaration of war against France in February 1793. In the eighth week, assign selections of readings from 1793 and onward, including Hannah More's *Village Politics*, Daniel Isaac Eaton's *Politics for the People*, and Wordsworth's "Letter to the Bishop of Llandaff." Have your institution's library make available for students Claeys's eight-volume collection, which brings together 128 titles and focuses on the years 1791–95. This collection, although it is minimally annotated and does not include substantial cross-references, can give students a sense of the breadth and variety of works that make up the Revolution Debate. At this point, I direct students' attention also to the effects of the Revolution Debate on other genres, such as fiction, in the event that any student shows interest in writing his or her final essay on a novel.[4]

In the ninth week, I interrupt lecture and discussion of later phases of the Revolution Debate to meet with a reference librarian, who can introduce students to some of the tools provided by digital humanities, such as *Eighteenth-Century Collections Online* (*ECCO* and *ECCO II*) and the *Oxford Text Archive* (*OTA*), which facilitate the study of how key words and phrases travel through the writings of the 1790s and provide students with a means of tracking and comparing uses of specific language. As professors of literature, we look for ways to teach careful reading, and studying the migration of key words and phrases of the Revolution Debate is an excellent exercise for demonstrating that words like *liberty*, *nature*, and *rights* are not transparent and unambiguous, whether for writers in the 1790s or today. Loyalists and radicals often use the same language to formulate their rival interpretations of the same concepts. A good assignment for the end of the ninth week is to provide students with a list of key terms to search on *ECCO* with prompts for a short essay comparing how at least two authors attempt to inscribe conflicting meanings on a single term. To take one example, the words *nature*, *natural*, *naturally*, and *unnatural* together appear more than 150 times in *Reflections*, prompting many of Burke's respondents to either deploy or interrogate the idea of nature. For the careful reader of the Revolution Debate, several other themes and tropes present themselves as options for investigation: there are Burke's "swinish multitude" (79) and gleeful uses by radical and plebeian authors of porcine metaphors, liberty trees, light and illumination, usurpers and usurpation, the Bastille, monsters and monstrosity,[5] cannibalism, the sublime, allusions to the Bible, and theatrical imagery. Again, looking forward to the final essay, this exercise will help students navigate multiple texts and experience in detail the struggle to fix meanings that characterizes much of the Revolution Debate.

In the tenth and following weeks, you should continue with lectures and class discussions of selected texts from later phases of the Revolution Debate, perhaps with a return visit from the outside lecturer to examine visual culture with more focus on the material covered during the intervening weeks. Spending a portion of a class meeting discussing and brainstorming essay topics may be a beneficial group activity and a spur to creativity. I always meet with students individually to discuss their submitted essay topics, and these meetings are also an opportunity to steer students in the direction of criticism and scholarship that can help them build better essays.[6] The penultimate week of term should be used for writing workshops and peer review, the final week for short presentations based on final essays.

Demonstration: William Blake's *The French Revolution*

Because the key texts of the Revolution Debate are not exhausted on a first reading and students will need to revisit these texts in any course of advanced study, I offer a model for further investigation of the intertextual nature of the Revolution Debate. It is also an opportunity to recuperate one of Blake's neglected works.[7] I illustrate how a theme from the first phase of the Revolution Debate, ancient liberty, operates in *The French Revolution*, not only as the simple incorporation of radical ideas but also as material for Blake's critique, correction, or elaboration.

The prominent radical publisher Joseph Johnson provided Blake with many engraving commissions during the 1780s and 1790s (Bentley 813–19). Even though Book the First of *The French Revolution* was never published and the other six books are unknown, the appearance of Johnson's name on the title page suggests that Johnson supported Blake's aspirations as an author in 1791.[8] Johnson is often remembered for the formation of the Johnson circle, a group of authors drawn to his bookshop and dinner table in St. Paul's Churchyard for professional as well as social reasons.[9]

The Johnson circle included a number of authors known for their radical politics and for their contributions to the Revolution Debate (e.g., Thomas Christie, Godwin, Paine, Price, Priestley, and Wollstonecraft). Reading *The French Revolution* in relation to their responses to *Reflections*, published in 1790 and 1791, reveals Blake's close engagement with and interrogation of their ideas; it may also make Blake's poem appear less idiosyncratic and obscure than the general scholarly neglect of it suggests.

Roland Barthes remarked that "discourse . . . moves, in its historical impetus, by *clashes*" (200), an observation peculiarly apropos for the present discussion, because ancient liberty, along with several other figures, images, and themes, evolved in the 1790s through the struggle to control their meanings that began with the publication of Price's *Discourse* and Burke's *Reflections* and continued with succeeding contributions to the Revolution Debate (Mee and Fallon 10–11). Burke and his radical respondents do not agree about the meaning of the liberties enjoyed by Britons (your students will also have a sense of this disagreement from their tracking of key terms). For British writers eager to appropriate the Revolution in France as an example supporting radical or reformist aims, events across the Channel could be interpreted as the restoration of original liberties after many years of living under the tyranny of the Norman yoke, a figure used by radicals and reformers to argue that Britons had lost the liberties and representative government enjoyed by the ancient Anglo-Saxons (Smith 51). In the fourth edition of his *Discourse on the Love of our Country*, for example, Price explicitly identifies Louis XVI as the "restorer" of French liberty (vii). Similarly, Christie argues that the new French constitution is "not an audacious novelty, but a glorious recovery of original rights . . . a restoration of the ancient system" (70–71).

Such arguments acquired urgency in response to Burke's emphasis on the ancient legal authority legitimating the British monarchy. Contrary to Price's interpretation of the settlement of 1688 as an assertion of the right of the people to choose their king, Burke claims that the Glorious Revolution was "made to preserve our *antient* indisputable laws and liberties, and that *antient* constitution of government which is our only security for law and liberty" (31). He insists that the British always based their rights on an appeal to laws and customs dating from the most obscure beginnings, even before the oldest historical evidence. Price (x–xi), Paine (116), and Priestley (viii) noticed Burke's sleight of hand, questioning his insistence that the "antient standing law of the kingdom" (32) precludes any assertion of the right of the people to alter their government. Blake's poem, ostensibly restating events in France during July

1789 and devoid of such analysis of British history as we find in Johnson's authors, nonetheless shares important features with their work.

In *Reflections*, Burke interprets the Revolution in France as a break with the past, driven by a "total contempt of . . . all antient institutions" (25), and Johnson's authors take particular issue with Burke's insistence on antiquity as the standard by which to judge the legitimacy of the British and French monarchies. Wollstonecraft claims that "there are rights which men inherit at their birth, as rational creatures, who were raised above the brute creation by their improvable faculties; and that, receiving these, not from their forefathers but, from God, prescription can never undermine natural rights" (13). Blake postulates a correspondingly ancient origin for the liberty of the French, as his King says to Necker,

> . . . the ancient dawn calls us
> To awake from slumbers of five thousands years. I awake, but my soul is in dreams;
> From my window I see the old mountains of France, like aged men, fading away. (286 [lines 7–9])

Burke suggests that if the recent leaders of France "appeared without much lustre," the French people "might have passed them by, and derived [their] claims from a more early race of ancestors" (36). He also describes the ecclesiastical institutions of France holding their property under "the accumulated prescription of a thousand years" (106). By characterizing the age of monarchical usurpation as the "slumbers of five thousands years," Blake urges the reader to reach imaginatively toward a moment that predates Burke's laws and tradition, thereby literalizing Paine's contention in *Rights of Man*:

> The error of those who reason by precedents drawn from antiquity, respecting the rights of man, is, that they do not go far enough into antiquity. They do not go the whole way. They stop in some of the intermediate stages of an hundred or a thousand years, and produce what was then done, as a rule for the present day. (65)

Blake's comparison of the National Assembly to "pillars of ancient halls, and ruins of times remote" (297 [line 258]) appropriates Burke's idea of "a more early race of ancestors" (36) while the reference to "ruins of times remote" suggests both their ancient legitimacy and the ruined state of French liberty before July 1789. Paine and Blake accept Burke's argument from the "accumulated prescription of a thousand years" yet suggest that Burke's sources are not sufficiently ancient.[10]

Ancient, one of Blake's most persistent epithets in *The French Revolution*, appears fourteen times, and this repetition might be construed as a mockery of Burke's own obsessive use of the term (more than fifty times throughout *Reflections*). Blake scatters the word throughout the speeches of his reactionary aristocratic party, with the suggestion that forms of ancientness are passing away and can provide no bulwark against the Revolution. As Blake's King first addresses the nobles, he describes the era of the Old Regime as five millennia but acknowledges that its ancient character alone cannot guarantee its survival:

> The nerves of five thousand years ancestry tremble, shaking the heavens of France;
> Throbs of anguish beat on brazen war foreheads, they descend and look into their graves.
> I see thro' darkness, thro' clouds rolling round me, the spirits of ancient Kings
> Shivering over their bleached bones; round them their counsellors look up from the dust,
> Crying: Hide from the living! Our b[a]nds and our prisoners shout in the open field,
> Hide in the nether earth! Hide in the bones! Sit obscured in the hollow scull.
> Our flesh is corrupted, and we [wear] away. We are not numbered among the living. (289 [lines 70–76])

By associating the line of "ancient Kings"—from whom the claims to the crown of George III conceivably also derived—with images of death ("Shivering over their bleached bones") and decay ("Our flesh is corrupted"), Blake questions the viability of leadership based on Burke's appeal to an unknowable past, as Wollstonecraft and Paine had done.

Blake's representation of the "ancientest Peer" (289 [line 83]), the duke of Burgundy, brings the poem even closer to the radical critique of Burke and of Burke's insistence on ancient values. Burgundy's address calls to mind a passage from *Reflections*, in which Burke responds to Price's belief in "the favourableness of the present times to all exertions in the cause of public liberty" (49) with a series of questions:

> Is our monarchy to be annihilated, with all the laws, all the tribunals, and all the antient corporations of the kingdom? Is every land-mark of the country to be done away in favour of a geometrical and arithmetical constitution? Is the house of lords to be voted useless? Is episcopacy to be abolished? Are the church lands to be sold to Jews and jobbers . . . ?

> Are all the taxes to be voted grievances, and the revenue reduced to a patriot contribution, or patriotic presents? Are silver shoe-buckles to be substituted in the place of the land tax . . . ? Are all orders, ranks, and distinctions to be confounded . . . ? For this great end, is the army to be seduced from its discipline and its fidelity, first, by every kind of debauchery, and then by the terrible precedent of a donative in the encrease of pay? Are the curates to be seduced from their bishops, by holding out to them the delusive hope of a dole out of the spoils of their own order? (54–55)

Blake's duke of Burgundy shares Burke's concern for the fate of the institutions and material forms of the Old Regime, likewise expressing his concern with a series of questions:

> Shall this marble built heaven become a clay cottage, this earth an oak stool, and these mowers
> From the Atlantic mountains, mow down all this great starry harvest of six thousand years?
> And shall Necker, the hind of Geneva, stretch out his crook'd sickle o'er fertile France,
> Till our purple and crimson is faded to russet, and the kingdoms of earth bound in sheaves,
> And the ancient forests of chivalry hewn, and the joys of the combat burnt for fuel;
> Till the power and dominion is rent from the pole, sword and scepter from sun and moon,
> The law and gospel from fire and air, and eternal reason and science
> From the deep and the solid . . . ? (290 [lines 89–96])

Blake's imagery of leveling, with the "marble built heaven" becoming "a clay cottage" and the royal "purple" fading to earthy "russet," transmutes to symbols Burke's detailed enumeration of what might be lost in the Revolution and echoes his concern that "all orders, ranks, and distinctions [might] be confounded." Like Burke, Blake's duke of Burgundy also notably expresses his anxiety for the fates of "the ancient forests of chivalry" and the legal system.[11]

Our examination of ancient liberty in *The French Revolution* obviously represents only one among many possibilities for study of the Revolution Debate and its wide-ranging effects on British literature in the 1790s and beyond. But it is a clear illustration of what an instructor can do with the Revolution Debate, both in terms of guiding students toward mastery of a complex and important body of texts and in terms of getting them to be demanding and discerning readers. When I first studied the Revolution Debate in the 1990s, there were few tools on offer from digital humanities, and my explorations of various discourses at work in writings of the 1790s were painstaking and accomplished by patient reading and rereading. The power of digital humanities means that students can now accomplish a great deal in a short period of time. If an instructor can show students where and how to look, they are sure to discover connections that we have not even imagined.

Notes

1. Jeffrey Champlin's contribution to this volume describes ways of using key terms from the age of the French Revolution, such as *nature*, *rights*, and *sovereignty*, as well as the works of Burke and Rousseau, in classroom discussion and student writing.

2. For a discussion of the French Revolution and propaganda, see Melissa Deininger's essay in this volume.

3. See the list of illustrations in Iain Hampsher-Monk's *The Impact of the French Revolution* (x). Much of Mary Dorothy George's magnum opus, the *Catalogue of Political and Personal Satires Preserved in the Department of Prints and Drawings in the British Museum*, is accessible through the British Museum's online catalog. For studies that contextualize contemporary visual culture, see her *Hogarth to Cruikshank*, Ian Haywood's *Romanticism and Caricature*, Ronald Paulson's *Representations of Revolution*, and Marcus Wood's *Radical Satire and Print Culture*.

4. Godwin's novel *Caleb Williams*, as well as the novels of Robert Bage, Thomas Holcroft, and Elizabeth Inchbald, should be considered. Morgan Rooney's *The French Revolution Debate and the British Novel, 1790–1814* demonstrates the continuing relevance of the Revolution Debate and illustrates new possibilities for student engagement with this important body of literature.

5. Note Blake's depictions of the members of the clergy and nobility as monstrous figures in *The French Revolution*. His rendering of monstrosity in poetic imagery would find companionable forms in graphic satire of the 1790s, such as Gillray's *Sin, Death, and the Devil* (1792). See Haywood 12–14, 28–32.

6. Mee and Fallon include a "Further Reading" list (191–97), which names almost every important scholarly essay and book relating to the Revolution Debate that was published before 2011.

7. Although Blake is now recognized as a major canonical author, his unpublished, fragmentary *The French Revolution: A Poem, in Seven Books* (1791) is an infrequently studied text and a bibliographic curiosity among his productions of the 1790s. It is extant today only as a single set of uncorrected printer's proofs bearing the imprint of his regular employer, Joseph Johnson.

8. The imprint on the title page of *The French Revolution* reads, "Printed for J. Johnson, N° 72, St Paul's Church-yard. MDCCXCI" (Blake 285).

9. Chard (61–62) and Tyson (66, 68, 118–22) provide brief accounts of the development of the Johnson circle.

10. Cf. Wollstonecraft's question: "Will Mr Burke be at the trouble to inform us, how far we are to go back to discover the rights of men . . . ?" (9).

11. Burke's lamentation, "the age of chivalry is gone" (see 75–77), was ridiculed by many of his respondents in the Johnson circle (Price viii; Wollstonecraft 14–15, 18; Lofft 49–55; Priestley 29–30; Paine 50; Christie 237–38). Bindman calls Burgundy's speech "a sublime parody of Burke's defence of aristocracy" (115).

Works Cited

Barthes, Roland. "Writers, Intellectuals, Teachers." *Image, Music, Text*. Translated by Stephen Heath, Hill and Wang, 1977, pp. 190–215.

Bentley, G. E., Jr. *Blake Records: Documents (1714–1841) Concerning the Life of William Blake (1757–1827) and His Family*. 2nd ed., Yale UP, 2004.

Bindman, David. "'My Own Mind Is My Own Church': Blake, Paine and the French Revolution." *Reflections of Revolution: Images of Romanticism*, edited by Alison Yarrington and Kelvin Everest, Routledge, 1993, pp. 112–33.

Blake, William. *The Complete Poetry and Prose of William Blake*. Edited by David V. Erdman, commentary by Harold Bloom, Anchor Books, 1988.

Burke, Edmund. *Reflections on the Revolution in France*. Edited by L. G. Mitchell, Oxford UP, 1993.

Butler, Marilyn, editor. *Burke, Paine, Godwin, and the Revolution Controversy*. Cambridge UP, 1984.

Chard, Leslie F., II. "Joseph Johnson: Father of the Book Trade." *Bulletin of the New York Public Library*, vol. 79, no. 1, 1975, pp. 51–82.

Christie, Thomas. *Letters on the Revolution of France, and on the New Constitution Established by the National Assembly: Occasioned by the Publications of the Right Hon. Edmund Burke, M. P. and Alexander de Calonne, Late Minister of State*. London, 1791.

Claeys, Gregory, editor. *Political Writings of the 1790s*. William Pickering, 1995. 8 vols.

Cobban, Alfred, editor. *The Debate on the French Revolution, 1789–1800*. Nicholas Kaye, 1950.

George, M. Dorothy. *Catalogue of Political and Personal Satires Preserved in the Department of Prints and Drawings in the British Museum*. British Museum, 1935–54. 7 vols.

———. *Hogarth to Cruikshank: Social Change in Graphic Satire*. Walker and Company, 1967.

Hampsher-Monk, Iain, editor. *The Impact of the French Revolution: Texts from Britain in the 1790s*. Cambridge UP, 2005.

Haywood, Ian. *Romanticism and Caricature*. Cambridge UP, 2013.

Lofft, Capel. *Remarks on the Letter of the Rt. Hon. Edmund Burke, Concerning the Revolution in France, and on the Proceedings in Certain Societies in London, Relative to That Event*. London, 1790.

Mee, Jon, and David Fallon, editors. *Romanticism and Revolution: A Reader*. Blackwell, 2011.

Paine, Thomas. *Rights of Man*. Edited by Eric Foner, Penguin, 1984.
Paulson, Ronald. *Representations of Revolution, 1789–1820*. Yale UP, 1983.
Pendleton, Gayle Trusdel. "Towards a Bibliography of the *Reflections* and *Rights of Man* Controversy." *Bulletin of Research in the Humanities*, vol. 85, no. 1, 1982, pp. 65–103.
Price, Richard. *A Discourse on the Love of our Country, Delivered on Nov. 4, 1789, at the Meeting-House in the Old Jewry, to the Society for Commemorating the Revolution in Great Britain*. 4th ed., London, 1790.
Priestley, Joseph. *Letters to the Right Honourable Edmund Burke, Occasioned by his Reflections on the Revolution in France*. 3rd ed., Birmingham, 1791.
Rooney, Morgan. *The French Revolution Debate and the British Novel, 1790–1814*. Bucknell UP, 2013.
Smith, Olivia. *The Politics of Language, 1791–1819*. Clarendon Press, 1984.
Tyson, G. P. *Joseph Johnson: A Liberal Publisher*. U of Iowa P, 1979.
Wollstonecraft, Mary. *Political Writings:* A Vindication of the Rights of Men, A Vindication of the Rights of Woman, An Historical and Moral View of the French Revolution. Edited by Janet Todd, U of Toronto P, 1993.
Wood, Marcus. *Radical Satire and Print Culture, 1790–1822*. Clarendon Press, 1994.

Ronan Y. Chalmin

How Should an Invisible Event Be Taught? The Haitian Revolution as Pedagogical Case Study

The desire to teach the Haitian Revolution to college students originated, in my case, from personal experience, because I knew relatively little about the topic until fairly recently. Having completed most of my education in France before coming to the United States to finish my thesis on eighteenth-century French literature, I had already studied in detail the Enlightenment, the French Revolution, and the French empire, but I had never touched on the Haitian Revolution.[1] The reasons for this persistent silence in the education that I, like others schooled in France, had received are analyzed by Michel-Rolph Trouillot in his insightful essay *Silencing the Past*. The silence, in striking contrast to the clamor of the French Revolution in world history, was the product of the unthinkability of the event itself: "The Haitian Revolution thus entered history with the peculiar characteristic of being unthinkable even as it happened." Trouillot finishes his reflection with a question of great importance: "How does one write a history of the impossible?" (73). This question can be reformulated to fit in the context of the classroom: How does one teach a history of the impossible?

Motivated by this simple yet challenging question, I elected to integrate the study of the Haitian Revolution into several undergraduate courses that had previously been dedicated solely to the study of the French Revolution (see Daut in this volume). By enlarging the geographic scope of the revolutionary era to include both France and her colonies, while remaining in the appropriate time frame (1789–1804), I provided an opportunity for students to learn as much about the Haitian Declaration of Independence of 1804 as they did about the Declaration of the Rights of Man and of the Citizen of 1789—that is, to discover Dutty Boukman, Toussaint Louverture, and Jean-Jacques Dessalines alongside Maximilien Robespierre, Louis-Antoine de Saint-Just, and Napoleon Bonaparte. It is generally acknowledged that France experienced its greatest restructuring and social renaissance in its revolutionary period, and that this restructuring propelled the nation into the role it has since played in global history. A similar (if not identical) sequence of events occurred in France's wealthiest eighteenth-century colony, Saint-Domingue, from August 1791 onward, but without acquiring the same global status or recognition. What is the cause of this difference? That question came up time and time again as I led students through discussions of documents centered on the birth of Haiti, the first black republic in history.

The Uprising

My students and I began by spending several weeks reading through works that were written during the French Revolution and that cover various social and political topics. We addressed the subject of the colonial problem using texts like Jean-Paul Marat's writings on the right to insurrection, Robespierre's works on the topic of slavery, Abbé Grégoire's works on the status of blacks in the colonies, and of course the decree of 4 February 1794, which marked the end of slavery in the colonies. We moved on to our Haitian Revolution unit, which spanned the period from the uprising of 1791 to the declaration of independence in 1804.

Before each class, I asked the students to read chapters of Jeremy D. Popkin's *Concise History of the Haitian Revolution*, which allowed me to focus in class on the literary and ideological aspects of the chosen texts. We went chronologically, using the divisions employed by Popkin: "The Uprisings, 1791–1793," "Republican Emancipation in Saint-Domingue, 1793–1798," "Toussaint Louverture in Power, 1798–1801," and "The Struggle for Independence, 1802–1806."

To start the unit on the Haitian Revolution, we discussed the voodoo ceremony led by Boukman at Bois Caïman on the night of 13–14 August

1791, which lit the spark of the flame that would ravage the colony, most notably the city of Cap Français in June 1793. I analyze for students select passages from documents written by contemporary writers (some of which can be easily located in the database at the John Carter Brown Library in Providence),[2] and from Popkin's *Facing Racial Revolution*. The description of events provided by the contemporary texts shows the revolution as a phenomenon that intermingled two very different emotions: the anger that led to the violence of the slave uprisings and a nostalgia for a world now being destroyed. In his *Récit historique du malheureux événement qui a réduit en cendres la ville du Cap Français* ("Historic Narrative of the Unhappy Event That Reduced to Ashes the City of Cap Français"), the colonial journalist H. D. de Saint-Maurice gives his account of things:

> Cap Français has ceased to exist; its inhabitants have been massacred or obliged to flee! . . . I owe my readers an account of the awful days of June 20, 21, 22, 23, and 24 [1793]. As a faithful historian, I owe them the story of the conspiracies that destroyed this capital—I almost said the colony—and that have cost France a source of wealth that seemed inexhaustible. (Popkin, *Facing* 186)

Saint-Domingue was soon to lose its status as *la perle des Antilles* ("the pearl of the Antilles").

The different eyewitness accounts we read in this unit explain the insurrection that occurred at Saint-Domingue: the main reason was the contradiction between the principles of the Declaration of Rights and the system of colonial slavery (certain colonists saw the declaration as an instrument of terror). The students were shocked by the intensity of the combat as well as by the destruction caused by the fighting between the colonists and the colonized. We had already tackled the question of violence in the unit on the French Revolution, particularly the part that dealt with the Terror of year 2, but the violence of the Haitian Revolution brought our study to a different place: it revealed the racial tension on the island between the whites in power and the black slaves. As François Carteaux, a plantation owner, declares in his *Histoire des désastres de Saint-Domingue* ("History of the Disasters in Saint-Domingue"), "The flames that devoured Le Cap were the complement of the *yellow caste*'s triumph over *the white race*, and the forerunners of the future primacy of the *blacks*" (Popkin, *Facing* 230). The racial and hierarchical composition of the Saint-Domingue colony at the end of the eighteenth century allowed the class to move to a broader discussion on the topic of racial tensions in the United States and the emergence of a movement today like Black Lives Matter.

Who Was Toussaint Louverture?

After exploring the first phase of the insurrection, during which the old colonial structures were destroyed and a great many colonists fled Saint-Domingue, we focused on the central figure of the event, Toussaint Louverture, much as we had attempted to understand the complex figure of Robespierre, and the debate that his actions during the Reign of Terror still generate in France, in our unit on the French Revolution (see Martin). Our study of Louverture included his origins, his personality, and, most important, his political ambitions. We emphasized the diversity of the texts and noted their different modes of expression—phonetic French, Creole, and of course modern French. These texts all created a vivid image of the complex character that was Louverture.

Born a slave (possibly in 1743) by the name of Toussaint Bréda, he was then freed and became the owner of a small plantation until the insurrection. His life was obscure before the famous proclamation he wrote at Camp Turel on 29 August 1793:

> Frères et amis, Je suis Toussaint Louverture, mon nom s'est peut-être fait connaître jusqu'à vous. J'ai entrepris la vengeance. Je veux que la liberté et l'égalité règnent à Saint-Domingue. Je travaille à les faire exister. (Césaire 146)
>
> Brothers and friends, I am Toussaint Louverture, my name has perhaps become known to you. I have undertaken vengeance. I want Liberty and Equality to reign over Saint-Domingue. I am working to make that happen. [He signed it, "your most humble and obedient servant, Toussaint LOUVERTURE."]

This text can be seen as symbolizing the birth of the person who would be referred to as the black Spartacus or the *premier des Noirs* ("first among the blacks"; see, e.g., Ferguson)—a hero of Haitian history and of emancipation movements worldwide in the nineteenth and twentieth centuries.

Raised in a highly politicized environment, Louverture decided to take charge of the island's destiny and strive for the recognition of equality in the wake of the French Revolution. He accomplished many things to realize that goal. The letter he wrote to the Directory, dated 5 November 1797 (4 Brumaire, year 6), shows the position he held as a military man on the island.[3] He criticizes the influence of the colonial party in France, calling them "enemies of the current system," and wants assurance that "France will not revoke her principles." To confront the increasing attempts to reinstate slavery in the colonies, he warns the Directory, "If [an attempt to] re-establish slavery in Saint-Domingue [were carried out], . . . then I declare to you it would be to attempt the impossible; we have known how to face dangers to obtain our liberty, we shall know how to brave death to maintain it." He concludes by reaffirming his oath to "remain loyal to France" (James, *Black Jacobins* 196–97). Note the shift: that the slaves would free themselves from the domination of their masters was once considered impossible; now, that these same masters would try to return the newly liberated people to slavery was considered impossible. This crucial reversal is symbolic of the change that took place in Saint-Domingue at the end of the eighteenth century.

Another document of importance to our understanding of Louverture's character is the Constitution of the French Colony of Saint-Domingue, 17 August 1801, written at Port-Républicain and sent directly to Napoleon. Louverture uses this document to expound on his political views regarding the island and to redefine his status. The most emblematic article is without a doubt article 3, which states, "Il ne peut exister d'esclaves sur ce territoire; la servitude y est à jamais abolie. Tous les hommes y naissent, vivent, et demeurent libres et français" 'There cannot exist slaves on this territory, servitude is therein forever abolished. All men are born, live and die free and French' (*Haitian Constitution . . . [French]*; *Haitian Constitution . . . [English]*). Following this are several articles that can be considered less progressive for the period, such as: "The catholic, apostolic, roman faith shall be the only publicly professed faith" (article 6); "[D]ivorce shall not take place in the colony" (article 10); and "Each habitation shall . . . represent the quiet haven of an active and constant family, of which the owner of the land or his representative shall be the father" (article 15). Together, the various articles of the document draw the portrait of Louverture as a "révolutionnaire noir d'Ancien Régime" 'black revolutionary of the Old Regime,' to cite the rather ironic term used by the French historian Pierre Pluchon.

The constitution also presents a series of resolutions about agriculture, which put into place what later would be known as *caporalisme agraire* ("agrarian militarism"), to permit the reconstruction of Saint-Domingue's economy after many years of war. Article 17 of the constitution declares, "The introduction of cultivators indispensable to the reestablishment and to the growth of agriculture shall take place in Saint-Domingue"; it also states, "The Constitution charges the Governor to take convenient measures . . . to ensure and guarantee the execution of respective engagements resulting from the introduction."

Even more noteworthy is article 28, which regards Louverture's own political status:

> The Constitution nominates the citizen Toussaint Louverture, Chief General of the Army of Saint-Domingue. Furthermore, in recognition of important services rendered to the colony in the most critical moments of the revolution, and in accordance with the wishes of its grateful inhabitants, he is entrusted with the direction thereof for the remainder of his glorious life.

The students I've taught tend to respond positively to the reading of the constitution. They enjoy its unique fusion of progressivism and conservatism, paternalism and liberalism. It and the other texts studied in this unit illuminate the many facets of Louverture. Some students begin to see resemblances of him to Robespierre, especially in the way that both men walked the line between defending new principles and leading the revolution according to their personal agendas.

To enrich the unit on Louverture, I used selected extracts from Louverture's memoir, which was written while he was imprisoned in France at the Fort de Joux in Jura; it was there that he passed away, far removed from the public eye, on 7 April 1803. The final lines of this long text, written in phonetic French and Creole and addressed to Napoleon,[4] are poignant:

> [P]remiere consul pere de tous les militaire juge integre defanseur des innosance prononcé dont sur mon sor, mes plai et tre profond, porté les remede salutaire pour lan péché de ne jamais ouverte vous et medecin, je conte entierement sur votre justice et votre balance, salut et respec. (*Mémoires* 168)

> First consul, father of all the military men, honest judge, defender of the innocent, decide on my fate. My wounds are very deep—employ the salutary remedies to prevent them from ever opening. You are a doctor; I rely entirely on your justice and your fairness. Salutations and respect. (*Memoir* 169)

His request, though legitimate, went unanswered, and Bonaparte pursued his plan to take back the island through military force. Louverture died without ever receiving the trial he demanded. This stunning text, in which Louverture bares himself through phonetic French, earned him the title of "the first of the black memorialists" (Desormeaux).

To complete the portrait of Louverture, we took a look at various literary works, mostly plays, that brought his story to life after the revolution ended. These works demonstrate how a historical figure was transformed into a literary hero. In the collective imagination of Haiti, Louverture came to embody the battle against slavery.

The first literary text that I had my students read was Alphonse de Lamartine's *Toussaint Louverture*, a drama performed for the first time in Paris on 6 April 1850. Lamartine himself recognized that it was less a literary work than a political one, that it was "un cri d'humanité en cinq actes et en vers" 'a cry from humanity in five acts and in verse' (v). This obscure text by the great French poet was an expression of commitment to the long battle for the abolition of slavery that ran through France in the nineteenth century—a battle in which Lamartine played an active role.

We then read selected passages from two twentieth-century plays: C. L. R. James's three-act English *Toussaint Louverture: The Story of the Only Successful Slave Revolt in History* (1934), which shortly predated his major study, *The Black Jacobins* (1938), and Édouard Glissant's *Monsieur Toussaint* (1961), the only play written by the Martinican writer. It is notable that Glissant strives to creolize the hero: entire speeches made by the characters are written in Creole, so as to better capture the reality (see, in this volume, the essay by Lau).

These excerpts from Louverture's literary posterity, which contributed to the construction of his mythical image as the great liberator of the slaves, have an undeniable pedagogical value. They permitted my students to see what was accomplished by literary treatments of that moment in Haitian history and by the fictionalization of the Haitian general.

The Birth of a Nation

Toussaint Louverture died in exile, leaving to his successors the task of giving a positive turn to the revolution. The signing of the Haitian Declaration of Independence on 1 January 1804 by Jean-Jacques Dessalines at the headquarters in Gonaives marks the end of the revolution.[5] What can this declaration teach us about the situation on the island as well as about the relation between this former colony and the metropole?

Entitling the piece "Liberté ou la mort" 'Liberty or Death' and addressing the "peuple d'Hayti" 'the people of Hayti [or of Ayiti, the old Amerindian name for the island],' the declaration begins, "It is not enough to have expelled the barbarians who have bloodied our land for two centuries . . ." (Dubois and Garrigus). Though short, the declaration has a shocking quality, because its language is so violent. It attacks the French for their long, harmful presence on the island: "Paix à nos voisins, mais anathème au nom français, haine éternelle à la France: voilà notre cri" 'Peace to our neighbors; but let this be our cry: "Anathema to the French name! Eternal hatred of France!"' It continues, employing dehumanizing descriptors such as "barbarians," "vultures," "tigers," and "assassins." The document further threatens "de dévouer à la mort, quiconque né français, souillerait de son pied sacrilège le territoire de la liberté" 'to put to death anyone born French whose profane foot soils the land of liberty.' Finally, Dessalines proclaims, "Jurons à l'univers entier, à la postérité, à nous-mêmes de renoncer à jamais à la France, et de mourir plutôt que de vivre sous sa domination" 'Let us vow to ourselves, to posterity, to the entire universe, to forever renounce France, and to die rather than live under her domination.' The message is clear: hatred for France but peace to the neighboring countries of Haiti. Students find the text even more striking when we compare it with other, more peaceful declarations of independence, like that of the United States.

Studying the declaration leads naturally to a discussion of the creation of the national flag of Haiti. It is useful to use a modern reproduction of this key event, such as the one executed by the modern Haitian painter Madsen Mompremier, *Dessalines Ripping the White from the Flag* (1995). Among other things, this painting offers a visualization of Catherine Flon, goddaughter of Jean-Jacques Dessalines, sewing the new flag (Girard).[6] The legend says that, in May 1803 Dessalines personally slashed out the white stripe of the French flag with his sword, and Flon, referred to as the Betsy Ross of Haiti, sewed the red stripe onto the blue hoist, making a new flag for the new nation. Today this moment of Haitian history is commemorated with a national holiday, the *jour du drapeau* ("Flag Day") on 18 May.

Our readings and discussions of the Haitian Declaration of Independence, as well as our discussions of the creation of the new flag, were the most successful and meaningful parts of the course. They functioned as a sort of culmination of our studies of the slave revolts and the emancipation. The students were able to gain a deeper understanding of the revolutionary process of a nation of approximately the same age as their own and of the process of decolonization, which was unusually intense for Haiti. Using the declaration as a lens allowed students to appreciate the hostility the Haitian people felt toward France at the time and the reasons behind it, which necessitated liberation without compromise.

Interpreting the Haitian Revolution

We ended the unit of the Haitian Revolution with two texts on its historical and philosophical outcomes: Michel-Rolph Trouillot's "An Unthinkable History: The Haitian Revolution as a Non-event" (chapter 3 of his *Silencing the Past*) and Nick Nesbitt's "The Idea of 1804." Reading these theoretical texts in tandem was sometimes more challenging for students, but it laid the groundwork for college students to explore a series of crucial questions: Why and how has this major event been considered a nonevent? What does this revolution, as well as the act of claiming independence in the Caribbean, represent in the course of global history, both at the time it occurred and later?

A question closer to home is, Why study the Haitian Revolution as part of a course dedicated to the Revolution of 1789? Nesbitt offers this answer: "The Haitian Revolution implemented a radically new conception of freedom that arose in the Enlightenment to receive perhaps its fullest realization on a small Caribbean island many thousands of kilometers from Paris"(14–15). If an event holds such importance in the history of humanity as a whole, how can we allow there to be such silence about it? Trouillot argues, "The silencing of the Haitian Revolution is only a chapter within a narrative of global domination. It is part of the history of the West and it is likely to persist, even in attenuated form, as long as the history of the West is not retold in ways that bring forward the perspective of the world" (107). Our course was a contribution to this unfinished task of retelling the history of the West.

The students enjoyed and benefited from the part of this course that was dedicated to the Haitian Revolution, because they had previously known little to nothing about these events in Saint-Domingue (later Haiti), about Louverture and Dessalines, or about the relation between France and its wealthiest colony during the age of the Enlightenment. Over a few weeks, we discussed a few texts about this revolution (their social and racial aspects), the importance of their creation and their meaning for future generations, the complex yet vital connection between the two revolutions (French and Haitian), the limits of the French Revolution with regard to colonial matters, the abolition of slavery, and finally the silence and denigration with which, all too often, people have treated "the difficult construction of an unqualified and *universal* freedom first concretized not in Philadelphia in 1776, nor Paris in 1789, but in the new state of Haiti on January 1, 1804" (Nesbitt 38). The experience, brief as it may have been, proved to be extremely fruitful—and gave the students who participated in the seminar the chance to engage in a task that was as challenging as it was stimulating: to think about the unthinkable.

Notes

This essay was translated by Benjamin Esposito.

1. Although the Haitian Revolution was long absent from the French university curriculum, it has assumed a significant place in that program over the last ten years, as my historian colleague Hervé Leuwers (Université Lille 3) confirmed during our recent conversations. There has also been a growing number of French-language publications and translations of English-language studies on the subject.

2. Among these documents are *Adresse de M. de Cambefort, colonel du régiment du Cap, à messieurs les colons de Saint-Domingue* (1790); *Observations importantes sur les troubles de Saint-Domingue*, by M. Blanc-Gilli (1791); and *Rapport de Philippe-Rose Roume* (1793). The library holds one of the world's biggest collections relating to Haiti (archive.org/details/jcbhaiti).

3. For further details about this crucial letter, see Chalmin.

4. Thanks to Philippe R. Girard, one can read the many versions of the manuscript and its transcription at annales.ehess.fr/index.php?283.

5. See the original version of the declaration at www.nationalarchives.gov.uk/dol/images/examples/haiti/0001.pdf. For an English translation, see Dubois and Garrigus.

6. The painting is in the Fowler Museum at the University of California, Los Angeles. For an image, see www.fowler.ucla.edu/wp-content/uploads/2016/03/X95-22-5_front_studio.jpg.

Works Cited

Césaire, Aimé. *Toussaint Louverture: La Révolution française et le problème colonial.* Présence africaine, 1962.

Chalmin, Ronan Y. "Ethique et rhétorique de la Révolution chez Gracchus Babeuf et Toussaint Louverture." *Modern Language Notes*, vol. 130, no. 4, Sept. 2015, pp. 836–62.

Desormeaux, Daniel. "The First of the (Black) Memorialists: Toussaint Louverture." *Yale French Studies*, no. 107, 2005, pp. 131–45.

Dubois, Laurent, and John Garrigus, translators. *The Haitian Declaration of In-*

dependence, 1804. ChickenBones: A Journal, www.nathanielturner.com/haitian declarationofindependence1804.htm.

Ferguson, J. A. "Le Premier des Noirs: The Nineteenth-Century Image of Toussaint Louverture." *Nineteenth-Century French Studies*, vol. 15, no. 4, Summer 1987, pp. 394–406.

Girard, Philippe R. "Birth of a Nation: The Creation of the Haitian Flag and Haiti's French Revolutionary Heritage." *Journal of Haitian Studies*, 15, no. 1, 2009, pp. 135–50.

Glissant, Édouard. Monsieur Toussaint*: Version scénique*. Seuil, 1986.

Haitian Constitution of 1801 (English). The Louverture Project, 10 Oct. 2007, www.thelouvertureproject.org/index.php?title=Haitian_Constitution_of_1801_(English).

Haitian Constitution of 1801 (French). The Louverture Project, 31 July 2007, www.thelouvertureproject.org/index.php?title=Haitian_Constitution_of_1801_(French).

James, C. L. R. *The Black Jacobins: Toussaint L'Ouverture and the San Domingo Revolution*. Vintage, 1989.

———. *Toussaint Louverture: The Story of the Only Successful Slave Revolt in History: A Play in Three Acts*. Duke UP, 2013.

Lamartine, Alphonse de. *Toussaint Louverture*. Michel Lévy Frères / Libraires-Editeurs, 1857.

Louverture, Toussaint. *Mémoires du Général Toussaint Louverture*. Edited by Daniel Desormeaux, Classiques Garnier, 2011.

———. *The Memoir of General Toussaint Louverture*. Translated and edited by Philippe R. Girard, Oxford UP, 2016.

Martin, Jean-Clément. *Robespierre: La fabrication d'un monstre*. Perrin, 2016.

Nesbitt, Nick. "The Idea of 1804." *Yale French Studies*, no. 107, 2005, pp. 6–38.

Pluchon, Pierre. *Toussaint Louverture: Un révolutionnaire noir d'Ancien Régime*. Fayard, 1989.

Popkin, Jeremy D. *A Concise History of the Haitian Revolution*. Wiley-Blackwell, 2012.

———. *Facing Racial Revolution: Eyewitness Accounts of the Haitian Insurrection*. U of Chicago P, 2007.

Trouillot, Michel-Rolph. *Silencing the Past: Power and the Production of History*. Beacon Press, 1995.

Marlene L. Daut

Teaching Perspective: The Relation between the Haitian and French Revolutions

The events that have come to be called the Haitian Revolution (1791–1804) and that led to freedom and independence for the former French-controlled colony of Saint-Domingue have often been seen as enjoying a causal relation with the French Revolution, whereby the *Déclaration des droits de l'homme et du citoyen* ("Declaration of the Rights of Man and of the Citizen"), ratified by the Estates General on 26 August 1789, directly led to a radical coming to consciousness for the enslaved Africans of Saint-Domingue. The idea that article 2's designation of the "natural and imprescriptible rights of man" to be "liberty, property, security, and resistance to oppression" (*Declaration*) could have reached enslaved Africans and consequently inspired them to rebel has provided the Enlightenment frame of reference used by many scholars to understand the Haitian Revolution. These events, spanning thirteen years, have been conceived of, then, as not simply the most successful slave rebellion in the world but the only attempt in the era to put into practice the democratic ideals of universal freedom and equality, ideals advocated for but not practiced by the creators of the *Déclaration*. Nick Nesbitt, for instance, tells the story of a plantation owner named Parham who claimed that a captured rebel slave hiding on his plantation had been caught with "pamphlets printed in

France, filled with commonplaces about the Rights of Man and the Sacred Revolution" (28–29).

The Haitian Revolution materialized the principles of democratic freedom theorized by the *Déclaration* by extending them to blacks. Yet connecting Haiti's revolution to a story about universal human rights that begins with the French *Déclaration* rather than with the Haitian Acte de l'Indépendance (Declaration of Independence)—students might read the two documents side by side for comparison—tends to elide the fact that the enslaved peoples of Saint-Domingue themselves rather than European philosophers were, as Laurent Dubois has written, the "central protagonists in the demolition of slavery" ("Enslaved Enlightenment" 3). "If we live in a world in which democracy is meant to exclude no one," Dubois elsewhere writes, "it is in no small part because of the actions of those slaves in Saint-Domingue who insisted that human rights were theirs too" (*Avengers* 3).

Although connecting the Haitian Revolution to the French Revolution may contribute to unsilencing the past by making more visible Haiti's struggle for independence, educators (particularly at the undergraduate level) must be wary of two things when teaching these historical events together: producing the belief that the Haitian Revolution is important primarily because it can be connected to the French Revolution and cosigning the idea that the Haitian Revolution can be definitively linked in fact rather than merely in people's minds to the European Enlightenment. Teaching perspective in the context of the age of revolutions means signaling that whether or not enslaved people were actually inspired by the *Déclaration* is not as important as that many planters and colonial officials believed that they were.

The belief that the French Revolution provided the lexicon necessary for the enslaved Africans of Saint-Domingue to seek their liberty may unwittingly contribute to the "silencing" of the Haitian Revolution described by Michel-Rolph Trouillot. Trouillot argues that the revolution was silenced as it unfolded because "[o]fficial debates and publications of the times, including the long list of pamphlets published in France from 1790 to 1804, reveal the incapacity of most contemporaries to understand the revolution on its own terms. They could read the news only with their ready-made categories, and these categories were incompatible with the idea of a slave revolution" (73). In other words, the French could understand the rebellion of enslaved Africans only by using European epistemological frames of reference.

One way to encourage a more capacious perspective of the causes of the Haitian Revolution is to assign Haitian-produced sources. Even though many French writers, like François-René de Chateaubriand, connected the Revolution of 1789 with the wholesale insurrection of the enslaved peoples of Saint-Domingue in 1791, writers of color from Saint-Domingue were not so quick to make that connection.[1] Julien Raimond contested the idea that future slave rebellions might be inspired by either the *Déclaration* or the budding transatlantic abolitionist movement when he wrote, "For two centuries the blacks have attempted uprisings in multiple regions; and yet there was not even a *société des amis des noirs*" (12). The antislavery group called the Société des Amis des Noirs ("the Society of the Friends of the Blacks") was formed in 1788 by a group of men that included Jacques-Pierre Brissot de Warville after the storming of the Bastille in Paris in July 1789. The development of this society has been associated with the Haitian Revolution because when the French king invited the people of France to submit their grievances at a meeting of the Estates General, the newly formed society seized on the opportunity to urge both an end to the slave trade and the gradual emancipation from slavery. Raimond, however, insisted on a much longer history of revolutionary consciousness, one that predated the French Revolution and the subsequent emergence of French abolitionist societies: "Oh! When the insurrection happens, we will really have to go so far as to point to the existence of this society in order to explain the cause? would it not be natural to fear that the blacks, in thinking about their own situation, would have wanted to demand their liberty?" (12). Introducing students to Raimond's interpretation can encourage the more perspectival approach needed to think about the Haitian Revolution beyond the European Enlightenment.

One of the best-known Enlightenment literacy narratives that unwittingly downplays the pivotal role that the twin brutalities of colonial slavery and colonial racism played in setting the terms for the revolution involves a tale about how Toussaint Louverture became radicalized by his reading of the black Spartacus passage of the *Histoire des deux Indes* (1770–80; "History of the Two Indies"), a collaborative work published under the name of the abbé Raynal. Many of the revolution's earliest historians, such as Marcus Rainsford, who produced the first known full-length history of the events in English, said that Louverture "had acquired the knowledge of new sources, and the relish for books of a superior order . . . the author of whom he became the most speedily enamored was the abbé Raynal, on whose history and speculations in philosophy he was intent for weeks, and never quitted" (152). The passage from the *Histoire* that allegedly inspired Louverture to believe that it was his "destiny" to "avenge the wrongs committed on his race" (154) reads:

> Your slaves do not have a need for your generosity nor for your advice to break the Sacrilegious yoke that oppresses them. . . . The negroes only want a courageous leader to transport them to vengeance and to carnage. Where is he this great man whom nature owes to her vexed, oppressed, and tormented children? Where is he, this new Spartacus? (6: 206–08)

In order for students to avoid a misleading symmetry that would mark Louverture as a legible revolutionary hero simply because he may have read Enlightenment philosophy, readings that tie the Haitian Revolution to the European Enlightenment, such as C. L. R. James's *The Black Jacobins*, should be counterbalanced by sources that promote an understanding of the Haitian Revolution that is tied to the daily experiences of ordinary enslaved peoples.

Understanding the revolution requires adopting a hermeneutic that is rigorously attentive to related historical events but at the same time remains sensitive to the material realities, particularities, and perspectives that drove the enslaved Africans of Saint-Domingue to create the first free and independent republic of the New World. Students can use Carolyn Fick's *The Making of Haiti* to that end, to explore the lives of "the mass of black slave laborers who participated in [the Haitian] revolution on their own terms and with interests and goals embodying their own needs and aspirations" (1). Jean-Pierre Le Glaunec's marronage database can be taught alongside Fick's work to encourage students to examine the relation of these goals and aspirations to the ongoing trauma of enslavement. The database, which contains nearly 13,000 ads for runaway slaves that were published in Saint-Domingue's most widely read periodical, *Les affiches américaines* ("American Notes"), between 1766 and 1790, is in Le Glaunec's vision a complicated but indispensable archive for gaining an interior vision of the lives of the enslaved. "A racist and disparaging source that refers to slaves as mere lost objects or stray animals," Le Glaunec writes, "the fugitive slave notice is nonetheless one of the most important sources for understanding the way slaves in the Saint-Domingue colony reclaimed their bodies and asserted their right to dignity, even temporarily." Because many of the notices in the database describe these fugitives by the forms of branding or marks of the whip covering their bodies, one way an instructor might flip the received perspective is to ask students to ponder whether the knowledge of violence against the enslaved, coupled with popular representations of slave rebellion circulating in the early modern world—as represented, for instance, in Aphra Behn's famous novel *Oroonoko* (1688)—could have contributed to the development of the ideas of freedom commonly associated with the French Revolution rather than vice versa.

Even though organized slave revolts had reportedly been "comparatively slight" on the island before 1791 (Geggus 4), runaway, formerly enslaved Africans, often called maroons, who created fugitive communities in the mountains of Saint-Domingue, had been raiding and devastating crops since 1719, particularly in the Sud-de-Cap region (Debien 109). Famously, a fugitive slave named Makandal had been using poison as well as a vast network of maroons in order to sow the seeds of rebellion in Saint-Domingue as early as the 1750s. On his capture in January 1758, he was burned at the stake, an act that was part of a series of high profile executions of maroon leaders in the eighteenth century. An eighteenth-century short story entitled "Makandal, histoire véritable" 'Makandal, a True History' circulated widely after it first appeared in the *Mercure de France* in September 1787 ("Account"). The story can be used in the classroom to demonstrate that slave revolts and other foms of rebellion were a reality long before the French Revolution or the emergence of transatlantic abolitionist societies.[2]

Teaching about the longue durée of the Haitian Revolution should invite students to reflect on questions not only of history (typically taught as a chronology) but also of perspective (understanding based on point of view). In this light, the French and Haitian revolutions might be considered to have a mutually constitutive relation that cannot be understood merely as cause and effect. Instead, we might ask students to think about how our perspective of the age of revolutions would change if we thought about the French and Haitian revolutions as parallel events occurring across "deep time" (Dimock 759). In other words, as events that, because they share a certain simultaneity, had ricocheting but uneven longitudinal consequences not only for the specific geographic locales in which they occurred but also across the world.

Combining sources about the everyday trauma of enslaved life with sources about everyday slave resistance before the French Revolution promotes an understanding of Haitian independence and the subsequent universalisms that it brought into existence—for example, that slavery should be outlawed unequivocally—as the result of a longer experience of defensive violence in the colonies or "an enslaved Enlightenment" (Dubois, "Enslaved Enlightenment" 1). The writings of Baron de Vastey, a former free person of color from Saint-Domingue who became one of the best-known politicians and writers in newly independent Haiti, cataloged with incredible detail the myriad forms of abuse perpetrated against the enslaved by specific enslavers in eighteenth-century Saint-Domingue. Reading the slave testimonies collected by Vastey in *Le système colonial dévoilé* (1814), which has recently been translated into English as *The Colonial System Unveiled*, confronts us with the fact that planters in Saint-Domingue practiced some of the cruelest punishments of enslaved Africans in the Atlantic world. These tortures including burning and burying the enslaved alive; severing limbs, ears, and other body parts; bleeding these human beings to death; and nailing them to walls and trees. Sexual assault also took many forms. Such cruelty not only caused the planters of the colony to constantly fear revenge from the enslaved, which is precisely what we learn by reading Malick Ghachem's historical study *The Old Regime and the Haitian Revolution*, but also produced perpetual terror among these captive laborers, a perspective that can be gleaned by reading Sara Johnson's *The Fear of French Negroes*. The physical violence used by the enslaved against the planters during the Haitian Revolution may have ended the tortures of enslavement in Saint-Domingue, but it did not end racism against people of color.

The Haitian Revolution forced the global public sphere to openly confront and debate questions of racial liberty and equality. As such, it was perhaps the most visible historical attempt to destroy the foundations of racism in the nineteenth century. The racism that writers of color like Raimond and Vastey had complained about in their numerous writings exposed not only the dire political consequences of color prejudice but also its dire material consequences. The revolution posed serious moral questions about the relation of freedom not only to race but also to the violence used to achieve it. A character in Victor Hugo's 1826 novel about the Haitian Revolution, *Bug-Jargal*, proclaimed, "[T]he *philosophes* fathered the philanthropists, who gave birth to the *négrophiles*, who produced the eaters of whites" (68). Haitian writing, on the contrary, signals that the violence the enslaved used against whites was less the kind of racial violence described by Hugo and more a reactive violence aimed at ending the permanent state of war of chattel slavery.

Teaching Émeric Bergeaud's posthumously published *Stella* (1859), the first Haitian novel, alongside *Bug-Jargal*, can help students gain perspective about the otherwise potentially shocking violence used by people of color in Saint-Domingue to rid the island of both slavery and colonial rule. Hugo focuses on painting the violence of the Haitian Revolution as the result of misguided Enlightenment philanthropy, which in his words became a "poison in the tropics" (68). Bergeaud in contrast describes the utter brutality experienced by enslaved Africans, and especially enslaved women, as the primary motivation for the Haitian Revolution. The rape and murder of an enslaved woman named Marie is described by the narrator of *Stella* in explicit detail:

> . . . the terrible whip resounded; a scene of horror commenced, the details of which will make you tremble. To the multiplying noise of the blows were mingled sharp, heart-rending cries that weakened little by little until they descended into a moan. The whip hits, hits for two hours. The victim jumped, writhed, grated her teeth. Her mouth foamed, her nostrils flared. . . . There was no more life, but her body was still quaking and the whip was still striking, stopping at last on an inert cadaver. (19)

Although the notion that Haitians view the causes of their revolution differently from the French may be obvious to many scholars, it is probably not obvious to many students, and they should be encouraged to consider descriptions like Bergeaud's at every turn.

Standard history textbooks have tended to reproduce the dominant (French colonial) perspective and discount the subaltern (Haitian) perspective. The perpetuation of this tendency can be actively discouraged precisely by teaching about the Haitian Revolution through literature and the arts. Fiction and other forms of artistic representation can teach us about people who lived in different eras in a more humane way[3] than immersive approaches, which involve asking students to role-play as either enslaved people or enslavers, a practice that has been documented as inciting trauma (Dozono 38).

The history of sexual violence in colonial Saint-Domingue is traumatic, but not speaking of rape contributes to the broader silencing of the lives of the everyday people who experienced and contributed to the Haitian Revolution. The many tragedies of enslavement must therefore be included when we teach the importance of perspective. In order to provide context and mitigate ongoing trauma, stories about the revolution involving rape and other forms of sexual and physical assault, such as Victor Séjour's serial "The Mulatto" (1837), can be taught alongside scholarship that defines, details, and historicizes the complications of consent and agency in the lives of enslaved women and men. Saidiya Hartman's "Seduction and the Ruses of Power" and Deborah Jenson's *Beyond the Slave Narrative* can be particularly useful in asking students to think about whether or not a sexual relationship between an enslaver and a person he enslaves could ever be consensual from the enslaved person's point of view.

Finally, any perspective of the Haitian Revolution would be incomplete without paying attention to the resultant fact of Haitian independence. Two paintings from artists of different eras invite reflection on contrasting interpretations of the transformation of colonial Saint-Domingue into independent Haiti: Guillaume Guillon-Lethière's *Le serment des ancêtres* (1822; "The Oath of the Ancestors") and Madsen Mompremier's *Dessalines Ripping the White from the French Flag* (1995). Guillon-Lethière's painting depicts an almighty white God reuniting Haiti's General Jean-Jacques Dessalines (the founder of Haitian independence) with General Alexandre Pétion (one of Dessalines's former rivals and a future president of Haiti) under the new constitution of Haiti. In the painting, we see Dessalines and Pétion swearing an oath to unite against Napoléon Bonaparte, making Haitian independence more the work of a fantastic God than of the very human revolutionaries. Mompremier's painting, in contrast, depicts Dessalines surrounded by members of his army and ripping the white out of the tricolor French flag in order to create the current Haitian flag, which is red and blue. The work of national independence is appropriately linked here to (black) Haitian volition and not to supernatural (white) Christian powers. A possible assignment involving these paintings is to break students into two groups and have each group develop an interpretation of Haitian independence based on the painting assigned to its members. At the end of the exercise, students might gain insight into what it means to think about revolution from a religious perspective versus a secular perspective and how understandings of Haitian independence are racialized differently in the separate paintings.

In the end, recognizing the world-historical significance of the Haitian Revolution means constantly signaling its importance in an age of revolutions that also included those in the United States and France. All these events are crucial in the annals of world history, yet they have not been afforded the same sense of universality in the popular imagination (the Hollywood actor Danny Glover, for example, continues to be unable to find financial support to produce a film about the Haitian Revolution

[Obsenson]), and they have not been researched with the same sense of urgency by historians. In a world in which the history of transatlantic slavery is constantly being disavowed—note the backlash caused when the first lady of the United States, Michelle Obama, publicly acknowledged that the White House was built by slave labor (French)—the importance of the Haitian Revolution should not be underestimated. It was an integral part of the making of modern democracy, and it should be a centerpiece in our reconstruction of the histories of enslavement and freedom, racism and civil rights.

Notes

Translations from the French are mine unless otherwise indicated.

1. In *Le génie du christianisme*, Chateaubriand showed his disdain for the Haitian Revolution in writing, "[W]ho would dare to plead the cause of the blacks after the crimes they have committed?" (1: 164).

2. In February 1788 "Le Makandal" was translated by the London-based *Universal Magazine of Knowledge and Pleasure* as "The Negro Makandal, an Authentic History."

3. Over two hundred novels, poems, and plays about the Haitian Revolution were published in the nineteenth century. See haitianrevolutionaryfictions.com.

Works Cited

"Account of a Remarkable Conspiracy Formed by a Negro in the Island of St. Domingo." *Common-Place*. Edited by Duncan Faherty. jto.common-place.org/wp-content/uploads/sites/2/2016/01/Makandal-text-JTO-version.pdf.

Bergeaud, Émeric. *Stella*. E. Dentu, 1859.

———. *Stella: A Novel of the Haitian Revolution*. Edited by Lesley Curtis and Cristen Mucher, New York UP, 2015.

Chateaubriand, François-René de. *Le génie du christianisme*. 2 vols., Garnier-Flammarion, 1966.

Constitution impériale de 1805. Haiti-Référence, haiti-reference.com/pages/plan/histoire-et-societe/documents-historiques/constitutions/constitution-imperiale-1805.

Debien, Gabriel. "Marronage in the French Caribbean." *Maroon Societies: Rebel Slave Communities in the Americas*, edited by Richard Price, Johns Hopkins UP, 1979, pp. 107–34.

Declaration of the Rights of Man. 1789. *Avalon Project*, avalon.law.yale.edu/18th_century/rightsof.asp.

Dimock, Wai Chee. "Deep Time: American Literature and World History." *American Literary History*, vol. 13, no. 4, 2001, pp. 755–75.

Dozono, Tadashi. "Historical Experience and the Haitian Revolution in the History Classroom." *Social Studies*, vol. 107, no. 1, Jan. 2016, pp. 38–46.

Dubois, Laurent. *Avengers of the New World*. Harvard UP, 2004.

———. "An Enslaved Enlightenment: Rethinking the Intellectual History of the French Atlantic." *Social History*, vol. 31, no. 1, Feb. 2006, pp. 1–14.

Fick, Carolyn. *The Making of Haiti: The Saint-Domingue Revolution from Below*. U of Tennessee P, 1990.

French, Megan. "Bill O'Reilly Responds to Michelle Obama's DNC Speech: Slaves Who Built the White House Were 'Well Fed.'" *U.S. News and World Report*, 27 July 2016, www.usmagazine.com/celebrity-news/news/bill-oreilly-slaves-who-built-white-house-were-well-fed-w431154.

Geggus, David. "Slave Resistance Studies and the Saint-Domingue Slave Revolt: Some Preliminary Considerations." *LACC Occasional Papers Series, 1981–1990*, 1 July 1983, digitalcommons.fiu.edu/laccops/. Paper 4.

Ghachem, Malick W. *The Old Regime and the Haitian Revolution*. Cambridge UP, 2012.

Guillon-Lethière, Guillaume. *Le serment des ancêtres*. 1822. *Le serment des ancêtres*, 1 Jan. 2018, lesermentdesancetres.wordpress.com/about/. Blog of Nathalie Jolivert.

Hartman, Saidiya. "Seduction and the Ruses of Power." *Callaloo*, vol. 19, no. 2, 1996, pp. 537–60.

Hugo, Victor. *Bug-Jargal*. 1826. Edited by Gérard Gengembre. Pocket Classiques, 2004.

James, C. L. R. *The Black Jacobins: Toussaint L'Ouverture and the San Domingo Revolution*. Vintage Books, 1963.

Jenson, Deborah. *Beyond the Slave Narrative: Politics, Sex, and Manuscripts in the Haitian Revolution*. Liverpool UP, 2011.

Johnson, Sara E. *The Fear of French Negroes: Transcolonial Collaboration in the Revolutionary Americas*. U of California P, 2012.

Le Glaunec, Jean-Pierre. *Marronage in Saint-Domingue (Haïti): History, Memory, Technology*, www.marronnage.info/en/accueil.php.

Mompremier, Madsen. *Dessalines Ripping the White from the French Flag*. *The Public Archive*, 18 May 2011, thepublicarchive.com/?p=2389.

Nesbitt, Nick. "The Idea of 1804." *Yale French Studies*, vol. 107, 2005, pp. 6–38.

Obenson, Tambay A. "Danny Glover's Toussaint L'Ouverture Film That Never Was, but Could Still Be and Other Films on the Haitian Revolutionary." *IndieWire*, 31 July 2015. www.indiewire.com/2015/07/danny-glovers-toussaint-louverture-film-that-never-was-but-could-still-be-other-films-on-the-haitian-revolutionary-235064/.

Raimond, Julien. *Réponse aux considérations de M. Moreau, dit Saint-Méry, député à l'Assemblée nationale, sur les colonies*. 1791. *Internet Archive*, 20 May 2010, archive.org/details/rponseauxconsi00raim.

Rainsford, Marcus. *An Historical Account of the Black Empire of Hayti*. Edited by Paul Youngquist and Grégory Pierrot, Duke UP, 2013.

Raynal, Abbé Guillaume-Thomas. *Histoire philosophique et politique des établissemens et du commerce des Européens dans les deux Indes*. 3rd ed. 10 vols. Jean-Leonard Pellet, 1780–84.

Séjour, Victor. "The Mulatto." Translated by Philip Barnard. *The Norton Anthology of African American Literature*, edited by Henry L. Gates, Jr., and Nellie Y. McKay, W. W. Norton, 1997, pp. 353–65.

Trouillot, Michel. *Silencing the Past: Power and the Production of History.* Beacon Press, 1995.

Vastey, Baron de. *The Colonial System Unveiled.* Edited and translated by Chris Bongie, Liverpool UP, 2015.

———. *Le système colonial dévoilé.* 1814. *Internet Archive*, 12 Aug. 2008, archive.org/details/lesystemecolonia00vast.

Ourida Mostefai

Exile, Displacement, and Citizenship: Émigrés from the French Revolution to the Twenty-First Century

Following the advent of the French Revolution, a massive emigration from France displaced thousands of people throughout Europe, inaugurating a new regime of political exile. Between 1789 and 1794, approximately one hundred and fifty thousand French men, women, and children left their homeland.[1] This group was very diverse, including aristocrats and their servants, noble bishops and poor priests, merchants and tradespeople, writers and journalists, soldiers and sailors. They sought refuge in neighboring countries—most of them went to England[2]—and as far as North America. In their exile they were immediately perceived as refugees of a new kind. Indeed a new word was invented for them—*émigré*—to distinguish them from earlier groups, most notably from the French Protestants who had sought refuge a century earlier[3] as well as from the new citizens created by the Revolution. Through their exodus the émigrés exported the Revolution and gave it a truly global reverberation. Excluded as they were from participating in the building of the new nation, they produced a rich literature of exile—memoirs, novels, poetry, and plays. Thus Europe witnessed the emergence of the figure of the émigré as a literary response to the Revolution.[4]

This essay focuses on the phenomenon of emigration as a novel way of teaching the French Revolution in a global context. Analyzing the representation of the figure of the émigré allows for a different perspective on the Revolution and on the literature that emerged in Europe in the period. It highlights the role played by a new generation of writers—many of them women but all of them émigrés—in the shaping of the new nation or nations and of their literatures.[5] Viewing the French Revolution through the prism of exile also provides a historic context for current discussions and debates on migration and displacement in the West today. Students should be encouraged to reflect on the invention of the term *émigré* and its entry into European languages and on the diverse related vocabulary in use at the time: *émigré*, *emigrant*, *immigrant*, *refugee*, *exile*, *banishment*. The word might be fruitfully contrasted with the current use of the word *migrant*.[6]

A focus on the revolutionary decade and the early years of the nineteenth century, the so-called *tournant des lumières* ("Enlightenment turn"), helps bring to light a period during which political and philosophical debates were carried out not only in pamphlets but also in fiction. Reading the literature of European émigré writers and studying the ways in which they engaged with the debates on the Revolution through their novels show students how those discussions were conducted throughout Europe. Because the status of the émigrés was ambiguous and paradoxical—they were stripped of their citizenship yet still subject to French laws and condemned to death in absentia—their novels examine the possibilities for dialogue in a radicalized political context. Through their focus on emigration these novels reflect on the division and strife in French society but do so by transposing historical and political issues into the private sphere. Through exchanges between individuals separated by class, ideology, and geography, they seek to reconcile longing for the past with the desire for change. Exile, wandering, and homelessness become the new human condition: Charlotte Smith's banished man, Frances Burney's wanderer, and Goethe's refugees—all these émigrés embody the condition of modernity even as they voice antirevolutionary ideas and sentiments.

Recent scholarship has helped restore emigration in the historiography of the French Revolution and reestablish it as an important part of France's collective experience of the Revolution (see Aprile; Rance; Wahnich). This important work has uncovered the complexity and diversity of emigration as a social and cultural phenomenon, as well as its numerous paradoxes. To help my students understand this phenomenon, I start by retracing how emigration evolved and expanded during the Revolution. It began in July 1789, when members of the royal family—most notably the comte d'Artois, Louis XVI's younger brother, and his entourage—left France. In its first phase the exodus was essentially aristocratic and took the form mostly of a military engagement with foreign troops allied against France.[7] No laws prevented the crossing of borders, and official policy first consisted in encouraging those who had left France to return, often through exhortations from the king. The Revolution radically changed the definition and status of emigration.

The turning point occurred after the king's arrest at Varennes following his failed emigration attempt.[8] With the king deposed and thus unable to use his veto, new sanctions against émigrés were instituted, and a series of legislative measures criminalized emigration. In 1791, the Constituent Assembly defined the émigré pointedly as "celui qui porte atteinte à la sûreté autant intérieure qu'extérieure de l'État, et par conséquent à l'intégrité de la nation" 'he who threatens the internal or external security of the State and consequently the integrity of the nation' (Aprile 21). All émigré property was seized and later sold as national property (*biens nationaux*). Then, to facilitate this confiscation, a list of all émigrés was created in 1792: "Liste générale par ordre alphabétique des émigrés de toute la République" 'The General List in Alphabetical Order of the Émigrés of the whole Republic."[9] Exiles were banished in perpetuity and stripped of their French citizenship. Emigration, now redefined as a crime in a time of war, became punishable by death. In its second phase, after the Terror, emigration grew into a massive phenomenon that affected all strata of French society, and most émigrés now came from the lower ranks.[10]

Emigration officially ended with the amnesty granted by Napoleon in 1802, after which an overwhelming number of émigrés came back to France. Many enlisted in the Napoleonic wars, where they sometimes fought against their former allies and hosts. Throughout the nineteenth century, émigrés were gradually reintegrated into the fabric of French society, as is suggested by the passage from the Littré dictionary defining the category of émigré as one who intends to return to France.[11] When the law for their compensation—the so-called *milliard des émigrés* law or "billion francs" law—was voted during the Bourbon Restoration in 1825,[12] new quarrels broke out about the legitimacy of their claims for entitlement to public funds.

Throughout the late eighteenth and nineteenth centuries the figure of the émigré underwent major transformation and developed a complex layer of significations on the basis of the variety of political and social contexts in which the emigration took place. The counterrevolutionary fighters of the royal army and the victims of the Revolution faced death if they attempted to return and impoverishment because of the confiscation of their property. Their plight gave rise to a discourse of sympathy: unable to return home, and in need of hospitality, they were now seen as embodying the modern condition of displacement. That is what accounts for their overwhelming presence in Romanticism and especially in British Romantic poetry.[13]

Writers in and outside France—in England, Switzerland, and Germany—portrayed and interpreted the experience of emigration through literary forms that had emerged before the Revolution. Responding to the powerful and profound transformations catalyzed by the Revolution and to the public's desire to understand the events it was witnessing, writers depicted experiences of the Revolution through narrative techniques that had been developed more than a century earlier. In so doing, they created a literary legacy that extended beyond the revolutionary period. This largely explains why the emigration influenced politics, literature, and culture after the Revolution; why it remained in the collective memory of all nineteenth-century exiles; and why it became a recognized feature of modern political life. Thus Balzac's 1835 novel *Le lys dans la vallée* ("The Lily of the Valley") refers to M. de Morsauf as "la grande figure de l'Émigré, l'un des types les plus imposants de notre époque" 'the great figure of the émigré, one of the most imposing figures of our time' (345).[14]

Against the long-held prejudice against the literature of the French Revolution, recent scholarship on the late Enlightenment has shown that the Revolution, far from putting an end to the novel, actually helped revive it and renew the forms and contents of narrative fiction.[15] In this new context, traditional conventions were reprised and adapted to new purposes, thus providing the foundation for the emergence of the novel as a major literary form in the nineteenth century—in French, English and German. The Revolution provided the novel with greater legitimacy, giving it a new raison d'être. The freedoms granted by fiction—most notably by the epistolary novel—allowed a new political space to open for debate and polemic. The sentimental novel as it developed in the eighteenth century opened new opportunities for opposing parties to coexist and examine their contradictory positions. During the intellectual and social conflict of the period, the novel also suggested the possibility of finding solutions to the political crisis. Goethe's *Unterhaltungen deutscher Ausgewanderten*

("Conversations of German Refugees") is a striking example: a violent dispute over the French Revolution leads to a proposal that the refugees ban all political talk and instead recount personal stories. The strategy is effective, because as they exchange and discuss tales of ghosts, love, and renunciation, they forget their differences.

Novels of emigration construct an experience of exile that together with memoirs, testimonies, and autobiographies seeks to mitigate the great disruptions caused by the Revolution. As literature of displacement and homelessness, these narratives anticipate the modern literature of exile (see Fritzsche). Émigré novels convey not simply the anecdotal stories of individuals but also the universal experience of emigration and the fate of the nation. A focus on them and on the debates generated by the figure of the émigré will help students reflect on the nature of political conflict and the possibility of its resolution.

By situating the debate outside national boundaries while considering émigrés as legitimate parties to the political conflict unfolding in France, writers of émigré fiction pursued the French Revolution by other, aesthetic means. Their radical project was to establish a dialogue between people divided by politics and separated by geography—a diasporic version of the French *république des lettres* ("republic of letters"). They also pursued the dream of peaceful coexistence. In the face of exclusion and expulsion, they constructed a model of friendship, hospitality, and fraternity.

Hospitality is inscribed at the heart of many émigré novels: a wounded Jacobin cared for by the aristocrats in Vendée in Isabelle de Charrière's *Lettres trouvées dans des portefeuilles d'émigrés* ("Letters Found in Emigrants' Portfolios"); an injured Frenchman welcomed into a German castle in Gabriel Sénac de Meilhan's *L'émigré*.[16] This hospitality is not a mere topos reprising the tradition of the *roman d'aventures* ("adventure novel"); it presents the other side of exile and acts as a response to exclusion. The gesture of welcoming the stranger becomes a social, political, and economic model.[17] To overcome the geographic and ideological separation, the epistolary novel struggles to maintain the conversation among friends and strangers in Europe. This correspondence is essential to the survival of the characters: by providing them with a network and giving them a space for their existence, it becomes the refuge of the émigré. With the epistolary exchange a model of conviviality is established, one that replaces the conversation that cannot take place: "Vivons ensemble, chère Germaine, doutons, croyons, raisonnons, déraisonnons ensemble et ne nous quittons pas même à la mort" 'Let us live together, dear Germaine, let us doubt, make sense and nonsense together and let us not part even in death' (Charrière 97).

The émigrés dream of a refuge, a homeland, because they are in exile in this world. The frequent absence of closure leaves readers in uncertainty, just as the outcome of the political situation is uncertain. Readers are provided with fragmentary lives that can offer only hope and conjecture. Thus the correspondence in Charrière's novel is interrupted by the last letter, which announces Pauline's arrival in Amsterdam but gives no indication of the final outcome. Will there be a family reunion or not? In Sénac's *L'émigré*, the novel ends with the reprisal of the movement of migration: "Tout le monde part demain" 'Everyone leaves tomorrow' (436). Students should be encouraged to comment on the question of closure and how its lack affects the literary forms. As an example, Therese Huber's German adaptation of Charrière's novel, unlike the original, offers an optimistic denouement, the marriage of the lovers.

Émigrés are foreigners in the modern sense: they do not belong to the new society, which has constituted itself without them and on the basis of their exclusion. The paradox with which the heroes of the émigré novels are confronted is that they are neither French nor foreigners. They rise up against the country that abandoned them, all the while claiming their Frenchness and their *droit de cité* ("rights of citizenship"). Alphonse in Charrière's *Lettres trouvées dans des portefeuilles d'émigrés* claims his right to participate in the political life of the nation in this way:

> Nous aussi nous sommes des Français, et il nous est permis comme aux assemblées primaires, comme aux assemblées constituantes, de réfléchir, de délibérer, de faire des plans et des vœux. Qu'ils sont ardents et qu'ils sont désintéressés, les vœux que je fais pour ma patrie! (67)
>
> We too are French and we have the right—just as do primary and constituent assemblies—to reflect, to deliberate, and to make plans and vows. How passionate and disinterested are the vows I make for my country!

The literature of emigration raises the question of national identity: Are émigrés citizens, or are they *étrangers* ("foreigners," "strangers")? These novels bring to light simultaneously the difficulty and the necessity of a nuanced political engagement. By reflecting on what it means to be and to feel French, as well as what it means to be *étranger*, they provide an interesting perspective on the definition of French identity. A class on the émigré novel can thus encourage a reflection on how the émigré experience is relevant in the works of writers and filmmakers today whose parents come from North and Sub-Saharan Africa and who—although French-born—are still not considered wholly French. The class can provide a forum for exploring the question of national identity raised by the literature of emigration in the eighteenth century and by contemporary francophone novels.

A number of contemporary francophone novels echo the émigré experience. Among the works that can be selected for the class, Fatou Diome's *Le ventre de l'Atlantique* ("The Belly of the Atlantic") seems exemplary.[18] This novel tells the story of Salie through the lens of her emigration: instead of recounting the heroine's experience of coming to France, it focuses on the painful condition of African émigrés, torn between the necessity and the impossibility of exile. Uprooted from their communities, these exiles continue in their absence to haunt the minds of their countrymen, who stubbornly await and expect their return. Thus Salie, having lost her place in Africa without gaining recognition in France and unable to convey her suffering in either place, feels like an outsider in both cultures. She is a foreigner in Africa, where everyone dreams of immigrating to France, and in France, where she is seen as another immigrant seeking naturalization. Accused in Africa of betraying her roots and in France of usurping the status of citizen, she is now a stranger both in her homeland and in her new country. Reflecting on her condition, she sees herself as a "être hybride" 'hybrid creature' (254), a being that has the "amphibian" character of the revolutionary émigrés.[19] Her story, just like that of the émigré novels, shows that immigrants are first and foremost emigrants: their first experience is of exile and the loss of homeland.

The migrants of the Middle East who today are seeking to reach the shores of Europe are the new émigrés. The very term *migrant* that has been given them seems to deny them all ties to their mother country or any new land, thus condemning them to perpetual mobility. Émigré literature can provide a new perspective for examining contemporary debates over immigration and national identity at this time of global displacement. Viewed through the lens of the revolution and the emigration it caused, current anxieties about French citizenship and Frenchness (*Francité*) can be recontextualized historically and reconceptualized in the larger framework of the construction of modern citizenship, and it can help students assess some of the major changes that have occurred in the past thirty years in the wake of globalization. Good supplemental readings might be critical texts such as Tzvetan Todorov's *Nous et les autres*, Julia Kristeva's

Étrangers à nous-mêmes, and Amin Maalouf's *Identités meurtrières*. There are also contemporary films that deal with migration and exile (e.g., Tony Gatlif's *Exils*).

Notes

1. This estimate does not include the twenty thousand exiles to America or those displaced from the Caribbean after the revolution at Saint-Domingue (who were also referred to as émigrés).

2. The massive arrival of the French exiles in England created a veritable refugee crisis, and their presence became a contentious issue. While relief efforts were being organized on their behalf (by personalities such as Hannah More, Burney, and Edmund Burke), the increased presence of Catholics was very much feared, and many people of England objected to charity that benefited the French at the expense of the native poor.

3. The revocation by Louis XIV in 1685 of the Edict of Nantes, which had granted Protestants a modicum of toleration, led to a massive exodus of Protestants out of France.

4. European dictionaries date the noun *émigré* to the first years of the 1790s. The *Dictionnaire de l'Académie française* defines it as follows: "se dit particulièrement des François qui, sans y être autorisés, sont sortis de France depuis la Révolution, et qui n'y sont pas rentrés dans le délai accordé par la Loi." *The Oxford English Dictionary* refers to "A Frenchman who has left his country for another; *esp.* one of those Royalists who fled at the French Revolution."

5. Among these writers were Isabelle de Charrière, Germaine de Staël, Burney, and Charlotte Smith, thus providing a European perspective on the French Revolution.

6. For a critical examination of this terminology, see Brecht.

7. A caricature by Isaac Cruikshank offers a satire of this early emigration. The stereotype of émigrés as reactionary aristocrats was common in the French popular imagination: newspapers such as *Le Père Duchesne* as well as prints and songs provide examples of such caricatures.

8. On 20 June 1791, Louis XVI was arrested at Varennes as he was attempting to leave France with his family to join the émigré army. Recognized despite his disguise, he was returned to Paris by the national guards, put on trial as a regular citizen (Louis Capet), and executed on 21 January 1793.

9. This list of about 145,000 names (with rank, profession, French residence, and property) was riddled with errors. It included the names of many who were dead or just happened to be absent from their homes at the time the list was compiled.

10. Of all émigrés, 51% were members of the third estate, 25% of the clergy, and 17% of the aristocracy.

11. The entry reads: "On donne le nom d'émigrant à tous ceux qui quittent le pays, au moment où ils s'en vont. Plus tard, quand le fait est accompli, on dit les émigrés. Ce mot alors ne s'applique qu'à ceux qui sont partis avec l'intention de revenir;

les autres sont devenus des étrangers ou des colons" 'The name *emigrant* is given to all those that leave the country, at the time of their departure. Later, once the fact has been accomplished, they are called *émigrés*. The name applies only to those who left with the intention to return; others have become foreigners or settlers.'

12. The compensation was voted on 28 April. On 17 April, a royal ordinance by Charles X had conceded independence to Haiti with the condition that the former colony agree to pay an indemnity of 150 million francs as reparation to former plantation owners. Students might be encouraged to compare the *milliard des émigrés* law and the law *Indemnité de St. Domingue*. For the links between the French and Haitian Revolutions, see the essays by Chalmin and by Daut in this volume.

13. See, for example, William Wordsworth's "The Banished Negroes," "The Emigrant Mother," and "The Exiled French Clergy" and Charlotte Smith's *The Emigrants*.

14. In *Le cabinet des antiques*, Balzac coined the phrase "déménagement social" 'social upheaval' in reference to the return of émigrés to France in 1800 (9).

15. See Astbury; Carpenter and Mansel; Douthwaite; Genand; and Seth.

16. For works that foreground the question of hospitality, see Fiévée: Goethe; and Shelley.

17. In Mary Shelley's *Frankenstein* the key episode in the formation of the creature occurs during his encounter with the De Laceys, a family of French exiles whose situation recalls that of émigrés fleeing the Revolution. See Douthwaite 92–93.

18. Another work that could be studied in class is Alain Mabanckou's novel *Bleu, blanc, rouge: Roman* ("Blue, White, Red").

19. For the use of the term "amphibie" in Charrière's works, see Delon.

Works Cited

Aprile, Sylvie. *Le siècle des exilés: Bannis et proscrits de 1789 à la Commune*. CNRS Éditions, 2010.

Astbury, Katherine. *Narrative Responses to the Trauma of the French Revolution*. Legenda, 2012.

Balzac, Honoré de. *Le cabinet des antiques*. 1838. Garnier, 1958.

———. *Le lys dans la vallée*. 1835. Gallimard, 2004.

Brecht, Bertold. "Über die Bezeichnung Emigranten" (1937). *Gesammelte Gedichte*, vol. 2, Suhrkamp, 1976, p. 718.

Burney, Frances. *The Wanderer; or, Female Difficulties*. 1814. Oxford UP, 1991.

Carpenter, Kirsty, and Philip Mansel. *The French Émigrés in Europe and the Struggle against Revolution, 1789–1814*. Macmillan Press, 1999.

Charrière, Isabelle de. *Lettres trouvées dans des portefeuilles d'émigrés*. 1793. G. A. van Oorschot, 1979. Vol. 8 of *Œuvres complètes*.

Cruikshank, Isaac. "*Salus in fuga*: La France se purge petit à petit." July 1789. Yale U Lewis Walpole Library.

Delon, Michel. "Lettres trouvées dans des porte-feuilles d'émigrés, ou l'éloge de l'amphibie." *Une européenne: Isabelle de Charrière en son siècle*. Éditions Gilles Attinger / Hauterive, 1994, pp. 197–205.

Diome, Fatou. *Le ventre d'Atlantique.* Librairie Générale Française, 2005.
Douthwaite, Julia V. *The Frankenstein of 1790 and Other Lost Chapters from Revolutionary France.* U of Chicago P, 2012.
Émigré. *Oxford English Dictionary*, www.oed.com/view/Entry/61179?redirectedFrom=émigré#eid. Definition 1.
Fiévée, Joseph. *La dot de Suzette, ou Histoire de Mme de Senneterre racontée par elle-même.* 1798. Desjonquères, 1990.
Fritzsche, Peter. *Stranded in the Present: Modern Time and the Melancholy of History.* Harvard UP, 2004.
Gatlif, Tony. *Exils.* 2004. *Internet Archive*, 25 Apr. 2016, archive.org/details/ExilsTonyGatlif20041.
Genand, Stéphanie, ed. *Romans de l'émigration (1797–1803).* Honoré Champion, 2008.
Goethe, Johann Wolfgang von. *Unterhaltungen deutscher Ausgewanderte.* 1795. Princeton UP, 1995.
Huber, Therese. *Briefe aus den Papieren einiger Emigrirten.* Voss, 1794.
Jaquier, Claire, et al., editors. *Destins romanesques de l'émigration.* Desjonquères, 2007.
Kristeva, Julia. *Étrangers à nous-mêmes.* Gallimard, 1991.
———. *Strangers to Ourselves.* Columbia UP, 1991.
Maalouf, Amin. *Les identités meurtrières.* Grasset, 1998.
———. *In the Name of Identity: Violence and the Need to Belong.* Penguin Books, 2003.
Mabanckou, Alain. *Bleu, blanc, rouge: Roman.* 2nd ed. Présence Africaine, 1998.
———. *Blue White Red: A Novel.* Translated by Alison Dundy, Indiana UP, 2013.
Rance, Karine. "L'historiographie de l'émigration." *Les noblesses françaises dans l'Europe de la Révolution*, edited by Philippe Bourdin. PUR / PU Blaise Pascal, 2010, p. 355–68.
Sénac de Meilhan, Gabriel. *L'émigré.* 1794. Gallimard, 2004.
Seth, Catriona, editor. *Mémoires d'une famille émigrée.* By Jeanne-Françoise Polier de Bottens, Slatkine, 2016.
Shelley, Mary. *Frankenstein; or, The Modern Prometheus.* 1818. Penguin Books, 1994.
Smith, Charlotte Turner. *The Banished Man.* Cadell and Davies, 1794.
———. *The Emigrants.* 1793. *The Poems of Charlotte Smith.* Oxford UP, 1993, pp. 131–63.
Todorov, Tzvetan. *Nous et les autres: La réflexion française sur la diversité humaine.* Seuil, 1989.
———. *On Human Diversity: Nationalism, Racism, and Exoticism In French Thought.* Harvard UP, 1993.
Wahnich, Sophie. *L'impossible citoyen: L'étranger dans le discours de la Révolution française.* Albin Michel, 1997.
Wordsworth, William. "The Banished Negroes." Wordsworth, *Poems*, vol. 1, p. 643.
———. "The Emigrant Mother." Wordsworth, *Poems*, vol. 1, pp. 695–98.
———. "The Exiled French Clergy." Wordsworth, *Poems*, vol. 3, pp. 417–18.
———. *The Poems of William Wordsworth.* 3 vols., Humanities-Ebooks, 2009.

Rosa Mucignat and Sanja Perovic

The French Revolution Effect: France, Italy, Germany, Greece

There are several challenges to teaching the French Revolution in a comparative literature context. Those (few) students who have previously encountered the French Revolution will likely have done so in a history department, where the conventional approach is a linear, chronological study of national events. The historical approach tends to divide events into a before and an after, into origins and outcomes. This overlooks the experience of the Revolution in its own present, both in the heroic sense of living in a new time and the importance of this epic quality in communicating revolutionary enthusiasm abroad. By contrast, literary history tends to leap from an internationalist European eighteenth century (a borderless republic of letters) to a nationalist European nineteenth century. Students rarely have the opportunity to read across national literatures in this crucial period when Europe's national borders were not yet consolidated. The challenge thus is threefold. How do we put literary agency, with its emphasis on emotions and intentions, at the heart of historical accounts of agency that focus on actions and effects? How can we understand the French Revolution as an ongoing presence—a continual aspiration—even after its (partial) defeat as a political project and historical event? Finally, how do we go beyond the mere instrumental use of literary texts as historical documents?

We address these challenges in the final-year undergraduate module we coteach at King's College London (equivalent to a ten- to eleven-week trimester in the United States but easily expandable to a fifteen-week semester; see appendix for details). Taught in translation, this module also responds to the pressures toward interdisciplinary teaching in modern language departments at a time of shrinking faculty and student numbers in both United States and United Kingdom institutions. Teaching in translation enables colleagues from different departments to guest-lecture and address students beyond their core constituency; it also gives us, the module conveners, access to new material and different perspectives on what we normally teach. The pedagogical method, alternating between lectures and small-group seminars, emphasizes close readings of texts in their entirety, texts chosen with an eye to problematizing revolutionary key words still in use—notably *rights* (individual and collective), *citizenship*, *nation*, and *equality*. At the same time, the comparative approach is used to resist the still dominant diffusion model of the Revolution, which assumes a strong original with weaker copies. We focus on the intellectual problem of temporality. How did countries on the verge of emancipation engage with the Revolution's idea of radical, man-made change? And how did the Revolution prompt European radicals outside France to reappropriate their own republican and democratic traditions creatively?

The module as a whole aims to complicate traditional chronologies about the causes and results of the Revolution and to incite students to see for themselves how ideas can flow in many directions at the same time. Our starting point is not America or France but Naples, Italy, with the excavation of Pompeii and Herculaneum. We then turn to documents that exemplify the "cascading" nature of revolutionary rights (Hunt 147, 212). But the module's main focus is tracking the Revolution's explosive outward radiation in the first half of the nineteenth century by investigating France's sister republics in Italy and Germany and the case of Greece. Italy's paradoxical position is highlighted as both the originator of an exemplary republicanism and a nation unable to emancipate itself. The German experience of revolution is examined through the moral quandaries posed by the Terror about what can be sacrificed to realize revolutionary aspirations. Greece is the most striking example of crossed temporalities in a revolutionary age. The Greek struggle against the Ottoman Empire (1821–32) reenacted the ancient battle between European freedom and Asian despotism, and its success galvanized liberals everywhere.

We adopt a comparative perspective that is both synchronic (between nations at the same time) and diachronic (between earlier and later writers). For instance, Ugo Foscolo's epistolary novel *The Last Letters of Jacopo Ortis* (1798), modeled on Goethe's *Sorrows of Young Werther*, is paired with Antonio Gramsci's reflections on "passive revolution," a term designating the necessity of slow cultural and political reform. Students are also encouraged to see connections with the Greek poet Dionýsios Solomós. Like Foscolo, Solomós was from the Venetian-controlled Ionian island of Zante or Zakynthos. His poem *Hymn to Liberty* features in Greece's national anthem. Solomós in turn is viewed in the light of Shelley and Byron's involvement in Greece and the international liberal response to the Greek-Ottoman conflict.

We begin with the semantic history of revolution, analyzing the original meaning of the word as a cyclical change and how the terms *renaissance*, *reformation*, and *revolution* were often used interchangeably (students read short texts by Burke, Koselleck, Ozouf, and Williams). Students reflect on why calling an event a revolution, regeneration, insurrection, or revolt influences how it is interpreted and understood both by contemporaries and by subsequent historical analysis. They are directed to the *Wikipedia* page describing recent media-baptized color revolutions: yellow (Philippines), orange (Ukraine), green (Iran), velvet (Czechoslovakia), and so on. How do these labels affect our perceptions of events? Why might a competing vocabulary—terms like *riot*, *uprising*, *civil war*—not be used?

If the first session focuses on conceptions of political and historical change, the second is devoted to metaphors of revolution. We track one image in particular, that of the exploding volcano. We first take the students back in time to Naples, circa 1738. This unorthodox choice is meant to sweep students into the exciting discoveries sparked by the excavations of Pompeii and Herculaneum, buried by Vesuvius in AD 79 and discovered nearly seventeen hundred years later. Students are introduced to the archaeological findings through texts and images—frescoes, sculptures, erotica, picturesque paintings of Vesuvius. We reflect on how the rupture of the volcano was perceived not simply as a destructive, terrifying event but also as a regenerative, positive force—fertilizing soil, constructing mountains, and preserving a long-lost civilization imagined to be closer to nature than ours.

We then go forward in time with a close reading of Percy Bysshe Shelley's 1820 "Ode to Naples," in support of the Neapolitan revolution of 1820–21. Set in Naples and Pompeii, the poem links the Greco-Roman democratic tradition to current aspirations to liberty. It suggests that Naples's former glory can be "restored" if the king of Naples accepts the liberal constitution implemented by the Spanish government in Cadiz, the first European constitution to successfully advocate universal suffrage. Shelley likens the Neapolitans to "volcanoes" and asks nature to intercede, but he is writing for the English readers of the *Morning Chronicle*, *Military Register*, and *Weekly Gazette*. The day after its first publication, the leaders of the Holy Alliance agreed on military intervention in Naples, and Britain did nothing. Students are asked to reflect on the problematic link between this natural-cultural idea of revolutionary change, where violence is creative and part of the natural order, and the subsequent experience of revolutionary action in Italy and elsewhere, which was violently repressed by both local and foreign powers.

The following two sessions focus on the new understanding of revolution that emerged in 1789, namely that "foundation comes from initiation" (Ozouf 809). Shelley's poem had already described the Cadiz constitution as "Spain's thrilling paean" to other nations. This lyrical understanding of constitutions is the departure for our reading of Emmanuel Joseph Sieyès's *What Is the Third Estate?* We then consider France's three constitutions (1791, 1793, and 1795) and how they open up what Reinhart Koselleck calls "a social space of expectation," as every revolutionary program strives for "realization in the name of freedom or equality or both" (52). We link Sieyès to what Hannah Arendt identifies as the new problematic: the ambiguous slippage between revolutionary nationalism and nationalist revolutions (158).

This incompatibility between the demand for either more liberty or more equality is explored in session 4, which pairs the Revolution's first communist manifesto, the "Manifesto of the Equals" (1796), with Alexis de Tocqueville's two speeches of 1848, "Je crois que nous nous endormons sur un volcan" 'I believe that we are sleeping on a volcano' (27 Jan.) and "Sur la question du droit au travail" 'On the right to work' (12 Sept.; "Tocqueville on Socialism"). The Conspiracy of the Equals was the first revolution against the revolutionary state and an acknowledged influence, through Philippe Buonarroti's involvement, on Italian Jacobinism. It exemplifies how journalism interacted with modern mass politics. It also underscores the issue of economic equality and the crucial rights to mass assembly and freedom of expression. Tocqueville's speech on the right to work is a mid-nineteenth-century rejoinder to socialism. Slamming this movement as a return to Babouvisme, he claims that liberalism (and America) is the Revolution's only future. The class is asked to analyze the differences in tone and intended audience between these two texts—one a manifesto and call to action, the other a parliamentary speech. We conclude by debating Tocqueville's assertion that the Revolution is nothing but "Christian charity applied to politics"; in other words, that duty toward the poor is acceptable but not a politics of, and in the name of, poverty ("Tocqueville on Socialism").

We then consider journalism in the effort to find a solution to the greatest pedagogical challenge of this module. This is the problem of how to communicate sufficient historical knowledge of revolutionary events to students who, for the most part, have a shaky grasp of the major dramatis personae and only a basic, if any, sense of the Revolution's time line. How do we climb down from the broad time span of intellectual and cultural history as described above to the specific time line of revolutionary events? In 2016 we were fortunate to visit the exhibition *Revolution under a King: French Prints, 1789–92*, curated by David Bindman and Richard Taws at the University College London Art Museum. Using a free teaching pack available online (dspace.jorum.ac.uk/xmlui/handle/10949/17553), students were assigned different prints to present to the class during the visit, each depicting an important revolutionary event (the fall of the Bastille, the march on Versailles, the flight to Varennes). This exercise gave students insight into the Revolution as a media event that amplified both good and bad feelings. One 1793 print contrasted French Liberty with English Liberty, the former a medusa-like figure presiding over the key words *atheism*, *rebellion*, *anarchy*, *equality*; the latter prosperous, holding the Magna Carta, seeing off a trading vessel sailing into the distance, and associated with the key words *prosperity*, *protection of property*, *inheritance*, and *justice*. Another print contrasted French Happiness and English Misery, the former starving; the latter represented by four feasting John Bulls or Jack Roast Beefs. In addition to this online resource, students at any university can explore the rich *Wikimedia Commons* site on revolutionary satire as well as the often underutilized print and newspaper collections of college libraries and local museums.

From this visual instantiation of the impossibility to separate historical fact from emotional feeling, we turn to literature. (Note that colorful maps are a crucial supplement to all lectures from this point!) We introduce Foscolo's *The Last Letters of Jacopo Ortis* through Maurizio Viroli's distinction between patriotism and nationalism (2). Foscolo's text is situated at a crossroads where the older language of republican patriotism, which might easily extend across borders with international patriotism, meets new discourses of ethnic-cultural nationalism, which are based on blood, language, and community. Here we encounter once more our key words—*rights*, *nation*, *equality*—but they are now inflected with pessimism. Foscolo was an exile from Venice. Like the fictional Ortis, he was forced to leave his homeland after the Treaty of Campo Formio, in which Napoleon, at first the great hope of young Italian radicals, gave Venice to the Austrians. Through Ortis, Foscolo promotes and eventually rejects patriotism as a passion that suspends disbelief, allowing people to overcome the natural impulse to self-interest. This novel stands out for its analysis of the "passive revolution" and for addressing the question, central to later theories of decolonization, of whether it is possible to have a revolution without a nation.

Our exploration of the dual languages of patriotism and nationalism continues with Solomós's *Hymn to Liberty* (1823). Celebrating Greece's revolution, the epic poem exemplifies the international character of European literature. Solomós's early poems were written in his native Italian before he turned to demotic or spoken Greek—the language of the people—which he did not in fact know very well. Although written in Greek for Greeks, the *Hymn to Liberty* was immediately translated into other European languages in full knowledge that the revolutionary struggle was taking place in a pan-European sphere. Our guest lecturer was Roderick Beaton, who made the case for considering the Greek Revolution more historically and ideologically important than is often assumed. The first successful national revolution in Europe and the blueprint for future European revolutions, it concealed its novelty to win approval from the European powers, which, by definition, were against revolution. *Regeneration* is the key term here, used to make a liberal revolution appear as a conservative restoration. Beaton contrasted Solomós's brand of nationalism with the rich intellectual discourse surrounding Hellenic republicanism. For example, Rigas Velestinlis's "New Constitution" of 1797 (based on the French Constitution of 1793) advocated a multireligious Hellenic republic established on civic notions of popular sovereignty. Adamantios Korais took a more ethnocentric approach, linking modern Greece to ancient Athens, the world's first democracy. Finally, both Byron's *Childe Harold's Pilgrimage*, canto 2, and Shelley's *Hellas* present the Greek struggle as a restoration of ancient liberty and a revival of a supreme point in European history.

After such high-minded cultural processing, Solomós's poem makes for somewhat uncomfortable reading. Unless prompted, students may be reluctant to discuss the violent imagery, the emphasis on Orthodox Christianity, and the negative portrayal of the Turks. To alleviate their discomfort, instructors might address the antagonistic aspects of identity politics; the need to evoke a common enemy, already present in Sieyès; and the tension between identity politics and revolutionary universalism.

Next we turn to the German-speaking lands. Friedrich Hölderlin's tragedy *Death of Empedocles* also uses Hellenism as a template for imagining revolution. We read the first version, written in 1798, at a crucial moment of radical politics in Swabia, shortly after the French retained the left bank of the Rhine. In staging the replacement of monarchy by a republican civil order, the play expresses the hope that the Holy Roman Empire, in place for over eight hundred years, could be reorganized along republican lines. Through the legend of Empedocles's leap into the volcano, it dramatizes the problem of the legislator: he who founds a new civil order but must remain outside it, lest he break the very law he founded. In representing an interregnum period, the play also highlights the ambiguous role of people power in any republican project. Are the people a chorus? a crowd? Are they liberated or duped by their leaders? Students interpret the play both with reference to contemporaneous events (France's prolonged constitutional crisis from 1789 to 1804) and in the light of the classical past. We pair the play with Diogenes Laertius's account of the historical Empedocles, Hölderlin's main source. This comparison provides an excellent context for asking, Does Empedocles renounce power in the interests of equality, or is he self-serving? Was his death by leaping into the volcano a fraud, chosen to set up his own legend, or was it spurred by the authentic desire to become one with nature? Why does Hölderlin's Empedocles never take the leap?

Political and rhetorical violence is also the theme of Georg Büchner's *Danton's Death*. The play marks both a continuity and break with our previous texts. Continuity can be found in Büchner's concern to reconcile the exercise of freedom, politics as active emancipation, with an overwhelming sense of futility. But it is equally important to emphasize what is radically new about the play: not simply the use of documentary evidence from the French Revolution but also how citation itself becomes a way of exploring what happens to language during a revolution. In our previous texts, the language of classics and nature served as a metalanguage through which to analyze revolution. Here the revolution is analyzed by means of its own language: violent, theatrical, and often inauthentic. As Büchner's contrasting use of street vernacular makes clear, the revolutionary watchwords of *rights*, *citizenship*, and *equality* trigger conflicts between state and society, idea and reality on the local level.

The last sessions are devoted to Stendhal's *Charterhouse of Parma* (1839). Through Fabrice del Dongo, Stendhal's half-Italian, half-French character, we return to our module's main theme: the differential European experience of the Revolution. Born in 1796, a time that the narrator describes as the first of Milan's two happiest years, Fabrice is an illegitimate child, the result of a love affair between his Italian mother and the French lieutenant Robert, a secret worshipper of Napoleon, the usurper of thrones. Fabrice embodies the revolutionary power to suspend time in a novel in which Restoration Europe otherwise appears as farce, in which there is privilege and no legitimacy, society and no state or system of justice. Both he and his aunt, Gina (who resembles the young Napoleon), reflect the experience of Napoleon as a fatal memory after which no one can be happy. But this novel also literalizes the conflicting temporalities, and sense of time out of joint, that characterize the Bourbon Restoration (1814–30). Stendhal suggests that the French Revolution might work better in Italy than in France, by reviving the inner values of freedom last experienced at the time of Italy's medieval republics.

Some colleagues consider teaching in translation a loss, but we consider it a gain, especially as few teachers or students are versed in all the languages represented here. We try to compensate for any perceived loss of original meaning through collaborative, research-led teaching. Where specialists of modern Greek or Italian might not be available, a similar module can be team-taught with colleagues from classics, Spanish studies, and German studies, not to mention specialists in British Romanticism and revolutionary history. For instance, the session on Greece can be approached profitably from the angle of Shelley and Byron, who are present on every university curriculum but appear here in a different light. In our experience, colleagues are keen to bring the perspective of their particular language area and discipline to new audiences. Each guest lecturer also provides a robust bibliography, enabling nonspecialist module conveners to advise on essay topics and eventually grade them. While the content of each session lends itself to many variations, the overall coherence of the course is ensured by a close focus on the core concept of temporality and on the key words of revolution: *regeneration*, *rights*, *freedom*, *citizenship*, *nation*, *equality*. However modest, we hope this module can serve as an example for both colleagues and students. For colleagues it is a chance to escape the siloes of academic life. For students it is a means to push back against a widespread frictionless view of literary and cultural production in which revolution and conflict no longer play an obvious part.

Works Cited

Arendt, Hannah. *On Revolution*. 1963. Penguin, 2006.

Büchner, Georg. *Danton's Death*. 1835. Translated by Victor Price, Penguin, 1998.

Burke, Peter. "Renaissance, Reformation, Revolution." *Niedergang: Studien zu einem geschichtlichen Thema*, edited by Reinhart Koselleck and Paul Widmer, Klett-Cotta, 1980, pp. 137–47.

Foscolo, Ugo. *The Last Letters of Jacopo Ortis, 1798–1802*. Translated by J. G. Nichols, Hesperus Press, 2002.

Gramsci, Antonio. "The Concept of Passive Revolution." *Prison Notebooks, 1929–35*. Edited and translated by Quentin Hoare and Geoffrey Nowell Smith, International Publishers, 1971, pp. 106–14.

Hölderlin, Friedrich. First Version. *Death of Empedocles*. Translated by David Farrell Krell, State U of New York P, 2006, pp. 35–110.

Hunt, Lynn. *Inventing Human Rights: A History*. W. W. Norton, 2007.

Koselleck, Reinhart. "Historical Criteria of the Modern Concept of Revolution." *Futures Past: On the Semantics of Historical Time*, Translated by Keith Tribe, Columbia UP, 2004, pp. 43–57.

Laertius, Diogenes. "Empedocles." *Lives of the Eminent Philosophers*, translated by R. D. Hicks, vol. 2., Harvard UP, 1925, pp. 366–91. Loeb Classical Library.

"Manifesto of the Equals." Translated by Mitchell Abidor, *Marxists.org*, www.marxists.org/history/france/revolution/conspiracy-equals/1796/manifesto.htm.

Ozouf, Mona. "Revolution." *Critical Dictionary of the French Revolution*, edited by François Furet and Ozouf, translated by Arthur Goldhammer, Harvard UP, 1989, pp. 806–17.

Shelley, Percy Bysshe. "Ode to Naples." *Bartleby.com*, Nov. 2011, www.bartleby.com/270/5/160.html.

Sieyès, Emmanuel Joseph. "What Is the Third Estate?" *Sieyès: Political Writings*, edited by Michael Sonenscher, Hackett, 2003, pp. 92–137.

Solomós, Dionýsios. "Dithyrambics to Liberty." 1823. Translated by Charles Brinsley Sheridan. *The Songs of Greece, from the Romaic Text*, edited by M. C. Fauriel, *HathiTrust Digital Liberary*, catalog.hathitrust.org/Record/008673517.

Stendhal. *Charterhouse of Parma*. 1839. Translated by John Sturrock, Penguin Books, 2006.

Tocqueville, Alexis de. "Je crois que nous nous endormons sur un volcan." 27 Jan. 1848. *Assemblee nationale*, www2.assemblee-nationale.fr/decouvrir-l-assemblee/histoire/grands-moments-d-eloquence/alexis-de-tocqueville-27-janvier-1848

———. "Tocqueville on Socialism." Translated by Ronald Hamowy, *Online Library of Liberty*, 13 Apr. 2016, oll.libertyfund.org/pages/tocqueville-s-critique-of-socialism-1848.

Viroli, Maurizio. *For Love of Country: An Essay on Patriotism and Nationalism*. Oxford UP, 1995.

Williams, Raymond. "Revolution." *Keywords: A Vocabulary of Culture and Society*, Fontana, 2013.

Appendix: Sample Teaching Plan

Background reading: Doyle, William. *The French Revolution: A Very Short Introduction*. Oxford UP, 2001.

Week 1: Visions of the Future

Burke, Peter. "Renaissance, Reformation, Revolution"
Koselleck, Reinhart. "Historical Criteria of the Modern Concept of Revolution"
Williams, Raymond. "Revolution"
Ozouf, Mona. "Revolution"

Week 2: Volcanic Ruptures 1

Shelley, P. B. "Ode to Naples" (1820)
Images of Herculaneum, Pompeii, and Naples from the British Museum, Tate Britain, and National Gallery. Online resource
Constantine, David. *Fields of Fire: A Life of Sir William Hamilton*. Weidenfeld and Nicholson, 2001.

Week 3: Constitutions

Abbé Sieyès. "What Is the Third Estate?"
Declaration of the Rights of Man and of the Citizen, 1789 and 1793
Arendt, Hannah. *On Revolution*

Week 4: Volcanic Ruptures 2: Cascading Rights

"Manifesto of the Equals" (1796)
Tocqueville, Alexis de. "Je crois que nous nous endormons sur un volcan" (27 janvier 1848)
Tocqueville, Alexis de. "Tocqueville on Socialism"

Week 5: Print Culture

University College London Art Museum French Revolution teaching pack

Week 6: Italy

Foscolo, Ugo. *The Last Letters of Jacopo Ortis, 1798–1802*
Gramsci, Antonio. "The Concept of Passive Revolution"
Optional: Maurizio Viroli, *For Love of Country: An Essay on Patriotism and Nationalism*

Week 7: Greece

Solomós, Dionýsios. *Hymn to Liberty* (1823)
Optional: Byron, *Childe Harold's Pilgrimage*, canto II (1812); Shelley, *Hellas* (1822)

Week 8: Germany

Hölderlin, Friedrich. *Death of Empedocles*, first version
Laertius, Diogenes. "Empedocles"

Optional: Hölderlin, Friedrich. "Bonaparte," "Empedocles," "Rousseau," "To the Germans." *Selected Poems and Fragments*, translated by Michael Hamburger, Penguin Books, 1998, pp. 5, 45–48, 49–50.

Week 9

Büchner, Georg. *Danton's Death* (1835)

Weeks 10 and 11: The Restoration as Farce

Stendhal. *The Charterhouse of Parma* (1839)

John Pizer

Teaching the French Revolution in Late-Eighteenth- and Early-Nineteenth-Century German Literature Classes

Undergraduate students without much historical knowledge often believe the twenty-first century is the first truly transnational age. In courses I teach on German literature of the late eighteenth and early nineteenth centuries, my emphasis on the seminal historical and literary influence of the French Revolution in Germany dispels this myth. This emphasis helps students understand the literature of Germany during that period in its cross-cultural historical context. The core pedagogical assumption guiding my teaching of these courses with respect to the Revolution is that students are unaware of its significance for the cultural, economic, and political life of Germany at that time, so that the teacher must convey a great deal of historical background material both at the outset of the course, when an overview of the period is provided, and during the discussion of the individual texts as the course progresses.

I teach two courses on German literature of the period during which the French Revolution took place. One is a survey course on late-eighteenth- and early-nineteenth-century German literature. I emphasize here the early enthusiasm of German peasants and intellectuals for the Revolution. Peasants welcomed French soldiers after battles along the borders, and they preferred to quarter the revolutionary troops from across the Rhine rather than their prisoners, German soldiers. I then discuss Goethe's *Die Kampagne in Frankreich, 1792* (written between 1819 and 1822; "The Campaign in France, 1792"). I focus on Goethe's proclamation to the German troops commanded by the duke of Brunswick, who had just suffered defeat in the Battle of Valmy in 1792, that they had witnessed the birth of a new epoch. I argue this assertion is an example of literary self-staging, Goethe's attempt to style himself as a prophet. I contrast his later characterization of the Revolution as the trigger of social chaos in his epic poem *Hermann und Dorothea* (written between 1796 and 1797) with Friedrich Hölderlin's ambiguous embrace of the French cause in his poetry. The importance of showing radically different perspectives on the Revolution among contemporary German intellectuals makes these texts by Goethe and Hölderlin particularly valuable in my survey courses. Another example of the seminal influence of the Revolution for German intellectual life at that time is its shaping of Immanuel Kant's perspective on cosmopolitanism and politics, as in his view that German enthusiasm for the Revolution was an edifying substitute for the actual spread of its principles to German soil.

In my fairy tale class, I draw on Robert Darnton's *Great Cat Massacre* not only to show the French origins of most of the Grimms' *Märchen*, which usually surprises students, but also to introduce how the French tale of "Little Red Riding Hood" evolved into "Little Red Cap." However, I also argue that Ludwig Tieck's play *Leben und Tod des kleinen Rotkäppchens* (1800; "Life and Death of Little Red Cap") played an important part in this evolution. The role of the red-capped Jacobins in Tieck's transformation of the "petit chaperon rouge" into "Rotkäppchen" is self-evident, but I emphasize that Red Cap's seduction by the wolf as a revolutionary agent is given greater metaphoric subtlety in the Grimms' tale, in which the heroism of the hunter, as a functionary of German royal authority, is underscored. In the second half of this course, when we transition from the Grimms' "children and house fairy tales" (*Kinder- und Hausmärchen*) to a focus on "art fairy tales" (*Kunstmärchen*), the elusive symbolism of Goethe's generic "Das Märchen" is clarified by articulating how the French Revolution shapes the tropes and narrative volition of this work. Because there is little awareness among students of the significance of the Revolution for the composition of both popular fairy tales as standardized by the Brothers Grimm and art fairy tales, the Grimms' "Rotkäppchen" as well as Goethe's "Das Märchen" are essential texts for the German fairy tale class. The following essay includes a discussion of the secondary materials on which I draw in teaching both courses.

The French Revolution at first had little effect on the German states as a whole because of the isolation in which the masses existed at the time in the highly fragmented political entities of the Holy Roman Empire's German-speaking territories. Intellectuals such as Beethoven and Friedrich Schiller first welcomed the Revolution, believing its early democratic reforms might have a beneficial influence at some point on the politics of the German states. Tales of famished French aristocrats pouring across the border into western German territories and preferring to die of starvation rather than accept the black bread of the peasants they encountered may be apocryphal. However, I note accounts by Goethe and the scholar-soldier Friedrich Christian Laukhard of what Thomas P. Saine terms the "black bread—white bread dichotomy" between the two lands, a dichotomy that had "nothing to do with aristocratism per se" but highlighted the vast divide between the French noble immigrants and the German peasants then (77–78). Whether or not Goethe was accurate in calling the white bread–black bread divide the "Schibboleth," indeed the "battle cry" between Germans and French (qtd. in Saine 77), a brief elucidation of this dichotomy provides students with a vivid and entertaining illustration of the deep cultural chasm at the outset of the Revolution.

One might tell students that the story of French émigré aristocrats' preference for starvation to eating German black bread is probably an exaggeration, but the story accurately conveys the obsessive class consciousness of these émigrés, an elitism that students today may otherwise fail to comprehend. An awareness of that elitism is essential in grasping what motivated the French middle class to bring about the Revolution. Despite its title, Saine's *Black Bread—White Bread* does not dwell on how the national class divide is illustrated by attitudes toward this staple; instead, his book treats at length the arrogance, condescension, avarice, and especially the politically ludicrous thinking of the French aristocratic émigrés in western Germany. Their behavior alienated not only the German peasants but also the German military allies of the French émigrés. The French prodded the allied German forces into the 1792 campaign in western France that proved disastrous. Before the campaign, of course, the émigrés' agitation also resulted in the manifesto issued by the duke of Brunswick that threatened Paris with destruction should the Republic in any way harm King Louis XVI or Queen Marie-Antoinette. The radical Jacobin faction used this manifesto to create the paranoia that helped them topple the moderate Girondins and instigate the Terror. The Brunswick-led campaign therefore paved the way for that development (see Saine, esp. 105–25).

Virtually all students are vaguely aware of the Reign of Terror, even if they know little else about the Revolution, but almost none are aware of the unintentional German contribution to it.

Citing Goethe's proclamation, dated 19 September 1792, on the eve of the cannonade at Valmy, to the troops that Goethe accompanied on the campaign in France provides an excellent transition point from describing the historical background of the French Revolution's immediate impact on Germany to an engagement with the imaginative literature of the period in its treatment of these events. For when Goethe tells the troops how he assesses the already somewhat dire circumstance of the allied forces by famously proclaiming, "Von hier und heute geht eine neue Epoche der Weltgeschichte aus, und ihr könnt sagen, ihr seid dabei gewesen" 'From here and today a new epoch of world history emerges, and you can say, you were there' (*Gedenkausgabe* 12: 289), the reader stands right at the intersection of history and literature, or at the intersection of "Dichtung und Wahrheit" 'truth and fiction,' as Goethe titled his autobiography. He wrote his diary some thirty years later, and virtually all scholars agree that his prophecy concerning the significance of a battle that did not even transpire until the following day is informed more by poetic artifice than historical reportage. As Saine notes, "The 'I' who tells the story of the campaign in France is not what we would call the 'real' Goethe, but a fictional one" (204). Knowing this, students are ready to engage with the first overtly poetic work we analyze in class concerning the Revolution, Goethe's *Hermann und Dorothea*.

Goethe composed his epic poem during the Revolution's bloodiest phase and was shocked at reports of the carnage. English-language translations of the poem are available in a number of editions in print and online, but as the introduction to a now out-of-print dual language edition of *Hermann und Dorothea* notes, the poem was largely inspired by the travails of Goethe's former fiancée, Lili Schönemann, who had a harrowing experience, as the wife of Strasbourg's mayor (who had escaped France earlier) crossing the border with her children into German territory in 1794 (viii). Schönemann's perilous adventure, Goethe's reading about the wanderings of Protestant exiles from Salzburg expelled earlier in the eighteenth century, and current events in France and western Germany inspired the author to write his epic romance of the stolid, plodding, but honest landed bourgeois Hermann and the refugee from the Rhine area, Dorothea, who braves the hardships created by the Revolution in selflessly aiding her fellow emigrants as they make their way east, to the outskirts of Hermann's village. *Hermann und Dorothea* is divided into nine cantos, each one bearing the name of a Greek muse as its title. The titular figures overcome much misunderstanding, theirs and that of Hermann's father, to become engaged at the tale's conclusion. The poem is driven by polarities; the chaos and anarchy plaguing the exile group, the difficulties constantly overcome by the undaunted heroine, are contrasted with the unchanging, orderly, placid milieu inhabited by Hermann, his parents, and their fellow villagers.

The poem is a must read in a class on German literature of the eighteenth and early nineteenth centuries that seeks to elucidate Germany's intellectual-poetic encounter with the Revolution, because it not only constitutes Goethe's most direct imaginative engagement with the event but also reveals that his attitude toward the Revolution is more ambiguous than some scholars (e.g., Wilson, *Goethe-Tabu* and *Goethes Weimar*) might concede. For by this point in the class I have demonstrated to students through a reading of certain of his lyric poems that Goethe saw the necessity of violent, seemingly anarchic upheaval; he viewed life as ruled by polarities, believed that truly stable order results only from initial chaos and that progress emerges only from tragedy. Hermann's parents came together when the father saved the mother from a fire, and Hermann claims, in trying to obtain his father's permission to marry Dorothea:

> Sollte nicht auch ein Glück aus diesem Unglück hervorgehn,
> Und ich, im Arme der Braut, der zuverlässigen Gattin,
> Mich nicht erfreuen des Kriegs, so wie ihr des Brandes euch freutet?
> (*Gedenkausgabe* 3: 202)

> Should not happiness also emerge from this misfortune, and I, in the arms of the bride, the dependable spouse, not also rejoice in the war, as you rejoiced in the great fire?

This passage, and the poem as a whole, shows Goethe's view of the Revolution as necessary and latent with positive possibilities.

To be sure, Goethe never overtly embraced the French Revolution. Only a few intellectuals at the time were unwavering in their support of it, especially after the Jacobins became the dominant power in the nascent French Republic. The best known German supporter was the ethnologist, naturalist, and explorer Georg Forster, who was actively involved in the leadership of the short-lived Jacobin Mainz Republic. A brief discussion of Forster and the Mainz Republic should be of interest to students, most of whom assume that the aegis of the Jacobin government was confined to

France. Friedrich Hölderlin was not an outspoken adherent of the Revolution, but some scholars, led by the eminent Germanist Pierre Bertaux, argue that he was a discreet believer in the Jacobin cause. Indeed, influenced by Bertaux, the twentieth-century German playwright Peter Weiß wrote a play, *Hölderlin* (1971), that pits a radical revolutionary Hölderlin against an arch-conservative Goethe (see Pizer 67–73). Hölderlin's private feelings about the Revolution will always be a matter of conjecture, but I discuss his canonic poem "An die Deutschen" 'To the Germans' (1798) in the context of this event. Hölderlin believed Western Europe in the late eighteenth century existed in an in-between time marked by deep division, alienated from the divine but yearning for, and possibly moving toward, the kind of harmony he felt the Ancient Greeks enjoyed in their relationship with their gods. "An die Deutschen" reflects both this hope and a sarcastically expressed disappointment that his fellow Germans are childishly behind in the active quest for such a new, holistic age. When he refers to the Germans in this poem as "tatenarm und gedankenvoll" 'poor in deeds and rich in thoughts' (386), it is virtually certain that he is tacitly contrasting his nation's intellectualism and quietism with the dynamic revolutionary activities of its western neighbor.

I do not assign any texts of Kant that reflect this philosopher's complex attitude toward the Revolution, but I point out that Hölderlin could have had Kant in mind in characterizing the Germans as "poor in deeds but rich in thoughts." For while Kant abhorred the possibility that his countrymen would pursue their own violent revolution, he applauded their enthusiasm as spectators of the events in France, a spectatorship that he believed could sublimate fanatic impulses that, when properly channeled through government oversight, could lead to moral improvement at both the individual and social level. Andreas Gailus's chapter "Crisis and Enthusiasm in Kant's Philosophy of History" in his monograph *Passions of the Sign* (28–73) is quite useful in helping formulate a pedagogical summary of this element in Kant's views on the Revolution.

At the outset of my course on the German fairy tale, I stress that the assertions of the Brothers Grimm that their fairy tale collections had a German peasant provenance and that they simply standardized the German-language source material were proved false by late-twentieth-century scholarship. The Grimms' source material derived from interviews with people who spoke French and whose origin was French or from the Grimms' reading of early French tales. I draw heavily on Darnton's *Great Cat Massacre* to describe the French tales' narrative intent and purport, both at their origin and in such collections as Charles Perrault's *Contes de ma mère l'oye* (1697; "Tales of My Mother Goose"), which were distinct from those of the Grimms' tales. This broad adumbration of French origins and an account of how the Grimms reworked their Gallic material provide students with a corrective to the belief, still widely held and often inculcated in childhood, that there is something primally German about the Grimms' tales.

A striking example is "Little Red Riding Hood," as it is known in English, a direct translation of the French "petit chaperon rouge." Most American students are familiar only with the Grimms' version of this tale, the title of which was actually "Little Red Cap" ("Rotkäppchen"). "Red Riding Hood" became "Red Cap" through the Grimms' adaptation of Tieck's *Leben und Tod des kleinen Rotkäppchens*, which represents the beguiling of German youth by French revolutionary agents such as those who had been operative in the Mainz Republic. The red cap worn by the young woman is clearly that of the Jacobins, who themselves repurposed the ancient Roman token of manumission. To cite just one example of the transparency of the tale's allegory, the wolf, in conversation with a dog, denies belief in an afterlife, characterizing such a concept as "Aberglauben" 'superstition' (Tieck 351). This passage mirrors the Jacobin tendency toward atheism. The hunter in Tieck's play is too late to save Red Cap and her grandmother, though he does kill the wolf. In the Grimms' version, the hunter reflects the status of those who held the position of royal agent charged with protecting the forest, so his successful defeat of the wolf and rescue of Red Cap and her grandmother project a royal overthrow of the Revolution. When, at the conclusion, the two women save themselves from another wolf through their own ruse, the tale provides a lesson on peasant cunning typical of the Grimms but also harking back to the French original. Although I convey some of this background to students in the fairy tale class directly through lectures, I frequently assign Tieck's play and its influence on the Grimms' "Rotkäppchen" as an oral report to be turned into a written essay.

Like *Hermann und Dorothea*, Goethe's "Das Märchen" narrates a tale of renewal possible not despite but because of the chaos, death, and destruction linked to the French Revolution (*Gedenkausgabe* 9: 369–402). However, unlike the poem, which was composed with a popular audience in mind, Goethe's art fairy tale cloaks the Revolution in a dense cluster of symbols that require somewhat detailed unpacking in the undergraduate classroom. This unpacking presents a pedagogical challenge, but including Goethe's "Märchen" in the German fairy tale course is important, not only because it is among the most canonic of late Romantic art fairy tales but also, as the title implies, because it attempts to constitute in its narrative a definition of the genre itself. Though Goethe does not actually provide such a definition, "Märchen" becomes a paradigm of this genre through its atmosphere of timelessness and its embodiment of alchemically inflected forces not subject to the concrete natural laws of the real world. It incorporates the fantastic according to laws immanent to what Goethe perceived as the fairy tale realm.

The French Revolution manifests itself in this work in two ways. First, "Märchen" is the last story in the narrative cycle *Unterhaltungen deutscher Ausgewanderten* (1795; "Conversations of German Refugees"). All the stories in this cycle are told among a group of German refugees fleeing the Revolution. The more or less natural realm of the tale is separated from a fantastic domain by a river plied by a ferryman. In the fantastic domain, the Princess Lilie suffers from a condition in which living beings die but nonliving things come to life at her touch. Her beloved, a prince, becomes a victim: unable to bear the impossibility of intimacy, he embraces her and dies. Through her love and the self-sacrifice of a magical serpent, Lilie and her party cross the river with the dead prince in tow. He is brought back to life through love and becomes king in a new, transcendent realm. He incorporates the attributes of four kings from the previous time, attributes that disparately and conflictedly exist in France on the eve of the Revolution. A clumsy giant, whose destructive power reflects the revolutionary anarchy unleashed in the 1790s, becomes frozen in the new kingdom into "eine kolosalle mächtige Bildsäule" 'a colossal ornamented column,' which becomes useful because its shadow reveals the hours (*Gedenkausgabe* 9: 401). In her book on the *Unterhaltungen*, Jane Brown notes that "Märchen" "describes the salvation and rejuvenation of a disrupted society through the combined effort of its members" (27). Through discussions that navigate, like the ferryman, the different realms of the fairy tale, students can see how it enacts a cooperative utopian postrevolutionary society. In writing it, Goethe responded to contemporary circumstances in a Germany threatened by the bloodshed convulsing its western neighbor immediately before Thermidor. It is this disrupted, bleak world that "Märchen" imaginatively transcends and overcomes.

Note

Translations are mine, unless otherwise indicated.

Works Cited

Bertaux, Pierre. "Hölderlin und die Französische Revolution." *Der andere Hölderlin: Materialien zum 'Hölderlin' Stück von Peter Weiss.* 2nd ed., edited by Thomas Beckermann and Volker Canaris, Suhrkamp, 1979, pp. 65–100.

Brown, Jane K. *Goethe's Cyclical Narratives* Die Unterhaltungen deutscher Ausgewanderten *and* Wilhelm Meisters Wanderjahre. U of North Carolina P, 1975.

Darnton, Robert. *The Great Cat Massacre and Other Episodes in French Cultural History.* Basic Books, 1984.

Gailus, Andreas. *Passions of the Sign: Revolution and Language in Kant, Goethe, and Kleist.* Johns Hopkins UP, 2006.

Goethe, Johann Wolfgang von. *Gedenkausgabe der Werke, Briefe und Gespräche.* Edited by Ernst Beutler, 24 vols., Artemis, 1948–54.

———. *Hermann and Dorothea.* Introduced and translated by Daniel Coogan, Ungar, 1966.

Grimm, Jacob, and Wilhelm Grimm. "Rotkäppchen." *Ausgewählte Kinder- und Hausmärchen: Gesammelt durch die Brüder Grimm.* Reclam, 1981, pp. 84–89.

Hölderlin, Friedrich. "An die Deutschen." *The Age of Goethe: An Anthology of German Literature,* edited by Stuart Atkins, Houghton Mifflin, 1969, p. 386.

Pizer, John. *Imagining the Age of Goethe in German Literature, 1970–2010.* Camden House, 2011.

Saine, Thomas P. *Black Bread—White Bread: German Intellectuals and the French Revolution.* Camden House, 1988.

Tieck, Ludwig. *Leben und Tod des kleinen Rotkäppchens: Eine Tragödie.* 1828. *Schriften,* vol. 2, De Gruyter, 1966, pp. 327–62.

Wilson, W. Daniel, editor. *Goethes Weimar und die Französische Revolution: Dokumente der Krisenjahre.* Böhlau, 2004.

———. *Das Goethe-Tabu: Protest und Menschenrechte im klassischen Weimar.* dtv Verlagsgesellschaft, 1999.

Yvonne Fuentes

The French Revolution's Echo in Spain through Literary and Satirical Representations

The long-term impact of the French Revolution in Spain is less connected to the events that transpired in 1789 than to those stemming from the incursion of the Napoleonic forces into Spanish territory in 1808. In Spain, because those two crucial episodes were not merely linked but often conflated, the nomenclature used to refer to the aftermath of the arrival of the imperial forces operated as either an overt or a veiled indicator of the political, religious, and philosophical position from which the French Revolution was interpreted.

Consequently, the three labels "Napoleonic wars," "Peninsular War," and "War of Independence" all refer to the same occasion, but each draws attention to discrete struggles, allies, enemies, and alternatives. "War of Independence" is perhaps the most frequently adopted in the Spanish context, because it reaffirms and renews in the collective imaginary a Romantic image of a passionate, courageous, and resolute people determined to defend the homeland against the most advanced war machine of its time. For many critics, however, the rejection of the Napoleonic regeneration renders these same people as grotesque, ignorant, and brazen fanatics eager to die for a despotic and degenerate king.

This essay proposes that we engage students with the events and the perceived causal relation among the French Revolution, the Napoleonic invasion, and the lingering view that Spain is different by exploring two distinct types of texts. The first comprises the objective and factual declarations of war, peace treaties, and official documents that offer seemingly clear margins between friend and foe.[1] The second is the satirical pamphlet literature—namely, the caricatures, lampoons, and images that seek to expose the folly and corruption of contemporary targets through wit or ridicule. The satire, however, poses a difficulty: although its viewers and readers seem complicit in the initial laughter, they often remain unsure of what alternative the satirist is proposing. The factual texts provide clear demarcations and firm footings; the satirical texts generate questions and ambiguity. I focus on two periods, pre-1789 to 1808 and 1808 to 1833, to facilitate understanding of Franco-Spanish relations before and after Napoleon and to help students gain the necessary background and context.

Employing two very different kinds of documents with such divergent communicative aims elicits classroom discussion regarding the value of an official narrative and the value of a sensational representation of news. Additionally, a close look at the language used in these often conflicting narratives reveals examples of the political and cultural functions of myth and memory. I suggest that students and instructors consider the following questions and topics as they explore the reverberations and legacies of the French Revolution in Spain. Which of the two representations of events, the official or the satirical, seems more credible and which might better be labeled "fake news"? Are the satirical images less authentic or permanent than the official ones? How does the manipulation and conflation of events contribute to an overarching narrative? What are the nuanced elements that confound or distort that narrative? What can students in interdisciplinary courses gain from texts with conflicting interpretations? How do we explain the widespread scatological motif present in both written and visual texts? Finally, how can these texts promote debate on current topics, such as the role of satire in society today or the fine line between free speech and hate speech?

Pacto de Familia and the Wars with Great Britain

The death of Carlos II in 1700 and the ensuing Spanish War of Succession signified the end of one dynastic era, the Hapsburgs, and the beginning of another, the Bourbons. Not long after, Louis XV and Felipe V signed and ratified the first Bourbon-Borbón family pact, which ensured the security of each monarchy and the glory of both houses (*Tratados* 277). The last article of this first of many pacts further guaranteed the perpetual and irrevocable close ties of friendship between his Catholic majesty and his most Christian majesty (281). In October 1743, the pact was renewed by Louis XV and Carlos III and then again in August 1761. Although their specifics differed, all iterations of the pact sought to consolidate the defensive union between both families by insisting that an attack on one constituted an attack on both, thus setting the stage for Spain's involvement in all French wars.

Despite the riots, the storming of the Bastille in July 1789, the Declaration of the Rights of Man and of the Citizen, the Civil Constitution of 1790, and the removal of the French monarch, neither Carlos III nor Carlos IV, his son, broke the pact or suspended diplomatic relations. It was not until the regicide of 1793 that Spain declared war against France, its possessions, and inhabitants as per the Spanish *Real cédula* ("royal decree") of 25 March. In May of that same year, Carlos IV of Spain and George III of England signed an offensive and defensive alliance, motivated by "their zeal and preoccupation over the safety of their respective States."[2] Their aim was to "conserve the general system of Europe [and] pose a barrier to the prejudicial objectives of aggression and expansion [of the French]" (*Tratados* 647).

Two years later, the economic cost of that war turned out to be an important reason for the 1795 peace treaty between Carlos IV, "the King our Lord," and the French Republic. The preface justifies it as follows:

> After sustaining a cruel and costly war, the King our Lord has the satisfaction of having procured peace for his vassals. His Catholic Majesty and the French Republic equally desirous to cease the calamities of this war which divides us, are convinced there are mutual interests that warrant the reestablishment of friendship and good intelligence between both Nations. . . . (654)

Particularly interesting and relevant to future relations between Spain and France are points 4 and 9 of the treaty:

> The French Republic restitutes to the King of Spain all conquests made in Spanish territory during the current war. French troops will withdraw within fifteen days of this treaty.
>
> In return for the restitution, the King of Spain cedes, abandons, and renounces on his behalf and his successors the Spanish part of the Island of Santo Domingo. (655)[3]

A cynic might regard the king's plea for peace as an example of empty rhetoric, considering that his vassals would soon after be entangled in an intermittent nine-year war, this time against the former ally Great Britain (peace was declared in 1802 and war again in 1804). An interesting note is that Citizen Joseph Bonaparte, the future king of Spain, appears among the signatories of the 1802 peace treaty.

These texts seem to support the idea that not before or even during the first decade of the Revolution were France or the French people perceived as an existential threat or an inherent danger to Spain, Europe, or Christianity. Despite the cordon sanitaire of 1791, which sought to curtail the introduction of seditious papers, local Spanish newspapers and diaries still portrayed France as a refined and progressive country. The unrest, the institutional changes, and the insurrection did not at first stir extraordinary commotion or awaken xenophobic tendencies in Spain or in other European governments, which were accustomed to such events. In the game of thrones and politics, political realignments and reassessments of alliances were considered primarily in relation to their ability to maintain or shift the continental balance of powers, as we saw in the treaty of 1795. The hegemonic ambitions of a newcomer like Napoleon, however, changed this status quo.

The War of Independence and Its Consequences, 1808–33

Although the French Revolution and its ideas neither heightened Spanish patriotism nor inspired great indignation against revolutionary thought, the same cannot be said of the events triggered by the invasion of 1808, when friendly imperial forces entered Spanish territory under the pretext of passing through on their way to Portugal, an English ally. Much happened that year: in March, disgruntled citizens first assaulted and then captured Prime Minister Manuel Godoy, aka Prince of the Peace, then compelled Carlos IV to dismiss him, and finally forced the king to abdicate in favor of his son, Fernando.

This trifecta of inefficiency in the form of a disengaged monarch, a dubious prime minister, and a resentful prince created a power vacuum that was filled shortly after when both Carlos and Fernando were persuaded to renounce the Spanish crown, which was then given to Joseph Bonaparte. Francisco de Goya immortalized the people's reaction against the invading French troops as well as the invasion's bloody aftermath in *El dos de mayo* ("The Second of May") and *El tres de mayo* ("The Third of May").[4]

Much of the contemporary pamphlet literature traced a causal relation between the ideas of the French Revolution and Napoleon's invasion of Spain, therefore fueling not only anti-Napoleonic but also strong anti-French sentiments. Eventually, Fernando VII, *El Deseado* ("the Desired"), returned to Spain after the defeat of the French forces and swore allegiance to the liberal constitution of 1812. However, it was only a matter of time before the tide turned, and in an ironic twist of fate it was an army of conservative French forces known as the One Hundred Thousand Sons of Saint Louis that helped Fernando reestablish absolute power in 1823. The actions of the following decade managed to temper democratic ardor: the constitution of 1812 was repealed, progressive acts and measures of the government were nullified, and *afrancesados* ("French lovers"), moderates, and *liberales* suffered retaliation.

Because of new and old alliances, it was no longer France or the French people who were the enemy but rather the demonic ideas of the philosophes and of all who shared that ideological inheritance. Consequently, the propaganda, be it early-nineteenth- or mid-twentieth-century, would anathematize as anti-Spanish not only all revolutionaries, all *bonapartistes,* and all *afrancesados* but also, and most tragically, most of the Spanish Enlightenment—as if all attempts to modernize were inherently foreign and alien, thus effectively denying the real engagement and exchange of ideas that took place between like-minded people. This inflated anti-Enlightenment discourse was espoused not only by absolute monarchs of the nineteenth century but also by demagogues who viewed the actions of 150 years earlier as precedents of contemporary conspiracies in the ongoing war between them and us.[5] It is interesting to note that even today the *Diccionario de la Real Academia Española* defines *afrancesado* as (1) one who admires excessively or imitates the French; (2) one who adopted the values of the French Enlightenment; (3) a Spaniard who collaborated with the Bonapartiste regime.

Reading the Revolution through Satire

Whereas historical treaties usually draw an unambiguous line between friend and foe, us and them, good satire seldom does. Instead, it often muddies the waters, makes us uneasy, and forces us to question our own response of shock or laughter as we see religious, political, and social icons mistreated, mocked, and desacralized. The following examples of written and visual satire seek precisely that: laughter, embarrassment, unease.

From the many satirical fables, sonnets, and pamphlets that circulated, I have selected two: a reactionary publication that appeared anonymously in 1811, *Diccionario razonado: Manual para inteligencia* (abbreviated as *Razonado*; "A Reasoned Dictionary: A Manual for Intelligence"), and the rebuttal published the following year by Bartolomé J. Gallardo, *Diccionario Crítico-Burlesco del que se titula Diccionario Razonado* (abbreviated as *Crítico*; "A Critical-Burlesque Dictionary of the Reasoned Dictionary"). By mocking key terms, these "dictionaries" seek to undermine the opposition's views while boosting their own. Words such as *liberales*, *democracia*, *Jacobinos*, and *patriotas* are defined in accordance with opposing political and cultural milieus.

The conservative *Razonado* likens *liberales* to clueless soldiers who are manipulated by the enemy to demolish splendid and ancient Spanish edifices (181). *Democracia* is likened to a packed and confusing wardrobe stuffed with stockings, leggings, three-corner hats, and other monstrosities (170). The answer from the *Crítico* is to dismiss the allusions to turmoil and deceit that originate from "sickly fantasies," "figures of whim," and "phantasmagoric spectacles" (121). At first glance, the vindication of *democracia* made by the *Crítico* seems somewhat bland, because it states the obvious: democracy is a form of government in which the people rule themselves. But the *Crítico* then surprises the reader when it flips the wardrobe analogy by proposing an equalizing option: everyone should wear the same uniform (87).

The conflation of key terms, people, and animals is common in satirical texts and in these dictionaries as well. The *Razonado*'s definition of *Jacobinos*, for example, describes the Jacobins as tigers with an insatiable thirst for human blood and as rabid *demócratas* who wish to de-Catholicize and Frenchify Spain (179). The *Crítico*, on the other hand, begins by expounding on the etymology, history, and usage of the term, then links the *Jacobinos* to the *repúblicos* of the elders and to the *patriotas* of today, skillfully establishing a seamless continuum between them (105).

It is disturbing to see accusations of conspiracy made against seemingly harmless social mores—some dictionary entries resort to images of anthropophagy to dehumanize the opposition—because violent rhetoric often leads to violent policies. In many of these texts of the early 1800s, we can see the beginning of what would become a profound religious, cultural, and ideological schism in the nation.

Visual accounts of violence and chaos are present in many of Goya's paintings and prints. *El tres de mayo* explicitly represents death and suffering, yet it is far from being a depiction of defeat or victory, or of losers and winners, because, despite the subject, it was meant as an indictment not of French soldiers but of war and its horrendous consequences. Goya's satirical works, however, are very different in nature and tone, and in the series of prints *Caprichos* (1799) and *Disasters of War* (drawn in 1810–15 though published in 1863) the darts are clearly aimed at many.[6]

Plate 6 of the *Caprichos*, *Nobody Knows Himself*, shows an elegantly dressed and masked woman curtsying to a man bowing before her while four monstrous male figures with striped witches' hats are visible behind him. Although the explanation accompanying the print reminds the spectator that the world is a masquerade where face and dress are feigned, it is not clear who the impostor is. We wonder whether the glamorous and beautiful do not, in fact, conceal a hideous face.

The topic of deceivers and charlatans reappears in many plates, remarkably so in plate 33 of the *Caprichos*, titled *To the Count Palatine, Who Accomplishes Nothing of What He Promises.* The count seems to be pulling teeth out of a peasant's mouth while two men are bent over vomiting or spewing blood. Here too, clothes, garments, and postures are crucial: the count is dressed a la mode and stands erect while the weakened and hunched men are identified as peasants. But the print compels us to reflect on who the target or targets might be: the charlatan who deceives or the fools who are deceived? Furthermore, we wonder, Do clothes indicate social class or defects in character?

Some anonymous Spanish prints target Napoleon, his brother Joseph, and Godoy in a more explicitly political way, but even in them the answer to the censured reality is not always clear. Juvenile scatological and physiognomic references recur in many of these prints. *The Manchego Painter*, an anonymous plate of 1812 (?), shows a mural of Joseph with a bottle of wine most likely from the wine-producing region of La Mancha, a reference that plays on the name for him as a wino, Pepe Botella.[7] What most captures our attention, however, is the group of locals watching the painter, because their gaze reveals insolence, mockery, and threat as they raise their swords at the image. Also in sight are a few banners, utensils, and a knife engraved with the words *dos de mayo* ("May 2") in clear reference to the rebellion. Memories of violence, bloodshed, and viciousness from a sneering, coarse mob are evoked rather than sentiments of patriotism, brotherhood, and righteousness from a civil populace who honor that day. Two other prints that rely on crude humor are *Satire against Napoleon* (1812) and *Spanish Caricature of Napoleon* (1802). The first features Napoleon in a valley writing a regenerative constitution for Spain while an English soldier looks on as a Spaniard drops fecal bombs on the emperor (bdh.bne.es/bnesearch/detalle/bdh0000030493). The second shows him on his knees being defecated on and given an enema by soldiers (bdh-rd.bne.es/viewer.vm?id=0000032823).

Since English satirical prints played such a central role as a weapon against the French imperial forces and particularly against Napoleon, I end with the 1808 *Ghosts of the Old Kings of Spain Appearing to Their Degenerate Posterity* (repository.library.brown.edu/studio/item/bdr:232391/).[8] Here we see the ghosts of four ancient Spanish kings passing judgment on Carlos IV; his consort, Maria Luisa; and the future Fernando VII. Complicit with the degeneration of Spanish posterity are Napoleon and Godoy: the former reaches out for the Spanish crown while the latter tries to hide incriminating correspondence as he feigns submission to the kings. By including Fernando among the degenerate posterity, the print casts an ominous cloud over Spain's future.

These once popular but now forgotten written and visual texts can be valuable illustrations of war as well as tools to help students understand the French Revolution's echo in Spain. Relevant still, these texts can serve as case studies on demagoguery as well as examples of how fear of military invasion is often succeeded and supplanted by fear of ideological invasion.

Notes

1. The original documents are in Archivo Histórico Nacional. There are digital copies of the 1843 compilation in *Tratados*. The online catalog of Legislación Histórica Española also offers digitalized copies (www.mcu.es/archivos/lhe). To navigate the database for documents related to foreign affairs, follow these headings: level 1: gobernación; level 2: corona; level 3: relaciones exteriores.

2. English translations are mine. A digital copy of the defensive agreement is in *Tratados* 646–48.

3. Among the signatories was Manuel de Godoy on behalf of Carlos IV, and although many considered the conditions of the treaty humiliating for Spain, Godoy was bestowed the title of Príncipe de la Paz in 1795. However, Fernando VII revoked the title in 1808.

4. Both paintings are in Museo del Prado and can be accessed online (www.museodelprado.es/coleccion/artista/goya-y-lucientes-francisco-de/39568a17-81b5-4d6f-84fa-12db60780812).

5. That the Counter-Enlightenment was an intensely Catholic movement and therefore an international one explains the dire warnings of a cosmic struggle between good and evil heard from Spanish, French, and other European pulpits.

What was different (and tragic) in Spain was that the apocalyptical rhetoric that severed what was genuinely Spanish from the ideals of the Enlightenment persisted in speeches made by General Francisco Franco and his followers until the end of his regime in 1975. For them, the true essence of Spain should be traced to its medieval past, to its chivalric golden age, to its fight against all infidels; in other words, Spain should be totally divorced from its enlightened renegades.

6. The eighty copper plates of *Caprichos* and the eighty-two of *Desastres* are in the Real Academia de Bellas Artes de San Fernando and in the online catalog www.realacademiabellasartessanfernando.com/es/calcografianacional/colecciones/goya.

7. The complete title is *The Manchego Painter, Grateful for the Benefits Received from Sr. José and his Satellites: Wishes to Perpetuate His Memory by Painting His Portrait on a Tavern Door* (c. 1812). The image is accessible at the digitalized collection of graphic material of Biblioteca Nacional de España (bdh.bne.es/bnesearch/detalle/bdh0000026991).

8. See the Brown University Library collection Napoleonic Satires from Britain and Continental Europe. This one is attributed to Charles William.

Works Cited

"Afrancesado." *Diccionario de la lengua española*, dle.rae.es/?id=10bbu6F.

Diccionario razonado: Manual para inteligencia de ciertos escritores que por equivocación han nacido en España. Biblioteca virtual del patrimonio bibliográfico, bvpb.mcu.es/es/consulta/registro.cmd?id=403936.

Gallardo, Bartolomé José. *Diccionario crítico-burlesco del que se titula "Diccionario razonado." Biblioteca virtual Miguel de Cervantes*, www.cervantesvirtual.com/nd/ark:/59851/bmc4q7r6.

Tratados, convenios y declaraciones de paz y de comercio que han hecho las potencias extranjeras los monarcas españoles de la casa de Borbón desde el año de 1700 hasta el día de hoy. Compiled by Alejandro del Cantillo, 1843, *Google Play*, play.google.com/books/reader?printsec=frontcover&output=reader&id=ersCAAAAYAAJ&pg=GBS.PP11.

Artwork Referred to in Essay

Goya y Lucientes, Francisco de. *Caprichos. Real Academia de Bellas Artes de San Fernando*, www.realacademiabellasartessanfernando.com/es/goya/goya-en-la-calcografia-nacional/caprichos.

———. *El dos de mayo de 1808 en Madrid o "La Lucha con los mamelucos." Museo del Prado*, www.museodelprado.es/coleccion/artista/goya-y-lucientes-francisco-de/39568a17-81b5-4d6f-84fa-12db60780812.

———. *El tres de mayo en Madrid o "Los fusilamientos."* 1814. *Museo del Prado*, www.museodelprado.es/coleccion/artista/goya-y-lucientes-francisco-de/39568a17-81b5-4d6f-84fa-12db60780812.

Satire against Napoleon, c. 1812, digitalized collection of graphic material of *Biblioteca Nacional de España*, bdh.bne.es/bnesearch/detalle/bdh0000030493.

Amy E. Wright

From Transnational Political Thought to Popular National Iconography: Latin America's Cult of *Liberté* in the Age of Revolution

The topic of the French Revolution's reverberations in Latin America offers many subtopics to incite students' interest: the transformation of sociability and public space (cafés, newspapers); contraband news and censorship; evolution of revolutionary lexicon; contemporary theories of government and revolution; and the role of elite criollos (a term used to designate the first generation of Spanish descent born in the Americas) versus that of the broader *pueblo*, a designation itself evolving from 1750 to 1850 in the Spanish-speaking colonies of the Americas.[1] Each of these themes can be mined with students in a variety of interactive projects examining responses to 1789 across that region, and this essay provides ideas to achieve that goal. As for methods, one of the most engaging I have encountered is Barnard College's Reacting to the Past, which consists of role playing that relies entirely on students' understanding of primary texts (for extensive modeling, see Carnes and Kates 38–44, 48–54). With it students can explore the period from 1750 to the 1850s from the varying perspectives of criollos, Spaniards, French émigrés, mestizos (a term first used during the colony to designate individuals of mixed European and indigenous descent), and members of the region's diverse indigenous cultures. Reacting to the Past enhances students' understanding of texts and contexts, drawing students deeper into the past and the ideas circulating in a given time period. In a class based on Reacting to the Past, the session is run entirely by students, while the instructor guides and advises, also evaluating their work (reacting.barnard.edu/about).

This essay on the context and consequences of the French Revolution in the Spanish-speaking Americas recommends several primary texts as a base from which students can begin to explore the complexities of *liberté* as an imported term, with an eye toward the different meanings that have been assigned to French-inspired revolutionary vocabulary according to different Latin American environments as well as social and political classes. For a readable and concise introduction to this complex sociohistorical context, I recommend John Charles Chasteen's *Born in Blood and Fire: A Concise History of Latin America* (chapters 3–5) and for a more detailed examination of the figures and events of the tumultuous period initiated by the 1807–08 Napoleonic invasions, Chasteen's *Americanos: Latin America's Struggle for Independence.* The material recommended below offers a Latin American perspective that can be included in general courses, with titles such as The Age of Revolutions or Revolution and Race, or foregrounded in the country- or region-specific courses suggested at the end of this essay. These suggestions are followed by an introductory bibliography with primary and secondary sources in English and Spanish.

In the first quarter of the nineteenth century, twelve new states replaced a centuries-old empire in the lands known as the Americas. Napoleon's 1807–08 incursions into the Iberian Peninsula provided the opening for a great wave of independence in the region. Inasmuch as these invasions can be seen as one outcome of the French Revolution, they offer the clearest example of the reverberations of 1789 in the region that today is Latin America. But the transnational cult of *liberté*—perceived as a new civic religion based on French-styled liberty, equality, and justice—ran much broader and deeper, affecting philosophies, actions, and an entire repertoire of symbols during the age of revolution and beyond (see Chartier; Fernández Sebastián). This cult of *liberté* fueled the political thought of various founding fathers, as well as iconographies popular among the sons and daughters of the nations to be. Struggles surrounding the incorporation of revolutionary language and images into national repertoires immediately raised the question of what role the *pueblo* might play in these new republics. Ultimately, a pivotal piece of the French Revolution's legacy in Latin America was the profound challenge it posed to the elite's relationship to the *pueblo*, a relationship whose evolution would prove crucial to the success of both independence and nation-state.

Certain aspects of the French Revolution resonated in the Spanish colonies to a greater degree than in North America. Much like France on the threshold of 1789, these colonies were entrenched hierarchies, based on a caste system more like the tiered *états* than the largely middle-class meritocracy under development in the British colonies. An excellent visual resource for examining this structure with students is the paintings of the castes, the eighteenth-century effort to establish racial taxonomy in New Spain (see *Castas*). Students can examine a contemporary (1772) text on the same topic in New Granada, "The Structure of Class and Caste," by the Spaniards Jorge Juan de Ulloa and Antonio de Ulloa, offering the colonizers' perspective on hierarchies established in their territories. Over their more than three centuries of existence, the Spanish colonies were under strict control of officials of the monarchy and the Catholic Church, a control that increased the disconnect between the impoverished masses and their privileged elite leadership (see Warren). The French Revolution came to be associated in Latin America with the unexpected uprising of these masses, the violent destruction of long-established hierarchies, and the establishment of a new society in which the people (*le peuple*) played a major role. Although there were several distinct phases of the Revolution, it was perhaps that first Jacobin phase that held the most lasting imprint on the hopes—and fears—of the varied sectors in Latin American society.

To understand why these associations were so influential in Latin America, students should know that for at least a century before 1789 France had been the single most important standard bearer of civilization and culture among the Spanish colonial elite. Coinciding with the eclipse of Spain's Habsburg monarchy and culminating in the reforms of the Bourbons, urban centers in the viceroyalties looked to France as the general cultural paradigm to be emulated.[2] This emulation was especially evident in the political philosophies of a transnational cohort in which a few privileged criollos began to take part (see Fernández Sebastián 215–22). For an interesting perspective on the period surrounding 1789, students can explore the diary of the Argentine independence hero Manuel Belgrano (1770–1821). A translated excerpt of this document is available, in which Belgrano relates his earliest exposure to the Revolution and the life experiences that transformed a young elite criollo into an ardent revolutionary:

> Since I was in Spain in 1789, and the French Revolution was then causing a change in ideas, especially among the men of letters with whom I associated, the ideals of liberty, equality, security, and property took a firm hold on me, and I saw only tyrants in those who would restrain a man, wherever he might be, from enjoying the rights with which God and Nature had endowed him. . . . (247–48)

Iberoamerican elites of that time were navigating a revolution in semantics, emanating from the French Enlightenment, in which the meaning of terms such as *liberty*, *equality*, *citizen*, and *the people* were changing drastically (Fernández Sebastián 138–40). By 1793, the very use of the word *liberty* made viceroys nervous (Rosas Lauro 144–47).

Jean-Jacques Rousseau and Voltaire were in vogue in Latin America among eighteenth-century *afrancesados*. (*Afrancesamiento* in Spanish refers to the love of all things French, while an *afrancesado* is a person exhibiting such love.) Their readings, however, did not immediately translate into a challenge to the colonial status quo.[3] On the eve of the French Revolution—by the end of the reign (1788) of the enlightened despot Charles III—the Spanish colonies had undergone numerous Bourbon reforms designed to improve conditions, and there was no significant upheaval in sight. The singular New Granadine criollo Francisco de Miranda (1750–1816) sought a full-fledged revolutionary experience outside the colonies in his grand tour of American and French battlefields. His diary from 1771 to 1789 is an anecdotal chronicle of these European experiences, particularly his complicated relationship with France in its early days of Revolution (177–94).[4] The rest of Latin America's revolutionaries would come of age decades after 1789.

As news of the storming of the Bastille began to arrive in the New World, the governing elites of Latin America discussed the events in private correspondence that compared the Revolution to a natural disaster, a cancer, or a plague. Colonial authorities feared contagion, and for the first time the throne and the Inquisition worked together to strictly prohibit news, as censorship under Bourbon reforms had been quite lax.[5] Spain's chief minister, José Moñino, count of Floridablanca, initially counseled his viceroys to adopt a policy of absolute silence on all matters relating to France, and the official gazettes at first said little about what was happening there. News gradually made its way into a larger portion of the *pueblo*, circulating via recently expanding circles of Enlightenment sociability, through the habit of gathering in public spaces to read aloud and discuss the latest news.[6] While elites shared access through travel to or correspondence with Europe, versions of revolutionary happenings filtered into the cafés and other public spaces where social classes mixed.[7]

The Reacting to the Past method in Mark C. Carnes and Gary Kates's *Rousseau, Burke, and Revolution in France, 1791* can be used as a template in which the café space of a given colonial city is reenacted, engaging students more deeply with primary sources and helping instructors bring these sources to life. The instructor will select a date that will plunge students into the political and ideological currents surging through that colony at that time. The instructor will also select a primary text. Students can discuss the role of the newspaper in the contemporary café by using suggested secondary texts, then a contemporary document in translation, such as those suggested throughout this essay. The instructor will then set up the structure of the debate by delineating the cast of revolutionary actors from the diverse social classes in contact in that space (i.e., members of various political clubs and social factions). Multilevel classroom debates then center around discussion of the primary text through reenactments and role playing. Different factions discuss the meaning of terms that appear in the article, such as *liberty*, *equality*, and *revolution*. What does the document mean by the term *citizen*? by the term *pueblo*? How do the meanings of each term differ depending on which social group generates the definition? Other debate questions can relate to the larger context: Should the king or the Catholic Church retain power, and if so, under what terms? Is it possible to maintain stability and at the same time introduce new freedoms? Is violence a legitimate way to change the status quo? Are people of other races or women entitled to the Rights of Man? These debates are contextualized by secondary readings, in which the instructor points out the threats and concerns of the historical moment (e.g., internal chaos, foreign invasion, censorship).

Students will learn that cafés throughout the Spanish colonies became hotbeds of political discussion and public opinion, in which rumors swirled about French revolutionaries' plans to decolonize America. At least one French deputy expressly incited the Spanish colonies to insurrection (Caillet-Bois 95; García Rigueiro 109), and the concern persisted that French revolutionaries would propagate their ideologies in the Spanish colonies (García Rigueiro 113). The first major aftershock to arrive, however, was not a conspiracy of the cult of *liberté* but a massive slave uprising in Haiti (1791), which alienated many criollos who otherwise might have sought limited reform, if only to improve their own socioeconomic position.

Increasing accounts of mob rule in Haiti, then in Paris, further turned the tide, as news of the king's and queen's executions (1793) reached colonial shores. The ensuing Reign of Terror (1793–94) alienated a conservative *pueblo* who generally believed in unity of God and king. By late 1793 Spain had declared war against France, and persecution of the French in the colonies began in earnest (Martí 659–60; Rosas Lauro 193–207). Official reactions promoted in the government-sponsored gazettes now channeled public opinion to fill war coffers. In Lima, for example, an official gazette (*La gaceta de Lima*) was revived in 1793 for the express purpose of creating counterrevolutionary propaganda (Rosas Lauro 54–55, 62–63). The official representations of the French Revolution consisted, edition after edition, in advertising Jacobin Terror. From their pulpits the members of the clergy mounted an intense campaign to associate *liberté* with the guillotine (Herrejón Peredo; Rosas Lauro 94–96). In this period of clergy-led backlash, the daring discourses of New Spain's friar Servando Teresa de Mier stand out as exceptional examples of free thinking, particularly the unorthodox 1794 sermon that earned him exile in Europe. Excerpts of his *Memoirs* from that exile (1795–1805) allow students to dip into his uniquely liminal perspective on Europe that included a critique of French culture and the Napoleonic reforms (18–41 ["From My Arrival in Paris to My Departure"]); students can also explore his observations on religion as a subset of the transgressive criollo thought that was soon to rock New Spain to its foundations.

Mier, however, was an outlier. By the time of Napoleon's declaration of the Revolution's end (1799), the clerical campaign in Latin America to denounce *liberté* would seem to have been entirely successful. Travelers to the Spanish American viceroyalties from Europe in the first years of the Napoleonic era (1799–1807) spoke little of instability (see Chasteen, *Americanos* 6–11), and newspapers—the foremost vehicle of criollo opinion in the last decade of Spanish rule—continued to espouse a muted version of Enlightenment that reinforced rather than challenged the colonial institutions of church and empire. To experience this temporary stasis on the cusp of upheaval, students can read an excerpt of the treatise by the respected scientist and editor Francisco José de Caldas (1771–1816), published in his *Semanario del Nuevo Reino de Granada* (1808–11), which espoused scientific study of New Granadine lands for the "glory of our monarch and the prosperity of our colony" (225).

Seeds sown from 1793 to 1807, however, would eventually bear more radical fruit. Curiosity about *liberté*, *fraternité*, and *égalité* as civilizing forces shifted underground into tiny sectors of the colonial population.

Pasquinades (broadsheets) with exalted slogans such as "Long Live French Liberty, and Death to Spanish Tyranny!" appeared in most of the viceregal capitals throughout this period as isolated expressions of counteropinion.[8] Contraband news continued to circulate as a parallel source to fear-based propaganda, allowing the public to cobble together counternarratives regarding faraway actors and distorted events.[9] Texts written by displaced and disaffected Jesuits, such as Peruvian-born Juan Pablo Viscardo y Guzmán (1748–98), exiled from the Americas in 1767 with the rest of his order, circulated first in Europe among the elite, then later reached the small literate colonial minority that was able to access them. A key example is Viscardo's "Letter to the Spanish Americans," sometimes called the "Declaration of Independence of Spanish America" (Stolley 126). Writing from London in the heady first years of the Revolution (1791), Viscardo culls some of his strongest arguments from French revolutionary thought as well as from Enlightenment luminaries such as Montesquieu in a document not distributed in the Americas until 1806. His statement of grievances against the Spanish crown and his plea for Latin American independence was addressed to the white literate ruling class, not to all *americanos.* In 1801 Miranda translated the document back into Spanish (that original had been lost after the author's death [1798], and only a French translation remained). Students can read Viscardo's passionate letter as the quintessential example of the circulation of the translated political tracts and reprints of contemporary newspaper articles among an influential transnational elite whose activities circumvented Spanish censorship.

Translations must be considered in any account of emerging print culture, yet the written word was but one single current in the complex circulation of revolutionary ideas. Republican orality and imagery were essential to the *pueblo*'s creation of counternarratives that sustained the appetite for uprising during the grueling decade of independence wars.[10] Indeed, new iconography was purposely designed to replace symbols of church and king, and a nearly religious fervor was cultivated through spoken oaths and political rituals. Javier Fernández Sebastián has demonstrated how sworn patriotic oaths were substituted for religious oaths (216), and Dorothy Tanck de Estrada has shown the many functions of political catechisms in Mexico.

The importance of popular articulations of liberty during this age of revolution became paramount:

> It mattered a great deal who could effectively portray what; whose values and interests were embedded in these characterizations; and by

> what means and to what political effect they were disseminated and absorbed by the culture. To a great extent, we may say that "liberty" was defined by its most successful portrayal. . . . The theatrics of power—whether in words, stories, ceremonies, flags, or liberty poles—is not just a reflection of power, it is its very lifeblood. (Rozbicki 4)

Beginning in 1793, Latin American spectators to the theater of revolution got to know the urban actors, the sansculottes: their dress (the red Phrygian cap; see other images of contemporary dress styles inspired by the French Revolution in Cruz de Amenabar),[11] their songs (La Marsellaise), and their symbolisms (the pike and liberty tree or pole). Emblems and slogans of popular revolt were emblazoned on imported souvenirs and distributed via contraband lithographs (Caillet-Bois 99; García Rigueiro 109). In 1793 the *Gaceta de Lima* reported the confiscation of French ships exporting packages of Phrygian caps, referred to as "the favored insignia of the Jacobine Sect" (qtd. in Rosas Lauro 154), and the viceroy of Peru issued a royal decree against the circulation of any object with inscriptions or images pertaining to "French Liberty" (189). Similar fascination developed with popular leaders such as Jean-Paul Marat and Maximilien Robespierre (Caillet-Bois 100–05), and the emblematic Lady Liberty made frequent appearances as a secular goddess championing her cult of *liberté* (Encina 110). Though the pike, cap, tree, and lady were all present in the symbology of 1776, their connections to popular emancipation and radical mass revolt intensified through the French Revolution (see Korshak). Anthems proclaiming liberty and sovereign rights of the people became popular in the years between 1789 and the early 1800s, their rhythms and lyrics serving as powerful propaganda tools in largely oral cultures. In the Latin American colonies, these new images and oralities awoke the imagination of the urban classes, involving them in the visual and verbal creation of meaning around events inspired by the French Revolution.[12]

Colonial uprisings in the countryside gave signs of simmering interest in French-style liberty that reached beyond a small group of urban elites. The largest uprisings occurred between 1795 and 1799 in the section of New Granada that is present-day Venezuela. Students can explore the anonymous "Song for *América*" for signs of French revolutionary discourse; several thousand copies of these lyrics were printed in 1797 as an anthem for the aborted Venezuelan uprisings. Revolutionary ideas from nearby Saint-Domingue had inspired local mulattos and blacks to rise up, but both Coro (1795) and La Guaira (1797–99) were isolated regional rebellions quickly put down because they were not supported by a large-enough criollo base. The freed-black leadership of Coro openly proclaimed "the law of the French, the Republic, the freedom of the slaves" (Bethell 46), while La Guaira's more broadly based conspiracy—some fifty criollos were reportedly involved (Michelena 100)—distributed copies of the Declaration of the Rights of Man and of the Citizen, the French Revolution's defining document. Yet there was no large-scale local buy-in in these and other outlying incidents, such as Miranda's liberating invasions of Coro (1806) and Buenos Aires (1806), orchestrated in collaboration with British and North American agitators.[13] Both of Miranda's 1806 efforts failed due to lack of local support.[14]

Still, small groups within the minority of criollo elite in different urban centers had begun to develop their own regional cults of *liberté*. These groups served as the motor behind the independence wars precipitated by Napoleon's 1807–08 Iberian invasions, aggressions that made France a sudden enemy of the Spanish throne and its colonies. This small cadre of criollos came of age after the French Revolution, had been avid readers of the Enlightenment philosophes, and exhibited a growing commitment to the sovereignty and rights of a broader sector of society. Antonio Nariño (1765–1823), Mariano Moreno (1778–1811), Juan José Castelli (1764–1812), Bernardo Monteagudo (1789–1825), and Miguel Hidalgo (1753–1811) responded to the events surrounding 1789 in a way that expanded rather than reduced their relation to the *pueblo*, even as prominent *libertadores* of the same generation—Simón Bolívar (1783–1830) and José San Martín (1778–1850)—favored more authoritarian or even monarchical models. On the issue of engagement and inclusion of the *pueblo*, we might see Bolívar at one extreme of the ideological continuum and Hidalgo at the other, with Nariño, Moreno, Castelli, and Monteagudo situated at various points in between.

No discussion of Latin American independence seems complete without mention of Bolívar, liberator of the vast region that is now Venezuela, Colombia, Ecuador, Bolivia, Peru, and Panama. The wealthy youth was undoubtedly heir to French Enlightenment thought through the influence of his principal tutor, Simón Rodríguez (1769–1854), a fervent adherent to *liberté* who used the teachings of Rousseau's *Émile* (1762) to instruct his young pupil. Bolívar's various forays into Europe (1800–07) deepened his knowledge of European thought and military history and increased his contact with the concepts of liberty and popular sovereignty that had triumphed in the French Revolution. One such foray (1805) was accompanied by Rodríguez, culminating in their ascension of Rome's Monte Sacro, where legend has it that Bolívar swore to his mentor that he would never rest until Spanish America was liberated. His travels also allowed him to witness firsthand Napoleon's meteoric rise to power—Bolívar received a personal invitation to Napoleon's 1804 Notre Dame crowning as emperor. During this period the young Bolívar was fascinated by Napoleon but also repelled by his unslakable thirst for power. In any case, Bolívar found an inspiring model in the admiration that Napoleon incited in his people (Masur 37–38). It is the Napoleonic aftermath to the Revolution (1799–1815) and not the early idealistic phase of popular upheaval that most consistently compelled Bolívar and inspired his actions upon returning to New Granada in 1807.

At first Bolívar was but one inspired Jacobin among many (Lombardi 137), but as he gradually amassed victories and then suffered defeats during the First and Second Republics (1812–14), his words reveal an emerging leader quite vocal in his doubts about the unfettering of Latin America's class-bound masses. He did consider slavery an evil, freeing first his own slaves in 1810–11, then decreeing in 1816 that all Spanish American slaves be freed (Bierck 365). To catch a glimpse of Bolívar's most Jacobin moment, students can examine his "Proclamation of Total War" (1813), which was made as fighting against the Spaniards intensified during his Admirable Campaign.[15] To see the contemporary backlash against this position, students need look no further than the 1816 letter written by Bolívar's conservative sister, María Antonia, as she pleaded with authorities to clear the family name of revolutionary radicalism so that she could return from exile to Venezuela in order to reclaim family lands.

Bolívar often expressed the opinion that the heterogeneous societies of Latin America required a firm hand and that compromises to individual liberties were necessary in order for a republic to survive in the region. He first expressed this attitude, which seemed to grow over the course of his career, in his "Cartagena Manifesto" (1812), the first of his political treatises, written after the fall of the First Republic. The rising leader wrote:

> Our compatriots are not yet capable of exercising their legal rights. They lack those virtues that distinguish the true republican. . . . Government must accommodate itself to circumstances, to the era, and to the men that [compose] it. . . . [W]hen they are dangerous and confused, government must prove to be formidable and ruthless without regard to law or constitution, until peace is established. (17–18)

In his "Jamaica Letter" (1815), written in exile after the defeat of the Second Republic, students can observe his support for a European (preferably British) protectorate in alliance with local elites, as he voices clear concerns about the readiness of the *pueblo* to assume an active role in self-government. Several years later his "Angostura Address" (1819) announces the Third Republic to an assembly gathered to draft the new constitution, declares Bolívar president, provides the legal framework for his ongoing military campaigns, and proposes a hereditary senate based on British law (which Bolívar greatly admired). Though he was most influenced politically by Rousseau's *Social Contract* (1762), students will note that here Bolívar qualifies the love of liberty: "Liberty is a succulent morsel, according to Rousseau, but difficult to digest. Debilitated by their long servitude, our fellow citizens are not yet up to the challenge" (139). In his "Message to the Congress of Bolivia" (1825), a conservative Bolívar at the peak of his power calls for a lifelong presidency (with the ability to select a successor), drawing directly from Montesquieu's *The Spirit of the Laws* (1748), which Bolívar cited in his earlier "Angostura Address": "[L]aws must be suited to the people for whom they are made" (140). In his final political writing, students can find arguments for a conditional form of democracy, one that takes the masses' inferiority into account and exerts control through a tutelary dictatorship embodied in Bolívar until death. His *liberté*, then, was a push for national independence that ultimately excluded certain sectors of the society from *égalité*.

Nariño, on the other hand, provides an earlier example of the interest among some New Granadine elite in a more democratic configuration of power relations. In 1793 he used his connections with the viceroy to found the printing press La Patriótica, on which he printed hundreds of copies of his translation of the French Declaration of Rights of Man and of the Citizen, intended for dissemination in both the capital and the provinces. During this time he became associated with seditious pasquinades appearing throughout Santafé de Bogotá that declared French-style liberty, and he was soon implicated in a conspiracy to provoke a lower-class urban uprising; the record of his trial provides a resounding defense of popular sovereignty in New Granada (Blossom 14–21).

An entire node of allegiance to the cult of *liberté* developed in the upper Peruvian highlands and filtered south to the Southern Cone in the activities of the Chuquisaca-trained intellectuals Mariano Moreno, Juan José Castelli, and Bernardo de Monteagudo. The prestigious University of Chuquisaca was an early incubator of independence ideals. Founded in 1624 by Jesuits in what is now Sucre, Bolivia, it served as the only regional law school during the late eighteenth and early nineteenth centuries. There Moreno set out to translate Rousseau, then wrote a dissertation that openly criticized indigenous abuses in the mines of Upper Peru. He later coincided with Castelli and Monteagudo in Mariquita Sánchez's French-styled salons in Buenos Aires, where Monteagudo had fled to evade imprisonment for the Chuquisaca Uprising (May 1809). In the 1810 juntas, these three men guided initiatives to radically restructure colonial foundations. Moreno founded a newspaper, which he inaugurated with his translation of Rousseau's social contract, advertising *los derechos de los pueblos* ("the rights of the people") to an American public. Each supported the abolition of the Inquisition as well as all titles of nobility; they shared an open hostility toward the Catholic Church and what they considered its enslavement of indigenous populations. In 1811, under this group's initiative, official decrees were issued proclaiming indigenous people and criollos equal under law.[16] Still, rural indigenous populations proved ideologically difficult to reach. Many individuals remained loyal to their king, as evidenced by the fascinating diary of the orphaned patriot drummer boy José Santos Vargas, in his biographical account of independence guerrilla fighting in the upper Andes. Vargas describes how rural slaves and indigenous peoples might take up arms with whomever offered the best deal and were often mistrustful of the urban elites who came to organize them. Students can directly explore the ambiguities of these developing relationships among diverse social sectors in excerpts from Vargas's diary spanning from 1815 to 1817.

Meanwhile Monteagudo, a firebrand ideologue, continued to espouse radical action among an ever larger group of citizenry, speaking out for liberty against tyranny in his writings as editor for various periodicals in South America's burgeoning revolutionary press, the primary vehicle of political education at a time when the region's independence was far from certain. Students can sample his editorials from *La gazeta de Buenos Aires* and *Mártir o libre* (1811–12; "Martyr or Free"), in which he appeals to citizens' powers of reasoning instead of habitual acquiescence to centuries of colonial obedience. More moderate members of the revolution accused Monteagudo, Castelli, and Moreno of attacking the foundations of traditional society and compared their radicalism to that of Robespierre and his Jacobins. Monteagudo was assassinated in 1825, at the age of thirty-five, but not before his eloquent "Essay on the Need for a General Federation of Hispanic American States, with a Plan for Their Organization" (1824) enthused his collaborator, Bolívar, with its vision of a united *América*.[17] In it students can read Monteagudo's connection of current events in Latin America with the legacy of the French Revolution:

> Each century brings with it the seed of developments that will occur in the following century. Each extraordinary epoch, whether in natural or human history, is the harbinger of another, rich in rare phenomena and prodigious combinations of events. The revolution that has swept through *América* in the nineteenth century stems from ideas elaborated in the eighteenth. Our triumph, indeed, is nothing more than the repercussions of the bolts of lightning that have recently struck so many European thrones, shattering monarchies that had extended their sway around the world. (186)

As late as 1910, Luis Alberto de Herrera, a prominent Uruguayan historian and politician, wrote of radical Jacobinism as the French Revolution's principal and most harmful legacy to South America.

Indeed, the term *Jacobinism* was used throughout the nineteenth century to accuse individuals of collaborating with the lower classes or encouraging anarchy in the *pueblo*.[18] There is no clearer example of the connotations of radical *afrancesamiento* than the legacy of New Spain's iconoclastic priest Miguel Hidalgo y Costilla (1753–1811), accused in January 1811 by inquisitorial edict of professing and spreading the heretical ideas of the democratic French Revolution (*Procesos* 261 [article 23]), among fifty-two other "crimes" (253–75), before his excommunication and death in July 1811. Hidalgo spoke at least two indigenous languages alongside Italian and French, and it was his reputation for helping the disenfranchised—in addition to the multiclass social gatherings at his home, locally nicknamed Little France—that caught the attention of militia officers forming a regional conspiracy in 1810. Conspirators thought talk of French liberty would alienate pious masses with no interest in overthrowing a king, so when Hidalgo addressed the hundreds of countryfolk gathered on fair day with a plea to join his uprising, he railed perforce against the godless French.[19]

Hidalgo, more so than other leaders, may have actually envisioned his uprising in French revolutionary style, an uprising in which the mobilization of the masses was necessary for the transformation of society. At its height his army reached between 80,000 and 100,000 (Hamnett 136), the largest amassing of *americanos* to that day, a force composed mostly of Indians, blacks, and *pardos* (people of mixed European and African heritage), with relatively few mestizos and even fewer criollos.[20] Hidalgo, before he was captured, outlawed portraits of the king, eliminated *royal* from all official documents, and called for the creation of a national congress. Although little written evidence of his intentions remain, one of his last acts (in December 1810, several months into the uprising and about a month before his defeat) was to establish a printing press to issue new laws in the *pueblo*'s name, focusing on the unconditional abolition of slavery (freed men would be equal to whites, and former slave owners would receive no compensation) and of the tribute required of all Indians (with restitution of all lands taken from indigenous peoples). Students can read the untitled decree issued under Hidalgo's name, which repealed policies that placed undue burdens on the colony's poorest (and nonwhite) inhabitants. Hidalgo made visible efforts to reconcile the criollo ideal of independence with social justice for New Spain's most oppressed classes, but many conservative Creoles resisted this call. A notable example is the response (Sept. 1810) of Hidalgo's former friend, Bishop Manuel Abad y Queipo, a European-born Spaniard who opposed the uprising and was horrified by the anarchy that ensued. Students will see that in addition to calling for Hidalgo's excommunication, Abad decried the French Revolution as the direct source of division and destruction in New Spain and across the globe, exhorting his parishioners to "resist anarchy with all your heart" (112).

In comparison with Hidalgo's laconic written proclamations, his successor, José María Morelos (1765–1815), articulated a full vision for New Spanish social justice in his "Sentiments of the Nation" (1813), presented to the wartime congress convened to write Mexico's new constitution. Its numbered articles include declarations such as "Sovereignty emanates directly from the People" and "All *americanos* should be equal. Only moral qualities should raise one person above another" in an article that says that slavery and caste distinctions should be abolished "forever" (116 [nos. 5 and 15]). These are but a few of the appeals of a brief (1810–11) but enormous popular uprising that preceded New Spain's decade-long guerrilla war inspired by French revolutionary ideals. One of the martyred Hidalgo's first (preserved) depictions appeared in José Joaquín Fernández de Lizardi's popular national calendar of 1824: the priest is nobly outfitted as a French insurgent, complete with sword, pike, and cockade, proudly brandishing his liberty flag (Brenes Tencio 36; see Brenes Tencio for competing images of an outlaw Hidalgo).

Latin American independence wars concluded by the mid-1820s, and the first decades of the republics under formation featured numerous efforts to assemble collective imaginaries that would unify their motley masses into nations. The French Revolution continued to feed elite and popular imaginations, evident in the gradual, decades-long implementation of the much contested, at times dogmatic cult of *liberté*. The specter of Jacobinism continued to be evoked—congresses were disparagingly compared with 1793's French convention, and orators were described as Dantons, Marats, or Robespierres by the opposition[21]—yet the French Revolution increasingly served as a source of imagery that allowed for a certain making sense of the violent process of independence in Latin America. The bloody excesses of popular uprising caused some revolutionary associations to be questioned and revised—for example, Luis Cánepa, in his history of Argentine national symbols, discusses the long controversy surrounding the appearance of a Phrygian cap on Argentina's national shield.[22]

It was nonetheless common for the new republics to adopt emblems associated with the French Revolution—the pike and cap, Lady Liberty, the occasional bundle of fasces, or the tricolor cockade—to populate their national flags, shields, commemorative coins, and patriotic anthems. The majority of countries used some combination of these emblems alongside representations of the pre-Hispanic past, as in most of the Southern Cone (Burucúa and Campagne 437–54). But in some cases, the autochthonous past was eschewed in favor of an entire symbolic universe replicated from the French revolutionary tradition. An example is the Paraguayan national anthem, which contains the lyrics "liberty, equality, and the Republic rest protected from tyrants' vile feudalism in the shadow of the red Phrygian cap" (Burucúa and Campagne 448; translation mine). When the French sculptor Albert-Ernest Carrier-Belleuse was selected to design José de San Martín's tomb with an allegory of the three liberated territories—as European females wearing red caps of liberty, civilization, and progress instead of the native races and climates originally proposed—his choice was defended by Argentina's foreign minister, Mariano Balcarce, who issued a public statement that it was these figures that best represented the aspirations of the new republics (469).

By the 1850s the cult of *liberté* had been fully assimilated into the cultural liturgy of the young nations. Even so, competing representations of and responses to the Revolution constituted an ongoing litmus test regarding political as well as cultural visions for Latin America's *pueblo* going forward:

> The French Revolution was omnipresent in the speeches, the words, the images that accompanied the ruptures with the metropolis and the creation of a new political order in the Americas in the first half of the nineteenth century. For some, the Revolution was the model that ought to be imitated, for others a danger to be rejected. (Chartier 50)

At the very center of this debate was none other than the remaining question of what role the masses should play in the evolving body politic. As such, the legacy of the French Revolution served as a crucial though controversial reference point regarding the ongoing struggle for inclusion of the *pueblo* throughout Latin America's long nineteenth century, and beyond.

Through the primary and secondary materials suggested in this essay, students are encouraged to imagine how symbols, clothing, anthems, and visual materials inspired by the French Revolution were adapted to local needs (see images of such symbols in Cánepa; Burucúa and Campagne). Iconography is presented comparatively to demonstrate the role of the symbolic as a tool in the exercise of power. Creative writing or rewriting activities using pasquinades and anthems, and role-plays using the Reacting to the Past methods suggested above, bring students into the mindset of the theater of that time and offer an imaginative component to their interaction with primary sources. Course topics such as "The French and the French Revolution in Latin America's Historical Novels" or "The Theater of Revolution in Latin America" foreground literary and archival texts from Latin America as well as ephemera (newspapers and political caricature), flags, music, uniforms, portraiture, and other memorabilia.

The French Revolution provides an undertaught, cross-sectional prism through which to understand Latin America's evolving relation with the European metropolis as well as the postcolonial configuration of power relations in Latin American nations. Reverberations of 1789 continue well into the twentieth century, with 1889 and 1989 as landmark years in which to revisit the Revolution. This approach can be used effectively in a course on the role of revolutions in different Latin American nations: a course on the role of revolution in Mexico, for example, could begin with the American (1776) and French (1789) Revolutions, follow through to Mexican Independence (1810) and the 1889 centennial, then take on the twentieth century with the Mexican Revolution (1910), 1968 (an impactful year of student revolutions in both France and Mexico), and close with the bicentennial celebrations of 1989 and 2010. In these courses and others, 1789 is a fruitful point of departure point to discuss ongoing issues in

Latin American nationhood, such as the role of the Catholic Church, land reform, inclusionary suffrage, and representation of the *pueblo.*

Notes

All translations are mine unless otherwise indicated.

1. See Guedea and Roldán Vera for changes in the term *pueblo* in late-eighteenth-century Latin America as a collective of republican political subjects opposed to an old regime. The term is now used ubiquitously throughout the region to refer to "the people" as a political entity related to broader mobilization and popular politics.

2. See Martí regarding New Spain's emulation of France during this period (657–58).

3. Encina corroborates this point (108–09). Roberts has argued, in any case, that neither Voltaire nor Rousseau would have advocated for popular sovereignty in practice, regardless of the way in which their writings were used in the rhetoric of the French revolutionaries (8–9).

4. Miranda, after fighting battles in the French Revolution, came close to a beheading when the Jacobins took power (Pérez Vila 131). (The frontispiece to his 1771–89 diaries promises a 1789 to 1812 continuation that apparently never made it into print.) After barely escaping Paris with his life, Miranda remained partial to the British and chose to reside in London from 1797 on. There he established the first transnational political society of its kind for men born in the Americas (*americanos*), the Society of Rational Gentlemen. He had read the French Enlightenment authors early in his life, and his difficulties in France did not keep him from disseminating the Declaration of the Rights of Man and of the Citizen when he attempted to liberate Coro in 1806, despite his professed preference for the North American Revolution of 1776.

5. For accounts of elite discussions in Peru regarding the situation, see Rosas Lauro 82–85; for a general account of censorship during this period, see García Rigueiro 108–12.

6. For details on the expansion of this sphere beginning in the late eighteenth century, see Guerra et al.; for the connection between the French Revolution and emergence of sociability practices in Río de la Plata from 1810 to 1815, see González. Rosas Lauro offers a similarly detailed description of this popular public sphere in Peru from 1789 to 1808.

7. For accounts of elite correspondence, see Caillet-Bois 97; García Rigueiro 108. For general examples of the way in which news on the French Revolution circulated orally throughout this period, see Caillet-Bois 98–99. For details on the political importance of cafés in late-eighteenth- and early-nineteenth-century culture in the Viceroyalty of Peru, see Rosas Lauro 161–64.

8. Pasquinades, or *pasquines* in Spanish, were political lampoons posted in public spaces. For details on the robust *pasquín* tradition in Peru during this period, see Rosas Lauro 79–82.

9. On the tendency toward long-distance distortion of these events, see Vovelle 15.

10. Starobinski and Agulhon have both written extensively on the agency of images in the unfolding of the French Revolution. Starobinski wrote, "Up to the death of Robespierre the Revolution unfolded in a symbolic language out of which its legend was made. . . . Crowd reactions, festivities, and emblems are the elements that go to make up this symbolic discourse" (58). Agulhon focuses on images and symbols of the French Republic from 1789 until 1880.

11. On the presence of French Revolution–inspired dress from 1800 to 1820 in Chile, see Cruz de Amenabar.

12. On the general importance of such symbols in the Viceroyalty of Peru, as well as on Lomné's work in New Granada, see Rosas Lauro 151–54.

13. Miranda made it a point to equip his ship with a small printing press to publish Viscardo's "Letter to the Spanish Americans" for distribution on landing in Venezuela. The document was copied and circulated by Miranda (Stolley 125), but according to Stolley relatively few Venezuelans seem to have been familiar with the letter. The reason may have been the illiteracy of the people in the Coro region, where Miranda landed and first disseminated the letter (125–26).

14. To see the preference that Miranda had for British over French leadership in the lead-up to these invasions, students can examine a set of three documents drafted over the decade from 1790 to 1800 (Chambers and Chasteen 51–58 ["Papers of a Career Revolutionary"]), consisting of various overtures to the British government that criticized the French Republic as "destructive" (54) while lauding Britain as "the wisest and most celebrated power on earth" (53).

15. This decree permitted all nature of atrocity against Spanish-born civilians who were not actively aiding the cause of South American independence. Spanish Americans, on the other hand, were exonerated, even if they had cooperated with Spanish authorities. This measure assured elites they would not be punished for previous collaboration with royalists.

16. For the particular activities of this triumvirate during the period surrounding the 1810 May revolution, see Goldman, "'Jacobinos.'" Guerra, however, has claimed that these men's Jacobinism consisted more in theoretical bases than in their actual mobilization of the *pueblo* (365).

17. The Spanish term *América* was used, in the eighteenth and nineteenth centuries, to refer to the whole of Latin America (the lands colonized by Spain and Portugal), not to the United States.

18. For more on the associations between *democracy* and *anarchy* that were beginning to develop in the late colonial period, see Rosas Lauro 148–50.

19. For an account of how religion and xenophobia, as much as the language of liberty, played a role in mobilizing the rural population of New Spain, see Van Young 245–46.

20. Van Young also speaks in detail about the different agendas of the elite versus the popular insurgents as well as about the ethnic composition of the insurgents (234–36).

21. For details about this process, see Burucúa and Campagne 436. On the contradictory impulses surrounding the use of the French Revolutionary repertoire, see Guerra 365; Harwich Vallenilla 547–48.

22. "[D]espite the dissension [the cap] has provoked, one thing has always been agreed on: it characterizes Liberty. . . . [T]he cap was raised by the masses, precisely, as a symbol of aspiration to greater rights and guarantees for each individual. . . . [L]iberty is lost . . . if the government does not have an authentic popular origin, with everyone equal under law, without privilege in bloodlines or hierarchies" (Cánepa 149).

Works Cited

Abad y Queipo, Manuel. "Decree of Excommunication." Chambers and Chasteen, pp. 108–12.

Agulhon, Maurice. *Marianne into Battle: Republican Imagery and Symbolism in France, 1789–1880.* Cambridge UP, 1981.

Alberro, Solange, et al., editors. *La Revolución Francesa en México.* Colegio de México, 1992.

Annino, Antonio, and François-Xavier Guerra, editors. *Inventando la nación: Iberoamérica siglo XIX.* Fondo de Cultura Económica, 2003.

Ávila, Alfredo, et al., editors. *Las experiencias de 1808 en Iberoamérica.* UNAM, 2008.

Belgrano, Manuel. "The Forging of a Rebel." Keen, pp. 247–50.

Bethell, Leslie, editor. *The Independence of Latin America.* Cambridge UP, 1987.

Bierck, Harold A., Jr. "The Struggle for Abolition in Gran Colombia." *The Hispanic American Historical Review*, vol. 33, no. 3, 1953, pp. 365–86.

Blossom, Thomas. *Nariño: Hero of Colombian Independence.* U of Arizona P, 1967.

Bolívar, María Antonia. "A Refugee's Petition." Chambers and Chasteen, pp. 132–36.

Bolívar, Simón. "Angostura Address." Chambers and Chasteen, pp. 136–46.

———. "Cartagena Manifesto." Fitzgerald, pp. 10–18.

———. "Jamaica Letter." Fitzgerald, pp. 27–44.

———. "Message to the Congress of Bolivia." Fitzgerald, pp. 95–105.

———. "A Proclamation of Total War." Chambers and Chasteen, pp. 117–19.

Brenes Tencio, Guillermo. "Los rostros de Hidalgo: Iconografía del héroe nacional, padre de la patria mexicana (siglos XIX y XX)." *Acta republicana*, vol. 9, no. 9, 2010, pp. 31–45.

Burucúa, José Emilio, and Fabián Alejandro Campagne. "Mitos y simbologías nacionales en los países del Cono Sur." Annino and Guerra, pp. 433–74.

Caillet-Bois, Ricardo R. "The Río de la Plata and the French Revolution." Humphreys and Lynch, pp. 94–105.

Caldas, Francisco José de. "Colonial Journalism in Action." Keen, pp. 224–26.

Cánepa, Luis. *Historia de los símbolos nacionales argentinos.* Editorial Albatros, 1953.

Carnes, Mark C., and Gary Kates. *Rousseau, Burke, and Revolution in France, 1791.* Pearson-Longman, 2005. Barnard Reacting to the Past Series.

Castas. Colonial Latin America, edited by Peter Bakewell, 17 July 1998, faculty .smu.edu/bakewell/bakewell/thinksheets/castas.html.

Chambers, Sara C., and John Charles Chasteen, editors and translators. *Latin American Independence: An Anthology of Sources.* Hackett Publishing, 2010.

Chartier, Roger. "¿Tienen orígenes las revoluciones? La ilustración, la Revolución Francesa y las independencias americanas." Chartier et al., pp. 15–74.

Chartier, Roger, et al., editors. *La Revolución francesa: ¿Matriz de las revoluciones?* Universidad Iberoamericana, 2010.

Chasteen, John Charles. *Americanos.* Oxford UP, 2009.

———. *Born in Blood and Fire: A Concise History of Latin America.* W. W. Norton, 2016.

Cruz de Amenabar, Isabel. "El traje, como signo de los nuevos tiempos: La Revolución Francesa y la moda en Chile, 1800–1820." Krebs and Gazmuri, pp. 179–224.

Encina, Francisco A. "The Limited Influence of the French Revolution." Humphreys and Lynch, pp. 106–10.

Fernández Sebastián, Javier, "Las revoluciones hispánicas: Conceptos, metáforas y mitos." Chartier et al., 131–223.

Fitzgerald, Gerald E., editor. *The Political Thought of Bolívar: Selected Writings.* Martinus Nijhoff, 1971.

García Rigueiro, Ovidio. "1789 y la América Española: Eco ultramarino de los acontecimientos franceses." Sociedad Estatal, pp. 105–13.

Goldman, Noemi, editor. *Imagen y recepción de la Revolución Francesa en la Argentina: Jornadas Nacionales.* Grupo Editor Latinoamericano, 1990.

———. "Los 'Jacobinos' en el Río de la Plata: Modelo, discursos y prácticas (1810–1815)." Goldman, *Imagen*, pp. 7–26.

González, Pilar. "La Revolución Francesa y la emergencia de nuevas prácticas de la política: La irrupción de la sociabilidad política en el Río de la Plata revolucionario (1810-1815)." Krebs and Gazmuri, pp. 111–36.

Guedea, Virginia. "El 'pueblo' en el discurso politico novohispano de 1808." Ávila et al., pp. 279–301.

Guerra, François-Xavier. *Modernidad e independencias: Ensayos sobre las revoluciones hispánicas.* Madrid: Editorial Mapfre, 1992.

Guerra, François-Xavier, et al. *Los espacios públicos en Iberoamérica: Ambigüedades y problemas: Siglos XVII–XIX.* Fondo de Cultura Económica, 1998.

Hamnett, Brian R. *Roots of Insurgency: Mexican Regions, 1750–1824.* Cambridge UP, 1986.

Harwich Vallenilla, Nikita. "La historia patria." Annino and Guerra, pp. 533–49.

Herrejón Peredo, Carlos. "La Revolución Francesa en sermones y otros testimonios de México, 1791–1823." Alberro et al., pp. 97–110.

Herrera, Luis Alberto de. *La Revolución Francesa y Sudamérica.* Dupont, 1910.

Hidalgo, Miguel. Untitled proclamation. Chambers and Chasteen, pp. 107–08.

Humphreys, R. A., and John Lynch, editors. *The Origins of the Latin American Revolutions, 1808–1826.* Knopf, 1965.

Keen, Benjamin. *Keen's Latin American Civilization: History and Society, 1492 to the Present.* Edited by Robert Buffington and Lila Caimari, Westview Press, 2004.

Korshak, Yvonne. "The Liberty Cap as a Revolutionary Symbol in America and France." *Smithsonian Studies in American Art*, vol. 1, no. 2, 1987, pp. 52–69.

Krebs, Ricardo, and Cristián Gazmuri, editors. *La Revolución Francesa y Chile.* Editorial Universitaria, 1990.

Lombardi, John V. *Venezuela: The Search for Order, the Dream of Progress.* Oxford UP, 1982.

Lomné, Georges. "La Revolución Francesa y la simbólica de los ritos bolivarianos." *Historia Crítica*, vol. 5, 1991, pp. 3–17.

Maniquis, Roberto, et al., editors. *La Revolución Francesa y el mundo ibérico.* Turner, 1989.

Martí, Óscar. "México y la Revolución Francesa: Antecedentes y consecuencias." Maniquis et al., pp. 652–728.

Masur, Gerhard. *Simón Bolívar.* U of New Mexico P, 1969.

Michelena, Carmen L. *Luces revolucionarias: De la rebelión de Madrid (1795) a la rebelión de la Guaira (1797).* Fundación Centro de Estudios Latinoamericanos Rómulo Gallegos, 2010.

Mier, Servando Teresa de. *The Memoirs of Fray Servando Teresa de Mier.* Translated by Helen Lane, Oxford UP, 1998.

Miranda, Francisco de. *Fragments from an Eighteenth-Century Diary: The Travels and Adventures of Don Francisco de Miranda.* Edited and translated by Jordan Herbert Stabler. Tipografía La Nación, 1931.

Monteagudo, Bernardo. "Editorials from the Revolutionary Press." Chambers and Chasteen, pp. 119–24.

———. "Essay on the Need for a General Federation of Hispanic American States, with a Plan for Their Organization." Chambers and Chasteen, pp. 185–91.

Morelos, José María. "Sentiments of the Nation." Chambers and Chasteen, pp. 115–17.

Pérez Vila, Manuel. "Francisco de Miranda, general de la Francia Revolucionaria." Sociedad Estatal, pp. 127–32.

Los procesos militar e inquisitorial del Padre Hidalgo y de otros caudillos insurgentes. Ediciones Fuente Cultural, 1953.

Roberts, Warren. *Revolutionary Artists: The Public, the Populace, and Images of the French Revolution.* State U of New York P, 2000.

Roldán Vera, Eugenia. "'Pueblo' y 'pueblos' en México, 1750-1850: Un ensayo de historia conceptual." *Araucaria*, no. 17, May 2007, pp. 268–88.

Rosas Lauro, Claudia. *Del trono a la guillotina: El impacto de la Revolución Francesa en el Perú (1789–1808).* Instituto Francés de Estudios Andinos, 2006.

Rozbicki, Michal Jan. *Culture and Liberty in the Age of the American Revolution.* U of Virginia P, 2011.

Shields, David, and Mariselle Meléndez, editors. *Liberty! Egalité! ¡Independencia! Print Culture, Enlightenment, and Revolution in the Americas, 1776–1838.* American Antiquarian Society, 2007. Papers from a Conference at the American Antiquarian Society in June 2006.

Sociedad Estatal para la Ejecución de Programas del Quinto Centenario. *Revolución, contrarrevolución e independencia: La Revolución Francesa, España y América.* Turner, 1989.

"Song for *América*." Chambers and Chasteen, pp. 58–59.

Starobinski, Jean. *1789: The Emblems of Reason.* Translated by Barbara Bray, MIT P, 1988.

Stolley, Karen. "Writing Back to Empire: Juan Pablo Viscardo y Guzmán's Letter to the Spanish Americans." Shields and Meléndez, pp. 117–31.

Tanck de Estrada, Dorothy. "Los catecismos politicos: De la Revolución Francesa al México independiente." Alberro et al., pp. 65–80.

Ulloa, Jorge Juan de, and Antonio de Ulloa. "The Structure of Class and Caste." Keen, pp. 155–57.

Van Young, Eric. "La época de la revolución atlántica: Comparaciones entre México, Estados Unidos y Francia." Chartier et al., pp. 225–74.

Vargas, José Santos. "Diary of a *Comandante* of American Independence." Chambers and Chasteen, pp. 147–56.

Viscardo y Guzmán, Juan Pablo. "Letter to the Spanish Americans." Chambers and Chasteen, pp. 60–66.

Vovelle, Michel. Prologue. *Del trono a la guillotina: El impacto de la Revolución Francesa en el Perú (1789–1808)*, by Claudia Rosas Lauro, Instituto Francés de Estudios Andinos, 2006, pp. 13–20.

Warren, Richard. *Vagrants and Citizens: Politics and the Masses in Mexico City from Colony to Republic*. Rowman and Littlefield, 2001.

Part VI

Resources

Melissa A. Deininger

French Revolution: Dates and People

Pre-Revolution

1774	Louis XV dies; Louis XVI's coronation
1776–82	Offices revoked and reinstated, cabinet reshuffled
1785	Affaire du collier ("Affair of the Diamond Necklace")
1787	Several parliaments disbanded
1788	Increasing riots

Revolution

1789

Widespread riots

1 May. Estates General convoked, the first since 1614; third estate numbers doubled, but voting is still by estate

17 June. Third estate proclaims itself National Assembly

11 July. Necker (minister of finance) dismissed—widespread public unrest and anxiety

14 July. Bastille prison taken by Parisian mob

26 August. Declaration of the Rights of Man and of the Citizen published

5–6 October. Women march on Versailles to force king to Paris

2 November. National Assembly takes over Church property

1790

Many tariffs and taxes abolished

19 June. Nobility abolished

12 July. Civil Constitution of Clergy

1791

20–21 June. Flight to Varennes

14 September. Louis XVI signs new constitution

17 October. Counterrevolutionaries killed at Avignon

1792

Royalist uprisings

10 August. Royal family arrested

21 September. Monarchy abolished; First Republic begins

22 September. First day of new calendar

1793

First Republic

Decrees concerning standardizations (methods of payment, universal schooling, wage and price caps, etc.)

21 January. Louis XVI executed

January–March. Europe declares war on revolutionary France

6 April. Committee of Public Safety formed; Jacobins in control

Summer 1793–Fall 1794. Period known as the Terror

22 September. Revolutionary calendar enforced by law

10 October. Government is decreed "revolutionary until the peace"

16 October. Marie-Antoinette executed

1794

March–July. Revolutionary writers and orators arrested and guillotined

27 July / 9 Thermidor. Robespierre and Saint-Just arrested, guillotined next day

Parisian Jacobin club closed

1795

5–6 October. Bonaparte's "whiff of grapeshot" to Paris crowd

1799

9 November / 18 Brumaire. Napoléon's coup d'état; creation of Consulate government

1804

December. Napoléon's coronation as emperor

Christopher Tozzi

Major Battles of the Revolutionary Period

20 April 1792. French revolutionaries declare war against the "king of Hungary and Bohemia," meaning the Austrian emperor. The war quickly expands as other powers join the coalition against France.

1 August 1792. Prussian forces cross the Rhine into France. The revolutionaries are now on the defensive.

20 September 1792. The Battle of Valmy is more a cannon duel than a pitched battle but shows that inexperienced French citizen-soldiers will stand their ground against seasoned grenadiers—a first in European history. Leads to Prussian withdrawal from France, removing the threat of immediate defeat for the French.

27 October 1792. French troops invade Austrian Netherlands. Now back on the offensive, the revolutionaries begin their conquest of what is today Belgium, which they complete by the end of the year.

24 February 1793. The National Convention orders the levy of 300,000 new troops, leading to a substantial increase in French military manpower.

14 April–23 July 1793. Coalition forces recapture Mainz from the French. Combined with defeats elsewhere, this setback ends the military momentum the revolutionaries enjoyed going into 1793.

8 September 1793. Battle of Hondschoote: French victory leads British to end their siege of Dunkirk.

1 June 1794. British navy defeats French fleet in Atlantic engagement. This weakening of French navy damages prospects for an easy French invasion of Britain.

26 June 1794. Battle of Fleurus: decisive French victory leads to definitive French conquest of the Austrian Netherlands and, later, French invasion of the Dutch Republic.

18 October–22 November 1795. Austrian troops capture the Rhineland city Mannheim from the French. Combined with other French setbacks in Germany in 1795, this defeat puts an end to the revolutionaries' efforts to advance deep into Germany.

15–17 November 1796. Battle of Arcola: Napoleon scores decisive victory over Austrians in Italy, leading to the signing of the Treaty of Campo-Formio the next year and cementing his popularity in France.

22–24 February 1797. Battle of Fishguard: French attempt to invade Britain with a small force of poorly armed troops fails.

21 July 1798. Battle of the Pyramids: Napoleon wins decisive victory over local Mamluk forces, raising his stature further.

1–3 August 1798. Battle of Aboukir Bay: British obliterate French naval forces supporting Napoleon's campaign in Egypt. Napoleon escapes back to France to launch the Brumaire coup d'état, leaving his isolated army in the Middle East to waste away slowly.

8 September 1798. Battle of Ballinamuck: British defeat a French force that landed in Ireland several weeks earlier and enjoyed initial success fighting alongside United Irishmen rebels.

18 November 1803. Battle of Vertières: Jean-Jacques Dessalines's Haitian rebels win final victory over French troops, leading to Haitian independence the next year.

Julia Douthwaite Viglione, Dominica Chang, Melanie Conroy, and Melissa A. Deininger

Filmography

Old Regime Dramas

Joffé, Roland. *Vatel.* Starring Gérard Depardieu and Uma Thurman, 2000.

Kaufman, Philip. *Quills.* Starring Geoffrey Rush, Kate Winslet, Joaquin Phoenix, and Michael Caine, 2000.

Leconte, Patrice. *Ridicule.* Starring Charles Berling, Jean Rochefort, Fanny Ardant, and Judith Godrèche, 2010.

Revolution-Based Films

Conway, Jack. *A Tale of Two Cities.* Starring Ronald Coleman, 1935.

Griffith, D. W. *The Orphans of the Storm.* Starring Lillian Gish and Dorothy Gish, 1921.

Renoir, Jean. *La Marseillaise.* Starring Pierre Renoir and Lise Delamare, 1938.

Rohmer, Eric. *L'Anglaise et le duc / The Lady and the Duke.* Starring Lucy Russell and Jean-Claude Dreyfus, 2001.

Scola, Ettore. *La nuit de Varennes / The Night of Varennes.* Starring Jean-Louis Barrault, Marcello Mastroianni, and Hanna Schygulla, 1983.

Thomas, Ralph. *A Tale of Two Cities.* Starring Dirk Bogarde, 1958.

Wajda, Andrzej. *Danton.* Starring Gérard Depardieu, 1983.

Fictions of Marie-Antoinette

Coppola, Sofia. *Marie-Antoinette.* Starring Kirsten Dunst and Jason Schwartzman, 2006.

Jacquot, Benoît. *Les adieux à la reine / Farewell, My Queen.* By Chantal Thomas, starring Diane Kruger and Léa Seydoux, 2012.

Van Dyke, W.S. and Julien Duvivier. *Marie-Antoinette*, starring Norma Shearer, Robert Morley, John Barrymore, and Tyrone Power, 1938.

Documentaries

C'est dur d'être aimé par des cons / It's Hard Being Loved by Jerks. Directed by Daniel Leconte, with Philippe Val and Elisabeth Badinter, produced by Pyramide Vidéo, 2008.
Empires—Napoléon. Starring David McCullough, produced by PBS, 2005.
The French Revolution. Produced by the History Channel, 2005.
Marie-Antoinette. Starring Philippe Altier, Antoine de Baecque, and Caroline Bernard, produced by David Grubin, 2006.
La Révolution française: Les années lumières et Les années terribles. Historical reconstruction, 324 minutes, produced by Alexandre Mnouchkine, 2010.

Other Relevant Films

Donner, Clive. *The Scarlet Pimpernel*, starring Jane Seymour, 1982.
Ivory, James. *Jefferson in Paris.* Starring Greta Scacchi and Nick Nolte, 1995.
Walkins, Peter. *La Commune.* Historical reproduction, 345 minutes, produced by 13 Productions and La Sept-Arte, 2000.
Yorkin, Bud. *Start the Revolution without Me.* Starring Gene Wilder and Donald Sutherland, 1970.

Beth S. Wright

Revolutionary Artwork

Books

Ben-Amos, Avner. *Funerals, Politics, and Memory in Modern France, 1789–1996.* Oxford UP, 2000.

Bordes, Philippe, and Régis Michel, editors. *Aux armes et aux arts! Les arts de la Révolution 1789–1799.* Adam Biro, 1988.

Censer, Jack R., and Lynn Hunt. *Liberty, Equality, Fraternity: Exploring the French Revolution.* Penn State UP, 2001. Includes companion CD-ROM.

A Chronicle of the French Revolution, 1788–1799. Edited by Jean Favier et al., Chronicle Communications, 1989.

Clarke, Joseph. *Commemorating the Dead in Revolutionary France: Revolution and Remembrance, 1789–1799.* Cambridge UP, 2007.

Crow, Thomas. *Emulation: Making Artists for Revolutionary France.* Yale UP, 1995.

Kennedy, Emmet. *A Cultural History of the French Revolution.* Yale UP, 1989.

Roberts, Warren. *Jacques-Louis David and Jean-Louis Prieur Revolutionary Artists: The Public, the Populace, and Images of the French Revolution.* State U of New York P, 2000.

Rubin, James H. "Disorder/Order: Revolutionary Art as Performative Representation." *The French Revolution, 1789–1989: Two Hundred Years of Rethinking*, edited by Sandy Petrey, Texas Tech UP, 1989, pp. 83–111.

Tulard, Jean. *The French Revolution in Paris Seen through the Collections of the Carnavalet Museum.* Paris-Musées, 1989.

Web Sites

Bibliothèque Nationale de France. Gallica.bnf.fr.

Digital Media Repository. Libx.bsu.edu/cdm/search/collection. Ball State University's pamphlets and books include frontispieces.

Domaine de Vizille: Musée de la Révolution Française. www.domaine-vizille.fr/401-telecharger-des-documents/.

French Revolution Digital Archive. Frda.stanford.edu/en/images. Stanford University / Bibliothèque Nationale de France.

Wikimedia Commons. wikimedia.org/wiki/category/Musee_de_la _Revolution_française.

Yale University Library Digital Collections. findit.library.yale.edu/catalog/ digcoll.

Works of Art

Allais, Louis-Jean. *Exposition du corps de L. Michel Lepelletier sur le piédestal de la ci-devant statue de Louis XIV place des Piques.* Aquatint. Paris: Allais, 1793. Bibliothèque Nationale de France, De Vinck 5026. Johnson, fig. 51.

Ben-Amos, Avner. *Funerals, Politics, and Memory in Modern France, 1789–1996.* Oxford UP, 2000.

Blanchard. *Five Stopping Places on the Procession for the Festival of Fraternity, 10 August 1793.* Colored aquatint. Bibliothèque Nationale de France, De Vinck 4911. Hould, cat. 138, fig. 66; Schnapper, fig. 77.

Boilly, Louis-Léopold. *Héroïne de Saint Mihier.* Black ink, gray wash heightened with white, on paper, 1794. Private collection. Bourdon; Siegfried, fig. 24.

———. *The Standard-Bearer of the Civic Festival (The Singer Chenard Dressed as a Sans-Culotte at the Festival of the Liberty of Savoy, October 14, 1792).* Musée Carnavalet, c. 1792–93. P 0008. Tulard, fig. 151; Siegfried, fig. 22.

———. *Triumph of Marat.* Oil on paper laid down on canvas. Lille: Musée des Beaux-Arts, 1794. Wintermute, p. 147, fig. 1; Siegfried, fig. 29.

Boizot, Simon-Louis. *An Allegorical Figure of the French Republic.* Gray-and-black wash on cream paper, c. 1792. Wintermute, cat. 6.

———. *Republican France Offering Her Breasts to All the French,* c. 1794, engraved by Clément, Bibliothèque Nationale de France, De Vinck 6074. Rubin, fig. 8.

Bouillon. *Marie-Antoinette's Trial.* Drawing, 1793. Musée Carnavalet D 5974. Tulard, fig. 230.

Bourdon, Léonard. *Recueil des actions héroïques et civiques.* 1793–94. *Internet Archive,* 15 Aug. 2016, archive.org/details/recueildesaction00bour_0.

Boze, Joseph. *Portrait of Mirabeau.* 1789–90. Musée Granet, Aix-en-Provence.

Brion, Étienne. *The Assassination of Lepeletier de Saint-Fargeau.* Etching, 1793. Bibliothèque Nationale de France. Crow, fig. 113.

Cazenove, Jean-François. *Trait de courage héroïque* (*Woman of Saint-Milhier*). Engraved by Jean Thouvenin. *Domaine de Vizille* 88.34, subject from Bourdon; Mainz cat. 76; colored version in Censer and Hunt.

Censer, Jack R., and Lynn Hunt. *Liberty, Equality, Fraternity: Exploring the French Revolution.* Penn State UP, 2001.

A Chronicle of the French Revolution, 1788–1799. Edited by Jean Favier et al., Chronicle Communications, 1989.

Clarke, Joseph. *Commemorating the Dead in Revolutionary France: Revolution and Remembrance, 1789–1799.* Cambridge UP, 2007.

Clay, Richard. *The French Revolution: Tearing Up History. YouTube,* 23 Aug. 2014, www.youtube.com/watch?v=4bTQv9ESk2c.

———. *Iconoclasm in Revolutionary Paris: The Transformation of Signs.* Oxford UP, 2012. Studies on Voltaire and the Eighteenth Century.

Crow, Thomas. *Emulation: Making Artists for Revolutionary France.* Yale UP, 1995.

Cruikshank, Isaac. *Salus in fuga: La France se purge petit à petit.* London: S. Fores, 1789. British Museum. findit.library.yale.edu/catalog/digcoll:550776.

Crussaire, Pierre Jean Joseph. *The Mysterious Urn.* Engraved by Jean-Baptiste Debret, Jagot, 1795. Bibliothèque Nationale de France, Hennin 11974.

David, François-Anne. *The Day of IV February MCDDDXC.* Etching and engraving. Bibliothèque Nationale de France, De Vinck 4232, Hennin 11044. Reichardt and Kohle, fig. 52.

———. *États Généraux de 1789, représentés par figures allégoriques: Accompagnées d'un précis des matières que l'on y a traitées pendant chaque séance présenté à monsieur, frère du roi* (Paris, 1789). Plate 1: *Ouverture des États Généraux 5 Mai 1789,* by Nicolas Lejeune, engraved by David; plate 2: *Scission des deux premiers ordres avec le tiers.*

———. *Histoire de France, représentée par figures accompagnés d'un précis historique; les figures gravées par F.-A. David, graveur de la chambre et du cabinet du roi, d'après les plus célèbres artistes de l'école française: Le précis historique par Ant. Caillot, ouvrage destiné à l'éducation de la jeunesse* [1788–91] (Paris, 1817–19), 3 vols. Plates separately published by Bibliothèque Nationale, Est. Ef. 61; planche 63: *Ouverture des États Généraux*; planche 65: *Louis XVI accepte la constitution an 1791.*

David, Jacques-Louis. *The French Citizen at Home,* drawing in ink and watercolor, 1794. Musée Carnavalet. Tulard, fig. 192.

———. *Louis XVI montrant la constitution à son fils.* Study, 1792. Musée du Louvre RF 36942, folio 39. Bordes and Michel, fig. 5.

———. *Marat at His Last Breath.* 1793. Oil on canvas, Brussels: Musées Royaux des Beaux-Arts.

———. *Marat at the Time of His Death.* Etching and aquatint engraving by Jacques-Louis Copia. Musée Carnavalet, De Vinck 5314. Hould, cat. 109.

———. *Michel Le Peletier de Saint-Fargeau.* Painting destroyed, known through a drawing by A. Devosge, 1792 (Dijon, Musée des Beaux-Arts) and an engraving by Pierre-Alexandre Tardieu, 1792. See entries for Devosge; Tardieu.

———. *Oath of the Tennis Court.* Graphite, pen, sepia wash heightened with white on paper, 1791. Versailles, Musée National du Château, on deposit from the Louvre RF 1914. Crow fig. 134; Schnapper fig. 50; Roberts, details in figs. 85–91, 94–95.

———. *Oath of the Tennis Court,* right fragment. Oil on canvas, 1791. Versailles, Musée National du Château, on deposit from the Louvre. Johnson, fig. 44.

———. *The People's Representative on Duty.* Drawing in ink and watercolor, 1794. Musée Carnavalet D 7059. Schnapper, fig. 84; Tulard, fig. 310.

———. *Le peuple français, le génie de la liberté et de la victoire offrant le sceptre et la couronne au roi,* study. 1792, Musée du Louvre RF 36942, folio 41. Bordes and Michel, fig. 6.

———. *The Triumph of the French People.* Project for an opera curtain or set, c. 1794. Musée Carnavalet. Johnson, fig. 61.

Debucourt, Philibert-Louis. *Almanach national, dédié aux amis de la Constitution.* Colored aquatint and etching, 1790. Archives Nationales, Paris, AE/II/3706. Hould, cat. 142; Taws, fig. 60.

———. *Preparations for the* Fête de la fédération, *July 14, 1790.* Wintermute, cat. 3.

Destroying Statues of the Kings of France: Henri IV at the Pont Neuf, Place Royale. Etching, 1792. From Prudhomme, *Révolutions de Paris*, no. 161, 4–11 August 1792. Musée Carnavalet, Est. Histoire PC 18 B, De Vinck 4921. Hould, cat. 61b.

Destroying Statues of the Kings of France: Place Louis XV, City Hal. Etching, 1792. From Prudhomme, *Révolutions de Paris*, no. 161, 4–11 August 1792. Musée Carnavalet, Est. Histoire PC 18 B, De Vinck 4920. Hould, cat. 61a.

Devosge, A. Drawing after David's *Michel Le Pelletier de Saint-Fargeau.* 1792. Dijon, Musée des Beaux-Arts. Crow, fig. 115; Roberts, fig. 104.

Domaine de Vizille: Musée de la Révolution française, www.domaine-vizille.fr/401-telecharger-des-documents/.

Exposition du corps de L. Michel Lepelletier . . . 24 Janvier 1793 . . . honneurs du Panthéon (Michel Le Peletier de Saint-Fargeau.) Bibliothèque Nationale de France Réserve, De Vinck 5026. Johnson, fig. 51.

Fougea. *The Funeral of Marat in the Former Cordeliers Church.* Oil on canvas, 1794. Musée Carnavalet. Crow, fig. 117; Tulard, fig. 216.

The French People Overwhelming the Hydra of Federalism. August 1793. Musée Carnavalet. Johnson, fig. 58.

French Revolution Game. Colored etching, 1791–92. Musée Carnavalet. Reichardt and Kohle, fig. 173.

Funeral of Jean-Paul Marat in the Church of the Cordeliers. Black chalk drawing heightened with white, 1793. Versailles: Musée Lambinet. Crow, fig. 116.

Game of the French Revolution, Modelled after the Greek Game of Goose. Colored etching. Bibliothèque Nationale de France, Est. 4 July–August 1790, M 100244. Hould, cat. 146.

Gérard, François. *The French People Demanding the Overthrow of the Tyrant on the Tenth of August 1792.* Graphite, pen, sepia wash heightened with white on paper, 1794–95. Musée du Louvre, Cabinet des Dessins. Crow, fig. 133; Roberts, fig. 97; Wintermute, fig. 8.

———. *The French People Demanding the Overthrow of the Tyrant on the Tenth of August 1792.* Preparatory oil sketch for unfinished painting, oil on canvas, 1795–98. Private collection on loan to the University Art Museum, Albuquerque. Crow, fig. 136.

Girodet, Anne-Louis. *Portrait of Citizen Belley Ex-Representative of the Colonies*, 1797. Château de Versailles et de Trianon. Crow, fig. 150.

Grasset de Saint-Sauveur, Jacques. "Spare My Father, Let Me Die Instead." *Fastes du peuple français et tableaux raisonnés de toutes les actions héroïques et civiques du soldat et du citoyen français.* Aquatint, 1796. Private collection. Hould, cat. 104.

Helman, Isidore-Stanislas. *21 January 1793, the Death of Louis Capet at the Place de la Revolution, Presented to the National Convention of the Thirtieth Germinal.* After Charles Monnet, etched by Antoine-Jean Duclos, engraving and etching, 1793. De Vinck 5188. *Domaine de Vizille* 83.319. Hould, cat. 75; Reichardt and Kohle, fig. 146; Roberts, fig. 102.

———. *The Fountain of Regeneration Built atop the Ruins of the Bastille, August 10, 1793.* After Charles Monnet, engraving, 1793. Private collection, Montréal. De Vinck 1720. Hould, cat. 138; Roberts, fig. 106.

Honneurs rendus à la mémoire de le Pelletier. Etching, 1793. From Prudhomme, *Révolutions de Paris*, no. 185, 26 January 1792. Bibliothèque Nationale de France. Ben-Amos, fig. 3; Clarke, fig. 9, Crow, fig. 114.

Hould, Claudette. *L'image de la révolution française.* Musée du Québec, 1989.

Janinet, Jean-François. *Project for a Monument to Be Erected for the King and Dedicated to the National Assembly.* After Charles Santoire Varenne, colored aquatint, 1790. Reichardt and Kohle, fig. 51.

Johnson, Dorothy. *Jacques-Louis David: Art in Metamorphosis*, Princeton UP, 1993.

Kennedy, Emmet. *A Cultural History of the French Revolution.* Yale UP, 1989.

Labrousse. *Charté ouvrier d'une fabrique de Salpêtre.* Illustration for Jacques Grasset Saint-Sauveur's *Les fastes du peuple francais: Tableaux raisonnés de toutes les actions héroïques et civiques du soldat et du citoyen français*, 1796. BN Qbl 1795. Mainz, cat. 75.

Lafitte, Louis. *Brumaire (October/November), Second Month of the Republican Calendar.* Engraved by Tresca, French, c. 1794. Musée Carnavalet. Mainz, cat. 46; with text, Perovic, fig. 9.

———. *Messidor (June/July), Tenth Month of the Republican Calendar.* Engraved by Tresca, French, c. 1794. Musée Carnavalet. Perovic, fig. 10.

———. *Ventôse.* Print. Musée Carnavalet G 14031. Tulard, fig. 240. (All twelve decade calendar illustrations in color are in *Chronicle*, pp. 388–89.)

Lagrenée, Jean-Jacques. *Translation de Voltaire au Panthéon 13 Septembre 1791.* Engraving and aquatint by Claude-Nicolas Malapeau and Simon-Charles Miger. Bibliothèque Nationale de France, Hennin 11013. Clarke, fig. 6; colored etching, Reichardt and Kohle, fig. 8.

Le Barbier, Jean-Jacques-François. *Le Courage héroïque du jeune Désilles.* Musée des Beaux-Arts de Nancy. Inv. 512.

Lejeune, "Fantasmagorie de Robertson dans la cour des Capucines en 1797." Frontispiece for Étienne-Gaspard Robertson [Robert]'s *Mémoires recréatifs, scientifiques et anecdotiques du physicien-aéronaute*, Paris, Wurtz, 1831. R-49301 gallica.bnf.fr; Wright, fig.18.

Le Sueur, Pierre-Étienne. *L'execution du tyran (Louix XVI), 21 janvier 1793.* Bibliothèque Nationale de France, Cabinet des Estampes, Hennin 11675. Crow, fig. 135; Roberts, fig. 101; Wintermute, fig. 9.

Le Sueur, Pierre-Étienne, and Jacques-Philippe Le Sueur. *Dechristinization.* 1791. Gouache on card. Musée Carnavalet D 9080. Tulard, fig. 154.

———. *Demolition of the Bastille.* 1791. Gouache on card. Musée Carnavalet D 9079. Tulard, fig. 32.

———. *Departure for the Frontiers.* 1791. Gouache on card. Musée Carnavalet D 9065. Tulard, fig. 194.

———. *Federation Day.* 1791. Gouache on card. Musée Carnavalet D 9064. Tulard, fig. 62.

———. *The Jacobin.* 1791. Gouache on card. Musée Carnavalet D 9085. Tulard, fig. 236.

———. *Manuel, Petion, Chaumette.* 1791. Gouache on card. Musée Carnavalet D 9093. Tulard, fig. 237.

———. *Model of the Bastille: Four Men Carrying the Model during Civil Processions.* 1791. Gouache on card. Musée Carnavalet D 9061. Reichardt and Kohle, fig. 7; Taws, fig. 57; Tulard, fig. 33.

———. *Municipal Officer Giving News.* 1791. Gouache on card. Musée Carnavalet D 9089. Tulard, fig. 273.

———. *Napoleon.* 1791. Gouache on card. Musée Carnavalet D 9104. Tulard, fig. 300.

———. *Patriotic Women's Club.* 1791. Gouache on card. Musée Carnavalet D 9092. Reichardt and Kohle, fig. 123.

———. *The Revolutionary Tribunal.* 1791. Gouache on card. Musée Carnavalet D 9047. Tulard, fig. 193.

———. *The Royal Family.* 1791. Gouache on card. Musée Carnavalet D 9045. Tulard, fig.133.

———. *A Soldier.* 1791. Gouache on card. Musée Carnavalet D 9083. Tulard, fig. 301.

———. *Volunteer Dragging a Cannon.* 1791. Gouache on card. Musée Carnavalet D 9064. Tulard, fig. 101.

———. *Young Men from the Departments.* 1791. Gouache on card. Musée Carnavalet D 9103. Tulard, fig. 272.

Mainz, Valerie. *Women at Work, Men in Labour: Work and Image in the French Revolution.* Exhibition Leeds: University Art Gallery, 1998. Vizille: Musée de la Révolution Française, 1999.

Montagne élevée au champ de la réunion pour la fête de l'Être Supreme le 20 prairial l'an 2eme. Colored etching. Bibliothèque Nationale de France. Hould, cat. 140; Taws, fig. 65.

National and Instructive Lesson; or, Exemplary and Amusing Lesson Given to the Good Citizens by Henri IV and Father Gerard. Colored etching, Basset, 1791–92. Reichardt and Kohle, fig. 174.

The People Destroy the Symbols of Monarchy and the Statues of Former Kings. Print, c. 1791. Musée Carnavalet, Ha 16 C 022. Tulard, fig. 140; version as colored aquatint *The Toppled Idol*, Reichardt and Kohle, fig. 60.

Perovic, Sanja. *The Calendar in Revolutionary France: Perceptions of Time in Literature, Culture, and Politics.* Cambridge UP, 2012.

Place Vendome: The Worst Tyrant Overthrown by Liberty. Colored etching. Musée Carnavalet, Est. Histoire PC 18 B, De Vinck 4925. Hould, cat. 61c.

Prieur, Jean-Louis. *Fédération générale faite à Paris le 14 juillet 1790.* Engraved by Pierre-Gabriel Berthault, plate 39 from *Tableaux historiques de la Révolution française*, 1791–94. Hould, cat. 134; Roberts, fig. 48; Taws, fig. 38.

———. *Statue de Louis XVI abattue, Place des Victoires, les 11, 12, 13 aoust 1792.* Engraved by Pierre-Gabriel Berthault, c. 1794, plate 68 from *Tableaux de la Révolution française.* Roberts, fig. 79; Taws, fig. 78.

Prud'hon, Pierre-Paul. *Liberty.* Engraving c. 1793. Musée Carnavalet. Kennedy ix.25.

Queverdo, François Marie Isidore, with Durvy and Claude Louis Beaublé. *La régéneration de la nation française, dédiée et présentée à l'assemblée nationale le 13 juillet 1790 comme pouvant être le modèle d'un monument public.* Geoffroy,

1790. Bibliothèque Nationale de France, De Vinck 2744, Hennin 10747. Kennedy ix.4.

Regnault, Jean-Baptiste. *Liberty or Death*. 1795. Hamburg, Kunsthalle. Rubin, fig. 4; Kennedy x.2; Reichardt and Kohle, fig. 97.

Reichardt, Rolf, and Hubertus Kohle. *Visualizing the Revolution: Politics and Pictorial Arts in Late-Eighteenth-Century France*. Translated from the German by Corinne Attwood and from the French by Felicity Baker, Reaktion Books, 2008.

Robert, Hubert. *La Bastille dans les premiers jours de sa demolition*. Oil on canvas, 1789. Musée Carnavalet P 1476. Taws, fig. 58.

Roberts, Warren. *Jacques-Louis David and Jean-Louis Prieur Revolutionary Artists: The Public, the Populace, and Images of the French Revolution*. State U of New York P, 2000.

Robespierre Guillotines the Executioner after Having Had All the Rest of France Guillotined. 1794–95. Etching and line drawing. Bibliothèque Nationale de France, Hennin 11742. Hould, cat. 89; Reichardt and Kohle, fig. 160.

Rubin, James H. "Disorder/Order: Revolutionary Art as Performative Representation." *The French Revolution, 1789–1989: Two Hundred Years of Rethinking*, edited by Sandy Petrey, Texas Tech UP, 1989, pp. 83–111.

Sablet, Jacques. *Blacksmith Leaving His Anvil to Go into Battle with His Hammer*. Subject from Bourdon, engraved by J. L. Copia, 1793–94. Mainz, cat. 75; Wintermute, p. 35, fig. 6.

Un sans-culotte instrument des crimes. . . . Etching, 1794. Bibliothèque Nationale de France, De Vinck 5223. Clay, *Iconoclasm*, fig. 60; frda.stanford.edu.

Schnapper, Antoine. *David*. Alpine Fine Arts Collection, 1982.

Siegfried, Susan L. *The Art of Louis-Léopold Boilly: Modern Life in Napoleonic France*. Yale UP, 1995.

Tardieu, Pierre-Alexandre. *Michel Le Pelletier de Saint-Fargeau*. Line engraving after lost painting by Jacques-Louis David, 1792. Bibliothèque Nationale de France, Est. Rés. AA Tardieu. Fragment of an unfinished proof before letters. Hould, cat. 111; Roberts, fig. 103; Rubin, fig. 5.

Tassaert, Jean-Joseph François. *M.ie A.ne C.te Corday*. Stipple engraving, after a drawing from life by Jean-Jacques Hauer. Bibliothèque Nationale de France, Cabinet des Estampes, De Vinck 5379, Hennin 11563. Hould, cat. 114.

———. *The Night of 9 to 10 Thermidor, Year II*. Stipple engraving after Fulchran-Jean Harriet. Bibliothèque Nationale de France, Cabinet des Estampes, De Vinck 6500, Hennin 11922. Hould, cat. 88.

Taws, Richard. *The Politics of the Provisional: Art and Ephemera in Revolutionary France*. Pennsylvania State UP, 2013.

Thévenin, Charles. *The Festival of the Federation on the Champ-de-Mars, July 14, 1790*. Oil on canvas, 1792. Musée Carnavalet, P 2342. Tulard, fig. 76.

Tulard, Jean. *The French Revolution in Paris Seen through the Collections of the Carnavalet Museum*. Paris-Musées, 1989.

Vallain, Jeanne-Louise (Nanine). *La liberté*. Oil on canvas, c. 1793–94. Musée de la Révolution Française, Vizille. Bordes and Michel, p. 124.

Villeneuve [publisher]. *Something to Reflect upon for the Crowned Jugglers*. Etching and aquatint, 1793. Bibliothèque Nationale de France, Cabinet des Estampes, De Vinck 5206. Reichardt and Kohle, fig. 68; Wintermute, fig.1.

———. *Traitor Louis XVI Read Your Sentence. . . .* Etching and aquatint, 1793. Bibliothèque Nationale de France, Cabinet des Estampes, De Vinck 5209. Reichardt and Kohle, fig. 66.

———. *View of the Six Different Stations of the Festival of the Unity and Indivisibility of the Republic (10 August 1793).* Engraving, 1793. Bibliothèque Nationale de France, Cabinet des Estampes, De Vinck 6171. Rubin, fig. 6.

Wintermute, Alan. *1789: French Art during the Revolution.* Colnaghi, 1989.

Wright, Beth S. *Painting and History during the French Restoration: Abandoned by the Past.* Cambridge UP, 1997.

Notes on Contributors

Katherine Astbury is professor of French studies at the University of Warwick. She is the author of *Narrative Responses to the Trauma of the French Revolution* (2012) and the editor of Pixerécourt's *La forteresse du Danube* (2016). She is currently preparing an edited volume on cultural policy during the French Revolution and the First Empire as well as a monograph on theater during the Hundred Days.

Habiba Boumlik is associate professor at LaGuardia Community College of the City University of New York. She is the author of essays on Tunisian activism in *Adult Education Quarterly*, women in STEM in *Science Education and Civic Engagement*, and "Muslim and European Encounters through Travel Writing" in *The Maghreb Review*.

Ronan Y. Chalmin teaches French culture and literature at Connecticut College. He is the author of *Lumières et corruption* (2010) and the editor of S.-A. Tissot's *De la santé des gens de lettres* (2018), in collaboration with Anne C. Vila. His latest research focuses on revolutionary France. He is currently working on Gracchus Babeuf and his journal, *The Tribune of the People*.

Jeffrey Champlin is professor of literature at the Barenboim-Said Academy in Berlin. He is the author of *The Making of a Terrorist: On Classic German Rogues*, the editor of *Terror and the Roots of Poetics*, and the coeditor of *The Technological Introject: Friedrich Kittler between Implementation and the Incalculable*.

Dominica Chang is Margaret Banta Humleker Professor of French Cultural Studies and associate professor of French and francophone studies at Lawrence University. Her research interests include literary, visual, and historical representations of French and francophone revolutionary movements, the Paris Commune of 1871, Flaubertian studies, critical media, and cultural studies.

Logan J. Connors is associate professor of French at the University of Miami. He is the author of *Dramatic Battles in Eighteenth-Century France* (2012) and the editor of Pierre-Laurent de Belloy's *Le siège de Calais* (2014). His next monograph, *The Emergence of a Theatrical Science of Man in France*, is forthcoming in late 2019.

Melanie Conroy is assistant professor of French at the University of Memphis. She is the author of articles in *Poetics Today*, *Nineteenth-Century French Studies*, *Médias 19*, *Romance Notes*, and the *Journal of Modern History*. She is currently working on cultural histories of the aristocracy and of European salons as sites of literary production. She is the codirector of the Salons Project, a part of *Mapping the Republic of Letters.*

Marlene L. Daut is associate professor of African diaspora studies in the Carter G. Woodson Institute for African American and African Studies and of American studies at the University of Virginia. She is the author of *Tropics of Haiti: Race and the Literary History of the Haitian Revolution in the Atlantic World, 1789–1865* (2015) and *Baron de Vastey and the Origins of Black Atlantic Humanism* (2017).

Melissa A. Deininger is associate professor of French at Iowa State University. She is primarily interested in how literature and cultural production can influence perceptions of group identity. Her research interests include French culture and history, modern French politics and culture, the Marquis de Sade, and art and architecture as cultural production. She is the author of articles on topics from eighteenth-century political figures to the 2002 election in France.

Yvonne Fuentes is associate professor at the University of West Georgia. She is the author of *El triángulo sentimental en el drama del siglo dieciocho* (1999) and *Mártires y anticristos: Análisis bibliográfico sobre la Revolución francesa en España* (2006) and the coeditor, with Margaret Parker, of *Leading Ladies: Mujeres en la literatura hispana y en las artes* (2006).

Jennifer Gipson is assistant professor of French at the University of Wisconsin, Madison. Her work on Louisiana Creole and the racialization of orality appeared in the *Journal of American Folklore.* She is currently preparing a book manuscript, "Phantom Storytellers: A Literary History of Folklore in Nineteenth-Century France," that explores how notions of folklore and literature construct each other.

Robin Kietlinski is associate professor of history at LaGuardia Community College of the City University of New York. She is the author of *Japanese Women and Sport: Beyond Baseball and Sumo.* She teaches global and East Asian history survey courses and has helped build LaGuardia's International Studies Program.

Matthew Lau is assistant professor of English at Queensborough Community College. His writings have appeared in *Comparative Literature*, in *The International Journal of the Kafka Society of America*, and on the Web sites *Lacanian Ink* and *Jacobin.* His book "Sounds like Helicopters: Classical Music in Modernist Cinema" is forthcoming. Away from academia, he is a violinist with the String Orchestra of Brooklyn.

Amaya Martin is adjunct professor of Arabic at the George Washington University. She is the author of articles on Arabic cultural and literary texts and modern Arabic language and media. Her academic interests include linguistic analysis of cultural and literary texts, especially works by or about minorities to discern the subtleties of their social status.

José A. Martin-Pereda is considered the father of photonics in Spain. He created the first optical communications school there and introduced this field into the curricula of engineering schools in Spain. He is the author of works on different subjects, including a biography about the Spanish mathematician and engineer Jose Echegaray. He holds honorary degrees from the Polytechnic University of Catalonia, Carlos III University, and the University of Cantabria.

J. B. Mertz has taught composition and English literature at Lindenwood University and Maryville University. He is the author of articles in *Blake*, *Modern Philology*, and *Notes and Queries*.

Amir Minsky is assistant teaching professor of history at New York University, Abu Dhabi. He is the author of essays on the experiences of German fellow travelers of the French Revolution, problems of the French revolutionary and Napoleonic administration in the Rhineland, and the development of sentimental perceptions of liberty in the political philosophy of the German Enlightenment. He is currently writing a book titled "The Rise and Fall of German Political Sentimentalism, 1780–1848."

Ourida Mostefai is professor of French studies and of comparative literature at Brown University. She is the author of *Le citoyen de Genève et la République des Lettres: Étude de la controverse autour de la "Lettre à d'Alembert" de Jean-Jacques Rousseau* (2003) and *Jean-Jacques Rousseau, écrivain polémique* (2016) and coeditor of *Approaches to Teaching Rousseau's "Confessions" and "Reveries of the Solitary Walker"* (2003) and of *Rousseau and l'Infâme: Religion, Toleration, and Fanaticism in the Age of Enlightenment* (2009).

Rosa Mucignat is senior lecturer in comparative literature at King's College London. She is the author of *Realism and Space in the Novel, 1795–1869* (2013) and the editor of *Friulian Language: Identity, Migration, Culture* (2014). With Sanja Perovic she is working on a project on translations of radical texts between Italy and France in the revolutionary period.

Erin A. Myers has taught French language, literature, and culture to undergraduate students since 2005. Her dissertation, completed in 2018, examines the ways in which eighteenth-century French natural history, *idéologie* of the revolutionary period, and the work of Jean-Baptiste Lamarck in particular influenced novels of the early nineteenth century.

Giulia Pacini is associate professor of French and francophone studies at the College of William and Mary. Her current research focuses on representations of the political and material significance of trees in revolutionary

France, with particular interest in the discourses that surrounded the acts of planting, pruning, felling, transplanting, and grafting.

Sanja Perovic is reader in the Department of French at King's College London. She is the author of *The Calendar in Revolutionary France: Perceptions of Time in Literature, Culture, and Politics* (2012) and articles on the aesthetics and politics of time, from the early modern period to the present. Her current book project considers how live art can be used to think critically about history.

Lauren Pinzka is senior lecturer at Yale University. She is author of essays on the French Enlightenment and nineteenth-century French literature. Her research interests include nineteenth-century French literature, gender studies, myth and memory in modern France, the representation of Paris in French and American literature, and psychoanalytic criticism.

John Pizer is professor of German and comparative literature and chair of the Department of Foreign Languages and Literatures at Louisiana State University. He is the author of *Ego-Alter Ego: Double and/as Other in the Age of German Poetic Realism* (1998), *The Idea of World Literature: History and Pedagogical Practice* (2006), and *Imagining the Age of Goethe in German Literature, 1970–2010* (2011).

Pratima Prasad is associate professor of French and associate dean in the College of Liberal Arts at the University of Massachusetts, Boston. She is the author of *Colonialism, Race, and the French Romantic Imagination* (2009) and a coeditor, with David Powell, of *Approaches to Teaching George Sand's* Indiana (2015) and, with Susan McCready, of *Novel Stages: Drama and the Novel in Nineteenth-Century France* (2007).

Séverine Rebourcet is an assistant professor in French studies at the College of Mount Saint Vincent. Her work focuses on literature by writers from minority groups in France. She is especially interested in examining *banlieue* culture and the notion of Frenchness. She has written on Muslim hip-hop artists (such as Abd Al Malik) and their thoughts on Islam and national identity.

Catriona Seth is Marshal Foch Professor of French Literature at the University of Oxford and a fellow of All Souls College. She is the author of *Les rois aussi en mouraient: Les lumières en lutte contre la petite vérole* (2006), *Marie-Antoinette: Anthologie et dictionnaire* (2008), and *Évariste Parny: Créole, révolutionnaire, académicien* (2014). She recently coedited an anthology of Enlightenment texts on the idea of Europe.

Antoinette Sol is a professor of French and vice provost for faculty affairs at the University of Texas, Arlington. She is a coeditor, with Sarah Davies Cordova, of Balzac's *Le mulâtre* and *Le nègre* and of Hippolyte Carnot's

Gunima: Nouvelle africaine du dix-huitième siècle. They are currently working on an edition of Elisabeth Guénard's *Blanche de Ranci* (1802).

Christopher Tozzi is senior lecturer at Rensselaer Polytechnic Institute. He is the author of *Nationalizing France's Army: Foreign, Black, and Jewish Troops in the French Military, 1715–1831* (2016) and *For Fun and Profit: A History of the Free and Open Source Software Revolution* (2017). His current book project, "'Revolutionary until the Peace': War and Political Culture in the French Revolution," examines how wars and rumors of wars helped shape the political imaginary in revolutionary France.

Julia Douthwaite Viglione is professor emerita of French at the University of Notre Dame. She is author of *The Frankenstein of 1790 and Other Lost Chapters from Revolutionary France* (2012), *The Wild Girl, Natural Man, and the Monster* (2002), and *Exotic Women: Literary Heroines and Cultural Strategies in Ancien Regime France* (1992). She is the editor of *Rousseau and Dignity: Art Serving Humanity* (2017).

Amy E. Wright is associate professor of Spanish at Saint Louis University. She is the author of articles on eighteenth- and nineteenth-century print culture in Latin America, an essay on early serialized literature in Mexico (2009), and an essay on early nation-building prose in Mexican literature (2017).

Beth S. Wright is professor of art history at the University of Texas, Arlington. She is the author of *Painting and History during the French Restoration: Abandoned by the Past* (1997) and of publications on eighteenth- and nineteenth-century French art, literature, and historiography. She is the editor of *The Cambridge Companion to Delacroix* (2001).

Index